∞

The Joyful Ways
of the Saints

Sister Mary Eleanore, C.S.C.

The Joyful Ways
of the Saints

And What They Teach You
About Kindness, Humility,
Courage, and Love

SOPHIA INSTITUTE PRESS®
Manchester, New Hampshire

The Joyful Ways of the Saints: And What They Teach You About Kindness, Humility, Courage, and Love is an abridged edition of *Troubadours of Paradise* (New York and London: D. Appleton and Company, 1926) and contains minor editorial revisions to the original text.

Sophia Institute Press®
Box 5284, Manchester, NH 03108
1-800-888-9344
www.sophiainstitute.com

Nihil obstat: Arthur J. Scanlan, S.T.D., *Censor Librorum*
Imprimatur: Patrick Cardinal Hayes, Archbishop of New York
May 10, 1926

Library of Congress Cataloging-in-Publication Data

M. Eleanore (Mary Eleanore), Mother, 1890-1940.
    The joyful ways of the saints : and what they teach you about kindness, humility, courage, and love / Sister Mary Eleanore.
        p.   cm.
    Abridgement of: Troubadours of paradise / Sister M. Eleanore. London ; New York : D. Appleton, 1926.
    Includes bibliographical references.
    ISBN 0-918477-35-2 (pbk. : alk. paper)
    1. Christian saints. I. M. Eleanore (Mary Eleanore), Mother, 1890-1940. Troubadours of paradise. II. Title.
BX2325.M15   1999
235'.2 — dc21   99-32622 CIP

99 00 01 02 03 04 05 9 8 7 6 5 4 3 2 1

To
Fr. Carrico
of Notre Dame

∞

Contents

Editor's note: The biblical references in the following pages are based on the Douay-Rheims edition of the Old and New Testaments. Where applicable, quotations have been cross-referenced with the differing names and numeration in the Revised Standard Version, using the following symbol: (RSV =).

∾

Preface

Dear saint of God, I cannot reach
Thy hand — do thou in charity
Stoop to take mine; then I can run
The road to Paradise with thee!

∞

While it may be true that the proper study of mankind is man, history seems to indicate that the most persistent quest of mankind is God. From the pagan who first learned of God as the lightning flashed about him and the thunder rolled like the angry voice of an offended deity, to the philosopher who looked into his own soul and read there the law graven by a Supreme Legislator, all men have lived on the constant watch for glimpses of the Divinity and, seeing them, have paused to worship.

For all about, in oak and meadowlark and storm-wracked ocean, in the strong, tender arm of a man and the loving, un-selfish soul of a woman, men catch faint, elusive, tantalizing gleams of God — gleams that inspire them with a desire to see more and more. Yet as they run after Him with eager feet, He slips from their outstretched arms; they feel Him about them permeating everything, but He hides Himself from their prying eyes.

So the ignorant pagan, weary in his quest for a god he can see and handle, bumps his forehead against the image he has made, and kneels adoringly before the moaning wind and the strength of the sacred ox or the white elephant. The sensual-ist stops short with the physical beauty or the wisdom that captivates his fancy, and makes the splendid athlete on the racecourse or the sage in the senate his god, and the lovely maiden of his heart's vain desires his goddess. To them he builds his altar and sings his hymns of worship. The egoist falls in love with himself and sits upon his own altar, at once priest, acolyte, worshiper, and god.

But the man of faith, knowing that eyes of clay can never look upon the infinite majesty that is God, finds fleeting images of God in everything and sighs confidently for the day when he shall round the corner and find himself in the presence of Supreme Beauty and Truth. For the present, he is content to learn, from the shadows that fall along his path, the contours of the reality, and to read some pale reflection of God's face in the rusted brass of earth's perfections.

∞

Christ shows us God's face

Only one person in all of history showed in His adorable person the beauty and charm of the Divinity: Christ Jesus, the Lord. That is precisely the secret of the inexhaustible attraction that makes Him the most studied person of all time. Believers and unbelievers alike fasten hungry eyes upon Him, catching clear visions of the splendor and lovableness of God in His exquisite grace of feature, in His affability and utter winsomeness, in His tender pity and awesome power, in His words of simple wisdom, and in His works of stupendous might.

The unending seeking of man for the face of God was most fully realized when the Second Person of the Blessed Trinity took our human nature and walked among us, smiling at us through tender eyes and raising fallen humanity as easily and graciously as He raised the buried Lazarus.[1] Divine power was with us in the miracles of Christ; divine wisdom expressed itself in His parables and counsels; divine justice knotted the cords that drove the sellers from the Temple;[2] and divine love clothed itself with the mantle of pulsing flesh that became the Sacred Heart.

Because Jesus Christ is not only man, but God as well, He is a subject that will never be exhausted, but will draw every generation of poets and thinkers and mystics; for here one touches, through the thin veil of an exquisite humanity, the God who is the one object that human nature ever seeks and never, in this life, satisfactorily finds.

The undying interest of mankind in sainthood has for its reason this same, tireless quest for the Divinity. One is sometimes astonished at the diversity of temperament that grows interested in saints — types as antipodal as G. K. Chesterton and Anatole France, Mark Twain and Thomas De Quincey, Bernard Shaw and Maurice Maeterlinck. One is even more astonished that a generation that worships wealth pays ungrudging tribute to the Poor Man of Assisi,[3] or that a race that prides itself in flashing achievements falls in love with the Little Flower[4] blooming in an obscure garden in a little French village. But the astonishment fades when one remembers that unending quest of mankind for clearer, sharper glimpses of the divine nature.

[1] Cf. John 11:43.
[2] John 2:15.
[3] St. Francis (c. 1182-1226), founder of the Franciscan Order.
[4] St. Thérèse of Lisieux (1873-1897), Carmelite nun.

The Joyful Ways of the Saints

∞

The saints reflect God

Of all people who have ever lived, the saints have come closest to the Savior and, by so doing, have come closest to Divinity itself. Like the artists they were, they set up in the workshops of their souls the exquisite figure of the God-Man and, stroke by stroke, flying chip by flying chip, until the sweat rolled from their brows and their arms grew weary from labor, they hewed themselves into replications of the divine model they had chosen. Once they had glimpsed the Divinity that dwelt in Christ, they shaped their souls patiently but ardently to the perfection they saw and adored.

So *saintliness* and *Christlikeness* have become interchangeable terms. The saints had no ideals that were not His and no desires save those for which He had coined away His life in tears and sweat and blood. Because Christ hated sin even to the infinite hatred of Calvary, they made war on it ceaselessly and relentlessly; yet because He was the compassionate Samaritan, merciful to the Magdalene and tender to the good thief,[5] the saints threw about the sinner the mantle of an inexhaustible gentleness, welcoming the sinner, although they scourged the sin. They might be Savonarola[6] in the pulpit; in the confessional, they were Francis de Sales.[7]

Their Lord had prayed long nights upon a solitary mountain; the saints would cover the mountain peaks with houses

---

[5] Cf. Luke 10:33-35; 7:37-48; 23:42-43.

[6] Girolamo Savonarola (1452-1498), Italian preacher and reformer whose denunciations were often severe.

[7] St. Francis de Sales (1567-1622), Bishop of Geneva, known for his gentle, pastoral spiritual direction.

of prayer and penance, where night and day the divine praises might rise to the Father. Since their Lord had offered Himself as a victim for the sins of the world, they craved suffering with insatiable avarice. His labors inspired their tireless wanderings wherever souls might be found caught in the brambles of sin. His poverty made them fling away their cloaks to any chance beggar lifting his trembling hand. They saw Him leave home and the company of His Blessed Mother, and so they turned away from all human affection to follow in His lonely footsteps.

No saint is even conceivable who has not made himself a miniature of Christ; and, in making himself a miniature of Christ, the saint has caught up and crystallized perfections that are God's.

So, mankind, always searching feverishly, although often unconsciously, for glimpses of God, has been interested keenly in saints whose faith it often denies and whose motives it often so completely misunderstands. The gleams of divine beauty and perfection that leap forth in their words and actions have fascinated men even more surely than the traces of God seen in the inanimate creatures of His hand.

For in the saints, men saw clear visions of the moral perfections of God. The stars might tell of His beauty, but the tenderness of Peter Claver,[8] lifting from their galleys filthy African slaves to wash their bodies and cleanse their souls, spoke vividly of the divine mercy. Men went to the ocean pounding against the headland for a sight of His power, but in

---

[8] St. Peter Claver (1581-1654), Jesuit priest who ministered to the slaves in the New World.

the exquisite romance of St. Rose or St. Catherine,[9] wearing His ring upon their fingers, they read the love that consumes the divine heart. The mind of Augustine[10] flashed at times with a wisdom almost godlike. St. Gregory,[11] in his beneficent rule of a disorganized empire and a struggling Church, gave momentary hints of God's Providence. St. John Capistran,[12] lighting with the fires of his relentless wrath the bonfire of vanities beneath his pulpit, made men tremble at the thought of the awesome Judge whose sentence was eternal. St. Vincent de Paul,[13] as he walked the streets searching for the sick of soul and body, was like the tender mercy of the heavenly Father, not watching from the hilltop, but patiently seeking, through a lifetime of waywardness, his prodigal son.

Many of the saints were significant figures in history: St. Benedict, St. Bernard, St. Dominic, St. Brigid of Sweden, St. Joan of Arc.[14] But even had they been as historically unimportant as the Curé d'Ars in his confessional or St. Mary of Egypt

---

[9] St. Rose of Lima (1586-1617), Third Order Dominican and first canonized saint of the Americas; possibly St. Catherine of Siena (c. 1347-1380), Dominican tertiary. — ED.

[10] St. Augustine (354-430), Bishop of Hippo.

[11] St. Gregory the Great (c. 540-604), Pope from 590.

[12] St. John Capistran (1386-1456), Franciscan friar.

[13] St. Vincent de Paul (c. 1580-1660), founder of the Lazarist Fathers and the Sisters of Charity.

[14] St. Benedict (c. 480-c. 550), father of Western monasticism; St. Bernard (1090-1153), Abbot of Clairvaux; St. Dominic (1170-1221), founder of the Order of Friars Preachers; St. Brigid of Sweden (c. 1303-1373), founder of the Brigittines; St. Joan of Arc (1412-1431), French heroine who led the French army against English invaders.

alone in her desert or St. Gertrude[15] looking upon the vision of Christ's wounds, the flame of divinity that burned in them with brilliant radiance would have drawn the attention even of unbelievers.

Since God's perfections are veiled from all except eyes glorified by the Beatific Vision, He has given us His divine Son and the legion of His saints to show us in the flesh His beauty, His unfathomable love, and His irresistible attractiveness.

∞

The saints are God's masterpieces

This volume is a sort of guidebook to the gallery of saintly perfection. Sr. Mary Eleanore has selected some of the exquisite qualities of the saints — qualities that mirror forth so clearly the genius of the divine Artist — and she leads us from saint to saint, allowing us to study in their souls how these qualities have appeared. And she is an excellent guide. First of all, she has for her subjects a love that makes her talk from her heart; she loves the masterpieces she has to show us, and she has her special favorites to which she takes us promptly and with infectious enthusiasm. She can talk of the masterpieces with tender appreciation, but always she brings us back to the genius of the Artist whose own tremendous perfections and powerful mind are exhibited in every stroke.

The reading of this book is a certain step toward knowing and loving the saints. But that is just one further step toward

---

[15] The Curé d'Ars, or St. John Vianney (1786-1859), patron saint of parish priests; St. Mary of Egypt, fifth-century penitent; St. Gertrude (1256-c. 1302), German mystic.

The Joyful Ways of the Saints

knowing and loving the Father of saints, whose hands have fashioned what the life of His blessed Son inspired. For the saints — the most perfect work that comes from the hands of the Creator — speak to us, through these pages, of the transcendent beauty and the matchless loveliness that they mirror. They satisfy, insofar as man can be satisfied while his soul is covered with the veil of flesh, our craving to look upon the perfections of God. From His masterpieces we come to know and to love the Master.

Daniel A. Lord, S.J.
Feast of the Sacred Heart

∞

The Joyful Ways
of the Saints

Chapter One

The Way of Example

Star of the King, let those brave lesser stars,
That Thou hast fired to flaming ecstasy
Of love, blaze on the darkened world, to draw
All hearts into the burning Heart of Thee!

The saddest thing in life, after loss of faith in God, is the loss of trust in one's fellowmen. In these days of ours, such loss of trust happens with fearful ease, because the world seems to have turned its back on God and His laws, and men who reject the bonds of religion are almost inevitably prone to make light of human loves and loyalties. We need constant stimulus to trust in humanity nowadays, and oftentimes we seek for it vainly in those with whom we live.

Some of us, therefore, turn for solace to fiction, wherein we find noble and beautiful characters who triumph over difficulties numerous and great; and often the memory of these characters lingers with us for days to encourage and strengthen us. Unhappily, in order to find such fictional characters, we must pass over the greater amount of contemporary literature as too materialistic and pessimistic, and turn to the literature of older times.

Although we may deduce that, since these great people in books did great things, there must be worthwhile qualities in human nature, deep in our minds is the consciousness that these fine men and women are after all only the creations of the author's genius and did not exist in real life. Reading of this sort is therefore more of an anesthetic than of a cure for the malady of hopelessness.

The Joyful Ways of the Saints

Why, then, do we content ourselves with imaginary people when there are, unused and dusty on our bookshelves, divinely real romances with true and inspiring people in them? Why do we not turn for comfort and encouragement to the romantically beautiful and dramatic lives of the saints? To me it seems very sad that the lives of the saints are so little known, although some of the reasons for their being neglected are not difficult to understand.

Our modern books are made up in such attractive style with large, readable print and clever illustrations that we, being spoiled, are repelled by the very appearance of many biographies of the saints, with their fine print and huge bulk. Then, too, the cumbersome and heavily pietistic manner of many biographers wearies us even before we have well started to read. Finally, the matter of the books is often a difficulty; a multiplicity of unnecessary details and of personal comments and reflections hinders the movement of the narrative, while the author's own ideas of piety are read, often unconsciously, into his interpretation of the saint. An author, for example, who thinks that love of God is so exclusive as to call for something like hatred of man carefully keeps from his biography anything in the life or writings of his saint that savors of an affectionate disposition, and he painstakingly emphasizes any reprimands the saint may have been forced to administer or any expression of detachment from the things of earth that he may have uttered. As a result, the biographer creates an inhuman and most unlovable caricature of the saint. He does not mean to be untruthful, and yet, in a sense, he is. He is not content to let his saint be himself; he makes him into what he thinks the saint should be.

The very first requisite for writing the life of a saint is to fall hopelessly in love with him. Love may be blind, but it is as a rule willfully so. Love is true love only when it is big enough to understand the beloved with his virtues and his weaknesses. Such love is necessary to any truthful biography, which portrays the development of sanctity.

One of the supremely great biographies of saints is that of St. Bernard by M. L'Abbé Ratisbonne, which is ended thus: "What will become of him [who writes these lines]? He loses, in the conclusion of this work, the dear object which has employed his thoughts, consoled his leisure, and softened his griefs, through many a year of suffering. He has become habituated, by a voluntary illusion, to live with the saint, to follow him everywhere, to seek his delight in his words, to take pride in his writings, his merits, his triumphs, as if he had been one of his children, as if he had the happiness of being reckoned amongst his disciples! And now death, pitiless death, tears away his consolation, and forces him to lay down his pen. O holy and beloved Bernard, receive my farewell, and deign to bless this book, and him who wrote it."[16] Here is a fine and cultured man writing of a chosen and beloved saint, and the secret of his success as a biographer rests in his love of his subject.

G. K. Chesterton's *St. Francis of Assisi* was born of love and, to my mind, is a masterpiece of his genius. Francis Thompson was deeply in love with St. Ignatius of Loyola,[17] and he teaches

---

[16] M. L'Abbé Ratisbonne, *The Life and Times of St. Bernard* (New York: P. J. Kenedy and Sons), 475.

[17] St. Ignatius of Loyola (1491-1556), founder of the Society of Jesus.

his reader the lesson of love. These authors loved their saints enough to be content to give them to us as they are, for they know that we, too, having been taught to know saints, must love them. God is the Artist who made the saint; the man who tries to improve God's handiwork can only spoil it.

∞

You must approach the saints with a childlike spirit

Love is so naturally joyous that even the pain that almost always accompanies it is more of laughter than of tears. Love keeps people young, and youth is always joyful when unspoiled. The saints, therefore, are always young and always joyful, although they may live long and suffer much. Children can read the lives of the saints with something akin to rapture, because they see in the glad eagerness with which saints run into suffering for God's love the common sense of youthful vision. To the adult, St. Simeon[18] on his pillar may seem to have had an insufferably dull and stupid time, but, to the child, there is something entrancing in the idea of dwelling on a pillar from which one can look with greater ease upward into the face of Heaven and with a broader view downward on the busy little people running foolishly about in material pursuits, in the manner of ants.

Bodily infirmities do not make a man's soul old; sin is the only thing that can age the soul. Saints are sinless either through preserved innocence or through sublime repentance, and therefore they are young enough to appeal to children.

---

[18] St. Simeon Stylites (c. 390-459), the first of the stylites, Christian solitaries who lived on top of pillars.

Children exult in monotony, wanting their stories told in exactly the same words every night; they know all about tumbling down many times and jumping up to brush their clothes off and start afresh in the scamper after someone or something they love; and so they do not find the repeated struggles of saints against their human weaknesses in the least boring. Children understand that love means sacrifice, for they live with the sacrificial love of motherhood wrapped about them, and they respond to it by being good for the smile in their mother's eyes. Therefore, children can understand how saints can throw away every other joy of life for the sake of the joy of a smile from God.

Now I want to make an appeal to you who are reading this book. Will you please forget that you are grown up — if, you are — just while you are letting me talk to you? Will you, for only an hour or two, try to become again an eager child and come with me into the library while I take down a few dusty books from the shelves and read from them some scattered paragraphs that, I hope, will make you love some of my favorite saints just a bit more? Then perhaps you will want to linger among the books after I have left you and you have forgotten me. Books can be such dear friends, especially the books that have the understanding hearts of saints between their covers. And so, with a very special invitation, I ask you whose heart is burdened with care and sorrow to come with me for this little visit with our friends the saints.

I am writing this book, not for theologians and nuns who know ever so much more of saints than I do, but for you who have not had many opportunities to become acquainted with the most admirable men and women who have graced our earth by living on it. To you, especially, who think the saints are unlovable caricatures of humanity written of in painfully stupid volumes, I offer this little study of the saints whom I know and love. It is not a profound treatise, but is rather a picture book of people who illustrate some of the qualities of genuine saintliness in an imitable way. I do not know many saints, but those I do know, I love and consider typical of all. And I want you to love them, too, and, for their sake, to desire to know and love all other saints.

∞

The saints lead you to God

Come, then, as children into my house of life for just a little while and meet some of those who keep my trust in humanity alive and who console me in my sorrows. When all the world is dark, they are as dear and comforting as the lights in a window, as the star above a Christmas tree, and as the flickering flames on the hearth. They are real people, near and warm, and the halos around their heads are formed of light and warmth and love. They are holding out welcoming hands to you, with assurance that they will take care of you and love you. With the understanding humility that looks on God and sees how He uses creatures to work His will, they know that you will love them when you know them, and they are eager for your love. They know what they can do for you by prayer and precept and example.

St. Bernard, who was at the same time mystic and man of the world, recluse and churchman, contemplative and crusader, wrote thus to his sister, "The example of the saints contributes wonderfully to rouse the courage of sinners and to fortify the courage of the just. . . . Consider, every day of your life, what they did to please God — with what submission, what firmness, what austerity they walked in His ways. Let us follow the road which they have trodden. . . . They are our masters, we must learn in their school; they are our brothers, we must resemble them; they are our fathers, we must imitate them. Let their life be a model to ours."[19]

This saint taught truly that life is a school in which we may, if we wish, have the elect of God for our teachers. If some of the weighty biographies that are our textbooks seem hopelessly dull and tiresome, nevertheless let us in these pages wipe the dust from the pictures with patient fingers and then see their beauty. The saints are in the books, and their sweetness, lovableness, and loveliness shine through the maze of words like scattered gold.

I rejoice with all my heart when I find the life of a saint written in the manner of a breathless adventure, told as of one who goes through life with a laugh in his heart and a song on his lips, and runs at last into the arms of death, a lover too long withheld from his beloved.

A saint is a saint because he is in love with God. Saints know nothing of the only crushing sorrow in the world — the sense of unforgiven sin — because, if they commit sin, they run with childlike trust to ask their Father's forgiveness. Utterly trustful and childlike love of God is the one true joy in the world, and so saints are the happiest people imaginable.

All the world loves a lover, and so the world would love the saint if it were not too blind and stupid to understand his

[19] Ratisbonne, *The Life and Times of St. Bernard*, 483, 486.

The Joyful Ways of the Saints

exalted kind of loving. In the beautiful old days of chivalry, knights rode bravely and joyfully against the enemies of God and their king. They dared every danger for the sake of love's high fealty and the honor of their knighthood, and the world laid its homage at their feet because they were brave and fine and strong. Saints are in a truly ideal way the knights of God, who ride unafraid through the darkness of suffering and the strange silence of death — content with the far radiance of a Star in the East for guidance to their journey's end, for they know that it will lead into the Light and the Love of Heaven's morningtide.

And as the knights of God ride on and on, over the dusty highways of earth and through its shadowed places, they call back over their shoulders to you and to me: "Come along, come along with us to Paradise! You may find the way hard, but dawn is just over the farthest hill, and Love, dear Love, waits at the end."

Love, dear Love,
guide us all through the wind and the rain
and the night under the stars to where You wait at the end!
The way is dark and cold, but grant us to keep laughter in
our hearts and starlight in our eyes — laughter that shall break
into song when at last the starlight melts into the sun.

Chapter Two

∞

The Way of Kindness

Of Courtesy, it is much less
Than courage of heart or holiness,
Yet in my walks it seems to me
That the grace of God is in Courtesy.

Hilaire Belloc
"Courtesy"

∞

Old sayings and proverbs sometimes become so changed by the vicissitudes of time as to receive a meaning that is almost opposite to the original one. As an illustration, there is the instruction "Feed a cold, starve a fever," which was stated originally, "If you feed a cold, you will have to starve a fever."

Now, I think that the statement "It is difficult to live with a saint," has also been evolved from a theory entirely different from the common interpretation of this saying. In all likelihood, the author of the statement meant that it is difficult for critical people of easy conscience and lax morals to live in close contact with a person of heroic virtue, not because the saint himself is difficult and unkind, but because he is a constant reproach by his example. Many writers of spiritual books, however, and even biographers of saints have used this statement in the sense that the saint himself is the cause of the difficulty, and they have left us under the impression that holy people are difficult people to get along with, whereas surely the very opposite is true.

To be a saint is to be like Christ, and, as Stevenson said, "Christ was always a perfect gentleman." One needs only to read through the Gospels to learn the lesson of kindliness as taught by word and example, for kindliness is the outstanding feature of all our Lord's dealings with others. There can be no sanctity where there is no charity; and the flower of charity is Christian courtesy, or kindliness. Being an effect of sanctity, kindliness is, of course, less than its cause, and yet most of us can discern and appreciate the courtesy more than we can the holiness.

Why should saints be considered the sort of people who make others miserable, when it is emphatically true that charity is patient and kind, does not envy, does not deal perversely with others, does not seek its own, is not provoked to anger, and does not provoke others; bears, believes, hopes, endures all things, and never falls away?[20]

I suppose the reason some biographers of saints dwell at length on the cutting remarks and unkind acts of which certain saints were guilty (and for which, in all probability, they did secret penance) is that the rest of us, seeing them to be human like ourselves, may be encouraged to imitate their virtues. But I wonder whether there is not something wrong with the philosophy of these writers. Does it do us good to have the feet of our idols continually scratched that we may see the clay? May not the clay feet, because of our human perversity, occupy too prominent a place in our vision? It seems to me that it is better for us to have the ninety-nine kind little acts emphasized rather than the one burst of a temper too hardly tried. When we read of the rare explosion of that same temper, we are inclined to forget what the poet Robert Burns pathetically bids us remember: "What's done we may partly compute / But know not what's resisted."[21] And we are inclined to lay the

---

[20] Cf. 1 Cor. 13:4-5, 7-8.

[21] Address to the Unco Guid.

flattering unction to our souls: "Well, perhaps I'm not so bad, after all."

Among the hundred exquisitely beautiful things said by Chesterton concerning "the dear little saint in the old brown coat," none is sweeter or truer than this. When St. Francis of Assisi, inspired almost equally by the desire to spread Christianity and the desire to obtain martyrdom, went into the dwelling of the sultan in the city of Damietta, and then returned as freely as he entered, there seems to have been but one sufficient explanation: "Men liked him too much for himself to let him die for his Faith; and the man was received instead of the message."[22] Francis seems indeed to have "walked the world like the pardon of God. I mean that his appearance marked the moment when men could be reconciled not only to God but to nature and, most difficult of all, to themselves. . . . It was in fact his whole function to tell men to start afresh and, in that sense, to tell them to forget."[23] God's forgetfulness of forgiven sin is man's hope.

The saint, above all other people, possesses the wonderful power of restoring hope and confidence to those who have by sin merited misery. The saint uses his natural attractiveness to lead others to do their utmost for God. One who reads the life or the writings of St. Francis will understand — as much as one can understand God's ways in using people to accomplish His designs — why it was that the "little poor man" organized a crusade, in which were enlisted the sons of the noble and powerful rich, whose soldiers wore on their sleeves, not the

[22] *St. Francis of Assisi*, ch. 8.
[23] Ibid., ch. 10.

ribbon of a lady who dwelt in a palace, but the rag of Lady Poverty, whose dwelling was a cavern in the rocks. It is easy to believe that St. Francis, who, as a richly attired young man, tore through the streets after a beggar in order to load him with coins and who got down from his horse to hold a leper to his breast while he gave him money, flung his clothes at his father's feet and, clad in a hair shirt, went into the wilderness to get away from riches. If he had regrets, they must have been simply that he no longer had money to bestow upon the needy. And because he was so lovable in his simple bravery and his fine, young strength, other young men were inspired also to scatter their wealth among the poor and to run unencumbered along the hard ways that lead ever upward to the heavenly home of the poor Man of Galilee, who had on earth not even a stone whereon to rest His head.

∞

Sanctity calls for kindness

Among all the saints who have accomplished tremendously great things since apostolic days, the palm must be handed to that other Francis who, inspired by a zeal equal to that of the Francis who turned all Europe into a monastery for the poor friars, turned the Orient into the Catholic Church. St. Francis Xavier,[24] the "giant of the missions," although such a dreadful man in the eyes of Satan, was most gentle and lovable in himself, and saw the necessity of kindness in his fellow religious who were to labor in the vineyards of the Lord.

---

[24] St. Francis Xavier (1506-1552), Jesuit missionary known as the Apostle of the Indies.

In a letter to St. Ignatius that he wrote from India, he advised, "Anyone whom you are to send to be rector of the college at Goa, where he will rule the native students as well as our own people, must have, besides the other qualities which are necessary in rectors, two recommendations in particular. In the first place, let him be conspicuous for singular obedience. . . . In the second place, he should be very easy and gentle; affable in behavior and speech, rather than grave or severe, so as both to desire and to be able to bind to himself in every way the hearts, of all, and especially of the students and brethren whom he is to rule. . . . He ought, in short, to be such a man as even in giving an order seems rather to desire to do what he is told than to command."

During a few weeks spent in Venice, St. Francis was appointed to the Hospital of the Incurables. There he was the servant of all, waiting upon the sick and ministering to the lepers, making their beds, sweeping their rooms and cooking their food — and all this in addition to his priestly duties in their regard. Surely caring for lepers is the last word in kindness, especially if one happens to be delicate and refined by nature. He seems to have spent the greater number of his nights sleeping on the floor or earth — when they were not nights of prayer or care for others — while his own bed was occupied by a sick person.

∞

Humble kindness commands
others' love and respect

Everyone is attracted by real saints, just as inevitably as flowers lift their faces to the sun. Real saints do not go about with a stern and forbidding manner, donned for the purpose of demanding due respect for their personal dignity. In the first place, the genuine saint is entirely convinced that he has no personal dignity. True saints are humble, with the touching humility of unspoiled children. St. Francis Xavier wrote to St. Ignatius on his knees and signed one of his greatest letters to his brethren, "the useless servant of all my brethren of the Society of the Name of Jesus."

In the second place, the only kind of respect that a saint could desire — the respect for him as a temple of the Holy Spirit — is as a rule freely offered by those around him, and therefore he does not need to demand it. Not all the saints were granted the stupendous grace of martyrdom; many of them were held in honor even during their lives.

There is a strange perversity in us human beings that makes us delight in pricking the bubble of assumed dignity, or pompousness, and makes us respectful to the humble. We love the kind and humble person, and where there is genuine love, there is always respect. Then, too, in an all-embracing friendliness, there is a mantle of protection that repels the assaults of familiarity even more than the sternest severity is able to do.

Saints are always ready to be "bothered" by the tiresome petitions and confidences of others, for they are like Christ, who heard the beggars and the sick and the sinful when they cried after Him in a crowd that was acclaiming Him king. St. Lawrence[25] managed a smile and jest for his executioners, because he had before his fainting eyes the picture of a Cross on a

---

[25] St. Lawrence (d. 258), deacon and martyr.

hill, while in his ears there sounded a voice saying, "Father, forgive them, for they know not what they do."[26]

But the strange paradox seems to be that the greater number of hermits were men who had the tenderest love for others and a charm of personality that drew many after them into the desert. Their hovels in the rocks became beacons to the sin-darkened world. Genuine saints draw the hearts of men to God, for it is easy to see the tenderness of our Brother Jesus in their tenderness. The harsh and forbidding person never makes others think of God, whereas the love awakened by the god-like person is a love that leads to God.

Although we are prone to think of hermits as most austere men, whose voluntary exile from the ways of ordinary living among others made them most unsympathetic and unloving as well as most unlovable, the exact contrary seems to be the truth. It is a truth that should receive emphasis.

Of St. Anthony the Hermit,[27] who spent a great part of his time in hand-to-hand fights with devils and would therefore seem fated to be most ungracious in his ways, St. Athanasius wrote, "He was, in fact, like a healer given to Egypt by God. For who went to him in sorrow and did not return in joy? Who came mourning for his dead and did not quickly put aside his grief? Who came in anger and was not changed to kindness? Who sought him desperate in his poverty and, hearing him and seeing him, did not learn to despise wealth and take comfort from poverty? . . . Who came to him tempted by devils and was not freed? Who came with troublous thoughts and

[26] Luke 23:34.
[27] St. Anthony of Egypt (c. 251-356), hermit.

gained not peace of mind? . . . From foreign lands, too, men came to him, and having received help with the rest, returned as if sent forth by their father."[28]

One does not wonder that so frequently in his narrative St. Athanasius wrote, "and Anthony smiled and said" his words of peace and joy and healing, nor does one wonder that people ran to him "as if drawn by his eyes." We are never so blinded by our tears of sorrow as to mistake the unkind for the kind face, never so weighed down by our burden of grief as to be unable to run into arms outstretched for our comforting, never so old as not to become little children again at the voice of under-standing tenderness, never so weak and sinful as not to draw new strength from a great and Christlike heart that will send us forth unafraid to do battle. St. Anthony's cavern in the rocks shone through the darkness of the surrounding country as a lantern shines through the night, to tell the needy that somewhere they could find light and love and warmth.

∞

Holiness produces cheerfulness

Anthony was the most joyous of men, and his unfailing cheerfulness so found expression in his face that he drew the sad of heart to himself as a magnet draws steel. To be cheerful when one is sick in body or heavy of heart is to practice heroic kindness.

Even among the saints who are presented to us by pietistic biographers as lachrymose and sour-visaged, many have left

[28] St. Athanasius (c. 296-373; Bishop of Alexandria), *Life of Saint Anthony*, sect. 87, 88.

us writings bright and happy as can be, and when they have been allowed to speak for themselves on the tearful pages of their biographies, they have spoken in the manner of optimistic Catholics rather than in the pessimistic manner of their puritanical biographers.

Why should saints *not* be cheerful, since there is no joy in the world like that born of a happy conscience and a pure heart? Sin is the only legitimate cause of pessimism. All other sorrows are really the "shade of God's hand outstretched caressingly."

St. Gabriel Possenti[29] was wont to say, "Well, you know things might be much worse. There are so many good and pleasant things that happen to us; let us think about them, and overlook our little disappointments." Now, we must not forget that St. Gabriel was the victim of pulmonary tuberculosis and suffered very much. He was, however, always joyful and serene, and so personally attractive that his associates were constantly trying to be with him and to wait upon him. His little cell was the most popular spot, after the chapel, in the monastery, and his brethren vied with one another to be appointed to remain with him. One of them said that it was something more than fraternal charity that made them eager to care for Gabriel; it was his joyousness, which cheered and warmed them like sunshine.

Most of the men who have done great things as leaders of others were cheerful men. Our Lord was a man of sorrows and was acquainted with grief,[30] and yet we know that He was not

---

[29] St. Gabriel Possenti (1838-1862), Italian Passionist known for his cheerfulness.

[30] Isa. 53:3.

morose. If He had been so, the children would not have run to His arms, for children are afraid of gloomy people.

Brotherly love and its outward expression in affectionate courtesy or kindliness is the mark of the ordinary Christian. "By this shall all men know that you are my disciples," said the Master, "if you have love one for another."[31] All men were to understand this sign, and therefore our Lord meant by brotherly love something that manifests itself toward others unmistakably. He did not mean that peculiar kind of brotherly love which is locked so deep in its owner's heart that only he knows of its existence; He meant the love that bubbles out onto others, as from a living spring, in smiles and kind words and deeds.

∞

Kindliness springs from love

If this kind of love is required from the ordinary Christian, we may expect boundless love from the saint. St. Bernard wrote thus concerning the virtue of charity that flowers in kindliness: "In our neighbor, we should love his virtues and not his vices; to do otherwise would be to hate and not to love him. Have you no charity toward your brother whom you see before you? I doubt, then, whether you have any for God, whom you do not see. We are, then, under an obligation to love each other; and God, who has commanded it, is the source of this fraternal affection. He is its beginning and end. If we are without love of our brethren, who are visible and manifest to the eyes of our body, it is in vain that we seek God and charity with the eyes of the soul — neither of them dwell

---

[31] John 13:35.

with us. The one cannot be there without the other; for God and charity are one and the same. We are under obligation to love our kindred, if they be good people and servants of God; if they be not so, we owe more affection to strangers in whom we may meet with these holy dispositions — the bonds of nature not being so strong as those of grace, and the blood which flows in our veins less to be loved by us than the precious blood of Jesus Christ."

St. Bernard practiced what he preached. One of the chroniclers of his life tells us that during his stay in Milan — the scene of many of his miracles — he had no time for rest, because all who were troubled "found their rest in his labor and weariness." There was an uninterrupted succession of persons coming to see him and to beg his favors. It would be easy to excuse the saint if he had shown a little impatience at the crowds who selfishly thronged upon him with their importunities, for he was at the time suffering greatly in body, and in his soul he harbored an almost unbearable loneliness for his cloister home. One can readily understand how the exhortations of such a man won rich men and poor into the Crusades.

The Church, from the day her Founder drooped His thorn-torn head in silent anguish on a Cross of shame, has forever been the champion of causes that the blinded world calls lost, and yet from every bodily defeat has come a victory for her soul. St. Bernard was the true son of Christ and His Church in his understanding of what victory can be drawn from defeat. Our Lord told us of the joy in Heaven over one sinner who does penance.[32] To see in every human soul the brother of our

---

[32] Cf. Luke 15:7.

Lord, and, seeing, love and serve for love — this is charity, the virtue by which we shall be judged.

The kindliness or courtesy that springs from a heart Christ-like in its love of humanity is not at all the same as the courtesy born of good breeding and good taste or of worldly prudence. Christian kindliness is to be found among the uneducated as well as among the educated; it abides in the hovel as well as in the palace. Charity of the heart aided by education and good breeding is perhaps more charming in the eyes of men, but not a bit more holy or pleasing to God, we may be sure, than the charity of heart that lacks these external aids to perfect expression of itself.

Christ our Lord, the humble Son of the carpenter of Nazareth, shall ever be to us, as to Stevenson, the one truly perfect gentleman, for He was the one true Lover of all. And in proportion as a man resembles Christ in this matter of loving does he deserve the grand old name of Christian gentleman — which, perhaps, ought to be written as two words: gentle man.

Among all the saints, none deserves the name of Christian gentleman more than St. Francis de Sales, whose philosophy of life was colored throughout by the sunshine of brotherly love. Although, in some ways, his *Treatise on the Love of God* is to be considered his masterpiece, his personal correspondence, especially with St. Jane Frances de Chantal,[33] gives us a most satisfying understanding of his deep, abiding love of others. The system of direction by which he prepared Mme. de Chantal for her share in the work of founding the Order of the

[33] St. Jane Frances de Chantal (1572-1641), founder of the Order of the Visitation with St. Francis de Sales.

Visitation was in great measure built on this principle: "Live joyously and be generous. God, whom we love, and to whom we are consecrated, wants this of us." In another letter he writes, "Be joyous in serving God, I beseech you; joyous without forgetting yourself, confident without being arrogant."

This great bishop understood well the real cause of joy: the peace of a good conscience. "You would not," he tells Mme. de Chantal, "for the whole world, offend God. And is that not enough to make you rejoice?"

These were not mere platitudes addressed to one whose soul was always basking in the sunshine of spiritual consolation; St. Jane Frances de Chantal suffered from scruples and from spiritual dryness just as others do. Her saintly director taught her the distinction between the affective, or involuntary and fluctuating, elements of the soul, and the effective, or voluntary and fixed, elements. "Don't be anxious," he bids her. "Everything is going on very well. Darkness, yes, but we are very near the light all the same. Powerlessness, yes, but we lie at the feet of One all powerful." Again and again, he bids her be cheerful and trustful; at the end of his life, he is still saying to her, "Oh, how blessed are those souls who live on the will of God alone!" Cheerfully and bravely he led this unusual woman up the mount of Calvary; cheerfully and bravely she followed, for he was more than a director, being a friend to whose hand she could cling when the way was most difficult and dangerous.

∞

Kindliness manifests itself in serving others
St. Francis taught Mme. de Chantal how to practice the virtue of kindliness, as he practiced it. He tells her that if

someone interrupts her meditation by a request for help, she must come away from it with a bright face and a gracious heart toward the person who has interrupted her, because it is all the same serving of God, whether she meditates or bears with her neighbor.

The holy bishop would have had little patience with those pietistic people who spend long hours in prayer, only to make others unhappy the moment they come forth from the chapel. There can be no true love of God in the heart that cannot love its fellowmen, as the Master told us so often during the three years that He walked publicly on earth's ways and showed us how to live and how to love. He told us to love one another as He loves us, which means with even a greater love than self-love, with a love that is willing to lay down life itself for the beloved.[34] Such is the love that set a Cross on Calvary, that sent Francis Xavier into the Orient, and that struck the body of Fr. Damien[35] with leprosy. Such is the love that flowers in the heart of every real saint and scatters its perfume over the dark and lonely valleys of human suffering and despondency.

Tradition tells us that St. Francis de Sales, on the occasion of his first visit to Rome, met St. Philip Neri,[36] who embraced him tenderly and kissed him on the forehead, saying that he was destined for greatness in the service of God. It seems fitting that these two saints, who were such living personifications of the kindliness of sanctity, should have met and loved.

---

[34] Cf. John 15:12-13.

[35] Fr. Damien (1840-1889), leper missionary.

[36] St. Philip Neri (1515-1595), Italian priest who founded the Congregation of the Oratory.

In his biography of St. Philip, Cardinal Capecelatro writes, "Now, if I do not deceive myself, Philip and Francis of Sales resemble each other so closely that we might at times almost mistake one for the other. . . . We find in both the same glowing love of God, the same gentleness and meekness, the same sunny smile, the same winning sweetness of speech, and the same intense zeal for the salvation of souls; even the charms of natural disposition, and the serene beauty which comes of unsullied purity of heart, were alike in both; and in both we find that unlimited kindness and considerateness which is not weakness, but the perfection of self-sacrifice."

Only the person who constantly immolates self on the altar of God's love can attain the serenity of soul that flowers in untiring considerateness for the needs of others. One who can enter into the sorrows of others without allowing his own heart to be unduly disturbed has really modeled himself on the Master, whose inner serenity was untroubled while He wept with Mary and Martha for their dead brother.[37] Understanding sympathy from the strong and serene of soul is the most healing spiritual medicine in man's power to give. The one who can give such sympathy is a magnet to the souls of others. The attractiveness of understanding sympathy was one of St. Philip's outstanding qualities.

"All he did," writes Cardinal Newman, who had such tender devotion to him, "was to be done by the light, and fervor, and convincing eloquence of his personal character and his easy conversation. He came to the Eternal City, and he sat himself down there, and his home and his family gradually grew up

[37] Cf. John 11:33-35.

around him, by the spontaneous accession of materials from without. He did not so much seek his own as draw them to him. He sat in his small room, and they in their gay worldly dresses, the rich and the well-born, as well as the simple and the illiterate, crowded into it. In the mid-heats of summer, in the frosts of winter, still was he in that low and narrow cell at San Girolamo, reading the hearts of those who came to him, and curing their souls' maladies by the very touch of his hand."

One does not think of Newman as in the least inclined to write extravagantly, and so this tender tribute has the greater weight. St. Philip's biographer Pietre Bacci confirms the idea of saintly kindliness; he says that Philip was "all things to all men. He suited himself to noble and ignoble, young and old, subjects and prelates, learned and ignorant. When he was called upon to be merry, he was so; if there was a demand upon his sympathy, he was equally ready. . . . In consequence of his being accessible and willing to receive all comers . . . his room went by the agreeable nickname of the Home of Christian Mirth." Beautiful nickname! Home of cheerful kindliness, home of friendship, wherein the sad and the friendless were welcome — how it speaks of Heaven!

∞

Sanctity is kind and cheerful
Who can say truthfully that it is difficult to live with a saint? I admit that some of the people who pray much seem to have very sharp tongues, but I am convinced that there is something wrong with their prayers. If they prayed earnestly to be able to become like our Savior, then, as surely as the sun rises, they would become kind to their brothers and sisters in Christ.

We have seen in this little visit among the saints that sanctity is the kindest, happiest, cheeriest thing in the mind of man to conceive, that sanctity is unselfish and deeply affectionate, with such unselfishness and affection as make true friendship possible, that sanctity takes its delight in spending itself prodigally for others, because it loves them for the sake of God. We have seen that sanctity can see others preferred without a throb of jealousy, that it can endure hardship and monotony without tears and complaint. We have seen that sanctity cares no more for homage and others' bowing to its dignity than did He over whom the laughing children played and after whom the sinners and the sick crept, crying for the help that came swiftly and surely.

In a word, we have seen that sanctity is kind. Sanctity is kind because it is born of the queen of virtues: the love of God. Let us who love God, then, ask the saints to teach us how to pour out our love in kindness to one another for His sake. For who is so brave that he can live without love, who so strong that he needs not kindness? Shall we whose hands are forever outstretched through the darkness toward the warmth and light of love bring nothing in return for all that love has to give?

Life is for so many a valley of tears. Shall we who bask in the light of faith not help to turn the tears into a rainbow that is like the smile of God? No matter what trials come to us, we can learn from the saints how to face them with brave and sunny hearts. We can learn from them to strip from ourselves all selfishness, even the sweet selfishness of grief for our dear ones who are dead that so often makes us forget the needs of our dear ones who are living.

The Joyful Ways of the Saints

See our Mother at the foot of the Cross, who at her Son's bidding takes all the suffering ones of the world into her arms to mother them.[38] See the Lord turn His eyes to look on Peter,[39] hear Him promise immediate joy to the repentant thief,[40] hear Him pray for His executioners,[41] and learn that He who is goodness and holiness and justice is also kindness. Study Him in His saints, and learn that holiness is kind. Where there is true sanctity, there is kindliness.

Dear God, make us kind.

[38] Cf. John 19:26.
[39] Cf. Luke 22:61.
[40] Cf. Luke 23:43.
[41] Cf. Luke 23:34.

Chapter Three

The Way of Wisdom

Behold my teacher and my rule;
Thyself, St. Francis, art my school;
God, give me grace to be a fool!

A significantly arranged group of letters attached to a man's name usually indicates that he has highly specialized knowledge of some particular subject. The letters, however, give no indication of his wisdom. He may be, in many senses of the word, a fool.

In a general way, wisdom means the ability to deal sagaciously with facts as they relate to life and conduct. There are two kinds of wisdom — worldly and spiritual — and the possessor of either usually brands the possessor of the other as foolish. Considered in its true meaning as one of the gifts of the Holy Spirit, wisdom is that disposition or quality of the soul that enables one to judge rightly of divine things and to esteem and love them according to the inspiration of the Holy Spirit. Wisdom teaches the four cardinal virtues: temperance, prudence, justice, and fortitude. There is nothing in life more profitable than these four virtues, because by them a man governs himself, and he who governs himself is ruler of the world.

St. Thérèse of Lisieux, that sweet Little Flower of Jesus, once said, "We have only the few moments of life to spend for the glory of God; the Devil knows it well, and it is for this reason that he endeavors to make us waste them in useless works." The use or misuse of time is sufficient to determine whether a person is wise or foolish in regard to things spiritual.

The Joyful Ways of the Saints

We all complain frequently that we have not enough time, forgetting that we have all the time there is. The trouble with most of us is that we do not "fill the unforgiving minute with sixty seconds' worth of distance run," as Rudyard Kipling puts it.[42] Many of us waste our time in waiting for opportunities to do big things of temporal worth, and thus let the little things of eternal worth go undone. We long to conquer the enemies of Christ, and we are not able even to bridle our own tongues. We wish to preach the gospel to all men, and we sulk if others are preferred before us.

During her short life on earth, the Little Flower made such good use of time in doing small things of eternal worth that now she has power to do tremendous miracles. Our Lord preached the necessity of using time well and of doing little things as perfectly as possible. One who fails to use time in accordance with the dictates of spiritual wisdom works blindly, like a scientific instrument, seeking after the fleeting joys of earth, incessantly trying to get rid of time, rather than to use it. Such a man forgets that time is given him to be used for God and the good of others; he uses time merely for selfish purposes.

∞

Only spiritual things endure

Another name for worldly wisdom is selfishness. It is the wisdom that works for power and gain, using others as mere stepping-stones to its ends. Selfishness defeats itself in the final reckoning, and the foolishness of the spiritually unwise is

---

[42] Rudyard Kipling, *Rewards and Fairies*, "If —."

in their failure to see this truth. No man is so truly a slave as the one who is a slave to himself. He is not only a slave, but is most unwise as well, for "he that trusteth in his own heart is a fool."[43]

There is one sentence among the "vain boastings of the wicked" in the book of Wisdom that shows particularly the stupidity of worldly wisdom: "Let us crown ourselves with roses, before they be withered."[44] The roses of earth must wither, even if they be woven into crowns while they are still fresh and beautiful. But the red roses of martyrdom and the white roses of purity that are gathered by the spiritually wise shall be woven into a crown of beauty by the hand of the Lord.

The spiritually wise may say of his wisdom, "By the means of her I shall have immortality and shall leave behind me an everlasting memory to them that come after me."[45] But the worldly wise men say truly, "Our name in time shall be forgotten, and no man shall have any remembrance of our works."[46]

Deep in every human heart, there is desire for immortality of some kind. The trouble with spiritually unwise people is that they desire the unattainable kind of immortality. They desire to live on in the memories of men because of merely artistic or material accomplishments. The memories of men, however, are fickle. Countless multitudes have lived on the earth, and yet few individual names have come down to us even from among those who have ruled nations or have created

[43] Prov. 28:26.
[44] Wisd. 2:8.
[45] Wisd. 8:13.
[46] Wisd. 2:4.

masterpieces of art. The passage of most men through the world is, in the words of Wisdom, "as a ship that passeth through the waves: whereof when it is gone by, the trace cannot be found."[47]

In devotion to the Holy Face, little Thérèse found earthly immortality along with heavenly. "There," she said, "I understood better than ever what is true glory. He whose 'kingdom is not of this world' showed me that the only enviable royalty consists in 'loving to be unknown and reputed as nothing,' and in putting one's joy in the contempt of oneself. Oh, like Jesus, I wished that my face was hidden from all eyes, that no one should recognize me on earth: I thirsted to suffer and to be forgotten."[48]

Here is a giant paradox — these words from one who is the dear lady of countless hearts today, whose beautiful face smiles from myriad photographs with flowers and lights before them. Truly the Lord puts down the mighty from their seats and exalts the humble. Sr. Thérèse once said that she would "never be able to take any rest until the end of the world" because she wished to pass her Heaven "in doing good upon the earth." We have every reason to believe that her wish is being realized. True immortality has come to this little unknown nun who gave up all that the world holds dear and sought only to be forgotten.

Among the parables of our Lord, one in particular points out the folly of preferring earthly riches to heavenly delights. A steward was about to be dismissed by his master and therefore

---

[47] Wisd. 5:10.
[48] *Story of a Soul*, ch. 7.

desired to provide for his future. He called together the debtors of his master and greatly reduced the amount recorded
against each one. "And the lord commended the unjust steward, for as much as he had done wisely" in thus making friends
who would receive him into their homes after his dismissal.[49]
This is the end of the parable but not its point. The Savior
also gave this warning: "No man can serve two masters; for either he will hate the one and love the other, or he will hold to
the one and despise the other. You cannot serve God and
mammon."[50]

One must make the choice between things of earth and
things of Heaven, and eternity is involved in the choosing. It
requires no small measure of heroism to obey the dictates of
the wisdom of saintliness, and yet Revelation tells us that
there are countless multitudes in Heaven, upon whose foreheads is the sign of spiritual wisdom.[51]

There can be found in the parable of the unjust steward another deep meaning. The steward acted as if he were the
owner of the goods that were in his control. Worldly-minded
people act thus, also, when, as a matter of fact, they own nothing. God is the Master and Owner of all things, and we are but
the stewards in whose charge they have been placed so that we
may use them for God's glory. One may understand how the
atheist can act as if he were supreme in his control of wealth
and faculties, but one cannot understand how the believer can
act so.

---

[49] Luke 16:8.

[50] Matt. 6:24.

[51] Cf. Apoc. 14:1 (RSV = Rev. 14:1).

∞

Humility lets you see yourself as you are

There are many apparent paradoxes in the Scriptures, and they become simple statements only in the light of the Spirit. St. Paul tells us plainly, "Let no man deceive himself; if any man among you seems to be wise in this world, let him become a fool, that he may be wise. For the wisdom of this world is foolishness with God. For it is written: I will catch the wise in their own craftiness. And again: The Lord knoweth the thoughts of the wise, that they are vain. Let no man glory in men. For all things are yours."[52]

The Savior, however, told us to learn of Him how to be meek and humble of heart.[53] He said that we can enter Heaven only if we become little with the humility of little children.[54] The humility of children makes them truly democratic, and in no sense respecters of social prestige. Therefore their judgments are usually sound.

Democracy is the most Christian thing in the world, for it is founded on the principle of the worth of the individual and his natural rights. Yet there is in democracy an element of dangerous thought. Democracy teaches me rightly that everyone is in nature just as great and noble as I am, but it teaches me also that I am just as great and noble as anyone else. If I have a small mind, this second thought may exalt me to a level that will swell my head. If, on the other hand, I have a great mind, it will serve to make me more humble.

---

[52] 1 Cor. 3:18-21.
[53] Matt. 11:29.
[54] Cf. Matt. 18:3.

Humility does not mean self-depreciation; it means seeing oneself as one is. It is the way of us human beings to constitute ourselves the center of our solar system and to expect others in our universe to revolve around us like satellites. The more earthly-minded we are, the more confirmed we are in this delusion. Only the spiritually wise person can see himself as he really is: a most small and unimportant satellite of the Sun of Justice, whose one duty it is to reflect the glory of that Sun.

In teaching the principles of religion, our Lord again and again insists upon humility and condemns pride. Even before His birth, that sweet lady of our dearest love, His Mother, sang in her immortal *Magnificat*, "He hath scattered the proud in the conceit of their heart. He hath put down the mighty from their seat and hath exalted the humble. He hath filled the hungry with good things, and the rich he hath sent empty away."[55] The little maid of Nazareth, who had to bring the doves of the poor when she presented her divine Infant in the Temple,[56] was already in fullest sympathy with the teaching of poverty and humility, at that time a most strange and new doctrine in the world.

∞

The saints resist the world's ways

Many years later, the Master, looking on a rich young man and loving him, said to him, "One thing is wanting unto thee: go, sell whatsoever thou hast, and give to the poor, and thou shalt have treasure in Heaven; and come, follow me." But the

[55] Luke 1:51-53.
[56] Luke 2:22-24.

The Joyful Ways of the Saints

young man was spiritually unwise, and "being struck sad at that saying, went away sorrowful, for he had great possessions." Jesus looked after him and then said to his disciples, "How hardly shall they that have riches enter into the kingdom of God!" The disciples, not yet fully enlightened, "were astonished at His words." But Jesus said to them, "Children, how hard is it for them that trust in riches to enter into the kingdom of God." So prevalent was the worldly spirit in those days that the disciples began to question, "Who, then, can be saved?" And Peter, who was usually the spokesman of the disciples, reminded Jesus, "Behold, we have left all things and have followed Thee." Then came the strangest and perhaps the most glorious doctrine ever announced to men: "Amen, I say to you, there is no man who hath left house, or brethren, or sisters, or father, or mother, or children, or lands, for my sake and for the gospel, who shall not receive a hundred times as much, now in this time, houses, and brethren, and sisters, and mothers, and children, and lands, with persecutions, and, in the world to come, life everlasting. But many that are first, shall be last, and the last, first."[57]

It is strange indeed that persecutions should be listed among the blessings, yet, in the light of history, persecution seems to have been truly a blessing, because ages of persecution have been ages of faith that have given countless saints and martyrs to the Church, and because, in times of peace, the fervor of the faithful has sometimes cooled almost to extinction.

Our Lord said, "Amen, amen, I say to you, unless the grain of wheat falling into the ground die, itself remaineth alone.

[57] Mark 10:21-31.

But if it die, it bringeth forth much fruit. He that loveth his life shall lose it; and he that hateth his life in this world, keepeth it unto life eternal."[58] To hate one's life in this world would seem a strange instruction from Him who came that we might have more abundant life, were it not interpreted from the spiritual point of view. The Master warned His disciples that the earthly-minded would find difficulty in understanding this doctrine and those who obeyed it, and He promised them that they would be persecuted for their heavenly doctrines. Never before had there been a teacher who made such strange promises to those asked to follow him: hardship, poverty, hatred, and persecution. The long list of martyrs shows that the promises were kept.

The promises are being kept today, also, although the hatred and the persecution use more insidious methods. We call ourselves Christians today with no fear of a cruel death as a consequence, but the world links arms with us and whispers its seductive wisdom into our ears. Sad indeed is it for those of us who do not understand that the Devil is the more to be feared when he comes in the guise of an angel of light.

The grand old Church of Christ, with the wisdom of the Holy Spirit behind her, must, more than ever before in her history, hurl her eternal "No!" in the face of the false philosophies that parade the earth in magnificent apparel today. When there is a well-nigh universal repeal of laws restricting divorce; when horrible and heretofore unmentionable crimes against the marriage bond are committed; when it is made a matter of patriotism that the right of educating children should be taken

---

[58] John 12:24-25.

from their parents and given to the state; when there [are] laws that permit doctors to kill children and hopelessly sick people; when labor extortioners salve their consciences by self-advertising gifts to charity, it is indeed a time when men who believe in God and their own immortal souls should heed the voice of wisdom speaking through the Church. It is indeed a time to remember that the servant is not greater than his Master, to remember that nothing in the world matters except the Master and the soul of the servant.

∞

Spiritual wisdom conquers worldliness

If ever in the history of Christianity there was a city given over to the worst phases of worldliness, that city was Ormuz, on an island in the Persian Gulf, in the days of St. Francis Xavier. The city was conspicuous for its vices in those days, and yet I think we have many like it today. Francis knew of the conditions in Ormuz, and so he sent Fr. Gaspar Baertz to convert the wicked people of the infamous city.

The instructions given by St. Francis to this chosen apostle are a remarkable illustration of true spiritual wisdom in dealing with the evil of worldliness, and they also afford us intimate glimpses into the soul of Francis himself, for we may be sure that he was writing from his own experiences. We learn from them how he imitated the Master in his dealings with sinners and hypocrites, how carefully he studied human nature and individual characters whom he wished to benefit, and how he trained the fathers and brothers who were given into his care.

St. Francis first exhorted Fr. Baertz, "Above all things, be mindful of yourself, and of discharging faithfully what you owe first to God, and then to your own conscience; for by means of these two duties, you will find yourself become more capable of serving your neighbors and of gaining souls. Take care always to incline, even beyond moderation, to the practice of the most abject employments. By exercising yourself in them, you will acquire humility, and daily advance in that virtue."

In emphasizing humility, St. Francis is in accord with the teachings of our Lord and the saints. Humility is the foundation of spiritual wisdom — not the alleged humility that pretends modesty, but the humility that sees things as they are. In the parable of the talents, the Master warned us against false humility that fails to make use of natural gifts for God's glory.[59] Although a little learning may be a dangerous thing in that it breeds conceit, great learning necessarily begets humility, for the more one learns, the more one realizes how little he can ever really know.

Being wise, St. Francis understood that the best way in which to provide for the future of Ormuz was through its children. He bade Fr. Baertz to instruct the little ones of the city, so that they at least may thus be saved, and told him to visit the hospitals, poorhouses, and prisons, to bring there the sacraments and the word of God. Saints are usually considered impractical and sometimes imprudent people, but no such accusations could be brought against St. Francis Xavier. He warned Fr. Baertz to take care in matters of restitution of ill-gotten goods on the part of his penitents and, where actual restitution could not be made to those defrauded, to give the conscience money to the Brotherhood of Mercy.

[59] Matt. 25:14-30.

From one who so loved his friends next came this advice to Fr. Baertz: to treat his friends as if they might someday be his enemies, and therefore never let them be aware of any word or act that could later be used to work mischief toward his work or business. "This consideration of the instability of men will also make you look more to God, despise yourself more, and cling to God, who is ever present to us, with extreme humility and sweetness of soul." Because of his close union with God, Francis knew exactly what to expect from friendship. Yet, although he understood the frailties of human nature, he never lost faith in humanity.

∞

Mercy and gentleness lead others to repentance

People who are very hard on themselves are usually most tender with others; whereas those who are most tender toward themselves are usually rigid with others. There is no more Christlike expression of wisdom than tenderness toward the weaknesses of others. The gentleness of the saints in dealing with sinners whom they hope to win to repentance is one of their outstanding qualities. The saints understand that most people are led more easily than they are driven. Harshness and cruelty are the worst kinds of stupidity, and so we seldom find saints harsh and cruel. Their conduct is modeled on that of Him who will not break the bruised reed or quench the smoldering wick.[60]

Here, for instance, are the words of the apostle of the Indies, who mortified himself almost beyond endurance: "In

[60] Cf. Isa. 42:3.

dealing with persons who are ashamed to confess their foul sins, we must sometimes go so far and so low, in order to loosen the chain of this miserable shame in these unhappy persons whose tongues the Devil has by his cunning tied up, as of our own accord to indicate in general the sins of our own past lives, so to elicit from these guilty souls the confession of the sins which they will otherwise hide, to their irreparable loss. For what can a true and fervent charity refuse to pay for the safety of those souls who have been redeemed with the blood of Jesus Christ?"

This makes one think of Him who was censured because "He was gone to be a guest with a man that was a sinner,"[61] and who, because He let a sinful woman come into the house where He sat at supper, to wash His feet with her tears and dry them with her hair, read in the mind of the Pharisee who had invited Him these words: "This man, if He were a prophet, would know surely who and what manner of woman this is that toucheth Him, that she is a sinner."[62] Those who criticized the Master could not understand that it was *just because* the man and the woman were sinners that Jesus was so kind to them. It was for the sake of sinners that He came to live among men.

To the worldly-minded, such conduct is utter folly; and even to the spiritually wise who have not attained true humility, it is difficult and perhaps abhorrent. Tempering justice with mercy is a method of correction that only the spiritually wise who have studied our Savior's life can use.

---

[61] Luke 19:7.
[62] Luke 7:39.

The Joyful Ways of the Saints

Spiritual wisdom produces happiness

Once, when he met a newcomer to the order, St. Ignatius said to him, "Francis, I see you are always laughing." I suppose Francis stopped laughing at that. But, far from getting the rebuke he expected, he heard, "I am glad of it; and while you are docile and faithful to your rule, I do not think you can be too gay. But remember, you must not be depressed by things that do not please you. I think I see in you the possessor of talents above the common; but if they are not of use because you lack humility, you will be sad."

The saint did not require of the novice the false humility that fails to recognize and use one's talents. He taught that to lack the humility that makes one's talents of use is a real cause of sadness. Herein speaks the wisdom of saintliness. It seems to me that laughter should come as easily to the pure of heart in maturity as in childhood. There is only one real reason for sourness and pessimism, and that is the consciousness of unrepented and unforgiven sin. It is certain that the devils in Hell weep, and it is equally certain that they do not laugh joyously.

Most of us are inclined to consider the life of the hermit as the last word in joylessness, forgetting that the closer a person comes to God, the more joy he must secure. Then, too, we forget the true meaning of contentment, which consists not in the multiplicity of comforts and pleasures, but in the ability to be satisfied with what we have — not in the multiplication of wants, but in the diminution of them. St. Anthony the Hermit is the embodiment of the contentment that springs from wisdom; he had nothing whatsoever, and so he had nothing to worry him.

St. Athanasius, who knew Anthony well, says of him, "If he was with a company of monks and someone wished to see him, who did not know him before, as soon as he arrived, he would pass over the others and run straight to Anthony as if drawn by his eyes. Not by appearance or figure was he different from others, but by his ordered character and the purity of his soul. For his soul being at peace, he had his outer senses also untroubled; so that from the joy of the soul, his face also was joyous. . . . He was never troubled, his soul being tranquil; he was never gloomy, his mind being glad."[63]

How dear a picture: "He would run straight to Anthony as if drawn by his eyes." It makes one think of the Master as He walked upon the hills of Galilee. We do not wonder that "many Greeks asked only to touch the old man, believing they should be helped."[64] Because their faith was great, they were indeed helped, as was the woman who touched the hem of our Lord's garment.[65]

The joyful peace born of the wisdom of holiness is the greatest of human charms.

The dear saint of Assisi, whose bodily sufferings would make the most heroic pause, was an apostle of the gladness that springs from holiness, and he bade his brothers leave sadness to the Devil and his disciples. St. Francis and his disciples were surely poor in the goods of this world, but who can doubt that they laid up treasures in Heaven?[66]

---

[63] *Life of Saint Anthony*, sect. 67.

[64] Ibid., sect. 70.

[65] Luke 8:43-44.

[66] Cf. Matt. 6:20.

The Joyful Ways of the Saints

∞

The saints teach you how to live in this world

All the saints of God learned from the Master the folly of putting one's trust in the things of earth and the wisdom of looking always toward Heaven and eternal things. They can teach us by precept and example how to make good use of our brief lives on the earth, how to battle against the seductive wisdom of the world that is forever trying to lead us astray, how to disregard appearances and look into the heart of things so as to evaluate them aright. They teach us how to seek only the earthly immortality that lives in the memory of a beautiful, helpful life, how to make and govern our friendships, and how to keep ourselves cheerful and happy no matter what sorrows come to us. The saints teach us how to guide our whole lives by spiritual wisdom.

To the rich, they teach the lesson of generosity toward the less fortunate and the understanding use of wealth as a thing of stewardship rather than of absolute ownership; to the poor, they teach the lesson of contentment; and to the religious, they teach the observance of perfect evangelical poverty. To all men, they teach the wisdom of meekness and humility. To priests in a very special way and to all of us in general, they show how we should act toward sinners so as to help them return to God.

I suppose the whole of spiritual wisdom may be summed up in the two great commandments: love of God and love of neighbor. When a man's heart is truly set on God, he is not likely to be led far astray by the allurements of the things of earth. When a man really loves his neighbor, he will not as a rule fail in charity. The most common sin in the world is, I think, uncharitableness, and yet our Lord told us plainly that we shall be judged by our charity.

In studying the saints, I have found that their most conspicuous virtue is charity. Much emphasis is rightly given by spiritual writers to the courage of the martyrs and the purity of the virgins, but in all justice, much more emphasis should be given to their charity. At one time, Blessed Jordan[67] consulted his brethren concerning an apostate whom he wished to reclaim. One of the brothers would not give his consent, until Master Jordan thus rebuked him: "Ah, Brother, if you had shed but one drop of your blood for this poor man, as Christ has given the whole of His, you would look on the affair very differently." Then the brother "fell on his knees to beg pardon, and readily gave consent."

Is it not strange that we who pray to our Father for exactly the same kind of forgiveness as we give to others who offend us are so prone to remember offenses and to harbor resentment? Let someone we know fall into error and disgrace, and we never forget it. What would we do if God treated us so? Yet we ask Him for such treatment whenever we pray the Our Father! Most spiritually unwise are we thus to squander the whole of our Lord's precious blood, while we treat our fellowmen as if we had water instead of human blood in our veins! In nothing are we more unlike the saints of God than in our cruel judgments and our unforgiving resentments, because the saints saw in others their Savior's beloved friends for whom He laid down His life.

---

[67] Blessed Jordan of Saxony (d. 1237), follower and biographer of St. Dominic.

The Joyful Ways of the Saints

Spiritual wisdom is sanctity, one may say, for the spiritually wise man understands and does all things in a holy way. Worldly wisdom seeks its rewards in this life, and usually it fails to obtain them. Spiritual wisdom seeks its rewards in the life to come, and always it obtains them.

Chapter Four

The Way of Friendship

Those friends thou hast, and their adoption tried,
Grapple them to thy soul with hoops of steel.

William Shakespeare
Hamlet, Act 1, scene 3

∞

Deep in every human heart, there is desire for permanent happiness in love. The instability of human love is, therefore, one of the chief causes of human sorrow and disillusionment. It would seem that God has given man every good thing that could be even dreamed of by him, and yet He has kept back the one really satisfying thing, which is assured happiness in love. At the last analysis, we may say, I think, that the only truly unhappy people in the world are those who are too selfish to love enduringly despite disillusionment, poverty, suffering, or disgrace.

The human heart is fashioned for love, and yet there is no perfect love in this world — even the most optimistic must admit this fact. Herein is divine wisdom most perfectly displayed. If man could answer the cravings of his heart for satisfying love here below, he would never seek it in Heaven. The human heart must seek God and obtain Him, or be forever unsatisfied. St. Augustine made immortal the statement that the heart of man cannot rest until it rests in God.[68]

Love is the most necessary thing in the world because it is the most ideally human thing on earth. The tenderest love, however, has in it an element of instability. Unselfishness is

[68] Cf. *Confessions*, Bk. 1, ch. 1.

the cornerstone of stability in love. Motherly love is, therefore, the most enduring of human loves. Someone said truly that the only unkind thing our mothers ever do is to die and leave us. They do die and leave us alone with our tears, and the greatest heartache is that they can no longer be the ones to wipe away our tears.

Is it any wonder, then, that we must turn to God for happiness? Realizing our unworthiness, we are driven to the One who knows all our weaknesses and yet loves us. We are indeed fools to prefer the fickle love of creatures like ourselves before such a lover as Francis Thompson describes in this immortal poem "The Hound of Heaven." We are wise only when we keep our divine Lover first in our affections, because, having done this, we shall love those dear to us for happiness and not for misery.

Unselfish love is the source of almost everything beautiful in life. The highest of Christian delights is mutual love. Love is the one truly godlike thing in human nature, because from love spring tenderness, sympathy, courage, self-sacrifice, and all the virtues.

Unselfish love is the hearth fire in the house of life, a fire in whose light there are warmth and peace and safety and in whose shadows there is sweet pain. Selfish love cannot be content with the genial, reassuring, little flames on the hearth; it heaps on all the treasures of the house until the flames escape from the grate and everything is burned to ashes. In the selfish love that is grasping or vicious, there is sin; but in unselfish love, there is virtue. Unselfish love may be — indeed it is — the door to the love of God. Unselfish love sees through the dear face of the loved one into the face of Him who made love possible. Unselfish love follows the loved one to the end of the world and into the shadows of death, enfolding the beloved in the protecting mantle of prayer.

Some people divide human loves into two classes: love of family, which includes the love of husband and wife, of parents and children, and of relatives; and love of friendship. Love of country is only an enlarged family love.

We find both of these kinds of love at their best in the lives of the saints. Many of the saints were called to the marriage state and sanctified themselves in it. Many of them surrendered every human attachment and went into the solitude of the desert to work out their sanctification. Many of them entered the religious state, to which only the exalted love of high spiritual friendship is suitable.

True friendship is rare indeed, as most of us must learn with sorrow, and yet it is very common among saints. Saints know how to love with understanding and forgiving love. They are perhaps the only people who know the true meaning of friendship and, realizing its worth, make the sacrifices necessary to be worthy of possessing it.

∞

Helpfulness is a quality of friendship
Helpfulness should be the motive of every friendship. This motive is illustrated in its perfection in the friendship of St. Thomas and St. Bonaventure.[69] Each found in the other what

---

[69] St. Thomas Aquinas (c. 1225-1274), Dominican philosopher and theologian; St. Bonaventure (c. 1217-1274), Franciscan theologian.

was wanting in himself. Bonaventure looked deep into the earnest, serene soul of Thomas and found peace for his soul. Thomas was stirred and brightened by contact with the ardent, self-outpouring nature of Bonaventure. The deep thinker and the tender poet combined themselves into a glorious union. Each of them recognized and gloried in the holiness of the other. Each encouraged the other to more ardent love of God and greater zeal in His service. Each tried to become worthy of the ideal the other held of him.

Living up to the ideal a friend has created is helpful to anyone. Human beings need human help as well as divine aid; in fact, it may be said, I think, that human inspiration is often a divine grace in a particular channel.

There is something magnetic in holiness that even the ordinarily virtuous person instantly perceives, as is evidenced by the multitudes who followed our Lord into the deserts and mountains, and, down through the ages, by the devoted admirers of the various saints. And so it is not difficult to understand the sudden and intimate friendships that arose between saints on the occasions of their first meetings. Holiness, as a rule, gives its possessor a keener insight into the hearts of others than is enjoyed by those who are not so close to the source of light and truth: the God who reads the innermost thoughts of men.

∞

The love in friendship is giving
The love between friends is unlike the love of passion in that it desires rather to give than to take; there is in it not the desire of possession but the pleasure of contemplation. It can

arise between those who have never even seen one another. Long before St. Bernard paid his first visit to the Abbey of Benedictines of Mount St. Ruppert, wherein St. Hildegarde[70] dwelt, he had begun to care for her, because of her writings, with an affection that developed to a greater degree with every succeeding visit.

What comfort there was in this friendship for St. Hildegarde we can well imagine, for she had endured much from those who considered the revelations she received to be either hallucinations of the brain, or deceits of the Devil. She was forced to accept constant and bitter humiliation for a long time before St. Bernard's promise to her was fulfilled. "My daughter," he said to her, "fear not the words of men, since you have God for your protector. Their vain discourses will vanish like straw; but the word of God will endure forever."

Being so close to God, St. Bernard was able to recognize the extraordinary work of divine grace in his friend, to which more earthly-minded people were blind. Hers was a difficult mission, to attack the vices and weaknesses of those entrusted with the government of Church and state, and one can but feel that God in His mercy provided St. Bernard — who also was involved in great matters and suffered much in executing them — to be her comfort and her joy, by his fine and affectionate sympathy.

Truly, saints know how to love, with the love that is not only stronger than death but stronger than life as well. It is

---

[70] St. Hildegarde (1098-1179), German mystic and abbess who received visions that included denunciations of the vices of the world and apocalyptic prophecies and warnings.

easy to forget the faults of those who live only in the memory, the tender memory of an irreparable loss; but it is easier to remember the faults of those whose many kindnesses to us are simply taken for granted. Love is true love only when it is big enough to endure the daily strain of living side by side, only when it can see faults that need correction and can be big enough to correct them patiently and tenderly. Such is the love of the saint, for he is like the God who loves us even when we sin against Him.

"I would find it very difficult to explain to you," St. Francis de Sales once wrote to Mme. de Chantal, "either the quality or the magnitude of the affection I place at your spiritual service. But this much I can say: that I think it is of God, and for that reason, I shall nourish and cherish it; and day by day, I perceive that it grows and augments notably. Behold me, altogether yours. God has given me to you. The bond of charity, of true Christian friendship which exists between us, is what St. Paul calls the 'bond of perfection.' And indeed it is that, for it is indissoluble; the longer it endures, the stronger it becomes; death itself has no power over it. This is our bond, our chains, which, the tighter they press, the more ease and liberty will they give us; for beyond the nature of other things are they pliant yet strong."[71]

St. Francis and St. Jane de Chantal furnish an ideal illustration of the much-abused term *platonic love*, which really means the kind of affection that existed between them. In their regard for each other, there was the pleasure of contemplation rather than the desire of possession, and each meant to

[71] Letter 223 to Jane de Chantal, June 24, 1604.

the other only an inspiration to greater love of God. They were spiritually wise, understanding well that every gift of God, including friendship, can be used for His glory and man's sanctification.

∞

Wisdom must govern friendship

Wisdom in friendship is always a supreme difficulty to us creatures of half head and half heart. Emotion enters to destroy the calm balance of persons of similar intellectual tastes; and intellectual friendships, kept such, too often become utterly tiresome.

In studying the saints, I have become convinced that they can teach us not only how to love God, but how to love our friends as well. There is an old saying that if a man makes one true friend who will share his troubles during life, he is most fortunate; and, although most of us do not believe there is such poverty of friendship when we are young and trusting, we come to believe it when we are older.

Even the Savior Himself could keep only one of His twelve chosen friends during His sorrowful humiliation and suffering. And yet he had warned them. When they were most humanly proud of being His chosen disciples, because "the fame of Him was published into every place of the country"[72] as a worker of miracles and because the multitudes followed Him everywhere, and the two sons of Zebedee came with their mother to ask for high places in His kingdom, he said, "You know not what you ask. Can you drink the chalice that I shall drink?"

[72] Cf. Matt. 9:31.

Although they answered, "We can," and although the other ten "were moved with indignation against the two brethren" because of their selfish request, when the trial came, "His disciples, leaving Him, all fled away"[73] — all except St. John, who kept his promise to share the chalice.

We need but to study the Gospel narrative, however, in order to understand that the only way to have friends is to be a friend. When Jesus was risen from the dead, He came to His terrified friends as lovingly as if they had not abandoned Him. There was no word of reproach except for Thomas, who could not be persuaded that He really had come again.[74] The Master knew, of course, that by their fall, His friends had been redeemed from their cowardice and had found themselves, and that they would indeed drink the chalice of suffering when their time for it came.

In reading the lives of the saints, one must be impressed by the wisdom with which they made and governed their friendships, and one must conclude that the only people who know how to love in the sensible and unselfish way that is necessary for friendship are the saints of God.

St. Scholastica[75] was established as abbess of a convent about five miles from the monastery of St. Benedict, her brother, and they had the opportunity of visiting together once a year in a house at some distance from the monastery, which she could not enter. On the occasion of their last visit, St. Scholastica entreated her brother to remain with her until

[73] Matt. 20:21-22, 24.
[74] Cf. John 20:27.
[75] St. Scholastica (c. 480-c. 543), Benedictine nun.

morning, but he told her that according to his rule, he could not pass the night out of his monastery. Although she pleaded with him lovingly, he would not yield — partly, I suppose, to edify her, as well as to keep his rule. She bowed her head on the table and prayed with tears. Almost immediately, so terrific a storm broke that St. Benedict was compelled to remain with his sister. "God forgive you, sister, what have you done?" He cried. And she answered, "I asked you a favor, and you refused it to me. I asked it of Almighty God, and He has granted it to me."

Three days later, St. Benedict saw the soul of his sister ascending to Heaven in the shape of a dove, and then he knew that the sweet favor she had won from God, despite his refusal, was the last favor she had asked on earth. God is so much sweeter than people are about the little things that make us happy.

∞

*Worldly persons often
misunderstand holy friendship*

Saints are, like the Master, "set for a sign which shall be contradicted,"[76] and in their friendships, particularly, they have been misunderstood.

One example of the worldly inability to understand such a saintly friendship is to be found in the attitude of their friends and neighbors toward St. Francis and St. Clare.[77] St.

---

[76] Luke 2:34.

[77] St. Clare (1194-1253), founder of the Poor Clares with St. Francis of Assisi.

Clare belonged to one of the noble families of Assisi. At the age of seventeen, she wished to enter the conventual life, but her parents refused their consent. She told St. Francis of her difficulty, and he helped her to escape. She escaped through a hole in the wall, fled through the adjoining wood, and was received at midnight in the Portiuncula, where St. Francis lived. He and his brethren met her with lighted torches, and, after a brief ceremony, St. Francis cut off her hair and gave her a piece of sackcloth for a habit. He then took her to the Benedictine nunnery of St. Paul.

In the morning, there was a great commotion in Clare's home, and her relatives and friends went to the convent to try to recover her by force. St. Clare went to the altar and clung to it so that they could not pull her away. Despite their reproaches, she remained firm. Later, St. Francis used her to found the Poor Clares.

Of their friendship, Chesterton writes, "If a man may well doubt whether he is worthy to write a word about St. Francis, he will certainly want words better than his own to speak of the friendship of St. Francis and St. Clare. . . . One night, the people of Assisi thought the trees and the holy house were on fire, and rushed up to extinguish the conflagration. But they found all quiet within, where St. Francis broke bread with St. Clare at one of their rare meetings, and talked of the love of God. It would be hard to find a more imaginative image, for some sort of utterly pure and disembodied passion, than that red halo round the unconscious figures on the hill; a flame feeding on nothing and setting the very air on fire."[78]

[78] *St. Francis of Assisi*, ch. 7.

There is, undoubtedly, something to be said for the parents of St. Clare and for her friends who simply could not understand this "elopement" as a romance altogether divine; and yet, how much happier everyone would have been if they could have understood. Most of the unhappiness in the world is caused by those who do not understand the actions of others and who do not wait for explanations before they condemn. What a Heaven on earth we would have if people were even half so scrupulous and worried about their own sins of rash judgment and uncharitableness as they are about the virtue of their neighbors!

St. Ignatius of Loyola was once put into prison because two ladies in whom he had awakened the love of diviner things set off on a pilgrimage. The mere fact that Ignatius happened to be absent at the time and therefore knew nothing of the pilgrimage was not taken into consideration as he was haled through the streets on the way to prison.

At another time, the saint was almost beaten to death for trying — and succeeding in his attempt — to reform a convent of nuns. These unpleasant events were compensated for, in some measure, by the fact that women were generous in aiding him to accomplish his work. Nor did he fail to appreciate their help.

∞

*The saints recognize and respect
the dignity of women*

There is something gratifying in the attitude taken toward women by the great saints of the Church, some of whom founded orders for women as well as for men, and even went so

The Joyful Ways of the Saints

far as to set women as superiors over monasteries of men. St. Hilda[79] is an important woman in ecclesiastical history. She was entrusted with the arduous task of governing both convent and monastery at Whitby, and her kindly sympathy gave the mighty genius of Caedmon[80] an opportunity to flower into song. Her monastery was a shrine of holiness and learning, and from it came forth several saintly bishops of the Church.

In the good old days of universal Catholicity in Europe, woman was considered rightly as an intelligent being and was given educational opportunities practically equal to those of men, in monasteries and convents. The fact was recognized that woman is neither an angel to be idolized nor a dullard to be petted or pitied. She was considered as a being whose friendship is worthy of cultivation. And, in reading the lives of the saints, one finds abundant evidence of the inspiration and help to be found in the friendship of intelligent and holy women.

St. Philip Neri had many beautiful friendships with both men and women. One of the most interesting was formed with St. Catherine dei Ricci.[81] St. Catherine was the niece of Fra Angelo Diacceto, Prior of the Minerva in Rome, who was an intimate friend of St. Philip; and Fra Angelo, seeing in these two saints the similarity of dispositions and tastes that induces friendship, told each of them so much about the other that they began a correspondence that drew them very close together in

---

[79] St. Hilda (614-680), Abbess of Whitby.

[80] Caedmon (d. c. 680), the earliest English Christian poet and a laborer at the Monastery of Whitby.

[81] St. Catherine dei Ricci (1522-1590), Italian visionary.

spirit. Prevented from meeting by circumstances, they longed unceasingly to see each other, and "pour out their souls in that sweet and heavenly converse which is chief among the solaces of the saints here on earth."

God granted their desire by means of a miracle. He brought them together in a vision in such a manner that each saw the other as a real living being, and allowed them to spend some time in conversation. Each was able afterward to describe the other perfectly, and each had a comforting memory to keep until their reunion in Heaven.

In the only letter that remains of their correspondence, St. Catherine writes, "I shrink into myself with confusion when I think that you, who are occupied without ceasing in so many great things for the glory of God, should set yourself to write to me, who am only a weak woman of no value, and a miserable sinner. May God reward you for the great charity you do me!"

It was like the humility of St. Catherine not to understand that St. Philip was not just being unselfishly charitable in writing to her; he was receiving his reward in her affectionate inspiration.

St. Catherine of Siena furnishes many examples of the power that a gifted and holy woman can exercise in friendship. Friar Bartholomew de Dominici of Siena, who was St. Catherine's confessor for many years, wrote, "When I commenced visiting her cell, she was young, and always wore a cheerful countenance. I was also young; yet not only did I not experience any trouble in her presence, but the longer I conversed with her, the stronger became my love for the religious virtues. I saw in succeeding times many laymen and monks who visited her and who all experienced impressions similar to mine. The sight of her, and all her conversations breathed and communicated angelical purity."[82] Her stainless soul taught him lessons of holiness, and her prayers brought him numberless graces. She never failed him in his needs, for God gave her the power to see him in all his movements, even when he was at a distance from her.

The Church has never had any difficulty in regard to the emancipation of woman; she has never considered her as inferior to man. Since the Church has placed so many women upon her altars, even those most skeptical about intellect in feminine souls must not be surprised at their displaying the same wisdom that has characterized all the saints, the wisdom of using everything, especially the power of the heart to love, for spiritual ends.

∞

The friendship of the saints is inspiring
Among all the beautiful causes for faith in humanity to be found in studying the lives of the saints, none is more comforting than their friendships. Many formed friendships that were like that of David and Jonathan, so close that their souls were knit in everlasting union, so close that each loved the other's soul as his own.[83] All the saints understand that "a faithful friend is a strong defense, and he that hath found him hath found a treasure."[84]

---

[82] Blessed Raymond of Capua, *Life of Saint Catherine of Siena* (New York: P. J. Kenedy and Sons), 344.

[83] 1 Kings 18:1 (RSV = 1 Sam. 18:1).

[84] Ecclus. 6:14 (RSV = Sir. 6:14).

The love of saints is constant and enduring, for it is unselfish love. It leads to the heights of spiritual sweetness, for it is pure love that desires to give rather than to take. It reaches its hands through the gates of death, for it is established in God.

Chapter Five

∞

The Way of Courage

Ah, see the fair chivalry come, the companions of Christ!
White Horsemen, who ride on white horses, the knights of God!
They, for their Lord and their lover who sacrificed
All, save the sweetness of treading, where He first trod!

Lionel Johnson
"The Martyrum Candidatus"

∞

There are many kinds of courage, physical and spiritual. Purity of heart is the source of the best and highest courage. We say rightly that there is high and noble courage in the heart of the soldier doing battle for his country; and yet we know that in the soul of every good man on the bloody field, there is always a second battle fought while his body is fighting: the battle between the ideal love of his native land and the sick and shuddering horror of his heart at the thought of killing his fellowman. Because he must thus overcome himself, is he less brave than the brute by his side who kills for the lust of blood?

True courage does not mean merely the lust to kill joined with indifference to personal bodily injury; it is something far more spiritual than this. Yet, strangely enough, this lesser kind of courage has been most heralded and sung. Perhaps this is not so strange, however, in view of the fact that never but once in the history of mankind was the whole world at peace, and that was on the night when the Prince of Peace was born. War and the brave deeds of war have been knit into men's thoughts with love and religion, as long as there have been men to think.

True courage does not necessarily mean stoic indifference in the face of pain. Men writhed and twisted and screamed on the rack in Elizabeth's England, while they kept the names of hunted priests from passing their lips. Missionaries moaned and cried at the burning stake in the trackless forests of America, while they pleaded with yelling Indians to hear the name of Christ. Christ Himself sweat blood in an agony of fear, while He waited for His executioners to come for Him.[85] The courage to suffer even unto death for an ideal is true courage. When the ideal is God and His truth, we have the exalted courage of holiness.

War and the brave deeds of war sometimes prepare the way for the exalted courage of holiness, as is seen in the life of St. Ignatius of Loyola. Lying on a bed of sickness and racked by the pain of a wound received in the breach at Pampeluna, Ignatius the soldier read Ludolph of Saxony's *Life of Jesus Christ* and also the *Lives of the Saints* — chiefly because he had nothing else to read. Straightway he resolved to abandon his military career and devote himself to the service of "that sweet Captain, Jesus Christ."

There is to me something especially beautiful in the fact that on the eve of the feast of Sts. Peter and Paul, St. Peter, to whom Ignatius had great devotion and in whose honor he had written a poem, appeared to the sick soldier and promised him recovery.

I think that there has always been something military in the religious order that Ignatius founded, with its martyrs and its fighters for truth. "Soldier of Jesus" it is a most fitting and beautiful title for the priest of the Most High God — soldier of the gentle Jesus, who held the little ones in His arms and yet drove the thieves from his Father's house! Holding in his arms

---

[85] Cf. Luke 22:44.

the little ones of the world, whether they are little from age or pain or sin, and driving from the holy places the robbers who would steal the treasures of faith — are not these the missions of the priest?

St. Ignatius, with the memory of the warrior and the genius of the saint, called the means he used to prepare his soldiers for their warfare against the world the "spiritual exercises." By them he has ruled through the centuries an army that has outlasted the armies of his native land and has journeyed for eternal conquests into every country of the world.

There has always been persecution of the Catholic Church, both physical and spiritual, and therefore there has always been a need for both physical and spiritual courage. In the early days, this persecution was largely physical in its expression and gave us numberless martyrs. During the later centuries, persecution has made use of more spiritual weapons, and it is against these weapons that the great army of Ignatius has made war. Then, too, his followers have journeyed into faraway heathen countries to carry the Cross of Christ, and from his ranks came that greatest of apostles since the first century: St. Francis Xavier. Many of these religious who went into heathen lands were driven there by the desire of martyrdom, and some attained it.

It is exceedingly difficult for me to understand the joy with which countless people have run to martyrdom. I marvel at those Christians of early days who calmly and happily, sometimes even with songs on their lips, stood in the arena and waited, while roaring lions or charging bulls descended upon them, for I shudder even at the forward movement of the most meditative-looking cow. I can work myself into a panic over an operation, yet little St. Agnes,[86] with undaunted eyes and unquivering lips, looked at iron hooks, the rack, and terrible fires prepared for her torture. Finally she went cheerfully to the block to be beheaded. Most of us run for cooling ointment when we have burned ourselves accidentally. How, then, could St. Lawrence, stripped, extended, and bound with chains over a slow fire, which broiled his flesh little by little, turn smilingly to the judge and say, "Let my body be now turned; one side is broiled enough"? Then he prayed until his last breath for the conversion of Rome.

If it is difficult to think of a saint's enduring torments for his Faith, what of the mother of the Maccabees? After having seen six of her sons suffering most excruciating agonies, she urged the seventh and last, a little boy, to show himself worthy of his brothers and receive death with constancy. She watched the executioners as they tore the tender body to pieces, little by little, and then she, too, offered herself for martyrdom. All this because the mother and her sons would not eat the forbidden meat set before them by the king.[87] Of what stuff these martyrs are made!

I find difficulty, too, in understanding those heroic men and women who have devoted themselves to the care of people with lingering and contagious diseases. Consider, for example, the heroism of Fr. Damien in going to care for the lepers, when he knew certainly, as he watched over the horrible, rotting bodies, that on some morning, he must inevitably discover the dreaded white spots in his own flesh. Most of us do all in our

---

[86] St. Agnes (d. c. 304), Roman martyr.
[87] Cf. 2 Macc. 7.

power to avoid contact with diseased people. And when we have the ordinary aches and pains that flesh is heir to, very few of us bear them cheerfully and silently.

Sometimes I pick up a stray prayer book in Church, and I find in it a prayer asking for the privilege of martyrdom or at least for much suffering before death. I cannot make myself read it, because I am so afraid God might hear me. So I just say to Him, "I am weak and afraid; just give me what You know I can endure." I do not see how ordinary people can read such prayers and mean them. But I suppose there must be those desiring to be martyrs even in these days. Somehow, however, I shall always believe that those who have so edified me by their beautiful courage and resignation when cancer is gnawing endlessly within them are the elect of God, to whom He gives the grace to endure some of their Purgatory in this life, whether they choose it or not.

Faithfulness requires courage

Although most of us despair of imitating the marvelous courage of some of the saints, we should remember that they furnish us with a really imitable example in the practice of the more ordinary moral virtues. They understood the value of the commonplace heroism that is modeled on martyrdom but does not go by that name.

One of the most heroic women I know will perhaps never be heralded as a martyr, but she deserves real homage. She wished to become a Carmelite nun, but her widowed sister died and left to her care four small children. Without a word of complaint, the young woman surrendered her beautiful dream,

obtained a job as a stenographer, and set herself to the up-
bringing and education of the children. The children are
grown now and have gone their ways. The woman is too old to
enter a convent. Her one consolation in her loneliness is the
thought: "It was the will of God."

There are in the lives of the saints hundreds of illustrations
of courage born of ideals. After martyrs for the faith, I suppose
the greatest number suffered in order to preserve their personal purity.

Conspicuous among these is St. Thecla,[88] called by the
Greeks the protomartyr of her sex. Some of the early Church
Fathers tell us that she was converted to the Christian faith by
St. Paul at Iconium in about the year 45. Inspired by his
preaching, Thecla determined to practice the virtue of virginity
and broke off an engagement to marriage with a rich, attractive young nobleman. Naturally he objected, as did everyone
else interested in Thecla. After enduring persuasions that
amounted to real persecution, she fled from her home and
sought help and comfort from St. Paul. Her lover pursued her
and, finding that she would not yield to his entreaties, delivered her into the hands of the magistrates, urging such accusations against her that she was condemned to be torn in pieces
by wild beasts.

Poor Thecla was exposed naked in the amphitheater, and
yet she waited joyfully while the madly roaring lions and tigers
were released into the arena. Suddenly, to everyone's amaze-
ment, the animals walked gently to the girl and, lying down
before her, licked her feet, while their roars changed to pleased

[88] St. Thecla, early Christian martyr.

purrs. The keepers prodded them with rods and tore them with hooks, but the lions and tigers ambled peacefully back to their cages.

Although Thecla was exposed to many dangers during her life, she was always miraculously delivered, and she spent many useful years in aiding St. Paul in his apostolic labors. He knew all about persecutions and difficulties, and he must have been proud of Thecla.

St. Paul almost personifies in himself the courage of holiness: "Are they servants of Christ? I am a better one . . . with far greater labors, far more imprisonments, with countless beatings, and often near death. Five times I have received at the hands of the Jews the forty lashes less one. Three times I have been beaten with rods; once I was stoned. Three times I have been shipwrecked; a night and a day I have been adrift at sea; on frequent journeys, in danger from rivers, danger from robbers, danger from my own people, danger from Gentiles, danger in the city, danger in the wilderness, danger at sea, danger from false brethren; in toil and hardship, through many a sleepless night, in hunger and thirst, often without food, in cold and exposure. And, apart from other things, there is the daily pressure upon me of my anxiety for all the churches."[89] And one may add to all these things a martyr's death near Rome. The author of the most perfect treatise on the virtue of charity[90] did not write mere platitudes; his was a charity tried in the fire, and he wrote from a heart that could see God even in his enemies.

[89] 2 Cor. 11:23-28 (RSV translation).
[90] Cf. 1 Cor. 13.

The Joyful Ways of the Saints

∞

Christ understands your fears

Joined in memory with St. Paul is the first Pope of Chris-
tendom. Because I love St. Peter especially, I have always
wanted to know what Jesus said to him when first they met after
the Resurrection. Because I believe in the exquisite and understanding sympathy of Jesus, I imagine that He must have said
something like this: "Grieve not, Peter, nor be ashamed. If you
could have seen how sore afraid I was in the garden of Olives,
you would not sorrow so because of your fear that made you
deny me. Let your heart be troubled no longer, nor let it fear.
You will do great things for me."

Jesus had indeed been afraid, for He was man as well as
God. He let Himself be afraid, so that He might understand
our fear when we must go down into the valley of the shadow.
The story of St. Peter is the epic of courage, of courage that developed from rashness into cowardice, and from cowardice
into heroism. Peter the man was a rash, unthinking blunderer;
Peter the saint was a prudent yet unfearing martyr.

On the eve of the first Good Friday, Jesus led His Apostles
to Mount Olivet and there told them, "All you shall be scandalized in me this night." Then Peter, presumptuous because
of his recent installation as head of the Church-to-be, and
rash with promises — as those who love always are — replied,
"Although all shall be scandalized in Thee, I will never be
scandalized." Jesus, sweet with pity for His foolish friend, told
him the hard truth: "Amen I say to thee, that in this night before the cock crow, thou wilt deny me thrice." It is easy to
imagine the horrified reproach in Peter's face and voice as he
protested, "Yea, though I should die with Thee, I will not deny

Thee."[91] I am sure that he believed himself, too. In fact, he managed to be brave enough to strike the servant of the high priest, and cut off his ear, when the rabble came to take the Master, although this was an act freighted with serious consequences. Perhaps to save Peter as well as to show His power, Jesus touched the ear and healed it.[92]

Peter, still believing in himself when all the Apostles except John ran away to hide themselves, followed the crowd to the court of the high priest and stood with the servants and ministers before the fire to warm himself, for it was cold. Yes, it was cold, and suddenly icy fear laid hold on the heart of Peter. The Master, He who was to be their king and free His people, was now a bound prisoner before the court of injustice. There was talk among those near Peter of the penalty that would be meted out to the one who had proclaimed Himself not only king but God. Such blasphemy deserved crucifixion. The word sent a knife through the heart of Peter. Then they began to talk of His followers. Perhaps they might be crucified with Him, for they had preferred Him to Caesar and seemed to believe Him to be God.

Peter listened, and while he listened, his fear grew into abject terror. He had seen people crucified, for such punishment was common in those days. He had seen men writhe and moan and plead for even a drop of water. Then he saw himself writhing and moaning on a cross. Suddenly, the attention of those near him was attracted to him, and a maidservant said, "Art not thou also one of His disciples?" Sick with terror, he cried,

[91] Matt. 26:31, 33-35.
[92] Cf. Luke 22:51; John 18:10.

"I am not!" Again and once again they tortured him with the question; again and once again he denied. Then he heard a cock crow. And the Lord looked on Peter, as if to say, "Peter, friend, beloved, what hast thou done to me?" And Peter, going out, wept bitterly.[93]

What, indeed, had he done? He had been a despicable coward; he had denied his friend, his God. Where now were all his boasts of loyalty? Through the long hours, his boasts taunted him mockingly, while he wandered about blindly, shaken with grief. It had been so easy to be brave and to make promises while he had been with the Master, for he had known that Jesus would protect him from his own rashness. Now he was alone with his shameful cowardice.

Peter had been asleep during Christ's prayer in the garden, and therefore he did not know that the Savior, too, had gone through agonies of fear and anguish that had caused a sweat of blood to run from his pores until the very ground beneath Him was wet. Yes, even the Son of God was afraid, and He begged to be saved from the awful death before Him, if it were possible.[94]

The Son of God let Himself be afraid, so that the wounded hand to which we must cling in our agony of death may be an understanding hand. Truly, it seems to me, God's supreme mercy to man on earth is a sudden and provided death.

Peter learned the meaning of tears that bring no relief. He was alone with his tears — tears that were to wash away every trace of self from his soul, tears that were at last to be wiped away by a tender, pierced hand, tears from which a new Peter

[93] Luke 22:56-62.
[94] Cf. Matt. 26:40; Luke 22:42, 44.

82

was to be born. Peter fell, only that he might rise to the heights of heroic sanctity. Never from the day of Christ's Resurrection did the newly made saint waver even for a moment in his heroism. Confirmed by God in his apostolic labors with the power of working miracles, the first Pope caused many conversions in Jerusalem and Palestine, and then traveled through the East as a missionary, until, late in life, he journeyed to Rome to establish there the Apostolic Primacy and to die the death of a martyr.

Peter the coward, who, at thought of a cross, had denied his Lord, voluntarily died on that cross with his head downward, because he did not consider himself worthy to be crucified with even the poor dignity of the Master. Peter the man was a boastful and cowardly creature; Peter the saint was a humble hero. Truly there is no courage like the courage of holiness, as is proved in the life of the simple fisherman who was raised to the highest dignity in the world.

∽

Holiness calls for physical and moral courage

The courage of holiness manifests itself not only in physical bravery in the face of suffering and death, but in moral bravery as well. Purity of soul rarely abides in the complete physical coward, and yet physical cowardice is not always a sign of moral cowardice. St. Louis,[95] King of France, furnishes a fine example of the ideal combination between physical bravery and moral courage, and an even finer illustration of the fact that homage is given most easily to the truly humble. This

---

[95] St. Louis IX (1214-1270).

splendid king dared to demean himself by washing the feet of the poor whom he served at table, and yet never was a monarch more universally respected. Although he governed his people excellently, he found time to recite the Divine Office daily, besides many other devotions. He fasted often and sometimes spent whole nights in prayer.

During his imprisonment among the Turks, while engaged in the Crusades, his true heroism was revealed in such a manner as to win the unwilling respect even of the sultan. Threatened with the bernicles, an engine by which every limb would be pressed and bruised and his bones broken, he calmly told his captors that since they were masters of his body, they might do with it as they wished, but his soul remained his own and God's. Although, on another occasion, he was threatened with crucifixion, he refused to deny the Christian religion. The crusade was a failure, but its very disasters showed forth the heroism of the great king, who gloried in the chains worn — because God willed them to be worn — more than he would have gloried in conquering the world.

The soul who can pronounce a *fiat* when the very God for whom he fights seems not strong enough to conquer His enemies is a soul brave with the bravery of Calvary. One does not wonder that St. Louis had a large crucifix set where his dying eyes could turn to gaze on it lovingly.

There are many among the saints of God who, like St. Louis, combine in themselves bravery that is both physical and moral. When one thinks seriously of the fact that the motive of high sanctity is love and the highest expression of love is sacrifice, one begins to understand in some measure how martyrs are made. I suppose that if we could really fall in love with God and could weigh our sins in the balance against a crucifix, understandingly and sorrowfully, even we ordinary people would run gladly into the arms of suffering and death for God's sake. Courage born of supernatural motives is beyond our comprehension — much less our possession, because we are not sufficiently supernatural. Most of us understand the courage of patriotism better than that of holiness.

Without doubt, the most difficult kind of moral bravery is that of bearing injuries with patience, and yet it was enjoined by Christ even upon the ordinary Christian. "Love your enemies; do good to them that hate you; and pray for them that persecute and calumniate you: that you may be the children of your Father who is in Heaven, who maketh His sun to rise upon the good and bad, and raineth upon the just and the unjust."[96] Easy to say, but difficult to do. The King of kings did it, however, as well as said it. Hanging on a Cross, while His enemies jeered at Him and gambled even for His garments, He prayed, "Father, forgive them, for they know not what they do."[97] Surely this is example from Him who taught us to say, "Forgive us our debts as we also forgive our debtors"[98] — from Him who had no debts to be forgiven but only debtors to forgive.

Sometimes it is difficult to distinguish the external difference between meekness and weakness, but the motives of the two qualities are entirely opposed. Never was there a person more gentle-mannered and forgiving than St. Francis of Assisi, and yet he was in no sense a moral coward. He was brave in

[96] Cf. Luke 6:27; Matt. 5:44-45.
[97] Luke 23:34.
[98] Matt. 6:12.

defense of principle. The greatest principle of his life was voluntary poverty, and it was the principle upon which he was determined that his religious order should be founded.

During his absence, a magnificent mission house of the Friars Minor was established at Bologna, and, on the occasion of its opening, a vast body of the friars and their friends surrounded it and gave praise. Suddenly Francis appeared on the scene and denounced the building, wondering indignantly since when the Lady Poverty had thus been insulted by the luxury of palaces. There is no other record, so far as I know, of anger on the part of Francis.

The wrath of the kind and just man is effective for good and is never a source of sin to himself. He rebukes others only to help them. The gentle Jesus Himself on a memorable occasion went up to Jerusalem and found in the Temple "them that sold oxen and sheep and doves, and the changers of money sitting. And when He had made, as it were, a scourge of little whips, He drove them all out of the Temple, the sheep also and the oxen, and the money of the changers He poured out, and the tables He overthrew. And to them that sold doves He said: Take these things hence, and make not the house of my Father a house of traffic."[99] Even in His anger, He remembered thoughtfulness, and did not set loose the doves of the poor.

∞

Courage makes self-sacrifice possible

Two hundred years after St. Francis established his order, when many of the monasteries had departed from the strict

---

[99] John 2:15-16.

rules of their founder, the daughter of a humble artisan of Corbie, in France, was called by God to the heroic mission of restoring the primitive observance. St. Colette[100] was forced to conquer difficulties of every kind, but she never yielded to sadness or discouragement. Compelled by God to leave her hermitage, she spent the greater part of her life in traveling from monastery to monastery. Clothed in a patched, coarse habit and with bare feet, she journeyed on the back of a mule or in a rude cart over the roads of Flanders, Burgundy, Auxois, and Picardy. Hers was a herculean task, and she did it well.

I suppose there is nothing more difficult than the reform of relaxed and apathetic religious, and yet God saw fit to inflict St. Colette with constant and severe bodily sufferings while she was accomplishing her reform. When I read of her personal fights with demons and her fearful sufferings in body and mind, I can but wonder the more at her unfailing cheerfulness and her overflowing sympathy. In truth, the more I study her remarkable character, the more I understand how an untrained woman of humble parentage calmly gave orders to popes and kings, to bishops and princes, to rich and poor, and why they obeyed her.

One of the bravest self-sacrifices I have found in the lives of the saints is to the credit of St. John of the Cross.[101] I am firmly convinced that the saint who was sent by God to reform the Carmelite Order was perfectly sincere when he made frequent petitions to our Father in Heaven to be granted three

---

[100] St. Colette (1381-1447), founder of the Colettines, a branch of the Poor Clares.

[101] St. John of the Cross (1542-1591), mystic.

privileges: that he might not pass one day of his life without suffering something, that he might not die a superior, and that he might end his days in humiliations, disgrace, and contempt. The fact that he fell into ecstasy when contemplating his crucifix is not so convincing to me that he was in truth in love with pain, as is the choice he made of the monastery in which he died.

St. John was very ill and was suffering intensely. The provincial ordered him to go to either Baeza or Ubeda. The first monastery was comfortable and convenient, and the prior of it was a close friend of St. John. The other was poor in every way, and its prior hated St. John vindictively for former corrections in the matter of reform. This made the matter of choice exceedingly simple for St. John; he set out immediately for Ubeda. His third petition to God was generously answered; the record of the treatment the saint received is not a pleasant story to read. How did he keep sweet and cheerful in the midst of it? I hope to be able to ask him, on some glad day.

St. John's courage in bearing the martyrdom of bodily pain and studied unkindness was not greater than his moral courage in dealing with those who preferred luxury and ease to the Carmelite rule. He dealt firmly with those whose lives were a detriment to the order and a scandal to society. He was but imitating our Lord, who told us that we must exercise bravery in dealing with those who give scandal: "If thy brother shall offend against thee, go and rebuke him between thee and him alone. If he shall hear thee, thou shalt gain thy brother. And if he will not hear thee, take with thee one or two more, that in the mouth of two or three witnesses every word may stand. And if he will not hear them, tell the Church. And if he will not hear the Church, let him be to thee as the heathen and publican."[102]

If it is well-nigh impossible to write of the martyrs in any adequate fashion, what shall I say of her who is their queen? With seven swords of sorrow in her heart, Mary stood beneath a Cross for three unforgettable hours, a Cross whereon was nailed the God who is her Son. Mary paid an immeasurable price for her divine motherhood. She began to pay that price even before Jesus was born.

The Gospel tells us that Joseph, not understanding the miracle of the Incarnation, was troubled about Mary. There was every human reason for suspecting her virtue; even her own silence seemed to add weight to the suspicions that troubled him. I have often wondered why God tried the two of them so sorely. Perhaps it was simply because He loved them, and the price of divine love is suffering. The reason for Mary's silence seems to have been her understanding that the mystery wrought in her was God's affair and not hers, and that she must therefore trust Him to make everything clear to Joseph. And so she, before whom the mighty Gabriel had knelt while he hailed her immaculate, was the cause of Joseph's sorrowful deliberation as to whether or not he must proclaim her publicly so that she might be stoned to death as a faithless wife. Being unwilling to do this, "he was minded to put her away privately."[103]

And Mary knew with her tender sympathy the thoughts in his heart. Even a woman of ordinary virtue can understand in

---

[102] Matt. 18:15-17.
[103] Matt. 1:19.

some measure what anguish this knowledge must have meant to the pure heart of the one truly sinless woman. Yet Mary waited until an angel of the Lord appeared to Joseph to explain her motherhood.

Beyond the example of that mysterious and heroic silence, there is nothing left to say of the courage of holiness.

Chapter Six

∞

The Little Way

No scepter theirs, but they are kings:
Their forms and words are royal things.
Their simple friendship is a court,
Whither the wise and great resort.

Lionel Johnson
"A Dream of Youth"

∞

Most of us, when we read the lives of the great saints who did such stupendous things in God's service, are prone to forget that saints are really people and to think of them rather as allegorical personages, personifications of heroic virtues far beyond the attainment of us ordinary folks. In order to rid our minds of this fallacy, it is good sometimes to look into the lives of the saints who never did anything extraordinary, but who did ordinary things extraordinarily well, simply for the love of God.

When, for example, I read of the great Teresa's[104] ecstasies and her reiterated demands for suffering, I simply wilt in despair at the thought of ever becoming a saint. But then I read that the little Thérèse was annoyed at prayer by a "sister who did not cease rattling either her rosary or I do not know what else," and that the saint "wanted to turn and give the culprit a look," but refrained, "first for the love of God, and then also in order to avoid giving her pain." And I realize that for us ordinary folks, sanctity may well be only the practice of conquering ourselves one moment at a time and of being positively virtuous one moment at a time, for love of the God who will

[104] St. Teresa of Avila (1515-1582), Spanish Carmelite nun and mystic.

supply, on request, the particular grace needed for the one moment.

∞

You can attain holiness by doing little things well

Truth is the only thing that can afford to be presumptuous, and therefore, although the preceding statement may seem presumptuous, I offer it as a challenge. The reason I — and perhaps you, too — do not become one of the saints who follow the little ways of sanctity is that, although I may at some particular moment muster up enough courage to keep from "giving the culprit a look," at the very next moment, I commit an act of self-indulgence that squanders the hard-won grace and leaves me too discouraged to try again before many precious moments have slipped irrevocably away. I am sure it would be a marvelous experience to have an ecstasy, and yet I would be content if I could just once say half my Rosary without distraction and then not be distracted during the second half with trying to understand how I accomplished the miracle.

The ecstasies of St. Teresa have overshadowed her daily mortifications to such an extent that most of us forget the long days between them, when her little acts of kindness and her delightful humor made everyone love her. Somehow or other, she managed to see fun in the midst of every trouble — and she had her share of trouble. At the last analysis, I am sure it can safely be said that, except in rare cases, even the stupendous grace of martyrdom was purchased by greatness in little things.

Although most of us have no hope of ecstasies and might run from martyrdom, we can, with God's grace, be great in little things. To say our prayers prayerfully, to bear our crosses bravely and without noise of words, and to be positively virtuous and kind — these small triumphs are for us to follow the little ways of holiness. Some of us sigh for heroic opportunities of proving our virtue, and then, by an actual tumble, brought suddenly to the realization that we yield to small difficulties and temptations, we are likely to become discouraged.

Often we make the mistake of thinking that saints were not tempted as we are, and then, when we read their lives showing unmistakably that they were, we think they came unscathed through temptation because of unusual grace and strength of will. As a matter of fact, the saints had just the same kinds of temptations that we have, and they overcame temptations just as we must overcome them: by prayer and mortification. Their temptations were, like ours, of two kinds: the kind that must be fought as untiringly as Hercules fought the mythological giant Antaeus, and the kind that we must run away from.

Antaeus gained new strength every time Hercules threw him to the ground. Hercules finally grasped his foe in his arms and squeezed him to death. It seems to me that an easier way out of the difficulty for Hercules would have been to hit Antaeus over the head with a big club, but if he had done this, he would not have deserved the immortality of poetry. The one thing necessary in temptations to pride and covetousness is to beat them over the head with the spiked club of humility and self-sacrifice — which really means beating oneself over the head.

The other kind of temptations, which have to do with purity of body and mind, should be run away from as fast as we can run. If we could but say, "Get thee behind me, Satan,"[105] and then run to hide under the lovely blue mantle of our Lady, which always sends the Devil scuttling down the nearest hole, how safe we would be! The demon of impurity is a safe thing to look at only from the shelter of the mantle, because he, too, often appears as an angel of light when one parleys with him in the open.

∞

You can attain holiness by becoming little

In regard to the matter of such temptation, the Little Flower used an incident of her childhood for an illustration: "One day a horse was standing in front of the garden gate and preventing us from getting through. My companions talked to him and tried to make him move off, but while they were still talking, I quietly slipped between his legs — such is the advantage of remaining small." Would it not be wonderful to become so small through humility that one could just slip between the legs of a temptation and run away to hide — surely there would be loving arms waiting to catch and hold the fugitive from all harm!

When the Master told us to become as little children,[106] He certainly meant that we should be not only pure and humble, but trustful of Him as well. Children believe that those whom they love can do anything. So, in resisting temptations, trustful prayer is especially necessary. We must never forget how much we please God when we go to Him with the simple

[105] Matt. 16:23.
[106] Cf. Matt. 18:3.

confidence of children to confide our troubles and ask His help. Every person in the world likes to be trusted. So does God. He is most anxious to help us become better.

I think one of the differences between us and the saints is that they understand this truth and profit by it, and we do not. We shall become virtuous only when we use God's aid as we should.

Faith without good works is no more dead than good works without faith. It has been my experience that the one person whom I can consistently and constantly deceive with the greatest ease is myself, and in nothing can I delude myself more successfully than in regard to the proper proportions of prayer and work. I wonder whether I am altogether an oddity. If so, the fact ought to be another inducement to travel down into the valley of humility instead of trying to scale the mountain of towering spirituality. If I ever succeeded in climbing the high, difficult hill of great sanctity, I am sure that when I reached the top, I would bid everybody, "Just look what I did!" Therefore I pray to travel down instead of up, and then, when I have gotten far enough down not to be able to see anything except my own nothingness and the greatness of God, I pray to be able to ask Him to stoop to the littleness that is I.

"Everyone," says St. Francis de Sales, "likes to have eminent virtues. For the most part, were the choice given us, we would all like to be endowed with fortitude, magnanimity, the grace of martyrdom, the love of suffering, generosity, and the like. How few, comparatively speaking, are the occasions for exercising these virtues! How often we puff ourselves up with fine thoughts about them, and build castles in the air as to how we will exhibit them; and, when the occasion presents itself, our great courage dwindles down, and we are glad to hide our heads for very shame."

Once when St. Francis was looking at a picture of St. Mary Magdalene, he exclaimed, "How much ought we to love those little virtues which grow at the foot of the Cross and are watered by the Blood of Jesus!" When he was asked to name these virtues, he replied, "They are humility, benignity, bearing with others, condescension, sweetness of manner when proceeding from a motive of charity, cordiality, compassion, simplicity, candor, and the like. They are like violets which blossom in the shade, and which have little show but an exquisite odor. Other virtues are doubtless much greater; but we must beware of loving them more if the reason we prefer them is at all because they make us more illustrious in our own eyes or those of others. There is less danger to self-love in lowly virtues."

One of the miracles in the life of every great saint is that he does not fall in love with himself. Take that dear, sweet Francis of Assisi, for example; he treated himself with dreadful cruelty, and I am sure that he was most deeply humiliated as well as glorified because God loved him so much as to give him the stigmata. The explanation is, doubtless, that St. Francis was not only humble enough to despise himself but even humble enough to know that God can do all things, among them the exaltation of the unworthy.

The great saints are little enough to feel that their mighty powers are perhaps due to the prayers of unknown saints, for the glory of God and the spread of the Faith. St. Augustine, we may be sure, never forgets that his exalted place in Heaven is in large measure due to the prayers of his mother.

One of the joys of eternity will be the friendships of the saints, and we may be surprised to see some little old man or woman who prayed endless Rosaries in an obscure corner of the parish church walking arm in arm with St. Peter along some paradisal stream. I selected St. Peter because he is my best-loved saint, and because he must especially love the humble, unknown people who are the lambs he was told to feed.[107]

❧

Holiness calls for obedience

Of no saint is it more literally true that he followed the little ways of perfection than of St. Aloysius Gonzaga,[108] for, despite his aristocratic dignity, he used to run down the corridors leading to the chapel, wherein dwells the Bread of Life that makes men strong and swift for the race to Paradise. When, for the sake of his exhausted brain, he was forbidden to pray outside the prescribed times, he would often enter the chapel, genuflect, and then, in something of a panic, hurry out, because his love of the Prisoner might make him disobedient. I wonder what he thinks of us who sometimes shorten or omit our prayers because we like other people and other places more than we like the Lord in His dwelling.

The young Polish prince Stanislas Kostka[109] followed happy ways of spirituality, although his actual journey into religious life is well symbolized by his famous journey along the road

---

[107] Cf. John 21:15.

[108] St. Aloysius Gonzaga (1568-1591), patron of Roman Catholic youth.

[109] St. Stanislaus Kostka (1550-1568), Jesuit novice.

from Vienna to Augsburg, weak and sick from the cruelties of his brother and his tutor, exhausted and starving from the length of the way and the lack of food, but determined to become a soldier of Jesus. When he saw a shrine or a crucifix at the end of a path, he ran ahead of his companions and said some prayers before they arrived.

Stanislas exemplifies perfectly the follower of the little ways of sanctity. His rules, most of them concerned with the little things in daily living, he copied in his handwriting and carried next his heart. Because he obeyed them, he was happy and satisfied to be as he was.

Hero worship is a most lovable boyish trait, especially when it is worship of a saint. Just eight years after Aloysius died, a child was born who was later to adopt him for a hero, to doff his hat at the mention of his name, and to strive in every way to imitate him. This child was John Berchmans,[110] the third of the lads who, within less than seventy-five years, followed the little roads of the Jesuit rule to sanctity.

There is only one thing in the world more beautiful than a boy's love for his mother, and that is a boy's love for God's Mother. John Berchmans was very much in love with our Lady, so much so that he spent most of his recreations in trying to twist the talk around to her. Stanislas did not think of doing great things for our Lady, being content just to love her, but John made far-reaching plans. He would learn the languages of the heathens and would journey into dangerous countries to tell the glories of Mary. But first he must perfect himself.

[110] St. John Berchmans (1599-1621), Jesuit novice.

So, in the novitiate, he slept with his rule book under his pillow, and made for himself the motto "Die rather than violate the smallest rule." When he really was dying, he said that he had never voluntarily broken any rule, and his fellow novices could witness the statement. John Berchmans is another proof that saints are not difficult people for earnestly good people to live with, for he was universally loved.

For one so young, this saint understood remarkably well the sacredness of confidences and just exactly how much one dares expect of friendship. "Listen, Nicholas," he once told a friend, "we are good friends, but never on that account tell me secrets which I can't speak about if I think I ought to." This is vastly different from what most of us hear: "Oh, tell me. I'll never tell anybody." Usually the people who wheedle us in this way are just the ones who do tell the confidences we have given.

John's idea of friendship was service, and as his friendliness was universal, so was his service. He was always doing something for somebody. No matter what were his preoccupations, he was always ready to help anyone who needed help. How he did so in addition to observing all the difficulties with which he hedged his daily living is almost impossible to understand. He had great energy and a determined will, and these powers seem to be the human explanation.

Like Aloysius, Stanislas, and John, Gabriel Possenti's holiness consisted in the perfect observance of his religious rule. After his death, a set of resolutions was found among his notes that anyone must consider a plan for heroic virtue. Two things in these resolutions are conspicuous: a perfect regulation of actions according to rule and a perfect charity for others. Never to excuse oneself, never to speak or judge ill of anyone, to regard everyone as superior, always to rejoice at the success of others, to close one's heart resolutely against sadness, to combat one's inclinations, never to ask the why of anything, to practice unfaltering faithfulness in little things — these are difficult resolutions, and they are only a few of those by which Gabriel regulated his daily living. For he kept his resolutions — let us not forget that.

Gabriel's life was uneventful and known only to those who lived close to him. But his death was swiftly followed by great miracles wrought through his intercession. It is forever true that the saints, little or mighty, show forth the wonders of God; and one of the greatest wonders of God is that those who lived for only a brief time on earth should accomplish great work on earth continuously through centuries. Because he uses time on earth so well, the timeless ages of Heaven are his for continued labors.

∞

All states of life offer
opportunities to grow in holiness

These four boy saints and the Little Flower used the brief space of their mortal lives moment by moment in the little acts of heroism that take only a moment. They ran tirelessly while there was yet time, because they knew there would be calm rest at the end of the race. Their retired conventual lives prevented them from climbing the heights of supereminent sanctity and miracle-working power at which the contemporary world could stand agape; and so they were content to follow the little hidden ways in the blessed valley of humility.

That they have been exalted to the altars of the Church has doubtless surprised no one more than themselves.

Any person who keeps the commandments for the love of God becomes a saint. Many of the canonized saints lived their lives in the midst of worldly occupations.

The queen of all the saints was dedicated to the service of God in the Temple, and yet she was told by God that she must become His Mother and must live in an ordinary home as the wife of a carpenter. The Son of God lived for thirty years in an ordinary home and worked as an ordinary laborer. He was pleased to hide Himself in the little ways for thirty years, and to manifest Himself as the God-Man for only three years. In all the Gospel narrative, St. Joseph speaks no word and our Blessed Lady speaks only four times. They loved the little hidden roads of holiness, because they knew the sweet rapture of holding in their arms the little One whose hands are over and under the universe.

Love of the littleness of Jesus in the sacrament of His love is the surest and sweetest way to the humility of holiness. What shall one feel before the ever-present fact of the God who stoops to the utter abasement of the Host? To be carried under the heart of our sweet Lady and then to be cradled in her arms would be unmeasured bliss, but to be held as a flake of bread between the fingers of a man, sometimes weak or actually sinful, and then to be locked into a dark, lonely tabernacle, bereft even of human senses, is a degradation beyond human contriving and even conceiving.

Love is the secret of the runners along the high roads and the little low roads of holiness. Love runs because it finds all burdens light.

The Joyful Ways of the Saints

Mothers who traveled down into the valley of death to bring back with them children for Heaven; fathers who toiled for the mothers and the children; soldiers who died bravely for what is right; priests with hands laden by souls they have saved; nuns with pure eyes and with beads in their hands — these are not among the canonized, but they will walk down the flowery paths through which the rivers of Paradise are flowing, because they joyously followed the little hard and thorny ways of self-sacrifice for God's sake that life offers to those who dare to choose them.

Chapter Seven

∞

The Way of Song

I have run the way of Thy commandments,
when Thou didst enlarge my heart.

Psalms 118:32

∞

When our Savior told us to be perfect as our Heavenly Father is perfect,[111] He meant that we should perfect ourselves in accordance with our natural resources, not that we should become as God. There are saints in every walk of life, gifted variously, subject to various weaknesses, and therefore there is inspiration for every person in their lives.

Saints are the idealists of a very real world. The glamour of romance that touches their lives is a glamour that belongs by right to all men, because all men were made by God for His love. The courageous way in which the saints run to perform the behests of Love is the most romantically beautiful thing ever dreamed of by man. The fearful prudence of the worldly wise is an unthought-of virtue among saints.

Life, after all, is a thing to be used, not to be hoarded. Gold kept in coffers has never been known to multiply itself; but gold used productively ceases to be a dead, unfruitful thing. So it is with life; hoarded or doled out grudgingly, it can never be productive of good either for itself or others. It is ever so much better to wear life out than to let it rust itself out.

I have tried to make you see the saints as stars in the darkness who are waiting for your friendship and your confiding

[111] Matt. 5:48.

love. If I have not proved this to be true, please understand that the fault is in the manner of the introduction and not in the saints introduced. If I have not made the saints attractive, please undo the harm by seeking them out for yourself.

If I have made them attractive, let me ask something in return. Learn from them a love of God that will make you courageous enough to become a saint like them. Choose some among them for your friends and guides, and let them teach you how to follow the way of sanctity that is marked out just for you.

If you are proud, study their amazing humility. Humility is the root of good, just as surely as pride is the root of evil. It was the charm of Mary's humility that drew our Lord down from His Father's bosom to rest beneath her heart. Humility is the strongest bulwark you can erect against the assaults of Satan. Humility renders the practice of charity easy, and charity makes every burden easy to bear.

Because they are charitable and humble, the saints run lightly under all burdens. So, too, may you and I run lightly under our burdens if we but learn to love and to be kindly humble. Our bodies may become sick and may grow old, but our souls can keep the lighthearted gladness of children.

And what of our influence? We, too, shall be stars in the darkness. Men with their eyes cast to earth do not see the stars, but heavenward-gazing men see them. To those who see us only with the eyes of the body, we may seem to walk with tired step, but those who have spiritual vision will know that we run, with the laughter of love-made song in our hearts and the fragrant glory of dawn in our eyes, up and up the high, steep hills of the spirit, up and up until we pass beyond the farthest star into the light of our Father's home. Seeing us, they may draw from the sight courage to follow.

To many of life's pilgrims, the road to Paradise seems indeed long and hard; and yet, measured by the mere yesterdays of mankind, the longest life is less than a breath on the untiring winds. Even were the road as long as it seems, it still would lead to the utter rest of secure happiness. Could they but keep the journey's end in view, the end where Love awaits their coming, they would find the way easy, for "they that hope in the Lord shall renew their strength; they shall take wings as eagles; they shall run and not be weary."[112] The inspiring figure of the road to Heaven with its untiring runners is used in the Scriptures perhaps more frequently than any other.

∞

The saints' message goes forth through all the world

Another beautiful figurative representation of the saints is as knights who ride unfearingly through all life's danger and darkness of sorrow and suffering into the morningtide that lights the shining towers of the City of God. St. John saw the martyrs thus in his vision, armies who ride on white horses following Christ their Captain, the King of kings and Lord of lords. And as they ride, forever rises the glory of song, "as it were, the voice of a great multitude, and as the voice of many waters, and as the voice of great thunders, saying, 'Alleluia: for the Lord our God, the Almighty, hath reigned. Let us be glad and rejoice, and give glory to Him.' "[113]

[112] Isa. 40:31.
[113] Apoc. 19:6-7 (RSV = Rev. 19:6-7).

The Joyful Ways of the Saints

It is the wonderful prerogative of saints to catch the echoes of this celestial song while they are still on earth. Saints do indeed walk with the music of Heaven sounding its sweet and comforting message in their ears. Loving less favored people as they do, they cannot rest until they have, in turn, given this music to their fellowmen for solace and courage. Some of the saints can speak only with the faltering tongue of the poor and unlearned; some of them can sing the rapturous songs of seraphim. But they all, in the way of the troubadours of old, must go through life with no abiding city of their own; their vocation is to carry far and wide the story of the greatness of their King and the wonders of His realm.

Loving all things human for the sake of God, for His sake, the saints surrender all things. Having surrendered all things, they possess all things in Him.

Whether the troubadour of Paradise looks out at his bit of sky from a narrow window in a monastic cell or sits upon the throne of a king, whether he guards sheep on a hillside or preaches from a marble pulpit, the poetry of his daily living comes at last to all ears. To the troubadour of Paradise, God has said, "And the nations that know not thee shall run to thee, because of the Lord thy God, and for the Holy One of Israel, for He hath glorified thee."[114]

The Little Flower of Jesus, for example, lived her brief life in a garden enclosure, but the perfume of her songful life has been caught by every wind that blows. Many of her poems, the poems of genius, have been translated into a dozen languages and have traveled to the ends of the world.

[114] Isa. 55:5.

It is the beautiful vocation of saints to be the singing stars of a world darkened by unbelief and sin. They are such stars as those hymned in the psalm: "There are no speeches nor languages, where their voices are not heard. Their sound hath gone forth into all the earth, and their words into the ends of the world."[115]

Saints have the glorious power, like the fabled Pied Piper of Hamelin, of luring with their heavenly music the children of God away from the hampering places and things of earth into the far, fair country of the soul. For the troubadours of Paradise can never die, and their songs will stir generations yet unborn. Although their way leads over stony mountains and thorny paths, with the laughter of dawn in their eyes and with song on their lips, they will irresistibly and forever draw the children after them. Only children can follow them, for of such is the kingdom of Heaven.[116]

Dear God, make children of us all,
that we may follow Thy saints into Paradise.

---

[115] Ps. 18:4-5 (RSV = Ps. 19:3-4).
[116] Cf. Matt. 19:14.

Sister Mary Eleanore, C.S.C.

(1890-1940)

∞

A relative of Betsy Ross and Mark Twain, Sister Mary Eleanore was born Katherine Mary Brosnahan in Pierceton, Indiana, in 1890. She was educated in public schools until she was eighteen and then attended St. Mary's College in Notre Dame, Indiana. In her junior year, she entered the novitiate of the Congregation of the Holy Cross. As a religious, she took the name Sister Mary Eleanore and earned a doctorate from Notre Dame University.

She became dean of English at St. Mary's College and superior and principal of St. Mary's High School in Michigan City, Indiana. In 1937, she was elected General Secretary of her congregation, an office she held until her death.

Sister Mary Eleanore published a number of books, including *On the King's Highway*, the story of her congregation; *Mary*, a popular book on Marian theology, history, and devotion; and *Love Folds Its Wings*, a book of poetry. Having worked with the young, she had a particular gift for writing for children and for all those with childlike hearts. Sister Mary Eleanore had special friendship with the saints — God's most childlike servants and a source of help, comfort, inspiration, and encouragement. With the skill of a poet, she gathers for today's Christians the joyful stories of the saints, who beckon us to follow them into Heaven.

∞

Sophia Institute Press®

∞

Sophia Institute is a nonprofit institution that seeks to restore man's knowledge of eternal truth, including man's knowledge of his own nature, his relation to other persons, and his relation to God. Sophia Institute Press® serves this end in numerous ways: it publishes translations of foreign works to make them accessible for the first time to English-speaking readers; it brings out-of-print books back into print; and it publishes important new books that fulfill the ideals of Sophia Institute. These books afford readers a rich source of the enduring wisdom of mankind.

Sophia Institute Press® makes these high-quality books available to the general public by using advanced technology and by soliciting donations to subsidize its general publishing costs. Your generosity can help Sophia Institute Press® to provide the public with editions of works containing the enduring wisdom of the ages. Please send your tax-deductible contribution to the address below. We also welcome your questions, comments, and suggestions.

For your free catalog, call:
Toll-free: 1-800-888-9344

or write:
Sophia Institute Press® • Box 5284 • Manchester, NH 03108

or visit our website:
www.sophiainstitute.com

Sophia Institute is a tax-exempt institution as defined by the Internal Revenue Code, Section 501(c)(3). Tax I.D. 22-2548708.

Critical praise for this book

'This learned book demonstrates that the globalization of the un-regulated market, driven by the accumulation of property, leads to the impoverishment of ever wider sectors of humanity and the devastation of the natural environment. . . . This can be stopped only by recognizing the conditional character of property, de-mocratizing the ownership of productive goods, and creating economic development that serves human well-being and protects the earth.' *Professor Gregory Baum, McGill-Queens University*

'This book is an interesting and significant contribution to the growing discussion on the adverse effects of the implementation of unbridled global market activities. It also has good ideas on what can be done to rectify the situation. I hope many people will read it and draw lessons from it.' *Martin Khor, Director, Third World Network*

'Faith-based groups are enormously important in the global jus-tice movement and they are on the move, as this penetrating and crucial text demonstrates. It is incumbent on us all to incorporate this dimension in our own analyses so that we can move forward in unity, secularists and faith-oriented together, in the common quest for justice. This book is a great step forward on that road.' *Susan George, author and campaigner*

'Here is a strong message, one that makes connections in politics, economics, philosophy and scripture. It is an encouragement for those who have been told that "there is no alternative", and urges upon us the claims of economic and political discipleship. It will bring excitement, challenge and controversy to any group.' *The Rt Revd Dr Peter Selby, Bishop of Worcester and Bishop to HM Prisons*

'I highly recommend *Property for People, Not for Profit*. Capitalism today is too often thought of as "natural" or "God-given" when a careful examination of the history of its development shows that there are other ways to think about how our economy and society should be organized. The most valuable contribution of this book, however, is to show how another world is possible.' *Dennis Howlett, KAIROS: Canadian Ecumenical Justice Initiative*

About this book

The issue of private property – how it is conceived and the bundles of rights it confers – remains almost undiscussed in the current wave of criticism of globalization and free market economics, and also in the alternatives that the global social justice movement is putting forward. Yet, as these authors argue, property lies at the heart of an economic system geared to relatively unfettered profit maximization and that has no regard for either the lives of human beings or the integrity of Nature. The reason for this, they suggest, is because under capitalism property is not related to its use-value for people, but to its exchange-value for the unlimited accumulation of money assets by those who have.

In this powerful exploration of the modern Western notion of private property, the authors – one an economist and the other a theologian – have combined forces to make clear the historically specific and self- consciously explicit manner in which it emerged. While constantly making clear the relevance of their discussion to present-day issues, they trace this history from earliest historical times and show how, in the hands of Thomas Hobbes and John Locke in particular, the notion of private property took on its absolutist nature and most extreme form – a form which neoliberal economics is now imposing on humanity worldwide by means of the coercive pressures of globalization.

Ulrich Duchrow and Franz Hinkelammert argue that the only hope of overcoming the destruction of people's ways of living and of Nature – and the vicious circle of imperial terror and fundamentalist resistance to it that has now emerged – is to reshape our notions of private property in accordance with people's concrete lives and the common good. What human beings have created, human beings can change. In this highly original and persuasive account, the authors look at practical ways in which we can re-define our notions and the legal forms of different kinds of property – personal property; property in the fundamental elements of land and water; and economic property in the means of production. Finally, they look at the possibilities of social and ecumenical movements to campaign for the implementation of alternatives.

It is difficult to exaggerate the importance of this pioneering book in both philosophical and political terms.

Ulrich Duchrow & Franz J. Hinkelammert

Property for People, Not for Profit
alternatives to the global tyranny of capital

translated by Elaine Griffiths with Trish Davie,
Michael Marten and Páraic Réamonn

Zed Books
LONDON · NEW YORK

in association with

CIIR

Catholic Institute for International
Relations
LONDON

The Catholic Institute for International Relations (CIIR) is an
international development agency working through skill-share and
advocacy for an end to injustice and the eradication of poverty. We
work with people of all faiths and none.

*Property for People, Not for Profit: alternatives to the global tyranny of
capital* was first published by Zed Books Ltd, 7 Cynthia Street,
London N1 9JF, UK and Room 400, 175 Fifth Avenue, New York,
NY 10010, USA in 2004, in association with The Catholic Institute
for International Relations (CIIR), Unit 3, Canonbury Yard, 190a
New North Road, London N1 7BJ, UK.

www.zedbooks.co.uk
www.ciir.org

Cover designed by Andrew Corbett
Set in Bembo and Futura Bold by Ewan Smith, London
Printed and bound in Malta by Gutenberg Ltd

Distributed in the USA exclusively by Palgrave Macmillan, a division
of St Martin's Press, LLC, 175 Fifth Avenue, New York, NY 10010

A catalogue record for this book is available from the British Library

ISBN 1 84277 478 6 cased
ISBN 1 84277 479 4 limp

Contents

Preface, by Konrad Raiser

Many books have been published in recent years offering a critical analysis of global capitalism. They have considered the historical and political conditions that have facilitated the emergence of economic globalization. Particular attention has been focused on the impact of economic globalization in the form of global capitalism on the disadvantaged sectors of the population, especially in the countries of the global South. Increasingly the discussion has moved from critical analysis to the exploration of alternatives. The World Social Forum has become the framework that enables the diverse approaches in searching for alternatives to join forces. Its slogan, 'Another world is possible', marks the transition from an anti-globalization movement to an 'alter-globalization' stance.

This book by Ulrich Duchrow and Franz Josef Hinkelammert is intended to strengthen this constructive perspective. However, the authors develop their proposals for alternatives against the background of a penetrating historical and philosophical analysis of the roots of global capitalism. They are convinced that the dynamic of global capitalism has arisen from a fundamental change in the understanding of property. Today the purpose of property is no longer determined by its use for the sustenance of human life in community but is oriented towards the production of monetary gain. Property that can produce profit has become capital. According to the authors, the philosophical and conceptual basis for this transformation of the traditional function of property in human societies was provided by John Locke after the 'Glorious Revolution' in England (1688) and was sanctioned through the American constitution. Thus, the door was opened for the unlimited accumulation of property which is the main characteristic of capitalism.

The central three chapters of the book provide a sharp critical perspective on the establishment of the 'total market' as a consequence of the globalization of capitalism. The evidence is taken partly from developments in legislation and economic policy in Germany, partly from experience in Latin America. The terrorist attacks on the Twin Towers of the World Trade Center and the Pentagon, and the subsequent declaration of the 'war on terrorism', are interpreted as a manifestation of the (self-)destructive character of global capitalism which releases a vicious circle of violence.

The authors share a long-standing involvement in social movements both in Latin America and in the European context, especially in Germany, and are inspired by the tradition of 'prophetic criticism' in the worldwide ecumenical movement. Against this background they seek to reinstate the economic and ethical validity of the understanding of property which has its roots both in Greek antiquity (Aristotle) and in the biblical tradition, and which was maintained as ethically normative until the late Middle Ages. Here the legitimacy of the use of property is to be judged by the criterion of whether it ultimately serves the common good of the community. The unlimited accumulation of property is considered a danger for the sustainability of human community.

A life-centred ethic which accepts the common good as the guiding value and seeks to promote the sustainability of life for human community in harmony with the natural life cycles thus becomes the yardstick for considering alternatives to the dominant system of a market society based on the treatment of property as capital. *Property for People, Not for Profit* captures well the central thrust of this investigation. Concrete life is lived in local communities. This is also the context where the interdependence between human communities and the natural life cycles is most obvious. The local-regional level, therefore, becomes the focus for developing alternatives to the spirit, logic and praxis of global capitalism. Of course, the search for alternatives that are meant to promote an effective change cannot be limited to the local level. All forms of property, from personal property to the ownership of essential factors of economic life such as land, labour, energy, water and air, but also knowledge and above all money, are subjected to this critical scrutiny with a view to rebuilding an order of property from below from the perspective of life and the common good.

The book concludes with a brief survey of the critical social movements and initiatives that have emerged in the context of the ecumenical movement. Particular emphasis is placed on the *processus confessionis* against worldwide economic injustice and the destruction of nature initiated by the World Alliance of Reformed Churches in 1997. This has become the basis of intensive cooperation between several ecumenical organizations and their member Churches in the different regions. Ulrich Duchrow here again addresses the question he discussed in earlier publications, i.e. whether the Churches should not consider the global structures of economic injustice a case that calls for a prophetic confession of faith like the total claims of national socialism or the system of apartheid.

The two authors have made a very valuable contribution to the critical discussion about global capitalism. Their focus on the crucial role of a changed understanding of property helps to deepen the critical discourse and offers essential criteria for ethical judgement. And even those who would consider complete reconstruction of the social and economic use of property as unrealistic and utopian will find in this book many realistic proposals that could prepare the way for an alternative social and economic order. But above all, the book is a powerful and convincing refutation of the thesis that there is no alternative to the system of global capitalism. And its message is one of hope and encouragement – for the sake of life.

Foreword

After many years of preparation, this book was written between August and November 2001 in Costa Rica. During that time 11 September happened. In Latin America this day recalls the fulfilment in 1973 of the Nixon and Kissinger plan for intensive destabilization in Chile which aimed to oust the democratically elected socialist president Salvador Allende (see Hitchens 2001). A disloyal military group, in cooperation with the CIA, succeeded in murdering General Schneider, loyal to the president. Then the air force bombed the 'Moneda', the seat of government in Santiago. Clouds of smoke rose up; Allende was murdered. General Pinochet, a dictator by the grace of Washington, hired Milton Friedman of the Chicago School of Economics to set up the first purely neo-liberal economic programme, even before Margaret Thatcher and Ronald Reagan instituted theirs. The phase of neo-liberal globalization, in which *The Economic Horror* (Forrester 1999) was able to grow and flourish had been ushered in with the aid of US state terrorism.

On 11 September 2001 there were again clouds of smoke in the sky, this time over Washington and New York, also caused by terrorist planes. In Latin America the mourning mingled with the memory of 1973. The question is this: how can we overcome the vicious circle of imperial terror, the global economy and the fundamentalist resistance to them? This book tries to find answers to the dilemma.[1]

It arose in the context of a four-month research seminar run by the Departamento Ecuménico de Investigaciones (DEI) in Costa Rica on 'Globalization and Human Rights'. Chapters 1, 2, 4, 7 and 8 were originally written by Ulrich Duchrow, Chapters 3, 5 and 6 by Franz J. Hinkelammert; they were then discussed and revised. We are grateful to our colleagues in DEI, Wim Dierckxsens, Germán Gutiérrez and Pablo Richard, and also to the seminar participants from different Central and South American countries. Thanks also go to Ulrike Duchrow for her criticism and suggestions and to the translators, particularly to Elaine Griffiths. Elaine not only translated Chapters 1, 3, 7 and 8, but also coordinated the translations of Páraic Réamonn (Chapters 2 and 6), Trish Davie (Chapter 4) and Michael Marten (Chapter 5).

The international character of this study is also evident in the fact that the issue has arisen from the campaigning of Kairos Europa, a grass-roots movement for economic justice, and the ongoing campaign *(processus confessionis)* of the World Council of Churches, the World Alliance of Reformed Churches and the Lutheran World Federation to counter global economic injustice and ecological destruction. We thank all those who have given us valuable suggestions, particularly Bob Goudzwaard and Martin Robra. We hope that the book will be a contribution to those ecumenical processes that invite the world's Churches to place themselves more clearly on the side of the victims of this system – for which there is a clear biblical basis. The Churches are invited to resist the system and work for practical alternatives, in alliance with social movements, thereby bearing witness to their faith in the God of life.

We dedicate this book to our grandchildren and the future of life.

Ulrich Duchrow and Franz Hinkelammert,
San José, Costa Rica

Note

1 See also the special issue of the Departamento Ecuménico de Investigaciones (DEI) magazine *Pasos*, 98, Nov./Dec. 2001.

Introduction

'Whoever is not with us is against us' *George W. Bush Jr,*
US President
'If there are only two alternatives choose the third'
Ancient proverb

In the period of the Cold War the property question was reduced
to the simple formula: private or state ownership, leading to the apparent only alternatives of a 'free' market economy or centrally planned
socialism. Admittedly, after the Great Depression of 1929 the economies in the rich industrialized countries made provision for social
welfare, at least until the advent of neo-liberalism in the 1980s. With
the fall of the Berlin Wall in 1989, however, all dams broke and the
ugly face of capitalism began to subjugate the globe again.

The devastating effects may be seen in all parts of the world,
particularly in countries that had hitherto been bled by European
colonialism and the plundering of their national resources. But also in
those countries of the North that had benefited from this there were
increasing signs of unbridled global market mechanisms, structural
unemployment, social exclusion and destruction of the welfare state.

Yet resistance to this is flaring up everywhere in different forms
among the people concerned. Movements of indigenous peoples,
women, farmers, the landless and unemployed, trade unions, ecological activists, solidarity groups and human rights organizations
– they all start at the point at which they experience the pain of
destruction particularly harshly. They all come up against the same
causes: an economic system geared purely to profit maximization and
thereby having no regard for the life of human beings and nature,
a political class that supports this system, and an ideology justified
'academically' by most economists and disseminated, consciously or
unconsciously, by most of the media. So their criticism and resistance are increasingly aimed at these systemic connections: the finance
system, the institutions that support it (the International Monetary
Fund – IMF – and the World Bank), liberalized world trade within
the framework of the World Trade Organization (WTO), or the self-
appointed world government of the G8 countries.

But what are the secret components of this system that we need to know about in order to be able to oppose them and develop alternatives? In asking this question we are struck by the fact that since the end of 'real' socialism the question of ownership has completely disappeared from the discussion. It seems as though the critics of globalization are avoiding this topic in order not to be suspected of continuing to hanker for the centralist model that has apparently historically refuted itself. So it appears that we are dealing with an 'untouchable' taboo.

This taboo must be broken. There can be no doubt at all that capitalism, which is surpassing itself at present in the form of globalization, emerged from the introduction of a certain, absolute form of private property – bound up with certain mechanisms of money and the market. So when it comes to resisting globalized capitalism for its destructive effects, and seeking constructive solutions, it is essential to understand the relationship of ownership arrangements to money and the market. How and where did they arise? What historical forms did they take and how are these connected to the present situation? What is the importance of some countries' constitutional guarantee of the social commitment of property, which – bringing in the environmental context – we here term a commitment to life? Going beyond the alternative of private versus state ownership are there other options? This book examines these questions.

Chapter 1 looks at the original introduction of ownership, money and related market mechanisms in the eighth century BCE and its consequences in the whole of the ancient Near East, particularly in Israel. The biblical traditions, particularly prophetic criticism and legal reforms, show an intensive engagement with related social effects. Jesus and the early Church continue this critique and the quest for alternatives.

In Chapter 2 we enquire about the new approach to a market society based on property after medieval, feudal times, this time in the characteristic modern form of capitalism. This time England is the seedbed. Thomas Hobbes, the English philosopher, first developed this theory of a new society in the early seventeenth century.

More effectively than Hobbes, John Locke legitimized with his theory of ownership the assumption of political rule by large (land)owners in the Glorious Revolution of 1688, as well as the imperialist conquest of North America and India. His importance, as we describe in Chapter 3, consists not least in the fact that his theories provide the basis for Western constitutions.

Through the struggles of the labour movement in particular, it became possible after 1929 to add to the liberal, comprehensive guarantee of property a social obligation related to the common good, which today needs to be called commitment to life. In Chapter 4 we therefore first examine its meaning based on the example of the German Basic Law (constitution). Globalization has the sole goal of liberating the accumulation of capital from all social and ecological barriers. The result is the total market, which is in the process not just of destroying life on earth but with it its own foundations.

This correlation between destruction and self-destruction is the theme of Chapter 5. The dramatic events of 11 September 2001 have apparently induced the West, under the leadership of the United States, to resolve to meet resistance to the total market with the totality of empire. It does not seem inclined to remove the causes of the counter-terror.

What alternatives are there to this situation? Chapter 6 raises this question specifically from the perspective of Latin America and a new version of dependence theory. The exclusive character of the property economy has driven large parts of the population into the informal sphere. So the question is whether their reinvolvement in the formal sector by means of the production of simple goods offers a prospect of renewal for the global economy which could help overcome overproduction and the migration of capital into speculative financial markets.

This approach is developed systematically in Chapter 7. The point of departure is a fundamental question: what are the criteria for a new ownership system rooted in real life and the common good? This will lead to the elucidation of a flexible approach 'from below', which can find expression in an abundance of forms of property. With the aid of Binswanger's model of constitutional reform in Switzerland, we examine a possible legal model and finally make practical proposals from the local to the global levels.

Finally, Chapter 8 places the results derived in the context of different campaigns mounted by social movements, particularly by the ecumenical campaign against global economic injustice and ecological destruction. Such campaigns ask whether the present globally life-threatening system should not be tackled as clearly and unequivocally as were the evil systems of National Socialism in Germany and apartheid in South Africa. This concerns the Churches themselves, in that they need to review their own handling of capital ownership. But they must also take a clear, public position. We have drafted practical proposals in this regard.

There is still hope of stopping this disastrous trend for humanity and nature. A central condition is for property to be liberated from its random, destructive function and to be committed not just to society but also to life.

ONE
Absolute property creates poverty, debts and slavery: the origin of the property economy in antiquity and biblical alternatives

§ There are different theories concerning the origins of private property. One thing is certain, though: the first forms of private property arose in the late eighth century BCE, gaining ground in Greece and in the whole of the ancient Near East. It is also certain that money originated around the same time (not yet in the form of coins). There is no agreement among researchers about how it originated, but at any rate the two institutions, property and money, must have had something to do with each other.

The first, most widespread assumption is that money arose from *bartering*, and was at the same time the means of increasing property. The first to present a developed theory was Aristotle (following Plato).[1] He distinguished two types of economy: one supplying households and the broader community (*polis*) with the goods needed to satisfy basic needs (*oikonomiké*), the other used to increase monetary property for its own sake (*kapiliké*, buying and selling as part of the artificial form of acquisition, *khremastiké*). This chrematistic economic form, according to Aristotle, arose from the former, natural form of economy since it, too, used money as a means of exchange for vital goods, first in the form of precious metals such as silver and gold, and later in the form of coins.

As a motive for the origin of the second, 'unnatural' form of chrematistic economy Aristotle — here too linking up with Plato — cited human desire (*epithymía*). The boundless accumulation of money creates the illusion in the individual person of accumulating infinite 'means of sustenance' and means of pleasure, and thereby living for ever. That means that the striving for more property, provided by monetary mechanisms, is based on the desire, transcending the individually desired object, for eternal life. Chasing after this illusion, the individual destroys community. As an antidote to this community-destructive behaviour Aristotle suggests, first, ethical education and, second, political prohibitions (i.e. protecting the good of the *polis*). This will be described in greater detail below.

The second theory connects the origin of money with the *sacrificial practice* of the temple and the collection of tribute by kingdoms and empires, where there is also an element of barter (see Veerkamp 1993: 32ff, following Kippenberg 1978: 51). According to Deuteronomy (14: 24f), this basically arose in the late seventh century. The Judaeans, who lived farther away from the central temple, were supposed to exchange their sacrificial gifts at home for silver, with which they could buy the right sacrificial animals at the temple in Jerusalem. Evidence of small sacrificial spears as early forms of money reinforces this theory of the emergence of money from temple operations. The great temple treasures also lead to the conclusion that the priesthood made a good profit from this business. In Jesus's later criticism of the temple (Mark 11: 15ff) it becomes clear that the sacrificial system introduced under King Solomon was a way of robbing the poor, and not just a means of facilitation through the use of money.

This sacrificial function of money became all the clearer in its use as a means for empires to raise *tribute* from their subjugated peoples. This was first reported of King Darius I of Persia (522–486 BCE). He introduced state-guaranteed money as a universal unit of account. In this way tribute could be raised over the whole year and not just at harvest time, and from all parts of the empire.

A third theory sees money deriving from the new *credit relations* that became possible with the emergence of private property (Heinsohn 1984; Heinsohn and Steiger 1996; Duchrow 2000a; Hungar 2000). G. Heinsohn and O. Steiger (HS) see things as follows:

1. The property economy arose in antiquity (and in the modern age) through revolution, with dependent farmers dividing the feudal lands among themselves in times of crisis; this took place in an egalitarian fashion and along patriarchal lines.

2. According to HS money arose from the credit contract. This was based on the new situation whereby owners could mortgage their property as debtors and 'burden' their property as creditors. Since the credit contract stipulated that the creditor had to 'burden' his property, and so could not use it himself, he allowed this renouncing of the 'ownership premium' (by analogy with Keynes's 'liquidity premium') to be paid for with interest. Yet the debtor not only had to raise this interest in addition to repaying the principle, but also to mortgage his own property, usually his land, as security. If the credit contract was written down this document (like a bill of exchange) could be used as

a means of payment. It was secured not only by the mortgaging of the debtor's property but also by the 'burdenability' of the creditor's property. So the documenting of the credit contract was a way of making money. In short, money was the claim on burdened property. Markets arose through the fact that the debtors had to sell their credit-financed production at as favourable a price as possible, and in competition with each other. Only in this way could they service their debt.

3. According to HS the property economy was originally egalitarian, but through the creditor–debtor mechanism within society it inevitably brought forth inequality (classes). Debtors who could not repay their credits lost their land, i.e. their means of subsistence, and had to go into debt bondage with their whole family in order to work off their interest and loan. For their part, the creditors accumulated land and wealth.

For our purposes it is not necessary to give a definitive outline of the historical emergence of property and money. Wherever and however these institutions and their related mechanisms may have arisen, they became increasingly common from the mid-eighth century both in Greece and in Israel, and later in the Hellenistic empires and the Roman empire.[2] We are primarily concerned in bringing out the specific economic, political, social and cultural constellations in Greece, Rome and ancient Israel, because they provide the categorial foundations for the modern development of property and money. They also provide us with options in the debate about alternatives.

Ancient Greece

An excellent, brief description of the conditions in ancient Athens is to be found in the article 'Property owners or citizens? Household, economics and politics in ancient Athens and in Aristotle' by Thomas Maissen (1998; see also Binswanger 1995). The Greek *polis* arose at the same time as the institutions of property and money. In order to understand this event in the late eighth and, above all, in the seventh century BCE, it is important to realize that *polis* does not mean a city but an agricultural region *with* a city – in the case of Athens, Attica. 'There are … no hierarchical differences between *town* and *country* … on the contrary: the citizen, the *polítes* … is generally a *land owner* and resident on the land, and *only a citizen can own land at all*. By contrast, land ownership was originally the formal precondition for the status of citizen' (Maissen 1998: 67). Herein lies the decisive change from the preceding age of warring nobility. In principle all farmers became landowners and together formed the area of the *polis*. They were therefore no longer dependent, through paying tribute, on the city-kingdoms.

They had slaves to farm their land, were self-sufficient and not dependent on any external assistance; they exchanged only at will in order to make their lives more comfortable. The place of this autarky was the household, the *oíkos*, the private economic and living space in which needs were met. Here the farmer ruled as head of the household (*despótes*) over slaves, women and children. On this basis farmers gained the freedom and leisure to meet as *polítes*, citizens, at the *agora*, the centre of the city, and to discuss and discharge the common affairs of the community. Trading took place here, as well as religious, judicial and sporting activities. The people's assembl y met here. In view of the time this required, it is clear why the full citizen needed leisure. Smallholders without slaves, or farmers losing their land, retained the heritable status of citizen, but they could participate in political life only to a limited degree. They were dependent on public money to be able to attend political events and the theatre.

Non-citizens – slaves, freedmen and metics (*métoikos*) – were distinct from citizens; they could not participate in political life. The metics were Greeks who had come to the city from other *poleis*. They were mostly merchants and craftsmen (*bánausos*), who – unlike the landowning citizens – had to pay a poll tax. In terms of property law the picture was as follows:

- citizens can own everything;
- slaves, although legally not even able to decide for themselves as an 'ensouled instrument', can possess movable goods to which their master has no automatic access;
- metics as non-citizens cannot possess land and generally cannot buy houses in the city. A metic can therefore not grant a loan to a citizen if offered land as security – what could he do if it fell to him? Metic property is mobile (money and valuables, clothes, tools, animals and slaves), but it is still unrestrictedly their own;
- what slaves earn belongs to them only with the consent of their masters;
- it is similar with women, who can enjoy the status of a free person and owner, but can neither enjoy legal capacity nor be entitled to

inherit or possess wealth without the consent of their husband or
male guardian;
* the same applies to children and minors. (Ibid.: 69)

Unlike HS, Maissen does not see a terminological or legal distinction between property and possession in the Greek *polis*, by contrast
with Rome (see below), although the differentiation apparently occurs
in practice (ibid.: 69f). The word for both is *ídion*, what 'is' (*eínai*) to
one, or what one has acquired (*ktéma* or *ktésis*), and it means 'the actual
power and rule over an object'. It would, moreover, be anachronistic to
envisage the *polis* as an integrated market with modern economic laws.
Actual economic activities in the modern sense, such as agricultural
production, urban crafts, trade and monetary transactions, were carried
out by non-citizens. But money gradually began to play a role in the
contractual organization of urban work with outside credit arrangements.[3] The full citizen was involved in economic matters only as a
landowner, mine lessor or lender for risky maritime trade (ibid.: 70).

Accordingly, his ideal was not the accumulation of wealth as such.
Freedom to involve himself in political matters was to be acquired
through having slaves working on the landed property, enabling a co-
financing of community service (*leiturgía*), i.e. that which was necessary in emergencies and for the organization of religious and cultural
events. Therein lay the glory and honour of citizens. The interest in
wealth of non-citizens was despised. This was Aristotle's concern in
his critical argument against limitless money accumulation at the
expense of what he called the 'common good'.

Already in the ancient *polis* there were developments indicating
that property not only provided the basis of the freedom of farmer-
citizens but also generated divisions in society. This was demonstrated
by Solon's reforms of 594 BCE. At the time, a good hundred years after
the emergence of the *polis*, many farmers had apparently not only lost
their land because they were not able to repay their loans, but had also
become debt slaves. By contrast, others had risen to the position of
large landowners. The losers called for a redistribution of land, proving
the historical possibility of egalitarian approaches in ancient Greece,
and for the abolition of debt bondage. The power base underlying this
demand lay less in revolutionary phenomena, however, than in the
newly introduced (in 700 BCE) war technology of the hoplite phalanx,
for which trusty freemen were required (see Breuer 1987: 138f). Solon

abolished the subjection of farmers and debt bondage, but expressly rejected land reform.

In this way there were many classes among those enjoying the political rights of citizens of the *polis*: the full citizens who, through the work of slaves on their properties, had the freedom and leisure to fully participate in the *agora*, the middle-ranking farmers who, while owning land, were forced to work themselves, and the landless, who had to hire themselves out as day-labourers but retained their civil rights. 'That is a political solution for a political problem: how can citizens remain citizens?' (Maissen 1998: 81). This political constitution related to property classes was called timocracy. Around the year 400 BCE about a quarter of the citizens of Athens owned no land (ibid.: 67). It is therefore noteworthy that this first form of democracy was expressly linked to (unequally distributed) property.

A. Künzli has compiled a list of the Greek sources since Hesiod (*c.* 750 BCE) in which property, money and greed are criticized as being destructive for the community; this is portrayed in myths, philosophy and comedy (Künzli 1986: 63ff). In many cases the abolition of private property and the introduction of common property is demanded – in Plato for the upper class of guards and warriors. Aristotle argues, by contrast, for different forms of property in juxtaposition: private and common. But even private property is subject to moderate and generous usage, meaning that the landowning citizen leads a good life only if he does his bit in respect of his socially compensatory, cultic and military community responsibilities. 'The Greek state, the *polis*, does not act economically, it acts politically in taking from the wealthy what it needs to survive in external defence and for social and ritual integration' (Maissen 1998: 79). And this is not legally regulated, it is a moral obligation. The 'profit' for the wealthy is prestige and reputation in society. So economics, politics and ethics are inseparably linked in Aristotle's thinking.

Both the criticism and development of utopias reveal that the connection between impoverishment and enrichment was experienced, and they also raise the issue of the economic and psychological, or anthropological, mechanisms causing this division in the context of this 'ancient class society' (see Kippenberg 1977 and 1978). Whole new developments ensued when the manageable framework of the *polis* broke down and Alexander the Great, a student of Aristotle, founded the Hellenistic empire (after 333 BCE, first under Macedonian then under Egyptian-Ptolemaic and Syrian-Seleucidic leadership). Without political and moral control the striving for possession and wealth expanded greatly. This was compounded by the tribute obligation of the subject peoples towards the respective empires and their administrations, and the consequent increased social conflicts. Hellenism therefore united two forms of exploitation: that of the monarchy or empire, and that based on property, interest, indebtedness, loss of land and slavery.

From the perspective of Judaea and the true faith in Yahweh, four elements, in particular, were responsible for the increasing social division in the Hellenistic period (until 64 BCE) (see Albertz 1992: 594ff):

1. The commercialization of landed property that according to Lev. 25 was prohibited for Jews was extended from Greece to the whole kingdom; this led to increasing concentration of land and, in turn, land loss.
2. The mechanism of property, interest and mortgaging led, moreover, to increased debt slavery.
3. The internationalization of the Hellenist world entailed a rising trade in foreign slaves. 'Palestine became a slave-exporting country to cover the enormous demand for slaves in the Graeco-Roman world' (ibid.: 595).
4. The intensification of the tribute system consequent on allowing local large landowners to lease the collection of taxes, levies and customs duties – on the understanding that they could keep all that remained for themselves after handing on the tribute squeezed out of the population. All this was a terrible change for a people that had emerged from the status of freed slaves and tribute-exempt farmers. The Book of Job reflects this process of the growing poverty of the Judaean population in Hellenism. (see Veerkamp 1993: 115ff)

Rome

What began in Greece and the Hellenistic empires came to a head in the Roman empire, where it took on a legal form that was to prove momentous.[4] The Roman empire introduced a basic distinction between possession (*possessio*) and property (*dominium* or *proprietas*). Possession is the actual having of a thing.[5] It can thus designate all possible utility rights to a thing, even if they are partial or temporary.

Property, by contrast, designates a comprehensive right to a thing, a 'full right' not limited in time. It also consists of renting, leasing and cession as pledge. It enables encumbrance to secure a loan. Property as *dominium* is characterized by different features:

- As a full right it covers the substance of the thing. A thing as a whole is exclusively allocated to a person who can use it with complete freedom to the exclusion of every other person. This right grants protection in five relationships: against withdrawal (*rei vindicatio*), against damage, against other effects; the owner enjoys complete freedom of use including sale and destruction; he can leave his property to his heirs. In a nutshell:'*Dominium est jus utendi et abutendi re sua, quatenus juris ratio patitur*' (Ownership is the right to use and abuse/consume/destroy your thing as far as compatible with *ratio*, i.e. the logic of the law).[6] *The core of this statement is the absoluteness of property and hence its designation as* dominium, '*dominion*'.
- The dominion is meant literally, not just metaphorically, and goes to the heart of the matter. The origin is probably the rule of the paterfamilias (Greek *despótes*) over the persons in the household and the furnishings. The *patria potestas* (power of the house-father) over the family (Latin collective term *familia pecuniaque*, i.e. women, children, slaves, livestock) entails, as they are like things, rights concerning life and death (*jus vitae necisve*). Gradually the *patria potestas* was differentiated into the power of family law (*manus*) over wife and children and *dominium* over slaves and animals. Precisely in the classical period, the *dominium* was related to landed property.
- The *dominium* contains no relational elements at all, e.g. in terms of the fact that there are owners and non-owners in a society, and that possibly the having could have something to do with the non-having of others. It is absolute rule over things (*jus in rem*), and as such works against everyone, above all *excluding them*.[7] To be distinguished is the *jus in personam*. This is about obligations and contracts of all kinds between owners.
- Partial rights to the thing are envisaged as restrictions on ownership, particularly pledge rights (the pledge goes into the possession of the creditor or serves without actual seizure as a mortgage) and the transfer of the security (*fiducia cum creditore*). The distinction between property and possession of security, as in Greece, made the lending business possible on the basis of credit collateral.

• Finally, Roman law distinguished between *patrimonium* and *dominium*.[8] Patrimonium is the property inherited from the father, which has to be passed on to the children. This actually excludes the possibility of the 'thing' wearing out or even being destroyed.

Through the extension of patriarchal–despotic rule to the emperor (in contrast to the republican period of Rome) the concept of *dominium* took on an *imperial* component. The system of Hellenistic empires was formed by unbounded territorial expansion and limitless, money-mediated market relations between owners, held together by the divine figure of the emperor. The system of the Roman empire was likewise a property-dominion pyramid, with slaves and animals (nature) at the bottom; but legally constituted. This juridically established dominion was absolute in a double sense: it excluded all those who did not submit to it (see Rev. 13: 16ff), and it expressly included the possibility of abuse and destruction. This approach was taken up again later in early capitalism and in the whole of the modern age. And, although characteristically modified, it stands for the bourgeois, capitalist possessive economy.

Ancient Israel, the Jesus movement and the early Church as counter-cultural experiments

The origin and spread of the property and credit economy from Greece in the late eighth and seventh centuries BCE encountered a quite different context in Israel (see Duchrow 1995: 121ff). The liberation of the Hebrews from the slavery of the Egyptian empire and the farmers from the tribute obligations of the Canaan city-kingdoms had taken place around 1250 BCE. The freed slaves had settled on the Palestinian mountains and organized themselves into independent families and clans. They organized their common affairs in egalitarian fashion at a general meeting, with explicit reference to the God to whom they owed their liberation, Yahweh (*qu'hal Jahwe*). When, for example, defence needed to be organized against attacks from outside, they did this with charismatic leaders chosen by Yahweh (Book of Judges).

As of around 1000 BCE the people had opted for the monarchy, against the resistance of peasant and prophetic groups. The consequence was increasingly oppression and exploitation of the peasant people by the king's court, his officials and the military (1 Sam. 8). Solomon behaved like an ancient oriental emperor. When his sons wanted to add to the burden already weighing on the people, the northern tribes split off from Judah and Benjamin, the southern tribes, and formed their own northern kingdom. This developed along the same lines, even to the point of the arbitrary confiscation of peasant land by the king (1 Kgs. 21). Despite the violent Jehu revolution, this remained a dominant trend right into the eighth century BCE.

In this situation the new mechanism of property-interest-money for the predominantly (small)holder producers was an additional dangerous attack on their livelihoods. Hitherto they had to pay taxes to the king, the temple and to maintain the luxury of the aristocratic upper class, above and beyond their production costs. Now competition arose among them. They did not take out loans in order to set up lucrative, credit-financed production lines in the modern sense, but out of pure hardship – for example, for seed when they suffered a bad harvest and had to eat the seed before the next seed time in the interests of sheer survival. The consequence was that they lost their land to the large landowners and, to add insult to injury, had to work as debt slaves for them. It may be assumed here that the new form of property economy with its credit mechanism seeped into the monarchic, feudal system and that the starting point was unequal land distribution. The decisive thing for the social history of Israel was that the farmers were exposed to another exploitative mechanism from the late eighth century, in addition to the royal and imperialist structures of tribute. This mechanism arose in their own midst and destroyed their solidarity. How did Israel react to this aggravation of the situation?

Kessler (1992; see also Kessler 2000) examined precisely the period in which the property economy was penetrating the society of the kingdom of Judah. The question may remain in abeyance as to whether this was due to external influences from Greece and Mesopotamia or to Jewish society itself. It is striking, at any rate, that this development took place at exactly the same time as the emergence of the property economy in the Greek *polis*. Perhaps the seafaring Phoenicians served as intermediaries between Greece and Palestine (see Hübner 1997).

Kessler shows that the basic contradiction arising from the property economy in Jewish society was between creditors and debtors. It led to a concentration of land in the hands of large landowners, and drove smallholders into debt. The former could live in luxury, mostly in town. Debt caused the latter to lose their land; they and their families were deprived of their freedom and self-reliance, having to work as day-labourers or debt slaves. At the end of the kingly period they were desperately poor. The important thing is that the nouveaux riches were able to achieve their property concentration quite legally by means of creditor–debtor contracts. But they formed an upper class in common with the civil service, military and the royal court. These groups together had the political power, not just the economic power, in their hands. Consequently they could manipulate the very law that, according to Israelite understanding, was supposed to protect the vulnerable and the poor.

The protest of the prophets It was precisely this unfortunate development in public and social life, caused by the new property economy, which called forth the protest of the great prophets in the last third of the eighth and the seventh centuries. Amos and Hosea (still in the northern kingdom before its destruction in 722 BCE), Isaiah, Micah, Zephaniah, Jeremiah, Habakkuk and Ezekiel called for law (*mispat*) and justice (*sedaqa*), which had been lost through the new property law. But above all repudiating justice and the rights of the poor meant rejecting the God of Israel. Knowing God is identical with creating justice for the poor (see, e.g., Jer. 22: 16). The later continuation of the books of the prophets after the downfall of the northern kingdom in 722 and the southern kingdom in 586 BCE – which they had prophesied – contains indications that are likewise interesting in terms of our theme. Let us look more closely at some of the texts, in the light of Kessler.

The prophet Amos appeared in the mid-eighth century in the northern kingdom. His central theme was the threat to the small farmers. They were losing their possessions through seizures, being sold into slavery for excessive debts, the women abused as debt slaves (Amos 2: 6–8), the smallholders deceived in credit deals (8: 4–7), and made to pay levies and fines (5: 11f). This was breaking the law that was supposed to protect the poor (5: 10; 6: 12). On the other hand, the prophet criticizes the well-to-do who enrich themselves at the expense of the poor, depend on the work of others and live a life of luxury (5: 11; 6: 4–6 *passim*). They are threatened with doom and downfall (9: 9f). By contrast, in the further record of Amos's words the victims are promised that they will enjoy the fruits of their labour themselves: 'They shall rebuild the ruined cities and inhabit them; they shall plant vineyards and drink their wine, and they shall make gardens and eat their fruit' (9: 14). That makes it 'clear that the property of idle land-owners based on exploitation and luxury was doomed, and the property of farmers based on their own toil was to have a safe future. The property granted by freedom is not in the abstract. Rather, idle property is to be removed and only the property based on a person's own work is to be blessed by God' (Kessler 2000: 70).

At the end of the same century the prophet Micah appeared in the southern kingdom of Judah, the time during which the prophecy of Amos was fulfilled and the northern kingdom was destroyed by the Assyrians (722 BCE). He pilloried the same mechanism of property-interest-seizure-debt slavery:

> Alas for those who devise wickedness
> and evil deeds on their beds!
> When the morning dawns, they perform it,
> because it is in their power.
> They covet fields, and seize them,
> houses, and take them away,
> they oppress householder and house,
> people and their inheritance. (Mic. 2: 1f)

> The women of my people you drive out
> from their pleasant houses;
> from their young children you take away
> my glory for ever.
> Arise and go
> For this is no place to rest. (2: 9f)

These texts make it clear not only that the farmers lose their land, house and freedom but also that their children also have to go into debt slavery – not just for a limited period but 'for ever'. The apparently purely economic event of executing a credit contract is here, for the first time, called theft. The rich who are to blame will meet their doom (2: 3). And indeed, the nobility of Judah were carried away by the Babylonians in 586 BCE. In this period and on their return the book of the prophet was continued – in the hope of obtaining a confession of sin from the rich and also from the ordinary people who had abandoned the practice of solidarity. Only through a change in the economic system could there be hope that, when beginning again after the exile, everyone would be able to live justly from the work of their hands (Kessler 2000: 77f).

In the seventh century the prophet Isaiah also criticized the expropriation of farming families and the accumulation of land in sharp terms:

> Ah! You who join house to house
> who add field to field,
> until there is room for no one but you
> and you are left to live alone
> in the midst of the land! (Isa. 5: 8)

He, too, calls the greedy landowners 'thieves' (1: 23) and the seizure of the land of indebted farmers taking 'the spoil of the poor' (3: 14). He too foretells the perishing of their booty (5: 9f). The Book of Isaiah was also continued in different phases. While the 'tyrants' and 'boasters' are exterminated the 'meek' and 'needy' are promised great fruitfulness (29: 17–21). 'Trito-Isaiah' (Isa. 65: 21f) then clearly states, like Amos and Micah:

> They shall build houses and inhabit them;
> they shall plant vineyards and eat their fruit.
> They shall not build and another inhabit;
> they shall not plant and another eat.
> My chosen shall long enjoy the work of their hands.

The legal reforms The original prophetic texts from the eighth and seventh centuries were not totally unsuccessful. This is clear from the different legal reforms from that period and afterwards. Prophecy and law are, in biblical tradition, two typical starting points when it comes to questioning and overcoming life-destroying (unjust) orders.[9] They represent criticism and vision on the one hand, and institutional transformation on the other. The first legal reform took place in the southern kingdom probably after the experience of the catastrophe of the northern kingdom (722 BCE). The written record is found in the Book of the Covenant (Exodus 21–3).[10] Prophets like Amos and Hosea had heralded this collapse as the result of social and economic injustice in the northern kingdom and called for repentance. Now the followers of the prophets came with the refugees from the North, reinforcing the voices of the southern prophets like Isaiah and Micah with the message: if you do not turn away from the idols of wealth and power to Yahweh and to justice, you will run into trouble like the northern kingdom.

Probably it was in this situation that the Book of the Covenant introduced several 'rules of seven' and a number of other economic laws combining social and ecological criteria with theological ones:

*   23:12: On the seventh day of the week (not yet called the Sabbath) the farmer is to rest and also give the day off to his cattle, slaves and the 'resident alien' so that they 'may be refreshed'.
*   21:2–11: In the seventh year the (debt) slave shall be released without a ransom.
*   23:10f: In the seventh year the fields shall lie fallow so that the poor and the animals can eat of it.
*   22:20–23: Foreigners, widows and orphans shall not be violently abused as were the Hebrew slaves in Egypt because God will hear their cry (Exod. 3:7ff) and destroy the oppressors as God once did the Egyptians.
*   22:24–26: Anyone who lends money shall not take a pawn or charge interest; for God hears the cries of those whose lives are threatened as God once heard the cries of the Hebrew slaves – God is compassionate.

We are therefore dealing with preventive and corrective laws. On the one hand, neither pawns nor interest shall be taken[11] in order to prevent land loss and enslavement on grounds of over-indebtedness. On the other hand, if (debt) slavery has occurred anyway there should be a periodic liberation. It is noteworthy that the owner is not to overuse the earth either, but to grant it a periodic rest. He should also be aware of how people and animals jointly make use of it.

To sum up, according to the Book of the Covenant, in view of God's solidarity with all his creatures, the needs of real life, including freedom from oppression, write the economic rules.

These approaches are confirmed and expanded in the second law reform under King Josiah in 622 BCE, which form the core of Deuteronomy.[12] Again it is about the preventive measures of banning interest and usury (Deut. 23:20) and the law on pledges or pawns (24:6 and 10ff): 'You shall not charge interest on loans to another Israelite, interest on money, interest on provisions, interest on anything that is lent' (23:19).

'It was sometimes pure hardship that led people to run up debts, and this could then lead to the loss of land and freedom. No one was supposed to benefit at the expense of such need ... most ancient societies ... disintegrated into a small class of wealthy people and many completely impoverished or enslaved people. These laws were intended to prevent that happening and there is evidence that in Israel they did, as long as it was possible to apply the main aspects of them' (Crüsemann 2000: 53).

The owners also had obligations at harvest time. They were not supposed to completely strip the fields so that those without any land could find basic sustenance (Deut. 24: 19). In addition, the owners were committed to give a tenth of their harvest in discharge of community responsibilities (14: 22). This was to enable the holding of a big festival every year which *all* were permitted to attend. Every third year, however, this tithe was to be given to those with no land, i.e. those who for different reasons had no means of production: widows, orphans, foreigners and Levites (who were seconded to perform cultic and educational duties). 'That is the first social tax in world history, the germ of legal and state responsibility for the most vulnerable from general tax revenue' (Crüsemann 2000: 51). It is interesting to draw a comparison with the Greek *polis*. Here it was expected that the rich should give generous support to poorer citizens and to community responsibilities – to their own honour and glory. In Israel, by contrast, the poor had a God-given right to assistance.

The situation regarding debt slavery is more differentiated. At about the same time, Solon completely abolished it in Greece for Athenian citizens – but only for citizens. In Israel slavery was not supposed to exist at all, in memory of the liberation from Egypt. The preventive laws were intended to ensure just that. However, if it did occur slaves were to be released in the seventh year. 'If a member of your community ... is sold to you and works for you six years, in the seventh year you shall set that person free' (Deut. 15: 12; cf. Jer. 34: 8ff).

Deuteronomy adds (15: 12ff) that the freed slaves are to be given starting capital for their new beginning as smallholders free from their 'masters'. 'As debt slaves serve as pledges to secure the debt this law breaks the internal logic of debt law' (Crüsemann 2000: 54).

This becomes even clearer with the 'debt remission', also to take place in the seventh year (Deut. 15: 1ff). What does it mean? The Hebrew term used here is *schmittah*, renunciation (see Veerkamp 1993: 65ff). The creditor is to renounce – as the fallow land renounces the annual yield of the seventh year – not just his receivable debt repayment but also the pledged property of the debtor, normally the land (complete with house), i.e. the smallholder's means of production. So after seven years it is not just the possible consequence of the debt – debt slavery of the family – which is removed but the cause itself – the debt and related seizure of their own means of production. This enables a new beginning in freedom.[13]

Both these events are without parallel in the ancient Near East and in Graeco-Roman antiquity. In Israel the absoluteness of property is rejected, as is the transformation of an enslaved person (a fellow-countryman) into absolute property. Deuteronomy is, moreover, of the opinion that, if the people of God held to the good laws of justice and mercy, no needy or poor person would need to live among them (15: 4ff). On the contrary, the community of the people as a whole would prosper because God's blessing would be upon them. All these laws are accordingly accompanied by words of blessing (14: 29; 15: 10; 15: 18; 23: 21; 24: 13; 24: 19) (Crüsemann 2000: 51ff). The core category is life. If the people keep to these laws of Yahweh they will live (Deut. 6: 24). If they run after the gods of other nations – i.e. follow their practice of not protecting the poor – they will be lost (6: 14ff).

This is precisely what happened with the destruction of Jerusalem and the deportation of the Judaean elite to Babylon in 586 BCE, after the successors to King Josiah had fallen back into their old practices. Only the landless and poor remained in Judaea and were now able, with the permission of the Babylonians, to occupy the land from which they had previously been excluded by the rich. Then all groups started reflecting on the causes of the disaster and the question of how social, economic and political structures were to be reorganized when the time came for a new beginning. They did not want to make the same mistakes. An important witness to this is the holiness code of the priestly writings in the Book of Leviticus. It sums up the socio-economic rules codified for the post-exilic new beginning in Judaea (see Veerkamp 1993: 86ff; Crüsemann 2000: 330ff).

Chapter 25 is particularly important. It focuses on a theological statement without which all else is incomprehensible. It states why Israel has to have a fundamentally different economic order from that of the surrounding peoples. They have law laid down by the king or by owners. In Israel law is laid down from outside – from Sinai (Lev. 25: 1), i.e. by God. The power is withdrawn from kings and owners in the interests of human equality and thus in the interests of the poor and vulnerable. God says: 'The land shall not be sold in perpetuity, for the land is mine; and with me you are but aliens and tenants' (25: 23).

The laws of Leviticus 25 rest clearly on the rejection of the absoluteness of property. Anyone wanting to follow the biblical God must accept God as the owner of the land. God can only give rights to use or lease the land (the means of production in an agricultural society) so that all can share in it. All else follows from that.

- 25: 2–7: In the seventh year the land shall be allowed to enjoy a 'shabbat' (the concept of sabbath is now introduced for the seven-year rhythms).
- 25: 8–13: After seven-times-seven years the 'jobel', the horn, shall be blown and all families shall receive the parcels of land due to them, so that all can again provide for themselves (the jubilee year) as in the pre-kingly tribal society.
- 25: 14–17: The purchasing price for land shall not be left to the market and thereby to speculation: instead the fiftieth year shall serve as a basis for calculating how many harvests (then to be paid for) a piece of land will still yield.
- 25: 25–28: If a brother and his family are at rock bottom, i.e. have to sell their land or house, the nearest relative shall redeem them (the Ge'ulah order).
- 25: 35–38: And if they have to take out a loan their fellow-country-men shall not charge them any interest (*neshek* = bite) nor take any additional payments in kind (*marbith* = increase).
- 25: 39–46: Members of the same people shall not be made into slaves at all – the reason here too is that God is their owner and God led them out of Egypt.

It should be mentioned that the priestly writings weaken the detail of Deuteronomic social laws. The freeing of slaves and reimbursement of the land lost through seizure are taken out of the seven-year arrangement and postponed to the fiftieth year. Moreover, the fact that the restitution of the land in the fiftieth year, historically speaking, crops up only once in the Hebrew Bible at this point is best explained by the fact that with the return of the exiled from Babylon fifty years after their deportation it was precisely this problem which was urgent: how was the land to be distributed now that the landless poor who had stayed in the country had taken over and farmed the estates of the deported nobility? Should the large landowners get back their land (taken from the people in the past by force or debt mechanisms)? Should they get no land at all?[14] The answer is offered by the jubilee year arrangement as a compromise reminiscent of the pre-kingly, egalitarian tribal society: every family shall come back to their land to provide for themselves.

Later, during the time of the Persians, the 'third Isaiah' in Isa. 61 takes up the jubilee year as a sign of hope in the future ('year of the Lord's favour'). This shows that the prophetic criticism and the legal transformations in Judah could not hold, as is clear enough in the Book of Nehemiah (ch. 5). Here the ordinary women and men complain to Nehemiah that they are losing their freedom and livelihood through the tribute payments to the Persians, on the one hand, and, on the other, through the mechanisms of interest, the seizing of their land and the debt enslavement by their rich compatriots. Nehemiah actually manages to save the non-owners by a ceremonial cancellation of their debt. But the trend is not broken, as becomes clear from later developments towards Hellenism.

If Veerkamp (1993: 115ff) is right the Book of Job is about this very question. Will Job, will Israel, adapt to the tyrannical, arbitrary gods of Greece, and the fate ruling over them, or not? Will they give theological legitimization thereby to the Hellenistic class society of owners and property-less, or not? Job refuses to budge from the reliable God of the Torah and God turns back to him, thus becoming again this reliable God.

Resistance to the absoluteness of the empire For the Judaeans this decisive question came to a head in 168 BCE, when the Hellenistic ruler Antiochus IV erected a statue of Zeus in the temple of Jerusalem, banned the Yahweh cult and thereby expressed the absoluteness of the empire. The Judaean population was divided. Some adapted to Hellenization, particularly the priestly aristocracy at the Jerusalem temple and groups of nobles. Another group, the Essenes, withdrew to the wilderness and formed a closed community with shared possessions. Yet another group, consisting mainly of farmers and rural priests, took up armed resistance under the leadership of one family, the Maccabeans; successful at first, they then took on Hellenistic, totalitarian leadership structures. One faithful group (*Chassidím*, the pious), finally adopted passive, non-violent resistance and expressed itself in apocalyptic underground writings.[15]

The most important document in this connection is the Book of Daniel. Chapter 3 tells the story of the resistance of the three men in the fiery furnace (see Veerkamp 1993: 243ff). The king had put up a statue, made of gold, the symbol of political, economic and ideological – i.e. Absolute – power. Subject nations had to bow down before it. They all did so; only three Judaean men refused. For this they were thrown into the furnace, but rescued by God. In this way the apocalyptic writings strengthened people in their resistance and gave them hope.

This makes it clear that the First Testament, the Hebrew Bible, has several approaches to presenting God's alternative in terms of the political-economic-religious power systems of the peoples, depending on the historical context and the opportunities available:

- *autonomous establishment* of an alternative in the sense of the solidarity of tribal society;
- after the invasion of a kingly, aristocratic and later property economy, *prophetic criticism* of injustice and the *legal transformation* of the situation on the basis of a vision of actual human life in community with the earth and all other created beings;
- *partial alternatives* in partially autonomous situations, as after the exile;
- *resistance* in the case of totalitarian oppression.

This was the inheritance of the Jesus movement and early Christianity.

The Jesus movement and the early Church Jesus of Nazareth links up with the prophetic, the legal and the apocalyptic traditions. It is typical of him, however, that the corrective measures planned to take place periodically in Israel were supposed to characterize daily life. The Lord's Prayer says basically: 'And forgive us our debts as we have cancelled the debts of those who owe us something.' In Luke (4: 1ff) Jesus takes up the predictions of the coming reality of the jubilee year in Isaiah 61. He then continues, however: with my coming this hope has become reality today, which means that every day the rules of the jubilee year can now apply.

The story that we sometimes romantically call the story of the 'rich young ruler' is in the tradition of the prophets and the Torah.

He is a large landowner, who comes to Jesus and asks him how he can obtain eternal life ('he had many possessions' – Mark 10: 17–22). Jesus answers, in part, by pointing to the decalogue as handed down in Deuteronomy. This is no accident – the Ten Commandments were developed in precisely the context we have been examining. In the name of Yahweh, who freed the people from slavery in Egypt, they address the free peasants and warn them not to place their freedom at risk by trying, through various legal and illegal mechanisms, to take landed property and freedom away from their brothers and their families (Crüsemann 1983). 'You shall not steal' and 'You shall not desire your neighbour's house, farm, field and all that is therein' are in themselves very clear statements. On the other hand, Jesus sharpens his answer by adding to 'you shall not steal': 'you shall not defraud'. This detail of the text is mostly overlooked. It clearly shows, however, that Jesus is here referring to the prophets who called the mechanism of property-interest-seizure-debt slavery by the name of theft or robbery (see Myers 1988: 272ff). Jesus therefore tells the rich landowner that it is about this problem. The latter does not understand, however, claiming that he has kept all these laws since his youth. Whereupon Jesus says to him that he lacks one thing – and tells him to sell his (stolen) goods and give the proceeds to the poor. Normally this is understood as an appeal to give charitable alms. Nothing could be farther from the truth. It is a matter of giving back what has been stolen not simply by individual wickedness but with the aid of economic mechanisms in society.

This becomes clear with a positive counter-story, that of the conversion of the rich tax-collector Zaccheus (Luke 19: 1–10). Following his meeting with Jesus he gives up a good part of his wealth to the poor, but also to those whom he had robbed through the taxation system he returns a fourfold sum.

The topic of systemic theft also plays the decisive role in Jesus's prophetic confrontation with the temple (Mark 11: 15–19; Myers 1988: 297ff). This is about the central question: which God rules? The God who legitimizes impoverishment through exploitative structures? Or the biblical God who protects and frees the poor, and calls for justice, not sacrifice? This conflict, which constantly surfaced among the prophets from Amos and Hosea onward, is radically sharpened by Jesus. He targets all the actors in this den of thieves. First he tackles those who harm the poor with the aid of the monetary system. Then he has a go at those who earn a profit with the exchange system of the market (the doves they trade are the sacrificial birds of the poor). Finally he confutes the whole system of sacrifices. It allows the priestly aristocracy, which collaborates with the Roman occupying power, to accumulate their temple treasure. And, what is worse, with the sacrificial system the priests replace God in the hearts of people with an idol that asks for sacrifices and even pulls the last penny from the pocket of the poor widow (Mark 12: 42ff).

John the evangelist (John 2: 14–16) goes even farther than Mark (see Hinkelammert 2001: 37ff). According to him, Jesus does not just call the temple a 'den of thieves' but a 'marketplace', a kind of shopping centre. The house of God is subject to the legalistic values of the marketplace. Here apply the iron rules of the highest monetary profit for those who produce with their property, trade and make interest-bearing loans – without considering the real lives of the people created by God.

It is no wonder that the profiteers of the system take this prophetic, symbolic action of Jesus as an occasion to plan his death. But it is precisely his readiness to risk his life for the justice of the kingdom of God which testifies to the fact that he does not serve any god that demands sacrifices from people in order to enrich his 'servants'. His God is one whose messengers struggle and give their all for the sake of the real lives and freedom of human beings.

In sum, Jesus puts the central issue as follows: 'Those who want to save their life will lose it, and those who lose their life for my sake, and for the sake of the gospel, will save it. For what will it profit them to gain the whole world and forfeit their life?' (Mark 8: 35f). This takes us back to Aristotle: boundless striving for wealth, permitted by the property economy, is the illusion of being able to preserve one's life for ever. The unintended, real consequence is, however, death. Conversely the rejection of utility calculations leads to life for the sake of the kingdom of God. Jesus goes beyond Aristotle, however, in introducing the dimension of God-idol into the understanding of property accumulation through monetary mechanisms: people fall prey to a fetish that takes them captive in the illusion of an unconnected, individual life, and thus meet their doom.

Matthew the evangelist (Matt. 6: 19–34) elucidates the same from the angle of 'collecting treasure' on earth. You cannot serve God and Mammon. Conversely all that is needed for life will be given to those who first seek the Kingdom of God and its righteousness – that is, a life in just relationships.

Early Christianity followed Jesus on this path. The classical text is Acts 4: 32–35. The congregation voluntarily shared its property. More exactly: those with land and houses sold them and placed the proceeds at the apostles' feet. This wording can be no accident. After all, it was precisely the accumulation of land and houses which had been attacked since Micah and Isaiah as a structural cause of the impoverishment of the farming population. And Jesus had called this robbery, in the same prophetic tradition, and demanded of the rich young landowner that he sell his accumulated goods and give the proceeds back to the poor (whose land had been stolen through the mechanisms of property-interest-bearing loans-debt). And this balancing out of property was expressly described as the fulfilment of the Deuteronomic Torah, as the text continues: 'There was not a needy person among them' (cf. Deut. 15: 4). At the same time, however, it says that they gave their testimony to the resurrection of the Lord Jesus. In this way Jesus came alive among them not by virtue of their using their property as their own, to maximize personal profit and accumulate property, but by the community living together in such a way that there was no hardship among them. Jesus's resurrection means – economically speaking – life in community without need. This is the fulfilment of the laws and the prophets in the First Testament.

Now we have acquired an overview of the biblical options in dealing with the economy and, specifically, with property. In the different phases of the history of Israel, and later of Judaea, we have seen the potential of prophetic critique and vision, lawful regulation of the system (as far as it could be transformed at all) and resistance in the case of the totalitarian empires. In this resistance Jesus demonstrated a further option: a new beginning in life is possible in that real people embark on the alternatives in small groups among themselves.

Jesus and the early Church were not solely involved with the intrusion of the Graeco-Roman property economy into dependent Judaean society but also directly with the empire and its economic structures. They therefore also knew of the option of resistance, including in the form of boycotts. For example, in the often misunderstood story of the Roman coin with the idolatrous image of the emperor, Jesus calls for a boycott of the Roman currency (Mark 12: 13ff; see Myers 1988: 310ff). In another example, according to the

Revelation of John the Christians were excluded from the market (buying and selling) because they were not willing to wear on their foreheads the 'sign of the beast' from the abyss (the absolute dominance of Rome headed by the 'divine' emperor; Rev. 13: 17). Not all congregations could bear this enormous pressure and withstand the temptations of the empire. In particular, rich ones conformed partially or completely (Rev. 2–3). Those loyal even unto martyrdom would endure in the certainty that the empire and its economy would fall (18), in order to make room for life, i.e. God's dwelling among human beings in justice and peace.

This began on a small scale. When, for example, the five thousand people gathered around Jesus became hungry the disciples wanted to go to the market and buy food (Mark 6: 30–44). Jesus asked instead: what have the people got with them? And when this was passed around to everyone it was enough. This story has a symbolic meaning. When the people in a community use their opportunities and work together in terms of basic needs there are alternatives – in the midst of a system shaped by property, money and the market, not to speak of political oppression. And at the same time the people are no longer victims but protagonists. The gospels are full of such stories in which Jesus empowers people to take their lives in their own hands. 'Your faith has made you whole,' he says to them.

Early Christianity spread throughout the whole Roman empire thanks to such encouraging cells of life. The oppressed and exploited people felt attracted by these new possibilities of life in solidarity.[16] We call this mission through attraction (in contrast with the later, perverse form of imperialistic dissemination of Christianity). There were already signs of networking among such local cells, as is shown by Paul's collection among the rich congregations for the benefit of the congregation in Jerusalem that had fallen on hard times (2 Cor. 8–9; see Georgi 1992).

This brief outline shows how many fruitful starting points can be found in the biblical traditions as they wrestled with those of Greece and Rome – ways of overcoming the absolutized, destructive mechanisms of property, money and market imposed by the empires. Before we can draw conclusions for today, however, it will be necessary to undertake a more thorough analysis of the historical roots of our present neo-liberal system in the modern age.

Notes

1 Aristotle, *Politics*, book 1, chs 8–13. See also Duchrow 1995: 20ff.

2 Heinsohn (1984: 116) considers it possible that a similar revolution introducing private property, or at least the transferability of creditor–debtor contracts, took place immediately after 747 BCE under Nabonassar in Babylon and Tiglat-Pileser in Assyria.

3 On the role of craftsmen and artists and the origin of the division of labour in the early empires and city-kingdoms see Hinkelammert and Mora 2001: 178ff.

4 In the following we gratefully draw on a paper written by Dr Dieter Conrad shortly before his death for a joint seminar at the University of Heidelberg in the winter semester of 2000/1.

5 See the German civil code §854: 'The possession of a thing is obtained through acquiring actual power over the thing.' In English law possession means, e.g., rights to landed property measured in time (life estate) or leasing over a number of years.

6 The source of this sentence is unknown; probably it is a didactic saying from the Middle Ages. The key thing is that it becomes basic to all bourgeois rights of the modern age (see below). See also Binswanger 1998: 128ff.

7 See Binswanger 1978: 21: 'Property (and thereby "having") was not understood legally as a relation between different persons (because one has, the other has not), but as a relation between a person and a legal object. Thereby property is legally not a having of a person in conjunction with a non-having of another, but only the having as such.' See also Luhmann 1974: 66 (German edn): 'The unity of "having" and "not having" is not reflected on in language or law. It is only construed as an owner's right of exclusion … The sociologically most relevant problem, the fact that any

growth in ownership automatically means a disproportionate increase in the non-ownership of the other, is not relevant in legal terms.'

8 See Binswanger, 1998: 131. He points to the ecological significance of this concept (see below).

9 On the Torah as a basis of theological economic ethics see Segbers 1999: 99ff.

10 See Crüsemann 1992: 132ff (especially 179ff, 217ff and 229: 'response to the experience of catastrophes').

11 Interest at that time cannot simply be identified with interest in the capitalist system in that no growth could be achieved with capital; the interest had to be paid from the principle. This means that interest is identical with what is described as usury. In a growth economy this would correspond to a situation where the real interest rate exceeds the growth rate – which, in fact, is generally the case. A recent comment on the biblical ban on interest is to be found in Leutzsch 2000.

12 See Crüsemann 2000: 50ff. We can disregard the question of which texts stem from that period and which arose after the destruction of the southern kingdom.

13 For a practical example on the basis of the seven-year rule see Neh. 5 and 10: 32.

14 This view is taken, for example, by those who elaborated on Micah (see, e.g., Mic. 2: 4f and Kessler 2000: 75).

15 *Apokálypsis* means revelation. To the faithful the apocalyptic scriptures reveal the coming decline of the apparently unrestricted imperial power and the victory of righteousness in the Kingdom of God (see, e.g., Dan. 7).

16 On the structure of this solidarity approach in the context of the ancient economy see Stegemann 2000.

TWO
Homo homini lupus:[1] the emergence of the capitalist possessive market society in the modern age

§ The emergence of the capitalist market society can be considered from different angles and on different levels. One can focus on the institution of the market and its changes, and go on from there to examine further pertinent factors and elements. The classic book by Polanyi (1945) adopts this starting point. It refutes the liberal and neoclassical economic theories which assume that the market is a universal social and even anthropological phenomenon that is found in the same form among all peoples and at all times. There are peoples and cultures that organize and coordinate their economies and economic relations completely differently, in the form of reciprocity or of redistribution, for example. Moreover, for a long time, even in the modern age, several forms of market existed next to each other – for example, local markets and long-distance trade markets. Even when the capitalist nation developed uniform domestic markets, these were for a long time still not integrated into a capitalist world market. Equally, the early long-distance trading capitalism of the twelfth and thirteenth centuries did not yet mean that the whole of society was determined by the capitalist market, as later in the time of the mercantilist nation, which the English philosopher Hobbes was the first to analyse in terms of their economic, political, anthropological and psychological implications.

Giovanni Arrighi (1994) chose another starting point in his book.[2] He examines the historical emergence of capitalism and its major historical phases in the different coalitions of high finance and political power. He begins with the banking and commercial city-states of northern Italy, starting from the time when, through the crusades, Venice brought trade with the Orient under its control. Then follows the phase when Genoan high finance, as developed in Florence, entered into an alliance with the political power of Spain. Here, especially, a central question becomes that of when and why productive capitalism was replaced in large cycles, 'long centuries', by finance-dominated capitalism.

What happened so that the specifically capitalist economic and social form, as distinct from the property–money economy of antiquity, became generally accepted in society? How could this new formation subject everything to its calculus of utility, and through the mechanisms of money and the market develop the individual who accumulates wealth and power? Obviously, several factors come together here.

The cooperation between the Roman Curia and the upper Italian commercial states in connection with the Crusades had already led to a lifting of the prohibition on (usurious) interest, in force from ancient and patristic times (see Le Goff 1986). A theological solution was found by developing the doctrine and practice of 'indulgences', the system whereby cash payments could replace the expiation in 'purgatory' of the punishments due to sin. For the Church this was a win–win game: those with capital could obtain the highest possible returns and the Church made money out of it. In this way, usurious interest was still regarded as a sin but, at the same time, people gained the firm impression that they could purchase with their riches the eternal welfare of their soul. In Florence, the city-state where financial capitalism was created, they went a step farther and introduced compound interest.

Likewise in Florence in the chapel of Santa Maria del Carmine in the mid-fourteenth century the *individual* appears for the first time in artistic form. Significantly, this famous picture by Masaccio portrays the story of the tribute money. This is exactly the era in which the modern age was born.

Zinn (1989) draws attention to two further factors, which precisely in this period shaped the specifically modern individuality of the European modern age: the Great Plague and the invention of firearms. The plague, which carried off half the population between 1347 and 1352, led to traumatic changes in human relationships. Contact with an infected person could lead to infection and one's own death. Loving one's neighbour thus became dangerous, while keeping one's distance improved one's chances of survival. Eating habits changed. People began to avoid eating from a common dish and to eat with their own cutlery. Firearms made it possible to kill from a distance, without meeting the enemy face to face. This lowered the threshold of the inhibition against killing.

Together, the plague and firearms brought about a new relationship to mass death. Not only does a mysticism of death emerge in

the fourteenth century, but a readiness to kill others in great numbers
also grew – a European characteristic that had been legitimized theologically and put into action in the most brutal manner at the time
of the Crusades, not only against Muslims but also against Jews and
Christians of the Eastern Church. However, in the *conquista*, the conquest of the Americas, it led to genocide on an unprecedented scale.
The growing interest in firearms had direct economic consequences
as well. Through arms production, the economy of the cities became
even more dominant in comparison to agriculture.

Property and its consequences

In this investigation, our interest is centred on the changing
political-economic-legal framework and on the institution of property, which is fundamental for capitalist development. Together with
money mechanisms, it is the material basis of calculating individualism. Not unjustly, therefore, Macpherson (1962) uses the term 'possessive market society' for developed capitalism. The capitalist market
functions only with the fundamental institutions of property and
contract. Accordingly, property is of central importance for the development of relations of production, money, capital, work and land.

The earliest and most important transformation of the feudal
manorial system into that of bourgeois property took place in England. It occurs in the same century – the fourteenth – in which the
other factors involved in the early modern age also became effective.
A substantial impetus came from climate change – the colder climate
in the North undermined the peasants' ability to sustain themselves
and thus disrupted the previously balanced system of tribute. In addition, the number of peasants was reduced by the plague. In 1381, the
Lollard revolt broke out, regarded by Heinsohn/Steiger as the beginning of the modern property society. This is because in its aftermath,
for the first time in the modern age, the serfs (*villani/villains*) were
freed, while the lords, deprived of serfs, became mere landowners
(Heinsohn and Steiger 1996: 108ff).

The change to bourgeois property in terms of land ownership that
began at this time meant a revolution in all life relations that cannot
be overestimated and is fundamental for the rest of the modern age.
Through enclosure, the village common land that the medieval
peasants cultivated together became private land. Polanyi gives an
impressive description of how this changed all the traditional relations

between people. The mutual assistance and the common work of the peasants were supplanted by relations of contract and competition mediated by money. Since not all peasants were successful in this new economic mode, they had to hire themselves out as wage labourers, in so far as they found work on the land or in the towns; privatization led to unemployment even in those days. At the same time the feudal lords transformed themselves into great landed proprietors, which offered them advantages in the new context of competition. With the help of the financially strong merchants and bankers, the large land-owners bought up common land in order to transform it into pasture for the sheep needed for wool production in the textile industry. Throughout Europe, all life relations became increasingly commer-cialized. Rifkin writes:

> Enclosure introduced a new concept of human relationships into European civilization that changed the basis of economic security and the perception of human life. Land was no longer something people belonged to, but rather a commodity people possessed. Land was reduced to a quantitative status and measured by its exchange value. So, too, with people. Relationships were reorganized. Neigh-bours became employees or contractors. Reciprocity was replaced with hourly wages. People sold their time and labour where they used to share their toil. Human beings began to view each other and everything around them in financial terms. Virtually everyone and everything became negotiable and could be purchased at an appropri-ate price. (Rifkin 1998: 40f)

In economic terms, it was a question of developing a commercial agriculture characterized by several factors:[3]

1. While the feudal lords transformed themselves into large land-owners, some free peasants became medium-size independent farmers through the privatization of the common land; admittedly, the majority of the former serfs became wage labourers and small artisans (so the new beginning was by no means more egalitarian). Personal relations were replaced by employment contracts and leases, legal relations mediated by money. The emergence of wage labour is one of the crucial differences between the modern and the ancient economy, which was based on the work of slaves and, at most, day-labourers.

2. Beyond self-sufficiency, the peasants and the great landowners produced for the urban market. The primary product was wool for

textile production, both for the domestic market and for export, because more money could be earned from this than from agricultural products.

3. It was no longer the high aristocracy which dominated the land but the 'gentry', consisting of both former knights and those who had risen from lower social strata.

At the same time trade and industry developed, particularly around the production of textiles. Already there had emerged both factories with wage hands and a division of labour, and domestic industry, in which the raw material and the product were the property of the entrepreneurs while the workers received piece-rate wages. In charcoal and iron production, cooperative organization was transformed into capitalist relations of production. In the seventeenth century almost half the inhabitants of England were pure wage-earners; if one includes domestic workers, then the figure increases to two-thirds (MacPherson 1962: 61, following earlier research). It is characteristic of England that this dependent class was distinct from a common property-owning class, drawn from the aristocracy, the gentry and the burgesses, which developed its common interests and defended them against the king – by contrast with the Continent, where there was no initial alliance between the aristocracy and the bourgeoisie.

In this context the crucial institutions of the market society – property and contract – developed, as the courts increasingly defended the absolute 'discretion' of ownership (Rittstieg 1975: 25ff). This description reflects the fact that English law is common law, based on custom and precedent, in which the law evolves through judicial decisions. Roman law was not adopted in England, as it was (for example) in the reform of the laws in imperial Germany in 1494. Rather the administration of justice reacted to the socio-economic changes themselves, above all to the transformation of common land into private property through the enclosures. In these enclosures the owners could deal at will with the land, without giving any consideration to the community. In the course of the development, the absolute right of property was extended to immaterial things such as bills of exchange, patents and copyrights, as well as to the enforceability of all private financial contracts, regardless of content (ibid.: 29). Thus in practice property was made an absolute, as in Roman law.

According to Renoux-Zagamé (1987), in an article on the theological origins of the modern concept of property,[4] the absoluteness of modern property does not derive directly from Roman law, but from the secularization of the idea that God is the absolute owner of creation. This idea was developed by the neo-scholastics of the sixteenth and seventeenth centuries on the basis of voluntarist late scholasticism. Thus, for example, Armacchanus writes: '*Divinum dominium est jus plenum possidendi mundum et ... plene AC libere utendi*' (Divine rule is the full right to possess and ... completely and freely to use the world; ibid.: 56). This lordship over property, the neo-scholastics believed, was conferred on humans by God. This conferred property was then stripped of its theological underpinnings by seventeenth-century natural-law theorists like Hugo Grotius, and so became an innate human right (ibid.: 311ff). This thesis proceeds, however, from the methodological assumption that history unfolds according to ideas. In actual historical development, modern property surely developed earlier than the neo-scholastics and the natural-law philosophers, whose theories contributed at most to the legitimization of bourgeois property.

The first comprehensive theory of the possessive market society: Thomas Hobbes

Thomas Hobbes (1588–1679) was the first philosopher to conceptualize the new economic, psychological, social and political conditions in a comprehensive, original and far-reaching way. Since Macpherson (1962: 9ff) presents an exact, detailed analysis of his theory, based on his complete works, we can represent it here summarily and systematically. Hobbes proceeds methodically in several steps:

1. He begins from a mechanistic theory of human nature, which he obtains from market behaviour.
2. In order to make his theory plausible, he speaks to people on the basis of their experience of the market society in seventeenth-century England.
3. From the facts of a market society he derives a market ethics.
4. From the struggle of all against all in the market, he infers the political necessity of a sovereign ruler (a 'strong state').

The struggle for power of the individual The first point concerns the struggle for power of the individual (ibid.: 17ff). To understand Hobbes's argument, one must be clear on two points. Often his theory of human nature has been understood as if it described a historically original state of nature; in fact, Hobbes develops his theory in such a way that it describes the actual behaviour of human beings of his time under the hypothetical departure from the obligation to obey the law. Second, his aim is to prove the necessity of a single sovereign force if the market society is not to degenerate into the open, violent struggle of all against all. Hobbes's state of nature is thus a logical, and not a historical, hypothesis.

Already in the introduction to *Leviathan*, the principal work outlining Hobbes's analysis, he says: 'whosoever looketh into himself, and considereth what he doth, when he does *think, opine, reason, hope, feare*, &c, and upon what grounds; he shall thereby read and know, what are the thoughts, and passions of all other men, upon the like occasions'. The reader is requested 'to consider, if he also find not the same in himself. For this kind of doctrine, admitteth no other demonstration' (Hobbes 1651: 82f). What does the reader discover during this introspection?

In the first chapters of *Leviathan*, Hobbes describes the physiology of the human being as a self-directing automated machine. The senses receive the pressure of other bodies and announce this to the brain and heart, which produce a counter-pressure. Imagination and memory convert the sensory impressions into compound experiences. This allows for causes to be sought and the probable result of possible actions to be calculated in advance. Language and reason help with orientation.

This machine (as with the law of gravity for heavy bodies) seeks to continue its motion. It does this by moving towards (good) things, which according to its *calculation* are conducive to this progressive movement (desire), and by moving away from (bad) things, which are a hindrance to it (aversion). All human states of mind can thus be reduced to desire. The calculation of the actions springs from, and aims at, the satisfaction of desire. With conflicting impressions, deliberation decides which action is finally wanted. The human being is thus defined as a calculating individual, or more exactly as a machine that examines everything for its usefulness in satisfying its desires and directs itself accordingly in its actions.

Two consequences follow for its relationship with other humans – with other machines of this kind (ibid.: ch. 8). First, the man-machines evaluate everything by comparison with what others have:

'For if all things were equally in all men, nothing would be prized.'
Second, different people are successful in different measures because
their 'desire of power, of riches, of knowledge and of honour' is differently developed. Some have a greater desire for these things than
others. These are for Hobbes the physiological prerequisites for the
struggle of all against all.

The possessive market society How do these prerequisites unfold in
society – by which Hobbes always understands the developed market
society (chs 10 and 11)? Here he moves in several steps from the general definition of power to arrive at the result that each strives for
ever more power over others. Power is therefore first of all 'his present
means, to obtain some future apparent good'. Then Hobbes distinguishes *natural* power, such as special physical and mental abilities,
and *instrumental* powers, i.e. tools such as riches, reputation and good
friends, with which one can win more power. From this he concludes
'that the capacity of every man to get what he wants is opposed by
the capacity of every other man'.[5] In the struggle that results, power
means finally the ability to command the services of other people.

Thus a power market develops, in which the power of a human
being is regarded as a commodity: 'The value, or worth of a man, is as
of all other things, his price; that is to say, so much as would be given
for the use of his power: and therefore is not absolute; but a thing
dependant on the need and judgement of another' (ibid.: 151f). Since
one person's power now opposes the power of others, even those
who do not strive for more power cannot keep out of the struggle:
it is forced upon them by those who do. They have to defend themselves in order not to lose the power they have. From this it follows,
according to Macpherson, that 'his postulate that the power of every
man in society is opposed to the power of every other man requires
the assumption of a model of society which permits and requires the
continual invasion of every man by every other' (Macpherson 1962:
42). So 'he must be assuming some kind of society which provides
peaceful, non-violent ways by which every man can constantly seek
power over others without destroying the society' (ibid.: 46). This
Macpherson calls the possessive market society.

It is defined by four properties that it shares with simple market
societies and by four further specific postulates:

a) There is no authoritative allocation of work.
b) There is no authoritative provision of rewards for work.
c) There is no authoritative definition and enforcement of contracts.
d) All individuals seek rationally to maximise their utilities.
e) Each individual's capacity to labour is his own property and is alienable.
f) Land and resources are owned by individuals and are alienable.
g) Some individuals want a higher level of utilities or power than they have.
h) Some individuals have more energy, skill, or possessions, than others. (ibid.: 53f)

From these premises stems the concrete social consequence that those who can use more property can acquire for themselves the property, including the work, of others, in order to increase their own property and power:

> Those who want to increase their level of utilities or power, and who have either greater possessions which they can use as capital (and the skills to use them profitably), or superior energy and skill by which they can accumulate capital, will seek to employ the labour of others for a price, in the expectation of getting from the labour they employ a value greater than its cost. Individuals who have less land or resources, or less skill, than can regularly give them a subsistence by their independent production, will accept wages that will give them a subsistence. (ibid.: 54)

This whole market, driven by competition and by prices established through competition, creates a class opposition between those who possess property in land and capital, on the one hand, and those who have only their work as property on the other. The first can acquire for themselves the net surplus of production. This was also found, of course, in earlier social models, in the form of tribute, slavery and day-labour. What is new, however, is the impersonal mechanism of the competition of all against all. This requires national regulation by laws that at least secure lives and property as well as guaranteeing the observance of contracts.

The seventeenth-century English society in which Hobbes lived came very close to the possessive market society sketched here as a model (ibid.: 61ff; Rittstieg 1975: 62ff). What is also remarkable is the fact that Hobbes rejects the concepts of justice of pre-capitalist social formations (Hobbes 1651: ch. 15). There is no other measure of value than the market price. 'Where all values are reduced to market values, justice itself is reduced to a market concept' (Macpherson 1962: 64).

Ethics from facts According to Hobbes, it follows from the physiological observation that all human beings strive to continue their motion, as well as from the social structure of the market society in which this happens, that no one could survive in the struggle of all against all if they did not recognize a sovereign power that prevents this struggle from turning violent (ibid.: 70ff). All rationally calculating human beings must therefore recognize a superordinate power. Thus Hobbes, in his political theory, is the first to deduce moral obligation from facts. He needs in addition only the postulate of original human equality. This consists, in the last analysis, in the equal ability to kill each other and in the equal insecurity that this entails. Macpherson rightly notes that Hobbes does not take into account here the fact that the insecurities are indeed quite unequal, in view of the different classes (ibid.: 85). Hobbes's observation is valid, however, inasmuch as all classes must subject themselves to the dictates of the market. In it they are equal – at any rate, so long as the model of the possessive market society is accepted (ibid.: 87f).

Politics and law Certainly, no self-perpetuating sovereign needs to follow from this, as Hobbes assumed.[6] The actual history that he surveyed showed that the all-penetrating market did not simply plunge all members of society into the same insecurity, but necessarily allowed unequal classes to develop, with the possessing class able, out of common interest, to form a sovereign power: the parliament of the owners. 'Those who possess substantial property need a sovereign state to sanction the right of possession. They must therefore authorise a sovereign body to do whatever is necessary to maintain the right of possession, and the sovereign body must have the right to decide what is necessary. But the men of property need not give up their right or power to choose the persons who shall from time to time be the members of the sovereign body' (ibid.: 94f). Without sovereignty there is, according to Hobbes, no property (Hobbes 1651: ch. 24).

To this it may be added that a sovereign is necessary 'to appoint in what manner, all kinds of contract between subjects, (as buying, sell-

ing, exchanging, borrowing, lending, letting, and taking to hire,) are
to be made; and by what words, and signes they shall be understood
for valid' (ibid.: 299). That is to say, these conclusions on the necessity
of a sovereign to guarantee property and contracts correspond exactly
to the anthropology of the calculating individuals that Hobbes developed for the market society.

People without property also have no alternative to acknow-
ledging the sovereign so long as they see no alternative to the possessive market society. After all, the sovereign protects their life.

We do not need here to pursue in detail the development of the
rights of property and of political power in seventeenth-century
England. 'Even in the 20th century the English parliament is not a
democratic institution, but the organ of the possessing classes. That
applies both to the upper house and to the House of Commons'
(Rittstieg 1975: 33). This is so even though formally the right to vote
of the person without property was fought for in the nineteenth century. In the debates about the first Agreement of the People (1647),
Cromwell himself and his Irish son-in-law Ireton opposed the extension of the right to vote on the grounds that this would destroy the
rights of property and lead again to anarchy (ibid.: 35). The Glorious
Revolution of 1688 then brought the large property-owning class
unambiguously to power. 'Not unjustly did one compare the parliament, whose seats represented – at least partly – assets accessible to the
highest bidder, to the general meeting of a corporation' (ibid.: 36).

Hence there is a difference between Hobbes's acceptance that an
absolute sovereign is needed to prevent the struggle of all against all in
the market from taking the form of violent warfare and the real historical development of parliamentary democracy controlled by large
property-owners. And this leads us to a further difference. Hobbes
accepts that (premised on a possessive market society) human beings
would kill each other if they were not forced by an absolute ruler
to adhere to the laws that ensure that the struggle for power in the
marketplace ensues within the framework of institutions and law. So
the state's function is above all to enforce the institution of property
and the binding nature of contracts.

The later arguments of Mandeville (1729) and Adam Smith (1795)
are different (see Gutiérrez 1998: 26ff and 2001: 187ff; Horne 1982).
Since the end of the seventeenth century, bourgeois humanism had
criticized the negative effect of the rise of commerce on the virtues

and the common interests of society. Mandeville responded to this at the beginning of the eighteenth century by pointing out that the prosperity created by commerce nevertheless benefited the whole of society. In his famous fable of the bees, he developed the claim that when all do nothing but industriously pursue their own interests, the common end result is precisely a gain in prosperity for all. He coined the phrase 'private vices, public benefits'.

This is exactly what Adam Smith says, at the end of the eighteenth century, when he speaks of the 'invisible hand' of the market.[7] He proceeds from the natural tendency of human beings to pursue their egoistic individual interests. Certainly they do this in a calculating way, with *prudentia* (prudence) and self-control – if they are intelligent. That is, they consider the rules of the market. These are based on the absolute validity of private property and contracts. To follow them is *justitia*, justice. To desire this is functional ethics. To protect the rules, there is the legal system; to enforce them, the state. Where the market prevails, it brings out of individual egoistic actions, without any intention on the part of the actors, the public interest, the wealth of nations – even as by an invisible hand. Smith explicitly compares these statements with Newton's view about the harmony of the cosmos, which results from the universal validity of the law of gravity.

The contrast with Hobbes is noticeable. Hobbes needs the visible hand of the absolute sovereign to bring the struggle of all against all within the rules and laws of the market, which permits the economic battle for wealth, power and reputation to be pursued by non-violent means. By contrast, Mandeville and Smith in their theory exploit a double change in the situation. On the one hand, the impressive development of the productive forces of capitalism feeds the impression that growing progress can bring prosperity for all. On the other hand, they can proceed from a legal and political order in which the bourgeois class and, in particular, the large property-owners exercise political rule and have established laws that protect property and the adherence to contracts. The invisible hand of the market thus seems to lead to prosperity, and the visible hand of power enforcing the laws of property and contract has become gentler, because it has managed to provide legitimacy as a politico-legal order.

The consequence of fascism This observation makes it possible to understand better a certain feature of the later history of capitalism.

Every time the bourgeois order is challenged, because the indirect effects of the market lead to an intolerable false distribution of property and its fruits, as well as to hunger, misery and death, the bourgeoisie switches from a democratic order controlled by property to dictatorial forms of rule. To put it differently: if the myth of the invisible hand turns out to be in glaring contradiction to reality, the visible hand in Hobbes's sense becomes absolute. In the context of world history, the classic form of this development is fascism. Johan Galtung rightly says: 'Nazism is western civilization *in extremis*' (see also Duchrow 1987: 117). A more current example is certainly the introduction of neo-liberalism in the 1960s and 1970s. Here the United States, as the 'leading power' of Western capitalism, introduced dictatorships all over the world, in order to help transnational capital make a breakthrough against all social and national resistances – for example, in Brazil in 1964 and in Indonesia in 1965–66. Since the murder of Salvador Allende, Chile's democratically elected president, and the military coup by Pinochet on 11 September 1973, this has happened in more Latin American countries, particularly in Argentina, Uruguay and Central America. These dictatorships allowed the transnational companies (TNCs) to take over national industry. They contracted debts, which then led to unending interest payments and the dependence of their countries. They prepared for globalization. Only after this had been introduced and the challenge of the Soviet Union had imploded was 'low-intensity democracy' brought in again.

At present, the empire is again becoming absolute, albeit in the new mode of direct military intervention, not only by using dictators as proxis. This is evident from the new US military doctrine of 'preventive war' and the concrete examples of the wars against Afghanistan, the former Yugoslavia and Iraq as well as from the massive militarisation of the economy. History demonstrates that whenever capitalism faces a major crisis it turns to violence and war (more on this in the following chapters).

But back to the seventeenth century. Two years after the Glorious Revolution, John Locke's *Second Treatise on Government* (1690) appeared. It not only legitimized the rule of large property in England, but also laid the foundation for the constitutions of most Western states, beginning with the constitution of the United States in 1787.

Notes

1 Plautus: Humankind to humankind is a wolf.

2 See the summary in Duchrow 1995: 23ff.

3 On the following, see the fundamental work by Rittstieg (1975:21ff), which critically surveys the history of property law from the Middle Ages to today.

4 I owe this reference to Michel Beaudin.

5 Macpherson 1962: 36. See Hobbes, 'Elements', part I, ch. 8, sect. 4:'And because the power of one man resisteth and hindereth the effects of the power of another: power simply is no more, but the excess of the power of one above that of another. For equal powers opposed, destroy one another; and such their opposition is called contention.'

6 Rittstieg 1975: 108ff. However, Hobbes mentions the possibility that the sovereign can be 'an assembly, or a monarch' (Hobbes 1651: 297).

7 On A. Smith see Gutiérrez 1998: 25ff; on the market 89ff.

THREE
The case of John Locke: the inversion of human rights in the name of bourgeois property

§ The US wars against Iraq and Afghanistan and NATO's Kosovo war have shown us again the ambivalence of the term 'human rights'. Whole countries were destroyed in the name of respect for human rights. Human rights were turned into humanitarian aggression: to violate the human rights of all those who violated human rights. Behind this idea is another, that those who violate human rights cannot lay claim to human rights for themselves.

Human rights are turned upside down when they are violated in their own name. There is a long history of this. The story of modern human rights is, in fact, the story of their inversion, with the violation of such rights being transformed into the categorical imperative of political action. The reason given for the Spanish conquest of America was that the local cultures engaged in human sacrifice. The later conquest of North America was likewise justified with reference to the human rights violations committed by the indigenous peoples. The conquest of Africa was portrayed as a war against cannibalism and the conquest of India was intended to put a stop to suttee, the immolation of widows on their husbands' funeral pyres. The subjugation of China in the opium wars also took place in the name of human rights allegedly being violated in China. The West has conquered, colonized, enslaved and humiliated the world, annihilating whole cultures and civilizations. It has carried out unprecedented genocide but has always done it in the name of human rights.

For this reason the blood spilled by the West leaves no stain. On the contrary, it is this blood which washes the West white and gives it the guise of a guarantor of human rights. Over three centuries of forced labour in the United States still stain the descendants of the black people who suffered it, while the descendants of the lords of this forced labour have a soul that is as white as snow. The gigantic ethnic cleansing that exterminated the vast majority of the indigenous peoples of North America still stains the few descendants of these people, who even today are slandered and insulted in westerns – films which always picture them as being to blame for their own annihilation. Some of these films are sheer propaganda for genocide. All the developing countries have to account for their human rights situation to those countries that unleashed the wave of colonialism and trampled on their human rights for centuries. The argument for human rights in the form of their inversion is the smokescreen behind which one of the greatest genocides of our history took place, and today it still dominates our whole historical interpretation of global colonization. The Western countries, by contrast, accept no responsibility for what they have done. Instead they collect payments for a gigantic foreign debt fraudulently generated by themselves. So the victims become the guilty ones, the debtors; they have to confess their guilt to their lords and masters, and if necessary pay their debts with their own blood. These lords are the lords of human rights, thanks to their inversion of human rights.

There is a method visible in this inversion, the results of which have turned the victims into guilty parties and the executioners into innocent judges over the world. It was developed by classical authors. The most important of them is undoubtedly John Locke, who at a decisive moment in the process of global colonization formulated this inverse interpretation of human rights. He thereby gave it the form in which it is found everywhere today in the politics of the empire, and which was also the basis of the Kosovo war. He discovered the pattern whereby human rights are inverted in the name of bourgeois private property.

The world of John Locke

The book in which John Locke expresses his thinking about property, democracy and human rights is the *Second Treatise of Government*, published in England in 1690. The book is a foundation text in the English-speaking world and to this day defines imperialist politics, back then in England and now in the United States. At the same time it is the basis of the articles on property in all Western constitutions.

The book appeared at a crucial historical moment. England had just witnessed a victorious bourgeois revolution, culminating in the Glorious Revolution of 1688. This was in fact a second revolution after that of 1648–49, marked by the beheading of the king. The Glorious Revolution was the Thermidor[1] of this first revolution, and transformed the people's revolution, as it was in the beginning, into a purely bourgeois revolution. It promulgated the fundamental right of habeas corpus (1679) and the Bill of Rights (1689). This emphasized human equality before the law and focused on parliament as the representative of the people and the guarantee of private property. John Locke drafted his political theory in the light of these events.

Such a theory was necessary because this proclamation of equality entailed a few problems for the bourgeoisie for which Locke offered the solution. England was in a phase of founding its empire. It was generally expanding as an imperial power and therefore in conflict with the existing imperial powers of its time, particularly Spain and the Netherlands. The most immediate conflict was with the Netherlands and was sparked by Cromwell's Navigation Act (1651). However, the expansion itself was primarily directed towards countries outside Europe. North America was the most important goal, and English immigrants were in the process of conquering it. But a further expansion to the Far East was already under way, aiming in particular at India and thereby leading to conflict with France, which also saw India as a desirable prize. On the other hand, England was striving for a monopoly in the most profitable trade of this period of the seventeenth and eighteenth centuries, the slave trade, hitherto in the hands of Spain. John Locke himself had invested his personal fortune in the slave trade, as Voltaire did after him.[2]

In Locke's time these lines of expansion were already clearly visible. In fact they set the tone for the eighteenth century in which, in the Peace of Utrecht of 1713, England acquired the monopoly of global slave trading between Africa and Spanish America. It likewise finally conquered North America and defeated France in India, which became its crown colony from the mid-eighteenth century.

In view of this imperialist situation, a new political theory was urgently needed. In the preceding period Europe had founded its colonial expansion on the divine right of kings and, before that, in the case of Spain and Portugal, on the papal concessions relating to the countries to be conquered. The Glorious Revolution abolished this divine right of kings, however, and reduced the king to a constitutional monarch put in place by parliament. So this type of legitimization of imperial expansion had lost its validity.

This was a conflict that had already broken out in sixteenth-century Spain after the conquest of America. Ginés de Sepulveda legitimized the conquest by a divine right granted by the pope, by which the Christian authorities had granted a universal right to rule.

By contrast, Francisco de Vitoria developed the first liberal political
theory that was to legitimize the conquest of America. This is evident
in the theory developed subsequently by Locke, who largely agreed
with Vitoria, although his theory went even farther. At the time the
divine right of kings was represented in England by Robert Filmer,
and it was to counter this view that Locke wrote his First Treatise of
Government.

The legitimacy problem surfacing at the time was unmistakable.
Habeas corpus and the Bill of Rights had posited human rights that
the bourgeoisie were not able or willing to forgo. It was their answer
to the divine right of kings, and there could be no other response.
These rights guaranteed the physical integrity of persons and property
in the face of political authority and transformed the latter into an
authority for the protection of these rights. Taking these rights literally, however, meant excluding forced labour through slavery and the
violent appropriation of the indigenous territories in North America.
Consequently these rights, indispensable for the bourgeoisie, came
into conflict with important, central goals of the colonial expansion of this same bourgeoisie. Such a direct interpretation, moreover,
matched the first English Revolution of 1648–49 up until the dissolution of the 'Saints' Parliament' in 1655, and was reflected in the positions of the most important revolutionary group, the Independents
and their most extreme wing, the Levellers.[3]

There was therefore a contradiction between the declaration of the
equality of all people before the law and the power positions of the
expanding bourgeoisie. It was Locke who showed a way out of this
situation. He did so by a great theoretical feat. He did not seek middle-
of-the-road solutions that might have allowed exceptions for specific
historical situations. Instead he completely inverted the human rights
established in the first English Revolution. This later led him to a conclusion that was quickly adopted by the English bourgeoisie and later
enthusiastically received by the bourgeoisie the world over. This result,
developed in his *Second Treatise of Government* (Locke 1690a), may be
summed up in a paradox that faithfully renders Locke's thought. He
says that 'all Men by Nature are equal'; this includes the 'equal Right
that every Man hath, to his Natural Freedom, without being subjected
to the Will or Authority of any other Man' (§54). Locke's theoretical
feat consists in his drawing the following conclusion: therefore slavery
is legitimate. And he adds: therefore the indigenous peoples of North

America can be unconditionally expropriated. And also India can be colonized with the use of force.

Locke considered all this violence to be legitimate, claiming it was precisely a consequence of the natural equality of all people. This use of force does not violate human rights but is the consequence of their faithful application. Stating the equality of all human beings is, according to Locke, exactly the same as declaring the legitimacy of forced labour through slavery. Guaranteeing property is just the same as declaring that the peoples of North America can be expropriated without condition or restriction. In view of these intellectual acrobatics, it is understandable that the bourgeoisie were so enthusiastic in espousing Locke's political theory. One can also see that Big Brother's slogan 'Freedom is slavery' in George Orwell's *Nineteen Eighty-Four* was not invented by him: it comes from John Locke.

This is a considerable feat. It results in the inversion that runs through all liberal interpretations of human rights.

Locke's central argument: eliminate those who encroach on property

Locke develops the prototype of his argument in his analysis of the state of nature. He sees this as being the backdrop of all life in society. The politically organized bourgeois society, which he calls 'civil' society, is nothing but the confirmation of what exists in a state of nature through a political authority that is essentially a judge. Therefore the state of nature and 'civil' society do not contradict one another; they are governed by the same natural law. Locke sees this quite differently from Hobbes, according to whom the state of nature describes a state of war of all against all, to be overcome by civil society which puts order into chaos. Locke, however, considers 'civil' society a perfection of that which already applies in the state of nature.

The state of nature therefore underlies civil society, but also prevails wherever there is no civil society. Therefore Locke can insist that in America (North America) there is still no civil society, so that it lives in an immediate state of nature, while in Asia civil society already exists. Locke uses the concept of civil society to mean a polity with institutionalized authority.

The state of nature is, according to Locke, a state of equality and freedom. 'But though this be a State of Liberty, yet it is not a State of Licence' (§6). An ethic of the state of nature follows: 'Every one as he

is bound to preserve himself, and not to quit his Station wilfully; so by
the like reason when his own Preservation comes not in competition,
ought he, as much as he can, to preserve the rest of Mankind, and may
not unless it be to do Justice on an Offender, take away, or impair the
life, or what tends to the Preservation of the Life, the Liberty, Health,
Limb or Goods of another' (§6).

*This statement is based on the definition of people as owners, which Locke
developed later.*[4] *Human beings as a species are triple owners: 1) owners of
their own person (including their labour); 2) owners of their goods; 3) owners of
their freedom. This property must be preserved and defended. That is the law
of nature, which 'willeth the Peace and Preservation of all Mankind' (§7).*

This law of nature implies respect for the physical integrity of
human beings and respect for their property. Locke sees this as obvious
and therefore elaborates no further. What he does develop in detail is
a right he derives from this law of nature: it is the right of everyone to
be a judge of this law of nature in the state of nature. He insists: 'the
Execution of the Law of Nature is in that State, put into every Mans
hands, whereby every one has a right to punish the transgressors of
that Law to such a Degree, as may hinder its Violation ... For in that
State of perfect Equality, where naturally there is no superiority or
jurisdiction of one, over another, what any may do in Prosecution of
that Law, every one must needs have a Right to do' (§7).

In this case 'every Man hath a Right to punish the Offender, and
be Executioner of the Law of Nature' (§8). Therefore it is not just
the victim of an offence against this law who has the right to bring
the offender to justice but everyone on earth – and naturally every
Englishman – regardless of where the offender is to be found. This
leads to a focus on the figure of the perpetrator of a violation of the
law of nature, of which everyone is judge. Locke shows this offender
to be a veritable monster: 'In transgressing the Law of Nature, the
Offender declares himself to live by another Rule, than that of reason
and common Equity, which is that measure God has set to the actions
of Men, for their mutual security: and so he becomes dangerous to
Mankind, the tye, which is to secure them from injury and violence,
being slighted and broken by him' (§8).

This means ' ... a trespass against the whole Species, and the Peace
and Safety of it, provided for by the Law of Nature ...' (§ 8). It is a
'Crime which consists in violating the Law, and varying from the
right Rule of Reason, whereby a Man so far becomes degenerate, and

declares himself to quit the Principles of Human Nature, and to be a noxious Creature ... ' (§10).

This individual, further, '... having renounced Reason, the common Rule and Measure, God hath given to Mankind, hath by the unjust Violence and Slaughter he hath committed upon one, declared War against all Mankind, and therefore may be destroyed as a Lyon or a Tiger, one of those wild Savage Beasts, with whom Men can have no Society nor Security' (§11).

This is an annihilation mentality. The offender is to be annihilated as a 'degenerate' human being to be killed like a wild beast. He has committed 'a trespass against the whole Species' (§8) and 'declared war against all mankind'. Not only does Locke say that the offender is himself 'degenerate', he adds that this individual 'declares himself to quit the Principles of Human Nature, and to be a noxious Creature' (§10). Further: 'In transgressing the Law of Nature, the Offender declares himself to live by another Rule ... ' (§8). Locke explains that the transgressor has no human rights, declaring through the very transgression that human rights do not apply to him. In his view, this is a person who has to be annihilated, but he puts it in such a way that the person declares through the crime that he is a wild animal to be killed. If he is destroyed this will be his own desire, and Locke only calls for this to be implemented. Annihilation is self-fulfilment for the offender, and Locke just helps him to achieve this.

Locke deals with the property of the offender in like fashion. There is a right to destroy him but this is not a right to appropriate his property and therefore a licence to plunder. The right of kings entitles the victor to plunder the property of the conquered. Locke cannot condone such a right, but he too wants the victor to be able to appropriate the property of the conquered. But it should be done legally. Therefore he insists that 'some other Man receives damage by his Transgression, in which Case he who hath received any damage, has besides the right of punishment common to him with other Men, a particular Right to seek Reparation from him that has done it. And any other Person who finds it just, may also joyn with him that is injur'd, and assist him in recovering from the Offender, so much as may make satisfaction for the harm he has suffer'd' (§10). And he adds, 'The damnified Person has this Power of appropriating to himself, the Goods or Service of the Offender' (§11). He will then proceed to state that this claim to the 'services' of the offender justifies a right to forced labour through slavery.

In this way the conquered offender is not robbed of anything, although the victor still obtains his property. But he obtains it by receiving the just compensation for the trouble caused by the offender and his being punished. Here Locke starts to envisage the dimension of legitimate slavery, itself resulting from the applicability of human rights.

According to Locke, this state of nature is in reality not a state of peace but one of constant threat through potential offenders – wild beasts and monsters all. Locke declares war on them in the name of peace. This war is the result of the fact that there are enemies seeking to harm the physical integrity of persons, and their goods and chattels.

But when Locke speaks of a state of nature he means the present, by no means the past. He talks of America, referring to it constantly in the text, in order to illustrate that there this state of nature prevails and by no means a polity or 'civil' society. But he also talks about societies that are civil societies, be it in England itself or in other parts of the world, including India, which he means when referring to Ceylon (Sri Lanka). Locke speaks of civil society as being one in which a political authority asserts the law of nature. Civil society is also subject to the law of nature as a basic order within which the whole of society is to be organized. Hence Locke can regard all resistance in the world to the expanding bourgeoisie as the enemy whom he has defined as the offender in analysing the state of nature. Those who have risen up against humanity are considered to be wild animals and harmful beings and have therefore lost all their human rights; they are enemies to be eliminated. On the basis of his theory of the state of nature Locke sees himself and the fellow-citizens as part of a crusade against enemies who have risen up against humanity by opposing bourgeois expansion.

For this reason he proceeds in the next chapters to analyse the state of war resulting from the state of nature.

The state of war

It follows from the above that society as seen by Locke is actually in a state of war. Wherever there is a state of nature as a direct state it has to be civilized in order to be turned into a civil society or polity (North America). Wherever there is a civil society or polity it is necessary to subjugate it to the natural law of the state of nature (the rest of the world, particularly India).

What Locke has developed regarding the state of nature and the transgressors of the law is here extended to the conflict with the whole world in which he and the bourgeoisie of his time considered themselves to be engaged. The state of nature has a key position in this argument. By reference to it, Locke can brand all resistance to the expansion of the bourgeoisie as being an aggressive war which it has to wage in the name of peace and the legitimate defence of humanity. (Locke always sees humankind as a species and never as flesh-and-blood human beings.) The bourgeoisie fights for peace against an aggression it sees springing up everywhere. A priori there are no conflicts in which the other side is not seen as degenerate, harmful, on the level of wild animals and rising up against humankind, reason and, consequently, against God.

All wars in the name of the bourgeoisie are now holy wars, crusades. The opponents have, however, through their resistance, declared that they have no human rights. Consequently one does their will in not ascribing human rights to them. Each war of the bourgeoisie is therefore a priori a just war, a war to defend humankind and all opponents of the bourgeoisie a priori wage such an unjust war. Therefore they can simply be destroyed with total legitimacy.

Human law being the law of humankind destroys the law-breaker. If he is conquered he will naturally have to pay the war costs of the one who has waged a just war against him. And that is the bourgeoisie and its government, who themselves estimate their war costs and collect them perfectly justly – without any plundering – by way of reparation.

Locke develops this in Chapter 3, where he addresses the state of war. In order to clarify the concept of the state of war he makes projections that allow him to construct a completely imaginary world. He starts from an 'I' and 'we' who are opposed to everything else. They are peaceful while the others declare they have designs on our lives:

> The State of War is a State of Enmity and Destruction; And therefore declaring by Word or Action, not a passionate and hasty, but a sedate settled Design, upon another Mans Life, puts him in a State of War... And one may destroy a Man who makes War upon him, or has discovered an Enmity to his being, for the same Reason that he may kill a Wolf or a Lyon; because such Men are not under the ties of the Common Law of Reason, have no other Rule, but that of Force and Violence, and so may be treated as Beasts of Prey, those dangerous and noxious Creatures, that will be sure to destroy him, whenever he falls into their Power. (§16)

The others have 'declared' that they have designs on our lives and so I, or we, can now destroy them as one destroys wild animals. Locke evokes a veritable mystique of destruction. But what have they done? What is this 'design' on our lives?

> For I have reason to conclude, that he who would get me into his Power without my consent, would use me as he pleased, when he had got me there, and destroy me too when he had a fancy to it: for no body can desire to have me in his Absolute Power, unless it be to compel me by force to that, which is against the Right of my Freedom, i.e. make me a Slave ... so that he who makes an attempt to enslave me, thereby puts himself into a State of War with me. He that in the State of Nature, would take away the Freedom, that belongs to any one in that State, must necessarily be supposed to have a design to take away every thing else, that Freedom being the Foundation of all the rest ... and so be looked on as in a State of War. (§17)

So whoever puts themself into a state of war with us will 'use me as he pleases', in other words make me, the owner of my own person and freedom, his property. But who are the people who would want to do that? On the one hand, they were the absolute monarchies of Locke's time. He refers to certain tendencies in contemporary England that wanted to return to the divine right of kings, but he also refers to the absolute monarchs of the continent of Europe and to 'Ceylon', which he mentions expressly, thereby showing that he is already thinking of India. All have placed themselves in a state of war against 'us' by depriving us of the freedom of the state of nature. They have declared war on 'us' without knowing us or having the slightest intention of doing so. On the other hand, Locke refers to the peoples living in a state of nature and opposing the transition to 'civil' society. He means the peoples of North America who have placed 'us' in a state of war by defending themselves. But this is an unjust war since in the state of nature all have the right to settle where they will. The European conquerers – so Locke sees it – come to North America with peaceful intentions. The peoples living there want, unlawfully, to thwart this. They put themselves in a state of war against these peace-loving conquerors. Here Locke even concludes that they want to make slaves of the conquerors. Consequently he concludes that these peaceful conquerors may treat the whole population like wild animals, and destroy them on the basis of the law of nature. It then turns out that only Locke and the bourgeoisie want to make slaves. Neither the absolute monarchies nor the population in a 'state of nature' have the slightest interest in this.

Who are this 'I' and 'we'? Locke does not simply mean the English conquerors or the English bourgeoisie. He means all those who defend humankind and the law of reason that God has placed in the human heart; in other words, those who assert the law of nature. This, however, includes John Locke and the English bourgeoisie, who are a kind of avant-garde of humankind. They can personify it; indeed, they are this personification by their very nature – they are the missionaries of humankind. They discover the fact that pretty well everyone has risen up against humankind except those who defend it themselves.

It is a very real state of war since between these fronts there is no judge. But, says Locke, where there is no judge everyone is the judge. The judgment is passed by the war, and Locke sees the latter as foreshadowing the Last Judgment:

> And therefore in such Controversies, where the question is put, who shall be Judge? It cannot be meant, who shall decide the Controversie; every one knows what Jephtha here tells us, that the Lord the Judge, shall judge. Where there is no Judge on Earth, the Appeal lies to God in Heaven. That Question then cannot mean, who shall judge? Whether another hath put himself in a State of War with me, and whether I may as Jephtha did, appeal to Heaven in it? Of that I my self can only be Judge in my own Conscience, as I will answer it at the great Day, to the Supreme Judge of all Men. (§21, also §176)

This reference to the Last Judgment, foreshadowed by war, is simply a reference to the power whose decisions are beyond criticism and which need not justify itself. Power as such becomes the prime criterion as long as it appeals to Locke's law of nature. If it does this it is right. It would even be hubris to want to bring charges against it since the last Judge has the last word.

Yet this state of war means that the war waged by this power that has written humankind on its banner is by definition a just war. Even if it does not go to war it has the a priori right to do so and it is always and by necessity a just war to defend humankind. Locke also includes the right to revolution even in the state of civil society, but this is only the other side of the right to intervention. After all, where there is no judge everyone is the judge. Even if there are judges in a state of civil society the right to go to war remains if these judges take decisions

that are in the service of powers opposing humankind. All decisions
of judges are illegitimate if they do not assert the law of nature that
Locke has in mind. Neither laws nor constitutions will then apply
as this law of nature is the true basic law: 'And 'tis the want of such
an appeal gives a Man the Right of War even against an aggressor,
though he be in Society and a fellow Subject ... Want of a common
Judge with Authority, puts all Men in a State of Nature: Force without
Right, upon a Man's Person, makes a State of War, both where there
is, and is not, a common Judge' (§19).

The political organization of civil society is also defined by
Locke's law of nature. But this means that it is only legitimate if it is
'civil'. If a civil society is not defined by this law of nature it places
itself in a state of war with 'us', the representatives of humankind.
Then there can be no judge because everyone is the judge and like
Jephthah can appeal to the Last Judgment. The right of intervention
follows, and every person in the world now has this right. All are
judges, not just the subjects. Therefore the English bourgeoisie and
the English government can legitimately intervene, on condition
that they defend humankind. They can therefore collect the costs of
war as reparation since the opponent has lost an unjust war and thus
has to make reparation. However, there can be no criticism as the
Last Judgment will decide.

*Locke legitimizes the war of the bourgeoisie to conquer the world and
acquire all its wealth. But its perpetrators also want this war to be a just war
and the unrestricted appropriation of the world's wealth not to be theft.*

For this reason, in the name of the bourgeoisie, he accuses the
whole world of putting itself in a state of war in order to be able to
wage a just war against everyone as a consequence. Locke accuses
the whole world of wanting to enslave the bourgeoisie so that the
bourgeoisie can enslave everyone in a just war. He accuses the whole
world of wanting to take the wealth of the bourgeoisie so that the
bourgeoisie can justly appropriate the wealth of the whole world. And
the whole world is nothing but wild animals which one can destroy
if they are in the way. And that is a consequence of what Locke pro-
pounds as human rights. By appealing to God as the final Judge, Locke
makes the bourgeoisie the final Judge, who, foreshadowing the Last
Judgment, condemns and punishes the whole world in the name of
the law of nature, humankind and the law of reason. Locke rejected
the divine right of kings but replaced it by an incomparably more

despotic law. What the bourgeoisie then proceeded to do could never have been justified in the name of any divine right of kings.

Locke thus formulated the classic prototype of inverting human rights that has since provided the fundamental categories within which even the empire represents its right to force its rule on the whole world. To this day all wars of the empire have been considered just wars – so just, indeed, that the opponents cannot claim any human rights. For opponents there are no human rights, and anyone else standing up for their human rights loses these rights, having thereby also risen up against humankind.

In the Vietnam War the US troops fought in a country thousands of kilometres away from the United States. The Vietnamese were fighting in their own country against these troops. Seen from the point of view of Locke, the Vietnamese were fighting a war of aggression against the US troops in Vietnam, and the US troops were fighting a war of defence against the Vietnamese.

The US government used similar legitimization for its war against the Sandinistas in Nicaragua. It declared its right and its duty to intervene with military force and did so in the name of Locke's law of nature. After all, the Sandinistas had risen up against humankind. The US government did not recognize the Sandinistas' human rights – although they had been democratically elected, like Allende before them in Chile. The war of the Contra was one of the most cruel wars ever waged in Latin America, and can only be compared with the present-day action of the paramilitaries in Colombia. Reagan himself stated that Nicaragua was suffering from a cancer that had to be excised. This expression stands for the annihilation of people and the denial of human rights, since a cancer obviously has none. The government of Nicaragua appealed to the International Court of Justice in The Hague, which condemned the USA for this aggression, whereupon the latter refused to recognize the judgment and withdrew its membership. To use the language of Locke, the US government is not subject to an earthly court but only to the Last Judgment and the Supreme Judge. The Cuban blockade is justified similarly, as is the recent denial of human rights to the captive Taleban and al-Qaeda soldiers from Afghanistan.

For more than a decade there has been a hunt for human rights activists in Latin America. They are threatened, forced to apply for asylum and frequently assassinated. This hunt is particularly fierce at present in Colombia. It is justified by the same schema we find in reading Locke, and it is often supported by the US government.[5] The reason is that anyone standing up for the human rights of those who are deprived of their human rights loses their own. That is why the US government has not ratified the major human rights instruments of the twentieth century. This includes not just UN conventions but also the American Convention on Human Rights (1969). The US government does not recognize them as legal obligations. It also rejects the establishment of an International Criminal Court.

John Locke is the classical thinker regarding this inversion of human rights that violates human rights in the name of these rights and even annuls the rights of all who offer resistance to 'civil' society and its logic of power. In our media this inversion is the prevalent form of reaction. Locke is still the thinker who, to this day, defines the categories used for interpreting human rights by the liberal empire.[6]

They are provided by the schematic nature of Locke's arguments. He produces a tautology. The question of who in a conflict is the aggressor is not answered by passing judgment on reality but by a deductive judgment. Whoever is right is right, so to speak. That is the tautology. It is also an apocalyptic schema. The war of those who wage a just war on its basis foreshadows the Last Judgment. 'Apocalypse now' begins with John Locke. At the same time it is a way of thinking that abolishes human rights precisely in their name. They simply become the rights of civil society and of those to whom it accords them.

The initial schema is very general. Locke elaborates it regarding two basic situations of his age. In one case this is the legitimization of forced labour by slavery, in the other the legitimization of expropriation and the virtual annihilation of the indigenous peoples of North America by the European conquerors. Locke comes to this conclusion as a result of his special way of recognizing human rights: the two examples do not violate human rights but are the result of their application. These two forms of legitimization are, however, based on Locke's analysis of the state of war.

The legitimization of forced labour by slavery

Locke's analysis of the state of war leads him in a very simple way to his legitimization of forced labour. It derives from his claim that every opponent who has waged an unjust war loses all his human rights as a consequence of his own decision to rise up against human-kind. Human rights are not taken from him but through his uprising he has declared that he has none. It is of his own volition that he cannot assert any human rights.

Locke, who inverts human rights against human rights, therefore begins by proclaiming the human right of all to be free from absolute, arbitrary power:

> This Freedom from Absolute, Arbitrary Power, is so necessary to, and closely joined with a Man's Preservation, that he cannot part with it, but by what forfeits his Preservation and Life together. For a Man, not having the Power of his own Life, cannot by Compact, or his own Consent, enslave himself to any one, nor put himself under the Absolute, Arbitrary Power of another, to take away his Life, when he pleases. No body can give more Power than he has himself; and he that cannot take away his own Life, cannot give another power over it. (§ 23)

Human beings are not just free, they have the duty to be free. They can never renounce their freedom and become a slave to someone. However, according to Locke, it is this freedom which legitimizes the forced labour of slaves. Human beings can lose this freedom although they cannot forgo it. They will lose it whenever they wage an unjust war, i.e. A war against the human species. Then they will be an enemy of freedom and there is no freedom for them: 'Indeed having, by his fault, forfeited his own Life, by some Act that deserves Death; he, to whom he has forfeited it, may (when he has him in his Power) delay to take it, and make use of him to his own Service, and he does him no injury by it. For, whenever he finds the hardship of his Slavery out-weigh the value of his Life, 'tis in his Power, by resisting the Will of his Master, to draw on himself the Death he desires' (§23).

The conclusion seems logical. If it is the case that the loser in an unjust war loses all humanity, then it follows that the victor acquires a completely arbitrary power over him. He can thus quite legitimately kill him but can equally legitimately 'delay' death and use his work as forced labour, doing him 'no injury by it': if the vanquished does not want to submit to this he remains free to commit suicide. Locke is cynical enough to allow dissidents only one alternative – that of forcing their masters to murder them. He calls this 'despotic power': 'Despotical Power is an Absolute, Arbitrary Power one Man has over another, to take away his Life, whenever he pleases. This is a Power,

which neither Nature gives, for it has made no such distinction between one Man and another; nor Compact can convey, for Man not
having such an Arbitrary Power over his own Life, cannot give another Man such a Power over it' (§172).

Locke unquestioningly accepts this despotic power, and for him it
follows from human rights that:

> … it is the effect only of Forfeiture, which the Aggressor makes of his
> own Life, when he puts himself into the State of War with another.
> For having quitted Reason, which God hath given to be the Rule
> betwixt Man and Man, and the common bond whereby humane kind
> is united into one fellowship and societie; and having renounced the
> way of peace, which that teaches, and made use of the Force of War to
> compasse his unjust ends upon an other, where he has no right, and so
> revolting from his own kind to that of Beasts by making Force which
> is theirs, to be his rule of right, he renders himself liable to be destroied
> by the injur'd person and the rest of mankind, that will joyn with him
> in the execution of Justice, as any other wild beast, or noxious brute
> with whom Mankind can have neither Society nor Security. And thus
> Captives, taken in a just and lawful War, and such only, are subject to a
> Despotical Power, which as it arises not from Compact, so neither is it
> capable of any, but is the State of War continued. For what Compact
> can be made with a Man that is not Master of his own Life? (§172)

And he adds: 'The power a Conqueror gets over those he overcomes
in a Just War, is perfectly Despotical: he has an absolute power over
the Lives of those, who by putting themselves in a State of War, have
forfeited them' (§180).

They are no longer the masters of their own lives although they
still live as prisoners of war. But this life no longer belongs to them,
it is that of the victor: 'Forfeiture gives the third, Despotical power
to Lords for their own Benefit, over those who are stripp'd of all
property' (§173). Since human beings are only real people if they
are owners, without property they fall prey to the total power of the
victorious owner. If the victor so desires, they will now legitimately
be his slaves until their death. 'But there is another sort of Servants,
which By a peculiar Name we call Slaves, who being captives taken
in a just War, are by the Right of Nature subjected to the Absolute
Dominion and Arbitrary Power of their Masters. These Men having,
as I say, forfeited their Liberties, and lost their Estates; and being in the

State of Slavery, not capable of any Property, cannot in that state be considered as any part of Civil Society; the chief end whereof is the preservation of Property' (§85).

But Locke is naturally worried about the goods of the vanquished: 'The Conqueror, if he have a just Cause, has a Despotical Right over the Persons of all, that actually aided, and concurred in the War against him, and a Right to make up his Damage and Cost out of their Labour and Estates, so he injure not the Right of any other' (§196). The victor's losses are therefore to be paid from the possessions of the conquered and the enslaved (§183). It is all strictly legal, nothing is stolen or plundered. The enslaved has to pay for the war waged by the lord in order to enslave him.

In this way Locke can champion a slavery that goes beyond all possible borders. Forced labour through slavery, as already introduced in North America, could thereby be practised with a good conscience. The conquerors could now accept the principle according to which 'all people are equal by nature'. It now justified the forced labour that they had introduced.

Locke went to greater lengths to legitimize slavery than any author before him in the whole of history. The Aristotelian legitimization of slavery seems downright paternalistic in comparison. Likewise he goes far beyond Hobbes, who simply took slavery to be a fact, without according it any legitimacy. Hobbes acknowledged no social contract including slaves or justifying slavery. Consequently he saw slavery as illegitimate and presupposed that the slave had a right to rise up. All this changed with Locke. He too did not acknowledge a social contract including slaves but believed that the law of nature condemned them legitimately to their estate.

Locke's position is infamous. In the name of law he opposed the divine right of kings and absolutism. He then, however, justified and legitimized a despotic power going much farther than the divine right of kings. Locke went to such extremes in justifying this despotism that finally the reality of world conquest seemed not so bad and therefore all the more justified. Conquerors have a free hand; all they do seems small in relation to what they may legitimately do.

The legitimate expropriation of the indigenous peoples of North America

Locke's argument again begins with the state of nature in which no one is a slave and there is no legitimate despotic power. From this he had deduced the possibility of forced labour through slavery and legitimate despotic power. Now he starts by arguing that in the state of nature the earth is common to all people, then concluding that some of them are allowed to monopolize it without restriction:

> God, who hath given the World to Men in common, hath also given them reason to make use of it to the best advantage of Life, and convenience. The Earth, and all that is therein, is given to Men for the Support and Comfort of their being. And though all the Fruits it naturally produces, and Beasts it feeds, belong to Mankind in common, as they are produced by the spontaneous hand of Nature; and no body has originally a private Dominion, exclusive of the rest of Mankind, in any of them, as they are thus in their natural state: yet being given for the use of Men, there must of necessity be a means to appropriate them some way or other before they can be of any use, or at all beneficial to any particular Man. (§26)

So the earth is given to humankind 'in common'. Consequently Locke seeks a justification for its private appropriation.

Property through work Locke develops a complicated analysis of what happened with the earth and its appropriation in the state of nature. He constantly repeats that this analysis refers to North America and the land owned by the people there. In his view, anyone who comes along can appropriate the land found to be without an owner. But people cannot take as much land as they want or feel like, but only as much as they can effectively work. It is a situation prior to civil society and the use of money. All that people can produce on this land is perishable. Therefore it is pointless to produce more than you need. The surplus would spoil. This only changes with the use of money, which enables an accumulation going beyond the needs of life. Therefore the actual working of the soil for the needs of the workers provides the measure in which there can be ownership over the land, in the state of nature, and each can only appropriate a small share of the whole available land. All other land still belongs to all the people in the world.

Locke sets great store by justifying this appropriation through work in the state of nature, since all this is meant as a basis for the legitim-ization of the conquest of North America: 'Thus the Grass my horse has bit; the Turfs my Servant has cut; and the Ore I have digg'd in any place where I have a right to them in common with others, become my Property, without the assignation or consent of any body. The labour that was mine, removing them out of that common state they were in, hath fixed my Property in them' (§28).

Anyone working the land is its owner. Locke does not care whether the labour is that of the actual owner or of his servant. If it is his servant it is still his property and not that of the servant. But Locke insists that this appropriation is severely restricted: 'As much as any one can make use of to any advantage of life before it spoils; so much he may by his labour fix a Property in. Whatever is beyond this, is more than his share, and belongs to others. Nothing was made by God for Man to spoil or destroy' (§31).

So far the conclusion is very simple. Since North America is in a state of nature the Europeans can come and appropriate the land they work. They have the same right as the peoples living there: 'Thus Labour, in the Beginning, gave a Right of Property, where-ever any one was pleased to imploy it, upon what was common' (§45). And he adds: 'Thus in the beginning all the World was America, and more so than that is now' (§49).

Within Locke's schema this argument has its particular significance. With respect to North America it means that the indigenous peoples are not owners of their land at all, but only of the part they are actually working on. Everything else belongs to all people 'in common', thus also to Europeans when they arrive and appropriate it. Should these peoples contest this, however, they place themselves in a state of war and wage an unjust war in which they can, entirely legitimately, be killed like wild animals and subjugated to a despotic power. In addition, the conquerors can now legitimately demand the reimbursement of their costs of war in order to indemnify the losses of the victor (§183). The indigenous peoples have thereby even lost their ownership of the land to the conquerors.

This explains why Locke so exhaustively analyses what prevails in a state of nature with respect to property ownership, before the emergence of a civil society. In his view there was no civil society in North America at the time so that he here outlines the relationship between the indigenous population and the European conquerors. But in reality Locke wants to go very much farther than this.

With the argument adduced so far, Locke can only justify the conquerors of North America having exactly the same right to the land as the indigenous inhabitants. They enter into the state of nature and each can only appropriate as much land as is needed for fulfilling personal needs, without exceeding this limit. All other land would continue to belong to all people. But for the conquerors that is not enough. Locke needs an argument to justify the way in which the conquerors accumulate land without any restrictions at all.

Accumulation of property through use of money Locke cannot presuppose a social contract to form a basis for a civil society. He presupposes that there is no such social contract yet. Were he to argue that it was now to be concluded he would have to include the indigenous peoples in this contract, so that it would be an agreement between equals, between the conquerors and the indigenous peoples. He avoids this possibility for obvious reasons and seeks a treaty that is independent of any social contract as a basis for civil society. Hence he claims: 'God gave the World to Men in Common; but since he gave it them for their benefit, and the greatest Conveniencies of Life they were capable to draw from it, it cannot be supposed he meant it should always remain common and uncultivated. He gave it to the use of the Industrious and Rational, (and labour was to be his Title to it;) not to the Fancy or Covetousness of the Quarrelsom and Contentious' (§34).

He seeks a reason why those who strive for the 'greatest conveniences' for their own benefit and therefore are the 'industrious and rational' should have access to this property. They are the ones who accumulate wealth and promise efficiency in the use of resources. In the state of nature, in which the earth is held in common by all, this is not the case, because this accumulation goes beyond the 'really useful things':

> The greatest part of things really useful to the Life of Man, and such as the necessity of subsisting made the first Commoners of the World look after, as it doth the Americans now, are generally things of short duration; such as, if they are not consumed by use, will decay and perish of themselves. (§46)

> There cannot be a clearer demonstration of any thing, than several Nations of the Americans are of this, who are rich in Land, and poor in all the Comforts of Life. (§41)

> An Acre of Land that bears here twenty Bushels of Wheat, and another in America, which, with the same Husbandry, would do the like, are, without doubt, of the same natural, intrinsick Value. But yet

the Benefit Mankind receives from the one, in a Year, is worth 5l. And from the other possibly not worth a Penny. (§43)

So he now construes a human agreement to precede any social contract and all society, and which is implicitly contained in the use of money:'... it is plain, that Men have agreed to disproportionate and unequal Possession of the Earth, they having by a tacit and voluntary consent found out a way, how a man may fairly possess more land than he himself can use the product of, by receiving in exchange for the overplus, Gold and Silver, which may be hoarded up without injury to any one, these metals not spoileing or decaying in the hands of the possessor' (§50)

The use of money breaks with the state of nature in the sense that it is justified to accumulate as much land as possible in the same hands since now the use of land brings forth a product that neither spoils nor perishes. With the use of money the industrious, rational agent has the right to accumulate an unlimited supply of land and to make invalid the natural limit of the state of nature. And he stresses that there are still large areas common to people and available for appropriation in unlimited quantities. Naturally he was thinking of North America: 'Yet there are still great Trails of Ground to be found, which (the Inhabitants thereof not having joyned with the rest of Mankind, in the consent of the Use of their common Money) lie waste, and are more than the People, who dwell on it, do, or can make use of, and so still lie in common. Tho' this can scarce happen amongst that part of Mankind, that have consented to the Use of Money' (§45).

So while the inhabitants that have not joined in using money are bound to the natural boundaries of the land the immigrants are not, for they have agreed to the use of common money. This agreement constructed by Locke applies 'out of the bounds of Societie, and without compact ... ' (§50). It is based on a 'tacit and voluntary consent' (§50). So its validity does not come from a social contract constituting a civil society but starts in a state of nature and applies from then on.

Here the use of money itself is equated with the right to the accumulation of wealth and increase of property, so that the use of money is not simply a means but a totality of production conditions containing in themselves an ethic. Using money and not accepting these production conditions and this ethic then seems a contradiction in itself.

However, as soon as a civil society is founded this lays down property rights: 'For in Governments the Laws regulate the right of property, and the possession of land is determined by positive constitutions' (§50). But there can be no doubt that this settling of the 'right of property' is subject to the state of nature transformed by the agreement on the use of money. Locke regards a social contract underlying civil society as secondary to this agreement on the use of money.

A global market before law and politics The agreement on the use of money for property accumulation is universal and makes demands on the whole world going beyond all state law. Neither laws nor constitutions are above it. Wherever the use of money penetrates it determines bourgeois society in terms of its production conditions and ethic of natural law. From the use of money for property accumulation is derived the true basic law that transcends all 'positive constitutions'.

There is actually a universalist attitude here which forms the basis of a global system. It is that of the global market. A total, global market *in statu nascendi* is discernible in Locke's works. Locke is therefore not an English nationalist, he is a champion of precisely this universalism. Yet Locke naturally had no doubt that if this universalism were imposed on the whole world, England, its proponent, would become a world power. It was in the name of the same universalism that the United States of America subsequently became a superpower.

This universalism, based in Locke's writings on such an alleged consensus on the use of money for property accumulation, still underlies globalizing capital today. It has marked the debate about the Multinational Agreement on Investments (MAI). Its protagonists openly talk of turning such an agreement into the true constitution on which the constitution of all states would have to be patterned. But this power takeover by multinational capital for its self-accumulation at the same time signifies the stabilization of the United States as superpower.

The monetary mechanism specifies the right to property that Locke declared to be the state of nature. It ceases to be an unrestricted right to property and, through the introduction of the agreement on the use of money, turns into purely capitalist property rights. Locke therefore distinguishes between the property serving to guarantee the needs of life (property in the state of nature) and the property used for accumulation (property according to the agreement on the use of money). The latter is capitalist property. Locke gives it absolute preference.

Locke was the first person to articulate this dominance running through the whole of the world market. However, for him it was primarily an argument in favour of the conquest of North America. He could thereby link up his theory that the earth originally belonged to all people with the right, preceding all polity and state organization, to accumulate the earth without restriction. The conqueror can now exploit the state of nature in order to occupy the land there, but is not bound to limits in using the land that Locke set the indigenous population. They have no right to resist. If they accept money they are forced to give 'tacit and voluntary consent' (§50) to the system and lose their right to the land. If they do not accept they also lose their rights. They have the alternative of being shot or hanged. Should they resist, however, they will rise up against humankind and may be treated like wild beasts. They are in a trap with no escape.

It therefore comes as no surprise that almost the whole indigenous population of North America was annihilated during the conquest. This corresponded to Locke's strategy.

Locke's method of deriving human rights from property

Locke gives no list of human rights, only principles outlining a framework from which all human rights can be derived. He expressly mentions four such principles: 1) 'That all Men by Nature are equal' (§54); 2) 'For a Man, not having the Power of his own Life, cannot, by Compact, or his own Consent, enslave himself to any one' (§23); 3) 'For Man not having such an Arbitrary Power over his own Life, cannot give another man such a Power over it' (§172); 4) 'God has given the World to Men in common' (§26).

Property is the foundation of humankind Locke's whole argument starts, in fact, from the orientation given by these four principles. Yet there can be no doubt that he did not invent them. They arose from the first English Revolution of 1648–49. They were put forward by the Independents and most radically by the Levellers. They were hoisted on the banners of this revolution, the most important slogan of which was equality. It was opposed to the despotism of the king and the nobility. It opposed slavery, which did not yet one-sidedly deal in black Africans but could strike anyone, regardless of the colour of their skin. The exclusive concentration of slavery on black people did not arise until the first half of the eighteenth century. But this re-

jection of slavery also included bondage. The Independents and Levellers likewise insisted that the earth had been given to all people and
thereby called for access to the earth for the peasants and the freeing
of craftsmen from the fetters of the guilds that restricted their autonomous activity. Their utopia was a society of small producers who all
had access to independent private property. Therefore it was crucial
for the right to property. However, the property they demanded was
not bourgeois property but one conducive to the independent livelihood of each of them. This utopia of small producers was a utopia
of a society in which all could satisfy their needs and lead a dignified
life. It was not a completely radical call for equality but an egalitarian
tendency thought out by those groups excluded from political and
economic freedoms.

Even if Locke started from the Glorious Revolution of 1688 he
had to work from the basic principles of the first English Revolution.
The Glorious Revolution was the Thermidor of this first revolution
and consequently claimed to be its legitimate successor. The Glorious
Revolution was the final victory of the bourgeois revolution over the
previous popular revolution. It was the victory of bourgeois society
and its imperial pretensions. Locke provided the corresponding political theory. The mere victory of the bourgeoisie could not be the last
word since it now had to present this victory as the legitimate expression of the whole English Revolution. John Locke solved the problem. His book was not about politics but one that was to make policy
and was intended to do so. It gave the bourgeois revolution its aura of
legitimacy and thereby greater stability.

In order to be able to do this, Locke inverted the human rights
framework that had underlain the popular revolution. He did this
by changing the proprietor of the human rights that he essentially
adopted. The proprietor is no longer the living, physical person but a
collective abstraction, the whole of humankind. It is now this humanity which has rights and the individual is the holder of these rights.
*But humankind is constituted by property. The individual has a share in
humanity through being an owner. Human beings have dignity only in so far
as they are owners.* The human being as a physical person, with needs,
is completely subordinate to property. This property is now a bourgeois property, governed by competition and efficiency. The enemies
Locke constantly has in mind defend their property, too. The indigenous peoples of North America defend their land as their property.

The English farmers and craftsmen also defend their property and strive for property. However, from Locke's perspective, this is another kind of property, one constituted by the opportunities in life of actual people. Locke inverts this relation into a relation of individuals constituted by the logic of the accumulation of property. From Locke's point of view, property constituted by human beings as persons is illegitimate and a barrier to progress. Macpherson speaks here of possessive individualism.

Between the first English Revolution and the Glorious Revolution legitimized by Locke there arises this clash of contrary conceptions of property and ultimately also of human rights. In fact Locke replaces human rights by those rights arising from the logic of a social system in which people are only supporting factors. As human beings and living, physical persons they lose all rights and can only lay claim to the rights resulting from the logic of the social system that is now the bourgeois social system. This system is absolute and it is God's will.

Locke takes this view to extremes. When starting from the state of nature before the consensus on the use of money he is aware of another two basic rights of people, the right to physical inviolability and the right to property. But this changes after he has introduced the consensus on the use of money. Then he knows only a single human right, the right to property. Locke now sees the inviolability of the body as a simple deduction from the right to property. There thus remains no trace of a human dignity going beyond the right to property and therefore beyond the system and its logic. So Locke can now assert that the chief end of 'civil society' is the preservation of property (§85). He therefore concludes that 'Despotical power [goes] to Lords for their own Benefit, over those who are stripp'd of all property' (§173). This power is despotic because those bereft of all property have also lost the ownership of their own bodies. They retain no right at all to the inviolability of the body as a consequence of the dignity of the human person as such. By being bereft of property they are completely at the mercy of their masters, who have the power to kill, torture, mutilate or enslave them. This is a consequence of Locke's concept of property in which it is not the human person who is the subject of human rights but property, and thereby humankind.

No property for the enemies of property The inversion of human rights performed by Locke can be summed up in a formula that Locke does not use directly but which reflects his standpoint: no property for the enemies of property. It is important to note here that the loss of property includes the loss of ownership over the body and therefore its inviolability. This formula covers all the inversions Locke carries out. It is the formula legitimizing all state terrorism by bourgeois society. It appeared in the French Revolution in accordance with the form given it by Saint-Just: no freedom for the enemies of freedom. Popper took over the same formula at the time of the Cold War and transmuted it: no tolerance for the enemies of tolerance. It is therefore no surprise that Popper became the court philosopher of the totalitarian dictatorships of national security in Latin America, particularly in Uruguay and Chile. In modified form, adapted to the system, the same formula recurs in the Stalinist purges of the 1930s and it can be found in the prosecution pleas of A. F. Wyschinski, chief state prosecutor of the Soviet Union between 1935 and 1940. *It is the formula with which modernism in all systems based on the recognition of human rights justifies the violation of these human rights in the name of human rights.*

It is the formula which legitimizes that 'despotic power' of which Locke speaks with such conviction, and which was always used to justify this violence. It eliminates the human rights of the human person that go beyond the right to property and therefore express human dignity, replacing it by system rights, then proclaimed as human rights. The formula is universal and can easily be adjusted to the differing situations in the history of the modern age. It is evident that the present strategy of globalization relates to the same formula and has again inverted human rights as rights expressing human dignity, turning them into the rights of the globalizing system overriding all human rights. This system also does this in the name of human rights. In this way the private bureaucracies of the large corporations seem to be the promulgators of Locke's 'law of reason' and therefore the true holders of human rights. They thereby take on that 'despotic power' of which Locke speaks.

From human rights Locke derived justifications for forced labour through slavery, the extermination of the indigenous peoples and the colonization of the whole world. The law of reason he deduced from this inversion was the unlimited accumulation of capital within the system of private property. When at the end of the nineteenth century, primarily from Max Weber onwards, private property was no longer called the law of nature, this was replaced by the argument of efficiency and competitiveness

in accordance with market laws. But subsequently it was possible
to reject human rights in the same way as Locke did, without even
changing the formalism. The logic of the system was substituted for
human rights in the name of human rights, while people were deprived of their human dignity. This mechanism, however, emerged
long before Locke in the very constitution of the patriarchy. Man, in
all his masculine glory, portrayed himself as the incarnation of humankind, as the law of reason that God prescribed for all human action,
so that Woman is transformed into a potential beast to be tamed or
destroyed. After Locke, racism came into its own in the eighteenth
century. Thereby the White Man adopted the law of reason by which
he declared himself to be the representative of humankind in dealings
with 'people of colour'.

On the other hand, this inversion of human rights is already
linked with utopianism in Locke's thinking. Locke gave expression
to a utopianism of technological progress. Interpersonal relationships
which need to be humanized, relationships of real people, are replaced
by the empty prospect of a technology designed to improve the world.
The promises of this progress are so infinite that no human rights
violation is even worth mentioning besides them.[7] The prospect of
boundless progress weighs on the possibility of representing tangible
human rights, since these rights always and of necessity appear to be
distortions of an accumulation capable of guaranteeing this infinite
progress. This utopianism has accompanied the whole history of capitalism and appeared in Stalinism with similar consequences. It is not a
matter of the problem of utopia as such but of its inversion, the process
by which utopia is turned upside down and then promotes the violation of human rights. This technological utopianism can even take the
form of utility calculation, as is the case with Hayek: 'A free society
needs morality that is ultimately reduced to the maintenance of life
– not the maintenance of all life, as it could be necessary to sacrifice
individual life in order to save a greater number of other lives. That is
why the only rules of morality are those leading to a "calculation of
life": property and contract' (Hayek 1981).

This calculation is hypocrital and deceptive as it presupposes
knowledge of the future. But apart from Hayek no one can know
about the future. Nevertheless, such an argumentation is an efficient
way of disputing all human rights. Human rights forbid the 'sacrifice
[of] individual life', as this would mean violating human rights. The

'calculation of life' mooted by Hayek accuses the defence of human rights of being an obstacle on the road to 'saving a greater number of other lives'. In this way it is again very easy for Hayek to denounce any defence of human rights as an attack on progress. Again 'humankind' represses human rights, and thereby human beings when they insist on human dignity.[8] The elimination of whole countries and the extermination of populations are thus transformed into a possible service to 'humankind' and to human rights – the latter no longer being perceived as real, existing human dignity but having been transformed into a simple myth.[9]

Regaining human rights in the context of postmodernism

One can only respond to the inversion of human rights by regaining the human rights of real people, as an expression of their human dignity. Let us start with a quote from Albert Camus, taken from *The Rebel*: 'The end justifies the means? Perhaps. But who justifies the means? This question leaves historical thinking open and rebellion responds: the means.'[10]

In fact, human rights are not an end to be achieved by seeking rationally expedient means. However, when they are treated like this the problem of their inversion inevitably arises. Striving to achieve them as an end can lead only to violating them by the means. The proprietor of human rights then, by necessity, becomes the system, the human species. Treated as an end, human rights must be made the object of rational action. Such ends, however, turn into institutions, and the human rights thus dealt with are guaranteed by the imposition of institutions. Institutions can be striven for by rational means, human rights cannot. Humankind hereby devours people. Instead of guaranteeing human rights one guarantees institutions, which today mean democracy, property, market, competition and efficiency. These themselves are now regarded as institutionalized human rights – jealous gods that suffer no other gods beside them. Hence, according to the prevailing view, they take precedence over human rights.

By making these institutions an end, one can seek the means to impose them. However, in order to impose them one has to violate the human rights in whose name one is acting. There follows an inversion of human rights that turns the violation of human rights into a categoric imperative.

By contrast, Camus asks about the means. If human rights are seen as an end, they must be violated with the means used for their realization. But precisely in this way the means reveal the true end and this true end cannot be human rights. Human rights as an end become pure rhetoric, behind which a quite different end becomes visible, that of imposing a certain system of institutions and thereby a certain dominance. It is the criticism of means which reveals the end and not the declamation of some kind of human rights. The criticism of means reveals a language of means that is the language of reality. It therefore reveals the extent to which the declared ends are lies.

The history of the West is the history of the annihilation of countries and the extermination of whole peoples and cultures. This is the language that unmasks the means. The language of the declared ends is, however, quite different. It speaks of the white man's burden, that of civilizing the world and bringing it culture and, of course, human rights. The history of the West is a history of hells created by the West in the past and in the present. In the language of rhetoric, by contrast, the West speaks only of the heavens it takes everywhere. These heavens cover the hells brought forth by the West. It is like the hell in which the devils torment the damned day and night. Yet no one torments the devils themselves. They even believe they are in heaven.

This contrasts with the language of means and denies the language of declared ends. Human rights can be regained only with the language of means. Human rights are not ends, but the challenge to the means calculated and used for arbitrary ends. A discussion of human rights must therefore be a discussion of the compatibility of means with human rights. Human rights therefore judge the means, not the ends. Even if the ends are justified by reference to human rights, human rights remain the criterion by which to judge the means.

In this sense the demand for human rights formulated by Camus is a rebellion. It is the rebellion of the human person as a living subject who refuses to be turned into an object of the system. But this person also rebels against human rights being turned into ends and thereby the domination of humankind over human beings.

In fact, we can trace from Locke a pattern for the inversion of human rights that has made history without interruption until the present day. For the modern age this is what French philosopher Jean-François Lyotard (1979) called a legitimation narrative. The pattern underlies the structures of modernism still and is constantly adapted to new historical situations. It is one of modernism's founding myths.

Precisely for this reason it is striking that when Lyotard speaks of the legitimation narratives of modernism he does not even mention this schema of Locke. He mentions two other legitimation narratives, derived from the thought of Rousseau and Marx. But he carefully conceals Locke's legitimation narrative which actually precedes the other two and to which Rousseau and Marx responded. Moreover, the thinking of Rousseau and Marx cannot be understood at all without this Lockean construct as a reference point. Rousseau and Marx are critics of this fundamental schema. Rousseau formulates his criticism starting from the concept of the citizen and Marx from the concept of the person as a needy natural being. But both of them reject Locke's schema.

Lyotard, by contrast, hails Rousseau and Marx as the founders of modernism. Hence his conclusion that postmodernism begins when their thinking begins to lose its previous validity. However, one must keep in mind that Lyotard does not use the names of Rousseau and Marx just to designate these thinkers – their names stand for all emancipatory movements of the nineteenth and twentieth centuries that opposed those unbridled forces of the modern age first schematized by Locke. These include the great movements to emancipate slaves which during the nineteenth century led to the abolition of forced labour in bourgeois countries, the emancipation of the Jews since the end of the eighteenth century, the labour movement, the women's movement, the peace movement, the emancipation of the cultures of the colonialized world and the independence of colonies.

Examining these great emancipation movements, one is struck by the fact that the great majority started with those human groups featuring in Locke's schema as a danger for 'the whole species', 'degenerate', 'noxious' beings who have waged 'war against mankind' and of whom Locke says that they are to be treated like wild beasts. Those who fought for their emancipation in the nineteenth and twentieth centuries are the wild beasts of the fundamental legitimation narrative of modernism derived from John Locke.

They are the ones who now assert the human rights denied them by modernism. Locke does not recognize human rights for any of them and says this expressly in the name of human rights. Locke does not attribute any rights to non-bourgeois cultures nor to peoples opposing colonization and conquest. They are nothing but wild beasts which the bourgeois conquerers can, and should, exterminate. However, it was precisely these emancipation movements that introduced human rights into the modern age in the first place. With these movements human beings first appeared as proprietors of rights that are not derived or derivable from any property but which they have merely because they are persons with human dignity. These rights then appear in the twentieth century in the great human rights declarations. By contrast, the preamble to the Declaration of Independence of 1776 (sometimes called the US human rights declaration) is not really about human rights. The Bill of Rights took matters farther by formulating basic rights which were then included in the constitution. The above-mentioned preamble is based on a natural law argument, largely taken from Locke (human freedom and equality, institution of government by the governed). So the rights postulated in the preamble and the Bill of Rights reflect the political philosophy of Locke, who was their true father. This also explains why the extermination of the indigenous population of North America could take place after this without there being any conflict with the Declaration of Independence and the US constitution. It also explains why the USA was able to remain a country with massive forced labour through slavery for almost another hundred years after the Declaration of Independence. If you consider that the human rights proclaimed in 1776 stem from the tradition of John Locke there is not the slightest contradiction. In the spirit of this declaration freedom is slavery and extermination.

The great emancipation movements then brought human rights into the modern age, leading up to the Universal Declaration of Human Rights which was adopted after the Second World War. The US government signed this declaration but has ratified few of the following human rights conventions. Signing has a declaratory character and does not involve any obligations, while ratification – in this case by the US Senate – makes them legally binding. Two key instruments were not ratified: 1) the International Covenant on Economic, Social and Cultural Rights, of 1966 (signed only in 1977); 2) the American Convention on Human Rights and Freedoms (1969), also signed but not ratified in 1977. But even in cases where human rights instruments were ratified the Senate imposed restrictive conditions that weakened their effect. That shows that the conflict is unresolved.

Lyotard identified modernism with these emancipation movements and the thought of Rousseau and Marx, which led up to the Universal Declaration of Human Rights; according to his definition of postmodernism, this document has lost its validity as a legitimation narrative. But what he calls 'postmodern' is in fact a modernism *in extremis*: it denies human emancipation any legitimacy and amounts to abolishing all the human rights that originated in the wake of the emancipation movements of the nineteenth and twentieth centuries. A naked modernism is arising which declares proponents of all human emancipation and all resistance to be wild beasts and therefore to be eliminated.

We then see that the thought of John Locke is by no means a theory of reality. It is something quite diffent. It creates a categorial framework that itself constitutes the reality. As it constitutes reality itself, however, we cannot refute it through reference to reality. It is therefore circular thinking. If one assumes this categorial framework then reality is what Locke claims it to be. Another reality cannot be indicated, unless one criticizes this thinking as a categorial framework. But nor can such criticism make any other reality visible to those seeing reality from the point of view of this categorial framework.

Yet this schema as a categorial framework for interpreting reality underlies not just all of bourgeois society but also all of modernism. Whenever modern society becomes total(itarian) this schema appears in its purest form. Locke formulates the framework as that of an absolute, bourgeois society, and any such society can only become total(itarian) in the way first shown by Locke's schema. In this sense this is not just an old, theoretical invention of John Locke, but a discovery. Locke discovers and formulates the categorial framework essential for a bourgeois society to become total(itarian) in the first place. Hence it is not just simply a matter of Locke's opinion, but the discovery of categories that are objectively part of bourgeois society itself. Locke discovered a fact.

Stalinist socialism also developed an analogous pattern in the process of its becoming totalitarian, based on the concept of socialist property. It transformed Locke's schema but retained it in its structure. In this case too it fulfilled the role of a categorial framework that created reality and could therefore not be refuted. But something similar happens in fascism, too. If you remove from Locke's schema his reference to 'mankind' and the 'law of reason', with which he performs the inversion of human rights, replacing it by the 'will to power', then Locke's schema appears in its fascist form. You will then see that all modernism constitutes its reality in terms of Locke's schema when, in the course of becoming absolute, it eliminates human rights understood as the rights of individual persons. This schema is then revealed as the categorial framework of all modernism, although there is scope for variation that Locke did not, of course, foresee.

If there is ever to be a society going beyond modernism it should be one that leaves this basic schema of modernism behind it. Many today have beome aware that this is necessary if human life is to continue to be possible at all. *But instead, in our present society with its strategy of capitalist globalization, a new type of absolutism is developing which is repeating the schema of Locke. Locke envisaged absolute bourgeois society as a project, but our society finally has the means to put it into practice, with all its bitter consequences.*

Notes

1 The deposing of Robespierre by the Directoire in the French Revolution.

2 According to Maurice Cranston, 1957, quoted by Macpherson 1962: 253, n. 4. For Voltaire see Poliakov, 1983: 110.

3 These positions are related to the radical reformation of the previous centuries in Europe. See Williams 1983. On the Independents and the 'Saints' Parliament' see Kofler 1974 and Macpherson 1962.

4 Book I, ch. 9; book II, ch. 5; see below.

5 In the documents of the conference of the intelligence services of American armies (CIEA) meeting in November 1987, parallel to the conference of American armies (CEA) in Mar de la Plata, Argentina, almost all autonomous human rights organizations referred to by the documents were branded as subversive and pro-communist. Since these organizations were of the opinion that even persecuted communists have human rights, they themselves were regarded as communist. The documents are published in Duchrow et al. 1990.

6 But not just of the liberal empire. When I (F.J.H.) was preparing this text I reread the speeches of the main prosecutor of the Soviet Union during the Stalinist purges of the 1930s. See Pirker 1963. Wyschinski's language is the lan-

guage of John Locke, adjusted to Soviet circumstances. Wyschinski also thought that the accused had risen up against humankind and concluded that they should be killed like 'mad dogs'. This expression has a life of its own. These 'mad dogs' also turned up when the US government carried out its air attack on Libya with the aim of killing Qaddafi. Then Vice-President Bush declared that Qaddafi should be killed like a 'mad dog'.

The Brezhnev Doctrine, too, is only comprehensible in terms of Locke's approach.

7 On the works of technical and economic progress Locke says: 'I readily agree the contemplation of these works gives us occasion to admire, revere and glorify their Author: and, if rightly directed, may be of greater benefit to mankind than the monuments of exemplary charity that have at so great charge been raised by the founders of hospitals and almshouses. He that first invented printing, discovered the use of the compass, or made public the virtue and right use of Kin Kina, did more for the propagation of knowledge, for the supply and increase of useful commodities and saved more from the grave, than those who built colleges, workhouses and hospitals' (Locke 1690b, vol. II: 352).

8 Colonel Paul Tibbet, who aged twenty-seven was the chief pilot of the

plane that dropped the atom bomb on Hiroshima on 6 August 1945, was interviewed as follows:

Question: 'What is the most important thing you have done in your life?'

Answer: 'Obviously the fact of being part of Group 509 that was trained to use the bomb. I can say that that saved the lives of millions of people ... the only thing I can add is that I would take the same decision today in order to save such a large number of lives.'

The interview was conducted by Andrés Jiménez for the Colombian magazine *Semana* and was published in *La Nación*, San José, Costa Rica on 22 August 1999. It is obvious that Tibbet sees the attack on Hiroshima as a service to human rights. He made a 'calculation of life' just as Hayek does. If this kind of calculation is considered justified almost any human bestiality may be portrayed as a service to human rights.

9 Hayek distinguishes two types of liberalism, a good one and a bad one. Good liberalism starts with Locke and bad liberalism with Rousseau. See Hayek 1952: 12.

10 *L'homme révolté*, 1951 (published in English 1953).

FOUR
The total market: how globalized capitalism is eliminating the commitment to sustain life

The struggle to make property-owners accountable to society and the example of the German constitution

John Locke's theory of property sums up the reality of bourgeois, capitalist society in all its aspects. As a result we gain a clearer picture, despite elements of continuity, of how this society differs from the property-owning society of ancient times. At that time property meant primarily ownership of land and slaves (i.e. their labour). Nevertheless, credit based on property, and then on the use of money, was already the principal means of increasing one's wealth. In the modern era, by contrast, accumulation of capital property has become the guiding principle for every element of the entire economic context, as formulated so clearly in Locke's definitions. Land ownership, and consequently all natural resources, are seen in terms of monetary value and are thus subordinated to the purpose of (unlimited) accumulation of wealth. Human beings, whose sole possession is their capacity to work, likewise become wage earners for the purpose of capital accumulation. Both land and labour, then, become the means by which capital owners increase their capital property. Capital property is thus the basis of indirect power over people and land. In so far as capital accumulation no longer takes place solely in the agricultural context of working the land, but also exists in an industrial context, employing machines and trading the finished products, fixed assets can now be added to the traditional means of production of land and labour. The ordering of all these elements with the aim of capital accumulation takes place via the capitalist market, which differs from the traditional market, where goods were exchanged on a basis of need, precisely because all transactions serve only one purpose: the accumulation of capital. It then becomes clear that the crucial and fundamental definition of bourgeois society first formulated by Locke is based on the linking of property with money-mediated accumulation, i.e. capital accumulation. This concept is not simply reflected in a single isolated economic phenomenon, but in all production relations. As we have shown, it takes on the status of natural law, rising above any political or legal constraint, and, applied to our present-day reality, underpins a global market for capital accumulation.

Any critical analysis and quest for alternatives will have to understand how bourgeois, capitalist society is organized both politically and legally. Given the fact that this system produces few winners and a great many losers, the winners cannot assume that the supposedly 'tacit agreement' of people with regard to the (unequal) accumulation of capital will simply continue. In order to implement their system of capital accumulation, they need political and legal instruments of power as well as economic ones. The economic losers, the wage earners, for their part also have to engage in political and legal activity in order to limit the power of the capital owners.

Locke's property theory also became the basis of Western legal systems and constitutions, starting with the United States in 1787 (Rittstieg 1975: 92ff). The original wording was 'Life, Liberty, Property', but 'out of liberty and property came the liberty of property' – at least until 1937 (ibid.: 134). Humankind is, according to Locke, a property-owning species. All human rights derive from property. Therefore, the sole purpose of the state is the protection of this hypostatized property. Since the aim of property – allied with a monetary system – was self-propagation even before the creation of a state, it is hardly surprising that the political-legal system from the beginning favoured large-scale ownership.

We find the same development in the constitution at the time of the French Revolution. The Declaration of the Rights of Man of 1789 refers to property as an inviolable and divine right (Article 17). Drawn from Roman law, the absolutism of property is given its most unequivocal wording in Article 544 of the Code Napoléon (Code Civil), which has formed the basis of nearly all civil codes since that time: '*La propriété est le droit de jouir et disposer des choses de la manière la plus absolue, pourvu qu'on ne fasse un usage prohibé par les lois ou par les règlements*' (Property is the absolute right to utilize and possess things, provided that one does not use them in a way that is contrary to the laws and statutes; quoted in Binswanger 1998: 130).

Since the nineteenth century, and particularly following the collapse of the classical liberal economy in the global economic crisis of 1929, campaigns have been waged in every Western country to make at least a minimum of social responsibility legally incumbent upon (large-scale) ownership. However, in the nineteenth century this social responsibility was extremely restricted in the Anglo-American sphere of common law (Rittstieg 1975: 142ff). With regard to the use of property, which was otherwise unrestricted, the law required only that no third party should be *unnecessarily* harmed and that monopolies should not hinder the functioning of the market. The first real change came in the USA with the New Deal and the ensuing 'constitutional revolution' of 1937 (ibid.: 148ff). There the majority in the Supreme Court shifted away from the laissez-faire ideology, recognizing the government's right to limit the rights of property-owners when required by the common good. Accordingly laws were passed to establish a minimum wage, trade union rights were accepted, and regulations were also introduced with regard to land use, prices and rents.

Of particular significance, however, was the state's right to taxation, which granted the state far-reaching freedoms even before 1937: these even allowed the removal of economic activities regarded as unnecessary or damaging, for example betting offices (ibid.: 168ff). In the case of expropriations it had only to be proven that these would serve a public purpose, and the state was also expected to pay fair compensation. Even the enormous concentration of power through the ownership of means of production in the industrial system was considered to be in the common good, especially since the state was seen as winning important gains for the economy through its provision of infrastructure (ibid.: 174ff). At the same time, the idea developed that new rights, such as employers' contributions, or income from public service salaries, should also be protected as property rights (ibid.: 191ff).

We see a similar development in Germany, even though here the development of unlimited bourgeois property came much more slowly than in France and the Anglo-Saxon countries (ibid.: 191ff). The move towards social responsibility with regard to property was first attempted in the Weimar Constitution. Article 153 states:

1. Property shall be guaranteed by the constitution. Its content and limits shall be defined by the laws. Expropriation shall only be permissible for the public good. It may only be ordered pursuant to the law. Appropriate compensation shall be paid provided that no other Reich [imperial] law dictates otherwise ...

2. Property entails obligations. Its use shall also serve the common good. (quoted in ibid.: 252ff)

This new constitutional approach was possible because of the strengthening of the socialist movement in both politics and society. In paragraph 1 the property guarantee is restricted initially by the proviso that the content and limits of this property shall be determined by the legislative body. Paragraph 2 even allows for the possibility of expropriation without compensation, should this be determined by a supreme law. Paragraph 3 provides for the possibility of intervention by the legislative body in cases of private use. Further articles strengthen this new approach. Article 154 permits the state to retain a portion of legacies. Article 155 makes land ownership subject to the public interest. Article 156 stresses clearly the right to nationalize.

With such legislature at its disposal, the Weimar Republic could have introduced decisive social and political changes even before 1929. This was thwarted, however, by the German Reichsgericht (supreme court), which, with a staff that had hardly changed since the Kaiser's reign, secured the maintenance of the status quo. In various final appeals, the supreme court extended the exclusive rights of the property guarantee while also imposing limits on the state's power to enforce a social obligation (ibid.: 255ff). This began with the rejection of housing controls after the First World War. It then extended to the recognition of the rights of the ruling class to income from their feudal lands and went on to justify the profits derived by big business from inflation. Even in relation to land use, the supreme court declared 'the wishes of the property owner in the context of maximising profits [to be] a matter of constitutional principle ... the exemplary model is the property owner who is maximising his profits without restraint, not the one who acts according to his sense of social responsibility' (ibid.: 267). Then, to top it all, National Socialism destroyed the unions as the independent representatives of wage earners.

Developments in Germany after the Second World War illustrate both the range of options available at that time to the economic system in general and the property system in particular, and the choices that were actually made. Following its catastrophic collapse, the classical liberal model was completely discredited by all political parties as well as the population at large (ibid.: 275). Both of the big parties in what later became West Germany – the SPD and the

CDU/CSU – argued the case for a system of 'social economy' in their respective manifestos in 1946 and 1947, with the CDU/CSU even expressly condemning the capitalist system. The constitutions of the federal states (Länder) drawn up in the same years permitted the transfer of entire branches of industry into public ownership, with the constitution of Hessen even making this compulsory. The American military administration responded by ordering a referendum. When this resulted in a yes vote of 72 per cent, representing an overwhelming majority in favour of nationalization, the military regime forbade the enforcement of the Hessen constitution until the German constitution came into effect. In addition, the USA, through the Marshall Plan, played its part in increasing the allure of the 'Golden West' as compared to East Germany under Soviet rule, dominated as it was by social restructuring and reparations. And so, with the German political entities both coerced and seduced by the USA not to undertake any nationalization, the economy actually began to reorganize itself on the basis of private enterprise.

In addition the CDU/CSU under Konrad Adenauer developed away from the original 'social economy' approach towards the 'social market economy'. Since both of the big parties had to be in agreement at the launch of the new constitution, it is not surprising that it is founded essentially on private ownership of the means of production. During the constituent assembly Carlo Schmid (SPD) tabled a motion to limit the guarantee of protection to 'property which serves to preserve a person's life or own work', but it was not passed (ibid.: 283).

How may we interpret the German Basic Law with regard both to property and in particular to ownership of the means of production? The crucial text is to be found in Article 14:

1) Property and the right of inheritance shall be guaranteed. Their content and limits shall be defined by the laws.

2) Property entails obligations. Its use shall also serve the public good.

3) Expropriation shall only be permissible for the public good. It may only be ordered by or pursuant to a law that determines the nature and extent of compensation. Such compensation shall be determined by establishing an equitable balance between the public interest and the interests of those affected. In case of dispute respecting the amount of compensation, recourse may be had to the ordinary courts.

However, further articles are needed to help us interpret the Basic Law:

Article 2: '1) Every person shall have the right to free development of his [sic] personality insofar as he does not violate the rights of others or offend against the constitutional order or the moral law.

2) Every person shall have the right to life and physical integrity. Freedom of the person shall be inviolable. These rights may be interfered with only pursuant to a law.'

Article 3.1:'All persons shall be equal before the law.'

Article 9.3:'The right to form associations to safeguard and improve working and economic conditions shall be guaranteed to every individual and to every occupation or profession.'

Article 12.1:'All Germans shall have the right freely to choose their occupation or profession, their place of work, and their place of training ...'

Article 15:'Land, natural resources, and means of production may for the purpose of socialisation be transferred to public ownership or other forms of public enterprise by a law that determines the nature and extent of compensation.'

Article 19.3:'The basic rights shall also apply to domestic legal persons to the extent that the nature of such rights permits.'

Article 20.1:'The Federal Republic of Germany is a democratic and social federal state.'

Article 28.1:'The constitutional order in the Länder must conform to the principles of a republican, democratic, and social state governed by the rule of law, within the meaning of this Basic Law.'

Three conflicting interpretations of these articles come to the fore (see Krölls 1998: 36ff and 348ff).

1. A conservative-liberal interpretation would claim that the Basic Law is to be understood in the liberal tradition, particularly that of Britain, as protection against interference by the state in the primarily middle-class society (see above). This means that bourgeois society, which is founded on both the freedom of the individual and the private ownership of the means of production (thus of waged labour), is organized as a political community in order to protect freedom and private ownership.

2. A left-wing school of constitutional law attempts to interpret

the statements regarding the social responsibility entailed by property and the idea of the welfare state in such a way as to imply that the Basic Law provides categorically for the possibility of casting off the capitalist economic framework as a matter of principle and replacing it with a socialist one.

3. Krölls and others critically analyse these positions by meticulously examining every detail of the texts. Krölls concludes that it is the state itself which sets the market economy system within the Basic Law, with the aim of abstract production of wealth, and that therefore the state has to guarantee the continued viability of the property-based market economy. In this way the state justifies not only its right to levy taxes, by which it has to maintain itself, but also the welfare state elements, which allow it to order economy and welfare in such a way as to avoid damage to the possessive market economy.

This third argument is convincing, not only because of its consistency in every detail, but also in the light of the climate surrounding the discussion of economic theory at the time of the drafting of the Basic Law. During this period there was unanimous agreement that there could not be a return to the pre-1929 classical liberal position, nor should there be. On the other hand, the rejection of Carlo Schmid's motion implies that the door was closed to any possibility of a socialist economic order. In Germany there were two dominant schools of thought: the ordo-liberal in the tradition of Wilhelm Eucken,[1] and Keynesianism. Each starts in its own way from the premise that the market can only function within politically established parameters and thus cannot function without state intervention. The ordo-liberals were concerned with the preservation of competition and the imposition of anti-trust measures. Keynes and his school concentrated on four main areas: state-imposed measures aimed at preventing economic fluctuation, so as to create full employment; a monetary policy that kept interest rates as low as possible; control of capital flows to avoid speculation; and finally a progressive taxation policy aimed at spreading the distribution of wealth within society in order to widen consumer spending power. All these Keynesian measures were meant in turn to facilitate economic growth and widen prosperity. It is notable that Keynes saw himself as a liberal theorist, by no means as a socialist. His argument gained its strength precisely because of the fact that it introduced measures designed to avoid the disasters brought about by capitalism, which had become all too evident in 1929.

The essence of the Basic Law lies in the relationship between Articles 2 and 14. 'By establishing the basic right to free development of the personality within the Basic Law, the authors of the constitution have standardised the individual's right to self-determination as a constitutional principle of the social framework in which they live' (ibid.: 73). At the same time the state protects individuals from the will of other individuals who do not respect everyone's right to self-determination. 'State protection of citizens in the pursuit of their freedoms over against those of others presupposes social conditions which are characterised by fundamental clashes of interest amongst members of that society' (ibid.: 75). It is therefore a matter of guaranteeing freedom in the *abstract*, independently of any material conditions of freedom and thus independently of access to the means of production. To this extent even Article 2.2 guarantees life only in the sense of existence.

This means that already in Article 2 of the Basic Law, which guarantees abstract freedom for the individual who finds him/herself in conflict with others' interests, a subsequent guarantee of private ownership of the means of production is taken for granted. For those who own the means of production, 'free development of personality' therefore means working in competition with other owners according to the property laws in order to increase wealth. To non-owners of the means of production 'freedom' is reduced to 'putting their capacity for work at the disposal of those in possession of the material prerequisites of wealth accumulation', simply in order to survive, and thereby 'creating more wealth for property owners' (ibid.: 82).

Article 3.1 ('All persons shall be equal before the law'), far from weakening this interpretation, actually confirms it. It merely guarantees an abstract equality before the law, while giving no such guarantee with regard to socio-economic equality.

By implication, the same status awarded by law to the abstract freedom of private and autonomous use of persons and property is accorded to *contracts*, which are guaranteed as one of the institutions of a liberal state system.

The contract is the form by which the state, in accordance with the concept of freedom, guarantees the existence of mutual exchange as a relationship based on consent ... The freedom of contract expressed in generalised form in Article 2 (1) of the Basic Law has its concrete guarantee in the specifically economic basic rights, with their inherent freedom of disposal in legal transactions. Accordingly

- freedom of contract with regard to contracts of employment is enshrined in Article 12 of the Basic Law;
- business transactions involving significant assets are covered by the rights laid down in Article 14 BL;
- freedom of association within society follows from Article 9 I BL;
- freedom of association with regard to the right to collective bargaining follows from Article 9 (3) BL.

As a 'conjunct institution' of a freedom-based system, the contract conveys the totality of economic relationships between competitors. (ibid.: 96f)

In light of the above, Article 14.1, the *guarantee of property*, is the central clause. How are we to understand it? (see ibid.: 109ff). In several rulings the Federal Constitutional Court has given the impression that 'property' here implies the material enabling of individual freedom. This so-called human rights argument, which takes up Hegel's idealist philosophy, has been rendered obsolete by the facts of the post-industrial situation. First, the overwhelming majority of the population have now been forced to become employees, having been excluded from the material conditions of property ownership as a means of making a living. Second, the dynamics of capital accumulation have given rise to business undertakings in the form of joint-stock companies, thereby reducing the ideal model of the owner-entrepreneur to a few exceptions.

As a result another argument has gained ground as a major justification for the capitalist market economy, associated with Adam Smith. It claims that the competitive struggle, where the 'invisible hand' of the market pits individuals against each other in an egoistic free-for-all, benefits everyone. The costs this model inflicts on society and the environment are simply brushed out of the picture.

The Federal Constitutional Court has used a 'trick' in order to overcome the lack of plausibility in its person-related legitimization of property by simultaneously incorporating rights under public law – such as pensions and workers' share in company decision-making (*Mitbestimmung*) – into the definition of property. It thus creates the illusion that ownership of the means of production and employee status are equivalent. Rittstieg (1975: 363) writes, therefore, with justification:

> If it is claimed that this constitutional article is intended to protect the domination of industry by managers and large share-holders, we may as well give up talking about human rights and their relation to the free development of personality. The function of the basic right would then be equivalent to the protection of feudal rule, granted by the king under duress to the English barons in 1215 in the form of the Magna Carta. In the same way that the villeins in the Magna Carta were accessories of the land they worked (albeit with the freedom to leave granted in law, if not always in fact), wage- and salary-earners would similarly be accessories of capital.

What is actually guaranteed by the term 'property' according to Article 14 (1)? It is 'the exclusive power of disposal regardless of whatever form of use it takes ... Thanks to the undisputed, universal validity of property the sum total of the material results generated in making a living is put to exclusively private use: therefore the acquisition of property becomes fundamental to the way of life of all members of society' (Krölls 1998: 116f). However, this means that the majority of the population are excluded from organizing their own livelihood and are thus forced into wage dependency on the property-owners. In other words, through its abstract guarantee of property, the state establishes a capitalist economic order in which the majority of people have no choice but to take up employment in order to support themselves, and thereby generate wealth for the property owners. 'The objective purpose of the production system guaranteed under Article 14 is the accumulation (by definition unlimited) of abstract, private wealth. Conceived in general terms, this wealth enjoys a separate existence: perfect, divorced from its use and reduced to a purely quantitative dimension in the state-authorised form of money (Article 73 [4] BL)' (ibid.: 120).

In constitutional law the term used for this abstract property is assets. In other words, property is measured in terms of monetary value. This once again makes it clear that property is seen not in terms of use justified by need, but in terms of abstract wealth and its increase.

Personal property is only a derivative of this abstract wealth. Citizens are placed on the same footing regarding the abstract concept of property, which gives them a semblance of equality. In this way the

Basic Law also appears to be neutral with regard to the economic order, whereas in fact it has clearly opted for the possessive market economy. Moreover, the guarantee of the law of succession ensures the perpetuation of the propertied class within society.

The state defines the *content and limits of property*. To what does this definition refer? (see ibid.: 125ff). By its monetary sovereignty the state establishes abstract wealth as the 'economic general purpose' of society. The state also lays down general ground rules and specific laws to deal with the relationship between economic subjects (actors) (Article 74 BL). It intervenes in the area of land ownership through spatial planning and support for agriculture (Articles 74 and 75 BL). It has the power to implement policies to protect the environment because, if left to itself, the purely possessive market economy destroys the natural resources needed for production (ibid.). Finally, the state has the right to levy taxes (Article 104aff BL), enabling it to cream off part of the wealth produced by society. All these state functions are oriented towards the smooth running of the possessive market economy.

There are three possible interpretations of the idea that '*property entails obligations*' and 'its use shall also serve the public good', as laid down in Article 14.2 BL.

1. The German Federal Court (BGH) represents the radical liberal position, turning the property-owner's desire into a constitutional principle and making restriction the exception rather than the rule – as did the supreme court of the Reich during the Weimar Republic (see Rittstieg 1975: 291ff and 393).

2. The Federal Constitutional Court requires the legislative body to implement a superficial, non-integrated compensatory policy 'in respect of rulings according to the spirit of Article 14 para. 1, clause 2 BL, in order to give equal weighting to both the constitutional recognition of private property in Article 14 para. 1 BL and the social requirement given in Article 14 para. 2 BL' (Federal Constitutional Court, JZ 1981: 828; see Krölls 1988: 130). Similar wording already existed in earlier regulations defining property: 'the interests of the community are to be weighed equally against the interests of the individual. The common good serves both as a point of reference and a limit to the restrictions placed on the property owner' (Federal Constitutional Court: 25, 112, 118; see also Rittstieg 1975: 393).

3. On the other hand, Krölls argues convincingly that this is really a state guarantee, ensuring that the pursuit of competitive interests

based on the property guarantee shall not conflict with the interests of the common good. This would of course threaten the possessive market economy in itself. It is, therefore, a question of maintaining the functional competence of an economic and social order founded on the private ownership of the means of production.

Once again the workings of the Basic Law become clear. On the one hand it remains consistent with the welfare state approach in accordance with ordo-liberal and Keynesian economic theory, in that it carries forward the liberal basis whereby the pursuit of individual interests theoretically serves the common good by increasing society's wealth. However, this hinges on the proviso that the state will provide a regulatory framework for this functional relationship within the capitalist market economy and will intervene when necessary.

We owe it to the struggles of the labour movement, as well as the catastrophic events of 1929, that a state-implemented social commitment to the common good on the part of private ownership became possible. However, we must emphasize once again that there is no implication here that the capitalist abstract accumulation of wealth should be relinquished: rather the opposite, its functioning should be safeguarded.

This becomes clear when we take another look at other articles of the Basic Law relating to the theme of property. Because of the obligation, reinforced by the case law of the above two federal courts, to provide compensation in cases of expropriation (Article 14 [3]) – according to market values – the social commitment aspect of private property recedes more and more in favour of preserving the value of private assets (Rittstieg 1975: 396ff and 411ff; Krölls 1988: 130f).

Article 74 (16) BL gives the state the right to legislate with regard to competition in order to 'prevent the abuse of economic power'. This implies that the classical liberal idea, i.e. letting the market work out its own way of dealing with competition, has been abandoned. It is accepted as a matter of principle that economic concentration of power will inevitably take place within the legally constituted capitalist economic order. Evidently this is not criticized in itself, so long as the abstract wealth of society – privately acquired and creamed off in part by the state – grows with it. The only practice to be prevented is abuse, and anti-trust laws are used, in keeping with tradition. In this way, as in the other instances of state intervention, it is intended that the workings of the possessive market economy shall be guaranteed by means of a compensatory mechanism.

Article 15 BL presents a particular problem with regard to the commons. The pivotal clause reads: 'Land, natural resources and means of production may for the purpose of socialisation [nationalization] be transferred into common ownership or other forms of public enterprise by means of a law that determines the nature and extent of compensation.'

The parliamentary group of the Social Democratic Party (SPD) pushed this article through in the Parliamentary Council, obviously with specific ideas in mind. However, after the SPD narrowly lost the first federal parliamentary elections and the private enterprise faction carried the day, thanks to the CDU/CSU (a long-standing coalition between the Christian Democratic Union and the mainly Bavarian Christian Socialist Union), this article lost importance. (Rittstieg 1975: 401; Krölls 1988: 169ff and 235ff). It was written only as a discretionary provision and therefore had no binding significance in the face of the universal guarantee of private property. This regulation thus became one of a number of compensatory powers which enabled the state to take on the role of economic protagonist, nationalizing property in order to safeguard the possessive market society. This has rarely involved the state removing lucrative investment opportunities from private industry; it intervenes in macroeconomic areas of activity in order to cut losses.

The same applies to the restrictions placed on land ownership. The focus here is on spatial planning, environmental protection (not included in the original Basic Law) and municipal ownership of land. With regard to the latter, Krölls goes so far as to say that the fact that ground rent is collected by the community rather than the landowner is irrelevant to the interests of capital (Krölls 1988: 179ff). At the end of the day, even in this instance the state is simply nurturing the overall reproductive capability of a possessive market society (based on private property).

Because the state guarantees this reproductive capability, it has the right to levy taxes (Articles 105 and 106 BL) and thus carry out property's obligation to society, as enshrined in Article 14.2. This is crucial to judging the constitutional legitimacy of the economic and political action in any given situation – a point to which we shall return later. During the ordo-liberal or Keynesian phase of the Federal Republic, at any rate once the Basic Law came into force, the state respected this constitutional mandate. By exercising overall control of the economy

and by introducing a progressive tax system, the state provided for
social balance to keep the property-based market economy afloat
(ibid.: 372ff).

The definitions of the FRG as a '*democratic and social federal state*'
(Article 20 [1] BL) and as a 'democratic and social state governed by
the rule of law' (Article 28 [1] BL) sum up the different elements
which give the state its role as guarantor of the possessive market
society. The welfare state requirement is not couched in anti-capitalist
terms, referring rather to the compensatory power of the state intended to keep precisely this economic system viable – which is
something.

A question that was given no consideration whatsoever in the
original Keynesian and ordo-liberal model was that of 'limits to
growth' with respect to the environmental effects of a growth
economy. It was only in later amendments to the Basic Law that the
foundations were laid for state legislation. In widening the idea of an
obligation to society (*Sozialpflichtigkeit*) to include nature, we therefore now speak of the obligation to sustain life (*Lebenspflichtigkeit*).
However, when the state imposed environmental restrictions on industry it was very careful to employ strategies that were compatible
with the market. The most recent example is the struggle over the
abolition of atomic power stations in Germany. The state had to agree
to a period of thirty years before they could be shut down, in order to
avoid facing impossible demands for compensation. The same applies
to the lowering of CO_2 emissions. This was taken to the extreme by
President Bush, who argued that the USA would not even sign up to
the already half-hearted Kyoto Protocol on climate change because it
would damage the American economy.

The destruction of nature and of social cohesion by private property in the context of neo-liberal globalization

It has become clear that the idea of property entailing a social
obligation within the capitalist economic and social order grew out of
various historical factors:
- the struggle of the labour movement, which had gained in strength;
- the competitive stance towards socialism;
- the experience of the catastrophic failure of liberalism in 1929;
- the interest of the Fordist economy in creating mass purchasing
  power;

- the relatively influential role of the nation-state;
- the exploitation of nature in the interests of economic growth, with apparent impunity.

The methods used by globalized capital to drive up profits What caused capital and politics to revoke this 'historic compromise'? (see Lisbon, The Group of, 1993; Roth 1999; Dierckxsens, 1998 and 2001). The touchstone of capitalist economics is the maximization of profit, i.e. the accumulation of capital (property), which is measured in money. The achievement of this fundamental aim depends on the success of competition with other capital owners in the production and marketing of goods. As markets are increasingly saturated with consumer goods, competition drives manufacturers to bring new products on to the market as fast as possible. However, in a highly developed technical age this means that time and time again new and costly investments have to be made before the earlier investments have had a chance to pay for themselves. It also means higher marketing costs. Simultaneously, attempts are made to cut costs by increasing the growth rate through higher productivity, but this of course means job cuts. As a result, both purchasing power and investment in the production of simple goods go by the board (see Chapter 6). The globalization of the market means that the nation-state has less and less power to intervene in economic policy when social considerations dictate. Instead capital employs every conceivable means to drive profits ever higher, without any consideration for people and the environment, and in this way evades the constitutional obligation to sustain life. Here are a few examples:

1. One method is *'just-in-time' production*, relating to out-sourcing of production units to subcontractors, also a form of *lean production*. As a consequence, smaller and medium-sized firms are put under pressure to compete with each other in order to take on the costs both of storage and of meeting supply deadlines. At the same time employees of such firms have fewer opportunities to organize themselves with the help of factory committees. Jeremy Rifkin has examined an advanced form of this subcontracting in what he calls 'hypercapitalism' (Rifkin 2000; see also Gorz 2001). According to him, many firms, for example Nike, no longer even have production plants and now supply only designs and names. Nike has shoes made in poor countries in the southern hemisphere, paying the lowest of wages and imposing in-

humane working conditions, only to market them at the highest possible prices. Other examples include fast-food chains like McDonald's, which likewise only sells the name, while forcing subcontractors to slavishly fulfil the prescribed conditions by exploiting their workers.

2. At the same time, large-scale capital ownership tries as far as possible to replace human labour with technology. The resultant structural unemployment is then used as a justification for lower wages and worsening working conditions. Here, consistent with its own nature, the *exclusiveness of private property* is heightened. This was used in the first stages of capitalist evolution to secure manpower: after all, those who had been excluded still possessed their own capacity to work, which they could then offer to the capitalist market. However, structural unemployment, while cutting capital expenditure, results in the exclusion of a growing number of people even from such limited participation in the economic process. In other words, private ownership of the means of production excludes the majority of the population not only from the material conditions needed to sustain life, but even from the opportunity to earn a living by working to increase profits to the benefit of the rich. In this way exclusion has, together with exploitation, become the dominant characteristic of the globalized capitalist economy. As a further consequence, the state, or more accurately those who (still) pay taxes, have to bear the social costs of capital accumulation.

3. Another way to increase profit is not to reinvest at all in the real economy, but instead to create shake-out competition by investing the profit in mergers. Another alternative is to accumulate capital by means of other *speculative finance* deals. The mergers and speculative finance deals produce no growth at all for the real economy and only an ever-increasing concentration of capital ownership, plus an ever-expanding financial bubble (casino capitalism). The high yields in this sector in turn exercise an additional pressure on the real economy to lower costs in order to guarantee a similar net product (see point 2 above). Most importantly, though, this creates the risk of financial crashes that could plunge the entire world economy into disaster, as happened in 1929.

4. However, the globalized capitalist economy simultaneously exerts *pressure on national governments* to improve their profits in various ways. It does this, first, by threatening to withdraw capital and invest it in other countries, where conditions can be exploited more

favourably, and, second, by promoting the blatant lie that jobs will be created through lower taxes and higher subsidies for capital. The mendacity of this argument was exposed as early as 1996, following the Human Development Report by the United Nations Development Programme (UNDP), entitled 'Jobless Growth'. In spite of this, governments still pursued the policy of supporting big business through subsidies and the lowering of taxes. Not only do further subsidies gained from tax revenues flow into structurally precarious production areas such as coal, shipyards and agriculture, but they are also poured into other areas, in particular high-tech industry. In Germany the proportion of taxes on profits in relation to overall tax revenue fell from 32.6 per cent in 1960 to 12.3 per cent in 1998. Wealth tax was abolished under the Kohl government. Under the red–green coalition, with its fiscal reforms, this trend continued unbroken. The government lowered the top rate of income tax, and abolished taxes on sales of company shares. The latter merely served to increase the merger frenzy, and naturally there was great approbation in the stock exchanges and large banks. In 2000 Jürgen Schrempp, the chairman of the board of directors of Germany's largest industrial corporation, DaimlerChrysler, boasted that the company didn't pay a penny in tax. Conversely the tax on earnings of dependent labour rose by 76 per cent between 1980 and 1995, exacerbated by the continual raising of value added tax, which particularly affects the poorer sections of the population. In its reform of pensions the red–green coalition government broke up the traditional solidarity-based system in two ways. First, it based part of the provision for old age on private capital investment. Second, it used tax revenue effectively to replace the legal requirement of an employer to contribute 50 per cent of pension insurance (a system based on parity).

5. By taking advantage of economic, especially financial, globalization to *evade tax*, property-owners evade the social obligation of ownership much more directly than by influencing legislation. It has long been known that transnational companies (TNCs) engage in price transfer manipulation, managing their accounts internally within the group so that large sums are dealt with in countries with low tax rates, and small accounts end up in countries with normal rates of tax. However, the worst example is the tax evasion of finance capital and, above all, the evasion of tax on interest payments. In Germany the trade union of inland revenue employees estimated an annual loss of

DM130 billion, which is likely to be lower than the actual figure. It was not only Helmut Kohl's own neo-liberal governments from 1982 to 1998 which capitulated to this – the next government followed suit by lowering taxes instead of employing more tax fraud investigators. In 1996 the leader of the German union of inland revenue employees wrote: 'Taking into account the deterrent factor, the addition of 7,000 new inspectors would bring in over DM30 billion in revenue.'[2] Clearly we are dealing here with a complicity between the state and capital owners. It is evident that this problem, particularly in respect of abolishing tax havens, has to be dealt with now – ideally on a global level, but at least within the European Union (EU). Yet apart from occasionally paying lip-service to the idea, western European governments show no sign of any real political will to tackle the problem. After all, Luxembourg, one of the principal tax havens, is part of the EU. Far from fighting tax evasion, countries refinance revenue loss by cutting social services.

6. The *national debt* itself is generated by business via the various mechanisms that have been described, and is the most perverse method by which property reneges on its obligation to society. In Germany the public budgets were in debt to the tune of DM2.3 trillion in 1997/8, and the debt mountain is growing every year (see Roth 1999: 175ff). In all, at least 25 per cent of tax revenue goes into debt servicing. In Belgium the figure is 30 per cent, i.e. nearly a third. 'This is how the state ends up paying by far the largest part of its debt interest to private enterprise' (Lafontaine and Müller 1998: 264). The few taxes that big business still pays are recuperated via loans to the state. In other words, tax evasion yields a double return. At the same time wage earners pay ever-increasing taxes – which they cannot avoid – including value added taxes on consumer products and services. This is tantamount to paying subsidies to private business.

7. The *privatization* of state-owned enterprises and public services is yet another means of reducing the social obligation of property. This is because, according to the rules of the game, only the 'prime investment choice' will be privatized, while necessary social services that yield no profit remain in state hands. In this way the state is no longer able to offset losses in one area with profits in another. On top of this, the federal government takes over debts and pension funds – as in the case of the privatization of the postal services and the railways – and this only increases the national debt. Add to this the job cuts

that follow privatization, which likewise have a negative effect on the public purse – not to mention the corruption that accompanies privatization – and we have privatized profits and nationalized losses.

8. This development reaches its logical conclusion in the *privatization of the environment and the elements basic to life*. Let us give some examples. Basic water supplies to populations are increasingly being privatized – which led to an all-out civil war in Cochabamba, Bolivia, because the poor were not able to pay the inflated prices (see Juhasz 2001; also Chapter 7). Air pollution is being turned into a tradable commodity by the Kyoto Protocol. Multinationals have long been stealing the few remaining indigenous seed varieties from developing countries, in order to alter a single gene, patent it and then sell the seed back to the farmers every year at a high price, along with fertilizers and pesticides. The most iniquitous example of this whole activity is inserting terminator genes, making it impossible for farmers to keep seed from their own harvests.[3] Genetic engineering holds out terrifying prospects for the future. The privatization of human genes exposes them to endless manipulation – with wholly unpredictable consequences (Rifkin 2000: 66ff).

What does this development signify from the point of view of property?

- at one extreme, an excessive concentration of capital in its various forms – indeed, ever-tightening control in the hands of the capital owners;[4]
- the disabling of workers (their ownership of their capacity to work) by making the labour market more 'flexible';
- the exclusion of those who are not able to make a living from either of the forms of ownership;
- the destruction of the natural basis of all forms of life on this planet by transforming it into an object of private capitalist interest;
- at the other extreme, the mutation of the state from a servant of the common good into a pawn of the interests of private capital.

The enforcement of neo-liberal globalization How did it arise, this model of capital ownership based on wealth accumulation without any social or environmental responsibility or any obligation to uphold the foundations of life? Which economic, political, military and ideological factors were responsible for its implementation? Any attempt to answer this will depend on one's understanding of the term 'neo-liberal globalization'. In view of the extensive literature that has since become available, we shall limit ourselves to an outline of the main features.[5]

The imperial beginnings of globalization, which were rooted in antiquity, were only able to gain ground as a universal force after the discovery that the world was round. Emperor Charles V described the first empire of this new era – that of sixteenth-century Spain – in these terms: 'The sun never sets on my empire.' The later colonial empires of the European nations followed, led first by Holland and then England, before the United States took over the hegemonic role in the twentieth century (see Duchrow 2000c: 392ff).

It was in 1944, at the international monetary and financial conference at Bretton Woods, that the USA began to set a course towards neo-liberal globalization (see Duchrow 1995: 95ff). Keynes had proposed an international ordering of the post-war economy which corresponded to the socially regulated market economy of Western nations. Among his proposals were: an independent international currency; a monetary fund on the model of a central bank; a structural fund to stabilize development, similar to the current European Regional Development Fund; and a world trade system intended to ensure a balance of interests in terms of development by taxing countries with a balance-of-trade surplus. This set of proposals was rejected by the USA and its chief negotiator, Harry Dexter White. Instead the USA imposed the idea of the dollar as a world currency, albeit linked to the gold standard and its exchange rate tied to the main currencies of Europe and Japan. The central bank became the International Monetary Fund and the development fund turned into a World Bank. As for the plan for an international trade system, all that remained in the following years was GATT, with its mission to achieve widespread reduction of trade restrictions.

This gave the powerful industrial companies and the large commercial banks of the USA the opportunity to begin their triumphal march into every country, except those with socialist governments. They turned into TNCs with their production centres and markets spread across all continents, financed with the help of the strong dollar. Following the collapse of the Soviet Union and the development of computers and communication technology, the TNCs have since developed worldwide component production networks (global sourcing) and global marketing, through which they can exploit the tiniest price advantage for each component in every corner of the globe, in order to put an end product on the market at the lowest possible cost and thus beat their competitors (see, e.g., Rifkin 2000: 16ff). Once they have achieved a monopoly through mergers and takeovers, or negotiated price agreements with the remaining oligopolies, they can dictate prices. In so doing they play unions, suppliers and governments off against each other in order to save on wages, storage, taxes and environmental protection costs. The single-minded aim of these companies is to maximize profits on their invested capital. Social and environmental obligations are largely eliminated.

If we turn now to the *finance sector*, the strong European banks had been trying since the 1960s to circumvent their own currencies and conduct their international transactions directly on the dollar markets. This led to the 'Euro-markets' (see Duchrow 1995: 69ff; Kairos Europa/WEED 2000: 12f). Excess cash flow on the dollar markets, over and above the inflation caused by the Vietnam War, forced President Nixon to revoke the gold parity – first in 1971 then finally in 1973. This resulted in the collapse of the system of fixed exchange rates. At the same time offshore centres came into being as non-regulated finance markets (see Kairos Europa/WEED 2000: 12 and 27f). In this climate the exchange rates were left to the markets, which led to ever greater extremes of speculation and uncertainty on the money markets. The insurance derivatives introduced to counteract this became themselves the object of speculation.[6] It was in this context that the term casino capitalism was coined, to describe a world economy dominated by speculative finance capital.

Another significant step towards a globalized casino economy came in 1979 with the decision by the US Federal Reserve Bank to introduce a *monetarist policy* (see Duchrow 1995: ch. III.2). The other central banks followed suit, reducing their interest policy to securing currency stability in the interests of the owners of capital assets. In addition, the interest on loans was left up to the markets. This, combined with Reagan's credit-funded militarism, led to a sharp rise in interest rates and to a historically unique period of high interest rates, i.e. to persistently high inflation-adjusted interest rates (see among others Kairos Europa/WEED 2000: 14f). Although the real interest rate did indeed fall to 1 per cent at the beginning of 2001, the fact remains that on the deregulated transnational money markets the interest rate continues to exceed the growth rate of the real economy, particularly with regard to debt rescheduling for developing countries. The result is a permanent redistribution from debtors to creditors – and not only from direct debtors but from the majority of the population, since, for example, in Germany these days the proportion of interest constitutes on average 30 to 40 per cent of all prices, rents and taxes. Only approximately 10 per cent of the population earn more interest that they pay indirectly (see Fischbeck 1996: 668). Moreover, this system also drives money into attractive financial investment instead of into investment in production.

Another well-documented, if indirect, consequence of this high interest policy was that every country that had run up debts using easy money before 1979 fell inextricably into the *debt trap*. And no matter how much they paid back – at ever-greater cost to their own populations – the debts grew larger. In 1982 Mexico was the first country to go bankrupt. This was when the International Monetary Fund (IMF) came into its own. The G7 group of the world's richest nations used the IMF to organize rescue packages from public revenue for the countries now plunged into crisis – a crisis that had been caused by the unscrupulous interest-earning tactics of the capital owners. But the rescue packages served only to bail out the creditors, not the people affected by the debt. (Let us not forget: at the same time that this was going on, business was paying less and less tax, which means that here too those dependent on working for the capital owners were, and are once again, being asked to pay up.) The IMF, on the other hand, imposed the famous structural adjustment programmes (SAPs) on countries whose excessive public debts had now made them dependent. These programmes force the countries first to reorient their economies towards imports and exports – in other words, towards the world market – and second to abolish controls on the movement of capital. Last but not least, they force countries to reduce their public services by imposing austerity measures, privatizing services and thus driving the majority of the population into poverty and misery. Even the World Bank has given credit only when countries stick to this policy of impoverishment in the short-term interests of capital ownership. As early as 1988 an African delegate at an ecumenical hearing asked the IMF representative what he would think of a doctor who dispensed as a remedy the very poison that had caused the illness. The cynicism of this policy reaches its nadir when the IMF and World

Bank try to offset criticism by claiming that their new policy is fighting poverty – when in fact poverty persists through the very structures of the SAPs.

However, as the example of Germany has already demonstrated, it is not only developing countries which are driven to excessive public debt by the various mechanisms of capital in order to make them submissive to the whims of private interests. The same happens even to rich countries themselves. Monetary policy, which is only interested in supporting currency stability, combines with its associated economizing measures to propel unemployment and social disintegration forward. Worst of all, the deregulation of the transnational capital markets and the associated tax havens are exploited for massive tax evasion. In other words, in all corners of the globe capital owners and managers are using the globalized economy to maximize their profits at the expense of the common good.

The international institutions – the G7/G8 world economic summits, the IMF, the World Bank, the Organization for Economic Cooperation and Development (OECD) and the World Trade Organization (WTO), which are dominated by the rich nations, are used as a political means to this end. These last two have been involved in pushing through a Multilateral Agreement on Investments (MAI), which forbids governments to place social and environmental obligations on invested capital. Such obligations on capital would even be punishable. Social forces were previously effective in preventing this kind of assault on the common good, and actually succeeded in convincing the French government to vote against this plan. And yet a new draft of the MAI is being prepared within the WTO.

The governments of the rich nations have used the same organization to launch yet another attack on the common good: the General Agreement on Trade in Services (GATS).[7] This involves transferring all public and particularly municipal services such as water, electricity and (local) transport into private ownership. As we have already seen, this leads both to price rises – which means that poor people especially are not able to pay for these services – and to a reduction in quality.

By using these undemocratic institutions, the rich nations led by the USA have succeeded in pushing the United Nations more and more to the margins. UNCTAD, ECOSOC and UNDP are only shadows of their former selves. And the arrogant behaviour of the USA at world conferences of the United Nations is unsurpassed. Its

representatives walk out when something doesn't suit them, as happened in 2001 during the conference to combat racism in Durban.
On 16 October 2001, during the preparatory stages of the UN
Conference on Financing for Development, the US representative,
Terry Miller, declared bluntly: 'We start with three commitments: a
commitment to peace; a commitment to freedom and rule of law;
and a commitment to capitalism. Governments that make these commitments have a chance to develop. Governments that do not have
no chance at all.'This is how he had earlier explained the commitment to capitalism: 'We need to be absolutely clear that when we talk
about financing for development, we are talking about the sustainable
development of economies in the capitalist model, for it is the only
model that we know works.'

Furthermore, the organizations of the UN are increasingly infiltrated by the TNCs. Everywhere powerful lobbies of capital sit in
the control centres.[8] The neo-liberal globalization of the possessive
market economy therefore not only has destructive economic, social
and ecological consequences but also destroys *democracy* itself. People
have fewer and fewer opportunities to influence the political decisions that determine their lives, and the 'political fatigue' which we
have increasingly witnessed grows from this. Electoral participation is
on the decline in most countries. What is the point of voting when all
the big parties have either dedicated themselves to neo-liberalism or
surrendered to it?

The hyper-capitalism of intellectual and cultural property But
over time capitalism discovered that the human mind itself, its body,
spirit and culture, could all be exploited for their accumulist potential,
and so they too were included in its strategy. This forms the thesis of
Jeremy Rifkin's latest book (Rifkin 2000; see also Gorz 2001: 33ff).

We need first to clarify the terms used. Rifkin asserts that the category of *property* essential to the foundation of classical capitalism has
been replaced by the term *access* in the new capitalism. However, the
examples he uses demonstrate that he understands property in terms
of industrial machinery and consumer goods. These are becoming
less interesting to the global players of capitalism. In the new forms
of capitalist economics the objective remains the relentless pursuit of
more *capital assets*. Property is even defined legally as assets. Thus the
multiplying of these assets through the commercial exploitation of

life's last remaining territories remains the unaltered objective of the new hyper-capitalist paradigm.

The networking of computer systems through the internet provides the technological basis for the new hyper-capitalism (Rifkin 2000: 16ff; Gorz 2001: 33). This is how the lean production mentioned earlier is made possible. The large TNCs which dominate the market maintain control and keep most of the profits using finance and distribution channels. At the same time electronic networking stimulates the perpetual innovation conditioned by competition, and consequently the lifespan of products is foreshortened. This then leads to a situation where products are sold less and less frequently, but are instead leased with follow-up services until the replacement product yields subsequent contracts. At the same time the process of making money invisible by using electronic systems and the associated 'financial services' misleads people into buying or leasing on credit rather than spending their savings – and because of the interest involved in these transactions, this means a double gain for the capital owners and increased dependency for the consumers.

Central to this shift is the colonization of intellect, life and culture by capital in its quest to accumulate more wealth. The 'knowledge economy' privatizes knowledge, which used to be publicly funded from tax revenue via the education and research institutions. By its very nature it builds on the work and experience of earlier as well as contemporary generations, and since knowledge is common property, it also prospers best in free exchange. The Internet, originally developed by the Pentagon for intelligence purposes, could ironically provide the vehicle for promoting the open communication that is so quintessential to knowledge. (Indeed, it performs this function within the various alternative movements, to which we will return later.) But within the capitalist society knowledge, as private property, has to serve the accumulation of assets, and so it must be made inaccessible to others. A direct example of this is the private companies' leasing of goods and services the production codes of which are kept secret (*franchising*). An indirect example is the *patenting of intellectual property* and the lucrative marketing opportunities this affords.

Patenting is defined by capitalist ownership's two primary features: the exclusion of others and the techniques for accumulating assets. The patent comes into its own in the new phase of global capitalism when we consider the *life-science industry*. This is directed at plants, animals and human beings themselves (Rifkin 1998: 37ff and 2000: 64ff; Lappé and Bailey 1998; Wörner 2000). Jeremy Rifkin ascribes the same importance to the privatization of life – its patenting with its dramatic long-term consequences – as to the enclosure of common land which, as we have already said, marked the beginning of capitalist development in the early modern age.

Originally humans abode by the maxim that nature could only be discovered, not invented. And this is also how the US Patent Technology Office (PTO) ruled in 1971 when the Indian microbiologist Ananda Chakrabarty, an employee of General Electric, attempted to file a patent on a genetically modified micro-organism that could eradicate oil from the surface of the sea. Chakrabarty appealed, and in 1980 the US Supreme Court ruled with a majority of one that *life is patentable*. The direct consequence: the shares of the life-science industry boomed. The indirect consequences of this watershed are unpredictable.

What had happened? The Supreme Court of one country had, with a majority of one, changed the world for ever. The first conclusion to be drawn from this is that property is a legal concept. In other words property, though fundamental to the capitalist economy, is not in itself an economic concept, and therefore cannot be regarded as part of the so-called autonomous economic laws. Rather, it is the sine qua non of an economy which then declares itself autonomous with the help of the market mechanism. This is important for our later considerations with regard to alternatives. Second, we see the common law of one country allowing a single court decision – and one that has been reached with a majority of only one – to unleash incalculable consequences not just for its own society, but for the whole of humankind, without even its own democratic institutions (let alone those of other peoples) having had the opportunity to discuss the likely consequences of such a decision and choose for themselves. The hegemonic role of the USA in the world economy and world politics, mediated through the multinational companies, is in itself clearly a threat to humankind.

Other rulings followed swiftly. In the USA the first patent was granted on a plant in 1985, followed in 1987 by the first on an animal, the onco-mouse. In 1990 the California Supreme Court ruled against a man called John Moore, whose rare blood protein had been passed on, patented and licensed to the Sandoz Corporation without his knowledge, by doctors treating him at the University of California. In Europe we see the European Commission taking the side of industry. The European Parliament in fact defended the non-patentability of life for a long time, only to enter into a compromise in 1998 with its biotechnology directive. Now in the European Union too human cells and genes can be patented along with genetically modified plants and animals, although a furious debate still rages in Europe over this issue.

A few examples should bear witness to the consequences, many of which are as yet incalculable.

In the context of plants the most brazen and ruthless form in which TNCs privatize and commercialize common property is bio-piracy. They finance expeditions to the southern hemisphere, exploiting indigenous knowledge in order to discover plants whose genes could be useful in pharmaceutical production or pest control (Wörner 2000: 38ff; Rifkin 1998: 48ff). They frequently destroy natural organic pesticides in the process, as happened in the case of *Bacillus thuringiensis* (Bt). This is because widespread planting of crops (maize, cotton, etc.) that have been modified using the Bt gene causes insects to become resistant so that the organic pesticides are no longer effective (see Lappé and Bailey 1998).

The most serious consequence of the privatization of plants as intellectual property has to be the *monopolization of seed* by the TNCs. Their aim is to bring the entire world's seed under their control. Already only ten transnational companies control 32 per cent of the world's seed. The largest of these, including DuPont, Monsanto and Novartis, spend billions every year on buying up seed companies in order to reduce even further the number of firms within the oligopoly. Monsanto, for example, already controls 85 per cent of the cotton market in the US (Rifkin 2000: 66f). The effect on food production in countries in the southern hemisphere is totally destructive. The seed is manipulated in such a way that it has to be bought in conjunction with fertilizers and herbicides from the same companies. Moreover farmers are either not allowed to take their own seed from the harvest – which would enable them to develop by cultivating the land themselves – or else the terminator genes have made this impossible. Consequently, farmers who are able to buy this seed become dependent on the TNCs by paying tribute to them, while the other farmers have to give up – which brings a massive threat to the nutritional security of two-thirds of the world. This example illustrates more vividly than any other the fact that the possessive market economy is death-bringing. The starvation and death of millions of people are accepted as the price of achieving the maximum accumulation of capital.[9]

That the privatization of plants deals in death becomes even clearer when we consider its effect on the *extinction of species*. For example, if small farmers normally work with species suited to their particular region, then seed monopolization means that biodiversity is permanently threatened. This process started in the early twentieth century with the introduction of more modern uniform varieties, then took off in the Green Revolution in the 1960s and 1970s. Since then 'around three-quarters of the genetic variety of plants beneficial to agriculture have been lost worldwide' (Wörner 2000: 30). In response to this gene banks were organized, with 93 per cent of the stored genetic material originating in the South. It was initially regarded as the 'common heritage of humankind'. Through the Biodiversity Convention of 1992 control of plant diversity in any given country was granted to the government of that country. Now the TNCs, if they are not engaging in direct piracy, are making strenuous efforts to reach favourable agreements with individual countries, in order to be able to exploit their genetic resources (ibid.: 46ff).

Increasingly the same mechanisms apply to the privatizing of animals through patenting. These no longer pass into the buyer's ownership, but are leased. For example, calves or lambs no longer belong to the farmer. Instead, for every newborn animal, a fee has to be paid to the firm that owns the patent as its intellectual property (Rifkin 2000: 69).

In the case of human beings the TNCs have begun a race to patent as many as possible of the approximately 50,000 genes that make up the human genome. Once they have these under their control, the next step is to examine the potential use for medicines and therapeutic procedures. Patented monopolization of intellectual ownership brings automatic profits to the tune of millions for the capital owners of the winning firms in the case of a human gene that proves to be successful pharmaceutically. On the other hand, public health provision is ever more threatened because the financing of medicines can no longer be guaranteed. The classic case between the South African government and the TNCs that produce the drugs to combat AIDS is a foretaste of what is in store worldwide. In this case, too, death is the consequence of a system which, through the exclusive right of ownership, places the capital accumulation of property-owners above the lives of human beings.

The main tool employed by transnational capital, supported by the rich industrial nations, to privatize life internationally is the WTO, or more precisely the *trade-related intellectual property rights (TRIPs)* (Wörner 2000: 56ff; Rifkin 1998: 51ff). The principal aim of the WTO, founded in 1994 as a result of the GATT talks in Uruguay, is the liberalization of trade. Signatory states may introduce trading restrictions only against products that have been scientifically proven to cause identifiable harm. Taking precautions in the case of suspected risks is not allowed. This is a preliminary decision based on Western knowledge which is claimed to be neutral but is in fact colluding with private industry – with potentially fatal consequences. Hans-Jochen Luhmann (2001), a researcher at the Wuppertal Institute, gave a remarkable lecture on North German Radio in 2000 entitled 'Certain knowledge – the god to whom we make human sacrifices today'. Using the examples of the sleeping pill thalidomide causing deformities, and a wood preservative containing dioxin causing severe harm to health, he demonstrated that, even after circumstantial evidence aroused strong suspicions, thousands more fell victim to these dangerous compounds because the companies threatened legal action. This is because legally only unequivocal 'scientific' proof counts. The perpetrators thus went unpunished because they simply maintained that in the absence of scientifically proven evidence they were not aware of any danger.

The purpose of the TRIPs agreement was to protect the economic and governmental interests of the industrial nations within the framework of the WTO, in particular by preventing the manufacture of imitation Western products in developing countries. As a result, 'the costs of health provision in developing countries rose by a factor of between five and ten' (Wörner 2000: 57). It is true that a country can exclude plant varieties from patenting in a so-called *sui generis* system, and that the poorest countries have been granted conversion periods up to 2005, but the disadvantages for these countries are enormous. First their sovereignty over their genetic resources is annulled by privatization. Second, their indigenous knowledge is exploited as a compass, guiding bounty-hunters to the discovery of pharmaceutically important genes – all of which is helped by the lack of clarity in the definitions of invention and discovery. Then the hard work of local farmers, who have developed useful plants over centuries, is totally disregarded. And above all, as we have already mentioned, the food security of developing countries is threatened. Any efforts on their part to achieve a revision of TRIPs were thwarted by various tricks employed by the USA and the EU – as happened again at the WTO Conference in 2001 (ibid.: 79ff).

The bio-sciences will be for the twenty-first century what atomic physics was for the twentieth. They will form the nucleus of the possessive market economy in the future, and it is from them that the major dangers for the future of humankind and the earth will emanate.

However, all this will not simply be forced on to individuals and populations directly; instead they will be seduced by *cultural capitalism*. Rifkin compares this process also to the enclosure of common land at the beginning of the modern age. Here he calls it 'enclosing the cultural commons' (Rifkin 2000: 135ff). Whatever was formerly established and nurtured in the close context of creative human relationships within their respective cultural communities is now the subject of global commercialization. It is not only the classic consumer culture which is responsible here, but also the marketing of prefabricated experiences, which applies equally to both tourism and the new shopping-centre culture. Counter-cultural forms of expression, such as the environmental movements, have also been incorporated into the new culture of fun and lifestyle. Even ethics and religion become useful promoters of commercialization, as Bolz and Bosshart (1995) have cynically described: 'Ethics sells better'. Thus the American way of life is becoming a global, homogenized culture.

The empire as the visible hand of the absolute possessive market The six global media giants have bought up the transmission frequencies from everywhere, with the result that in practical terms only their multi-media packages reach the far corners of the world (Rifkin 2000: 218ff). But of course, only those who can afford to pay have access to communication. Even in this area, private ownership either grants or denies access to people.

However, we must emphasize that the visible hand of the empire is still at work even in this instance. The secret strategic papers of the American military in 1987 and the policy documents Santa Fe I and II of the Reagan and Bush (Sr) administrations had already revealed that after the demise of Soviet power the objective was to wage a 'cultural war' in order to win the 'hearts and minds' of people for capitalism (see Duchrow et al. 1990).The victory of neo-liberalism cannot be explained other than in the context of the massive ideological war that was waged in schools, universities, the Churches and the mass media.[10] The neo-liberal ideology of the absolute market is presented as the only option, and all movements that resist it and its attendant injustices must therefore be opposed, including the international solidarity and human rights movements and liberation theology. For what is required is 'the domination and distribution of natural resources and of strategic raw materials' (ibid.: 55). In order to achieve this domination, neo-liberalism must wage its campaign at all 'levels of power', i.e. economic, political and military, and also on the 'socio-psychological' or cultural levels.

The Santa Fe IV policy document for President George W. Bush's government picks up this theme again.[11] It states among other things: 'The communists and leftwing activists of the United States are also gaining ground.They are following the agenda put forward several decades ago by Antonio Gramsci (1891–1937) and others in order to infiltrate this hemisphere.They do this via many channels: religion (liberation theology), the press, educational institutions through their links with culture (communism is alive and well in our universities), and through the justice system.'

It is to be expected that worldwide the new 'war on terrorism' will bring renewed pressure to bear on the protest movement against the 'economic horror' (Viviane Forrester). Instead of allowing the shock to change its view of the world and accepting an incentive to make a fresh start, the first global empire in the history of the world reveals its true colours as the vehicle for asserting the interests of absolute capital or – put another way – the dictatorship of property.We are no longer dealing with the imperialism of nation–states. Global empire and global capital are one and the same thing (see Negri and Hardt 2000; Negri 2001). If we summarize the various aspects of neo-liberal globalization, we reach the following conclusion:

Imperial globalization must eliminate every obstacle to total domination by the capitalist market, i.e. every obstacle to the ability of capital property to pursue unlimited wealth accumulation without any attendant obligation to sustain life.[12] As far as possible, every social and environmental restraint or obligation must be removed.

What does this mean? In German Basic Law these social and environmental obligations served no other purpose than to preserve the capitalist possessive market economy from the self-destruction suffered in 1929. Keynes had understood his interventions in the market economy in a similar way, i.e. that they were aimed at the self-preservation of liberal capitalism. If the accumulist model of neo-liberal globalization now seeks to tear down the protective walls against the mechanisms of social and ecological destruction that threaten both societies and the planet, then in so doing it is also bringing about its own destruction (see Mayer 1992). The total world market, nurtured and protected by its empire, threatens the whole of life on this earth. 'Destruction is self-destruction' (see Hinkelammert 2001a: 359ff).

Terrorism answers this neo-liberal, globalized terror of destruction and self-destruction using the same logic and providing the pretext for new direct imperial wars and the militarization of the capitalist economy in crisis.

Notes

1 Especially A. Müller-Armack and his student, Ludwig Erhard, the later minister of trade and commerce. The ordo-liberalists rejected laissez-faire liberalism in favour of a legally and socially regulated market economy.

2 *Die Woche*, 22 March 1996.

3 Rifkin 2000: 66 ff: 'The goal is to control, in the form of intellectual property, the entire seed stock of the planet.' See also Wörner 2000: 89f.

4 Neo-liberalism 'is the ideology by which power belongs to the strongest private interests in any given situation' according to Roth 1999: 387.

5 See, e.g., Altvater and Mahnkopf 1996; Duchrow 1995; Klingebiel and Randeria 1998; de Santa Ana 1998; Hinkelammert 1999a; Khor 2001; Koshy 2002; Mofid 2002.

6 For details of the speculative system today compare Kairos Europa/WEED 2000: chs 3 and 4; for derivatives especially, see 19ff. See also Dillon 1997.

7 See *Corporate Europe Observer*, 9, 2001: 11ff, and the international campaign Stop the GATS Attack, at<http://

www.citizen.org/pctrade/GATS/ GATSsignon. htm> and <http:// www.xs4all.nl/~ceo/gatswatch>

8 See the publications and website of Corporate Europe Observatory, Amsterdam, <http://www.xs4all.nl/~ceo/>

9 'If farmers can't plant the stuff that they harvest, and become totally dependent on this [i.e. seed that is limited to one year], you are really raising the ante on the possibility of mass starvation.' L. Busch, a sociologist at Michigan State University, quoted in Rifkin 2000: 69.

10 See Cockett 1994 on the meaning of think-tanks and Binswanger 1998b on the 'faith community of economists'.

11 See< www.geocities.com/ projectoemancipación>

12 On the totalitarian character of the capitalist market, see Hinkelammert 1984. Otherwise, for a more detailed discussion, see Kurz 1999: 524ff. On p. 524 he says: 'The modern concept of totality is only made possible at all when seen against the background of capital, with its inherent urge to become a total world force.'

I had trouble following the argument in this chapter

The fall of the Twin Towers: the enforcement of the total market through the absolute empire

§ The Bible of Bush against the Koran of the Taleban. The God of Bush against the Allah of the Taleban. What a world!

What has this to do with us? What has this to do with the possessive market economy? We live in an era of suicides.[1] It began in the 1970s with the collective suicide in Guyana, when in 1978 more than 600 followers of a sect from the United States led by Jim Jones committed collective suicide. Many others have imitated him. Later, in the 1980s, there were suicide murderers. They also appeared first of all in the United States. Initially they killed a great number of people they did not even know, and then they killed themselves. At first it seemed like a fashion in the USA, in schools, offices and on the streets. Shortly afterwards, suicide murderers appeared in the rest of the world: in Japan, China, Nepal, Africa, Europe, Ukraine and Russia. Soon after this murder and suicide were connected to political actions. The first Palestinian suicide attacks took place. In the USA, the Oklahoma bomber, Timothy McVeigh, appeared on the scene. Although he did not kill himself, he refused any opportunity for a judicial defence, and celebrated his execution as if it were a ritual. He portrayed himself (through the reading of the poem 'Invictus') as 'invincible'. Sometimes, suicide killers are religious people; their religiosity is founded in the monotheistic faiths. With the hope of a life after death they combine the hope that eternal life will be their reward for an admirable sacrifice of murder and suicide.

This connection between murder and suicide found its literary expression in the religious language of 1970s American Christian fundamentalists. H. Lindsey, one of the Rasputins in Reagan's court, mentions the Battle of Armageddon (Rev. 16: 16), taking it to mean atomic war. He says: 'When the battle of Armageddon reaches its feared high point and all earthly life appears to be on the verge of being extinguished, then just in that moment the Lord Jesus Christ will appear and will prevent total annihilation. As history moves ever faster towards this moment, I would like to ask the reader some questions: do you feel fear or hope for release? Your answer to this question will reveal your spiritual attitude.'[2] Here, collective suicide, connecting murder and suicide, is preached about as a spiritually heroic act. Lindsey's book was a bestseller in the 1970s in the USA, selling more than 15 million copies.

It is well known that in the 1970s Christian fundamentalists in the United States were chosen to stand by for the eventuality that the President would order the button that would initiate an atomic war to be pressed. Fundamentalists were chosen because it was certain that they would obey the commands. They even wished that such a command would come because they lived in the expectation of Christ's second coming. Atheists do not deserve such trust: they know only this life and are therefore not so willing to risk it.

In the case of Christian fundamentalists in the USA, the murderers commit murder and subsequently commit suicide, and expect to receive a reward in heaven for their actions. A very similar position was expressed by a German theologian several years before Lindsey. G. Gundlach (1958/59) said about a possible atomic war:

> Even for the possibility that the only result would be a manifestation of the majesty and order of God that we owe him as human beings, the duty and the right to defence of property is conceivable. Yes, even if the world should go under in the process, it is still not an argument against our thesis, firstly because we have the sure knowledge that the world will not last forever, and secondly because we are not responsible for the end of the world. We can then say that God the Lord, who has in his providence led or allowed us to end up in a situation where we need to show our faithfulness to his order, will also take responsibility for it.

From this it follows that religion – belief in God – is totally ambivalent. In the Christian religion too, the central thread of the Bible (i.e. God's solidarity with human beings, whose life is endangered through the idolization of power and riches) can be reversed. Then the God of life is transformed into an idol of death.

As far as 11 September is concerned, we find that the date has been historically significant twice. The first 11 September is that of 1973. Supported by the US government, the Chilean air force bombarded the Moneda, the seat of the Chilean government, and destroyed it. Salvador Allende, the elected president, was murdered in the presidential palace. The purpose was to prevent the democratic introduction of a form of socialism and to introduce a pure form of neo-liberalism for the first time. To this end Pinochet famously called on Milton Friedman of the Chicago School of Economics.

The attacks of the second 11 September in 2001, for which there can be no justification, destroyed the Twin Towers in New York and killed thousands of people. The murderers killed themselves in the course of their attacks. The attacks were regarded throughout the world as so shocking that they possibly represented a historical departure. We agree that this is in fact the case. But we have to ask ourselves why this is: in its own terms it is not so obvious. As an empirical fact, these attacks were not so very different from others that have occurred in the last one hundred years. There have been many worse attacks with much greater levels of destruction which people hardly remember now. Perhaps the attack on Hiroshima left a similar impression because it was recognized that the atom bomb, as a globally effective weapon, could destroy all of life on earth. But even in this case the condemnation was not quite so clear, no matter how shocked people were.

Why is this second 11 September so different from the other occasions? Surely because, for the first time, the world's superpower and the ruling centre of the empire was hit. Up until then, it had intervened with incomparable power in any country it disliked without ever having to fear a reaction. This time the centre itself became the target of a destructive attack from the air. Up until then only God in the heavens was greater than this god. With 'God bless America' and 'God's own country' this power held itself to be God's representative on earth, and in fact saw itself as godlike. If it is godlike, then it is an Achilles without an Achilles heel. The power that held itself to be godlike and was worshipped in the world as a god was badly hurt. This was parricide, regicide, deicide.

The Twin Towers were the holy shrine of this god. What the Vatican in Rome is for Catholics, and Mecca is for Muslims, these towers were for the bourgeois society based on property, money and capital. The towers were, on the one hand, a centre for worship as well as for business. The attack on the Pentagon – or the possibility of an attack on the White House – is of only secondary importance in comparison with the attack on the Twin Towers. From the perspective of finance people, the attack on the towers was a sacrilege. This is how global capitalism thinks. Parliaments and White Houses are simply a decoration peripheral to the hard core of property, money and capital mysticism, which regarded the Twin Towers as the royal throne and divine residence.

This is why what happened can be seen as a regicide for our times. This is how the whole world experienced it. A regicide that is simultaneously a deicide always counts as parricide, too. The air attacks were sacrilege, a revolt against God and the king. This is without doubt how it is seen. A regicide on its own is simply an ordinary murder. But because a king is involved it is anything but ordinary. Although an idol has collapsed, saying this is no consolation. There are still idols. Perhaps the sacking of Rome by the Goths in the fifth century left a similar feeling across the Roman empire.

When a king died, the French in the European Middle Ages always repeated the line 'The king is dead, long live the king'. But after the murder of a king one cannot repeat the second part of this line. After a murdered king there is no king of a similar kind. Everything has changed. Kings live in the heart, and with a regicide the king living in the heart dies. The hearts do not die, but the king who lived in the hearts dies. Attempts are made to restore their rule, but these succeed only rarely. Camus analysed this restoration better than most in his essay *The Rebel*. He already recognized that whoever kills the king must kill themselves.

Are the towers the king? Kings and castles can be exchanged when playing a game of chess. This is even more the case in our society in which things are the replacements for people – where people are transformed and become 'human capital'. For all these reasons the collapse of the towers has a much greater meaning than the murder of Kennedy. Kennedy was just the representative of the king who had his place in people's hearts. The towers *are* the king.

And at the same time this king is a god, and that is why we are also dealing with a deicide. However, the murder of those who commit deicide brings the murdered god back to life. This is why we are now once again dealing with the murder of those who would commit deicide, as has happened in all the Western empires in times of crisis since the European Middle Ages. The Second World War is usually connected with anti-Semitism. Anti-Semitism never had just the persecution of the Jewish minority as its aim, although persecution of Jews who represented a minority did happen. Rather, anti-Semitism was the means by which to explain any resistance to the imperial

rule as deicide, in that such resistance was described as 'Jewish madness'. This interpretation allowed for the murder of those who would
commit deicide to be extended to include any chosen group of
people. Up until the Second World War, Soviet socialism was seen in
all Western countries as 'Jewish Bolshevism'. In this way, the path was
cleared, allowing communists to be killed by reference to the murder
of those who would commit deicide, and then, under the banner of
anti-communism, killing Jews at the same time. National Socialist
anti-Semitism is misinterpreted if one overlooks the interpretation of
communism as the creation of Judaism.

Today we are again dealing with a deicide, although the language
is more secular. The words used again and again refer to the blessings
of God. But when President Bush proclaims the war of good against
evil, then the ethos of society is for him the good: peace, freedom
and free trade – and free trade means an increase in property for capital owners. One pursues war for these values and they represent the
most sacred of values; they are all incorporated into the concept of
'free trade' and there is no significant difference between them. When
Bush says 'God bless America' he means the god of these values whose
throne was the Twin Towers.

This god has been murdered and a murdered god rises again if one
murders its murderers. This is why there is a crusade, to use Bush's
language. Bush announced this on 7 October 2001 in the following
terms: 'I'm speaking to you today from the Treaty Room of the White
House, a place where American presidents have worked for peace.
We're a peaceful nation. Yet, as we have learned, so suddenly and so
tragically, there can be no peace in a world of sudden terror. In the
face of today's new threat, the only way to pursue peace is to pursue
those who threaten it.'[3] Again the talk is of peace, but the peace means
war. The defining words of Orwell's Big Brother are: peace is war. So
that peace can come, the enemies of peace need to be removed. So
that freedom can come, the enemies of freedom must be removed.
So that tolerance can rule, the enemies of tolerance must be removed.
So that free trade can flourish, the enemies of free trade in the capital
economy must be removed.

Like all despots in history, Bush in the same speech announces the
war that means peace with a reference to an innocent girl: 'I recently
received a touching letter that says a lot about the state of America in
these difficult times – a letter from a 4th-grade girl, with a father in

the military:"As much as I don't want my Dad to fight", she wrote, "I'm willing to give him to you."This is a precious gift, the greatest she could give.This young girl knows what America is all about. Since September 11, an entire generation of young Americans has gained new understanding of the value of freedom, and its cost in duty and in sacrifice.'

This sounds like cannibalism.The executioners sacrifice themselves when they take on the murder of other people.The crusade has begun but in a completely secular language.The god of George Bush, however, looks on this crusade with pleasure.

Fighting for all the power

What is the system actually fighting for? Many hypotheses have been mooted because many interests are at work here. On the one hand, there is the oil in Central Asia; to access this, control over Afghanistan is required. On the other hand, there is a desire to surround China, in order to be able to intimidate it from land bases, too. Finally, there are also, in many governments, so-called populist tendencies, for example in Venezuela: President Chavez is regarded as a dangerous enemy for the national security of the United States. There are therefore many reasons to be nervous. However, it would be a mistake to try to explain the current power politics of the USA in these terms, as if this or that single interest were to be regarded as decisive for the powers of the system.We think there is much more at stake.

The system never fights exclusively for single interests in a pragmatic sense: it is always fighting for power as a whole. Depending on the extent of this power, single interests in the system will be pursued as well. By appealing to the totality of power, interests are discerned and made into absolute values to be followed.The Parisian literary critic Tzvetan Todorov analyses how Hernando Cortés conquered Mexico.Todorov's analysis can be helpful to us in trying to analyse our contemporary problem:

> In Cozumel someone suggested to him to send some armed men to search for gold in the central region of the country. 'Cortés answered him, laughing, saying he had not come here for such trivialities, but to serve God and the king' (Bernal Diaz, 30).When he heard about the existence of the Aztec Kingdom, he decided not simply to satisfy him-

self with the extortion of riches, but to overthrow the entire kingdom. This strategy regularly caused concern with his soldiers who were hoping for instantly accessible profits but Cortés did not waver; so on the one hand we have him to thank for the development of a tactic of military conquest, and on the other hand for a policy of colonialism in times of peace. (Todorov 1985: 122)

Of course Cortés wanted the gold. But he had no interest in simply this one issue: he wanted everything – and therefore also the gold. He did not want to acquire riches in order to return to Spain wealthy and then live a life of leisure as a nobleman, he wanted everything, and that entailed a conquest that knew no end. The *conquista* led to wealth, but it went far beyond all levels of property. This is why Cortés rejects such 'trivialities', wanting to serve God and the king. This formulation means that the whole kingdom should be conquered, and after that all other kingdoms that are on earth. Cortés is not pursuing a personal interest but the whole. And this whole implies that all possible single interests are catered for for ever. And here, Todorov claims, modernity begins: it never has simply single interests at heart, but always the whole, and pursues the whole in order to serve current and future interests effectively. The interests transform themselves into metaphysical values. By appealing to these interests, the representative of these interests is prepared to sacrifice everything, even their own life. This is what Columbus meant when he said that gold is a material that can even open the gates of paradise.

The last Santa Fe document (Santa Fe IV) states this clearly and succinctly: 'Apart from this, the natural resources of the hemisphere should be made available to securing our national priorities. A "Monroe doctrine" if one wants to put it like that.'[4]

Of course, it is not simply about the natural resources of the hemisphere, which always include the human resources (the human capital), it is about the whole world. Today the system – with the United States at its centre – is once again engaged in a *conquista* for the whole and thereby serves its core interests: the increase in property of the owners of capital. One always acts in the knowledge that these interests are best served if one pursues the whole.

The accumulation strategy of global capitalism has achieved what even one of its disciples describes as a 'total market'. The total market is being pursued throughout the world. But it is still possible to identify resistance or interests that are not completely integrated; there are still movements that try to avoid the steel cage. There is a desire to resist the movements that criticize the strategy of capital accumulation – called globalization – these movements are active everywhere and mobilize people with a strength that might threaten the future of this strategy.

Even before the attacks it was clear that in the light of such uncertainties the politics of the total market could be continued only if they were complemented by a totalitarian political world power, which had the power to remove all 'market distortions'. Today we recognize that the reaction to the attacks on New York made this project possible by calling it part of the worldwide struggle against terrorism. Every last corner of the world is to be subjected to the absolute market of the capitalist property economy. The term terrorism is therefore defined widely enough for it to be possible to denounce any resistance to that strategy as terrorism if that resistance offers a limit to its subjugation. Bush's motto is: 'Whoever is not with us is on the side of the terrorists.' This motto has been shared by every totalitarian system in history. The American sociologist Mike Davis (2001) has stated clearly what this is all about:

> If there is a precedent that we can learn from in American history, then it is not 7 December 1941 – the attack on Pearl Harbor – but 23 September 1949. On this day, President Truman announced to a speechless American public that the Soviet Union had, three weeks earlier, succeeded in testing an atomic bomb. Shockwaves of fear and uncertainty spread through the United States. Truman's National Security Council reacted quickly with 'NSC-68', a blank cheque to create what President Eisenhower would later describe as the 'military industrial complex'. Simultaneously, Senator Joseph McCarthy and FBI director J. Edgar Hoover used the public's fear to initiate a merciless pursuit of an 'enemy within'. The onetime influential American left was extinguished. What convinced most Americans to join the authoritarian national consensus of the Fifties was less ideology than fear.
>
> Are we heading back to the future with George W. Bush? Will the war against terrorism mean the end for an openness towards immigration, for freedom in the internet, for protests against a global capitalism, the right to privacy, and all the significant civil liberties which have managed to withstand erosion by the war on drugs?

The new McCarthyism is today no longer restricted to the United States but pursues worldwide aims. Its tool, its weapon, is the supposed war against terrorism, which is appealed to in order to threaten any resistance movement with total war. The United States, the hub of power at the centre of the system, wants absolute power. It relies on the ability to threaten any opposition to the system with annihilation.

We are dealing with neither a clash of civilizations nor an anti-Islamic crusade. It is not about a 'clash of civilizations' as defined by the American political scientist and policy adviser Samuel P. Huntington; the Bush government leaves no doubt about this. This is a total clash with the whole world and therefore also, of course, with the Islamic world. Imperial globalization is, after all, not just about the economy in the narrow sense, it is also about the control of civilization or culture. The whole is always the aim, in order to be able to control each individual part. Every country in the world can become the target as soon as one believes that it distorts the total market of property accumulation; appeal will be made to the war on terror in order to make it a target. This is already noticeable today. While Afghanistan and Iraq are under attack various other countries are being lined up in the sights. It is all-out war. Vincente Fox, the President of Mexico, describes terrorism as a cancerous growth. This description used to be applied to communism; the war against terrorism has replaced the war against communism of the Cold War. This much is clear.

The new alliance against terrorism, which includes almost as many countries as the United Nations, threatens to replace the UN. The aim is to replace democracy worldwide with an anti-terrorist world government, the centre of which is the USA. This government represents the globalization strategy, and, using its position as a pre-eminent power over all other powers, pursues a worldwide McCarthyism. History becomes a world court with the USA as the judge. The struggle against the 'evil empire' which Reagan waged has been revived. The war against terrorism offers the opportunity to control every power in the world through one single power. For the first time we are dealing with totalitarian rule at a world level, rule that is no longer mediated through any other power and which cannot be opposed by any other power. The empire strives for omnipotence. It cannot comprehend that weak points keep breaking out the closer it comes to omnipotence. Ever more Achilles heels are becoming apparent.

The attacks on New York happened at a time when the prospects for a new worldwide totalitarianism were being explored. The propaganda about the war against terrorism has focused on one crucial point. To begin with, the attacks on New York were compared to Pearl Harbor. This comparison is truly frightening. As far as one can tell, the attack on Pearl Harbor was also an attack on itself on the part of the US government. Apparently it had information that indicated an attack was imminent, but decided not to prevent it. The disaster would be so bad that public opinion in the United States would see no option but to enter the war with grim determination. Hopefully what happened in New York was not a Pearl Harbor. But there are indications that something similar was going on. Should that be the case, then we would be dealing with the most stupid decision in the history of all political decisions in the United States, which does not lack absurd stupidities as far as the consequences of its actions are concerned.

The coordinates of good and evil collapse

We believe that 11 September 2001 has a further meaning which will be decisive for the future. The attacks struck the coordinates of good and evil of the entire Western civilization. Our confusion of languages became apparent. The towers of the empire collapsed. Empires themselves fall when their towers collapse. They do not fall because of bombs, but through confusion of language (see the story of the Tower of Babel, Gen. ii).

There is a terrible precedent, although it happened in a particular country and not in the globalized world: the Berlin Reichstag fire of 1933. Even today, nobody knows who caused it. The arson could have been the work of an anarchist or it could have been perpetrated by the Nazis themselves. In the eyes of the Nazis this was both regicide and deicide. With the burning of the Reichstag, the previously existing coordinates of good and evil went up in flames, not only in terms of a building, but also in terms of the soul. The Nazis offered no coordinates; rather they introduced the most disastrous and painful period of human history ever witnessed. All barriers were removed. A period without the coordinates of good and evil began, i.e. confusion of language.

Something similar happened on the first historic 11 September, that of 1973, with the attack on the Moneda in Santiago de Chile. Perhaps this even inspired the attack on the towers. Equally, there began at this time a cruel period in which the coordinates of good and evil were obliterated without hindrance. But the global empire still existed, and could support the subsequent restoration period.

Today the collapse is on a global level and nobody can say what is happening. We are witnessing a major catastrophe, but an alternative is not in sight. Civilization itself would have to be newly constituted, but who is available to build the new foundations? This is why the perspective for the future is so frightening. Once again all barriers and hindrances could be removed. But the empire no longer has any higher authority which could institute a restoration. That is why there is now no looking back to earlier experiences. Since there is now only one power that has any say in the world, there is no political power to oppose what is going to happen.

Together with the towers, the coordinates of good and evil that had established themselves in our society were struck and collapsed. This makes what happened so dramatic. They were hypocritical coordinates, but nevertheless they were coordinates. During the last one hundred years air attacks more calamitous than those on the Twin Towers of New York have taken place. But there are reasons to regard the attacks on New York as much more serious. All earlier catastrophes – Hiroshima, Hanoi, Baghdad, Belgrade, etc. – were situated in a meaningful context by the empire. It was a perverse context, a compass that only *appeared* to show a direction. But it was none the less a context. This is why the empire, following Locke, argued that these catastrophes served the implementation of his type of humanism. In this perverse perspective they were regarded as 'humanitarian interventions', and public opinion throughout the world accepted this, despite many protests.

This is no longer the case with the attacks on New York. Now the Devil is the origin. Perhaps the murderers of New York also regard their act as 'humanitarian intervention'. But there are no longer co-ordinates of good and evil which allow this attack to be classified under such a category. The Islamic world denies these to the attackers as well. We have to take the statements of their leaders seriously on this point. They cannot give these acts meaning, not even in a perverse sense such as the West has always done with its own wicked acts.

The contemporary globalized West regarded itself as an Achilles without an Achilles' heel. In Baghdad it killed hundreds of thousands of Iraqis in two wars, but suffered only a few hundred casualties itself. In Yugoslavia it killed thousands, but there was not a single casualty on NATO's side. The United States dreams of an anti-ballistic missile

shield that would make it the lord of the world, wielding absolute
despotic power that nobody in the world could oppose. But even
this Achilles had an Achilles heel, which is where the arrow struck. Is
there a shield against ceramic knives?

Where is the mistake? Have the secret services failed? Of course
they have failed. There are simply no secret services that do not make
mistakes. The secret services are also not an Achilles without an Achil
les heel. Are they allowed to make mistakes? Of course not. But they
will still fail. Should they try to make a minimal number of mistakes?
That is all that we can demand of them.

A wise old man once cursed his enemy with the threat: 'You will
live in interesting times'. Now these interesting times are coming. We
are cursed. But there are worse things than the failure of the secret
services. A whole world view has failed. All scientific-analytic activity has failed. Empirical sciences, which did not even recognize what
was reality, have suffered shipwreck. Hollywood's nightmares presaged
what would happen. But the scientists, who prided themselves on
their empiricism, had no idea. How this science would understand
these events can be seen using their own understandings. Let us study
what has happened using the perspective of Max Weber and the most
highly respected economic scientists. The analysis may appear cynical,
but this cynicism has been created not by us, but by the objectivity of
the discipline. The following happened:

Almost twenty people took control of four aeroplanes and directed
them towards the towers in New York, the Pentagon and the White
House. One aeroplane failed, the others reached their targets: they
destroyed the towers and hit the Pentagon.

What questions can science – at least, economics – ask, if it is empirical? According to Max Weber, the classical German economic
theorist of the early twentieth century, it can only assess the ends–
means relationship. In the language of economists, science judges only
the relations between means and preferences. If one examines these
relations more closely, it becomes apparent that these actions attained
a high degree of efficiency. The ceramic knives were apparently the
perfect means by which to take control of the aeroplanes. And the
aeroplanes became huge bombs, which reached the targets that the
attackers had selected perfectly. From the perspective of empirical
science this was an action which, 'viewed formally', was carried out
to the highest degree of rationality. The perpetrators had an end – or

a preference – in view, and they achieved what they wanted. Such efficiency is highly praised in our economy and our society. Empirical science declares such efficiency to be the only ideal capable of scientific proof.

If we now ask scientific economists who is to judge the result of the action and the preference of the perpetrators, the scientists, as empirical as they are, take their leave. Science can say nothing about this. It does not judge values, only rationality. The thought process of the scientists could be described in the following way. The perpetrators had various alternatives. They could fly their aeroplanes to another airport, land and go for a walk, go shopping or do deals. They could also blow up the towers. And why did they blow up the towers? The scientist answers: because they wanted to realize the preference they had decided upon. They made a formal, rational choice. But science can say nothing about the result of this decision between the various preferences. That is a value judgement; but science is neutral. Whether one prefers this or that depends on the relevant aspects of one's own preferences and taste. Nobody can argue about tastes. Whether one goes for a walk or blows up the towers – that is as much a question of choice as whether one prefers fish or meat.

Of course, these scientific economists do not dare speak like this today. But their science obeys this logic. It therefore comes as no surprise that this science cannot comprehend reality, because the reality is determined by the fact that these aeroplanes were hijacked and directed against the towers. But the scientist regards such an occurrence as external to science, as something that has nothing to do with science.

A few years ago, an economist was awarded the Nobel Prize because he had discovered a new formula for calculating stock market profits. The fact that for a whole week after 11 September 2001 the stock market did not exist is regarded by the scientist as a problem that is not something for science to deal with. Such vulgar facts – whether a stock market exists or not – do not influence the eternal truth of that formula. Even if there were to be no stock market, the formula would still be valid. Whether there is a stock market or not is a question of taste. But the formula to calculate profit is eternal – as eternal as the law of gravity with which the physicist can explain the collapse of the towers. But the towers did not collapse because of the existence of the law of gravity. They collapsed because someone made them collapse, someone who had rationally taken the law of gravity into account. But why were they made to collapse? No empirical scientist will set themselves the target of trying to explain this. The reasons are external to science, beyond scientific examination; this then also means that this science is external to reality, existing outside reality. Even German sociologist Niklas Luhmann had already discovered that a person as a subject is external to the system, i.e. exists outside the system. Does anyone seriously believe that the collapse of the towers in New York can be explained by referring to the law of gravity? Or by the formulas of the Nobel Prize-winner for economics?

This is not a cynical description of science; rather science behaves cynically, since it is precisely this systematic refusal to see real life that leads to the creation of such destructive indirect effects. This is why Viviane Forrester writes of 'economic horror'. If the sciences cancel themselves out, then one naturally needs to create a demon that brought about the towers' collapse with the help of the attackers. This is the view of George W. Bush, who believes in a fight between good and evil. But it is highly probable that the attackers also saw demons at work. In their conviction, demons were using the system and the towers. The towers' collapse was then part of their fight against the demons. What for some is a god is for others the Devil. Everyone fights the demons they see in others in an arena where science and reason have nothing more to say. Science says goodbye to reality and leaves it to the demons, can only observe the fight between the demons. But not just science; reason too takes leave of reality. Max Weber claimed that: 'Depending on the last position taken by the individual, one thing will be the Devil and the other God, and individuals have to decide which is God and which is the Devil for them. And this is how it is in all aspects of life' (Weber 1956: 329). What is God for some is the Devil for others. 'And fate rules over these Gods and their struggle but certainly no "science". It is only possible to understand what is divine for one or other, or: to understand where one or the other finds order. But at this point the matter is closed as far as a discussion in a lecture theatre and through a professor is concerned, even though, of course, the huge problems of life that lie therein are not closed matters. But powers other than university chairs have their say here' (ibid.: 330).

What is God for Bush is the Devil for Bin Laden. And what is God for Bin Laden is the Devil for Bush. Max Weber adds that it is not science but fate which determines these. Western society has done away with reason, the motive for its very foundation. The churches are full on pre-arranged days of worship, and people pray to a God who is supposed to replace the lost rationality. But there is no such God. Even atheists participate in such prayer days, but the God that can hear such prayers does not exist. Such a God-replacement can only make the situation worse.

Modern society has struggled for decades against utopias and alternatives. At the end of the 1980s it declared that it had finally won. And indeed, it really did succeed in destroying resistance movements, often in an unbelievably brutal way. But the argument was convincing. Almost everywhere, socialism perished. The system celebrated its victory on the ruins of human life and of the earth. A culture of hopelessness was implemented. It was claimed that whoever wanted heaven on earth created hell. Almost everyone believed in this assertion because nobody wanted to create hells. The hopelessness of this society, which claimed that there was no alternative, deteriorated into despair. Now we face a despairing world society. And promptly we see a hell, created not by demons but by despairing people themselves. But they are merely reproducing the hell that has already been produced for them. We are led to conclude: whoever does not want heaven on earth creates hell.

Hobbes presents civilized society as the order that replaces the struggle of everyone against everyone else. The order that has now been implemented results in the struggle of everyone against everyone else. This struggle does not belong to the past: it confronts us in the future.

The global civil war

The collapse of the towers marked the beginning of the global civil war, of which so much had already been said but only in terms of dire warnings. Now it has taken hold of people's hearts. But this war is not about positions. The attackers who brought down the towers want no other society and are not heralding a new project. But the capitalist possessive society that was attacked also offers no project. It proclaims itself as the end of history. This means only, however, that its own project is finished. It confirms only itself and the devastation it has created. It offers nothing more, but makes a project for the entire future out of the misery of the present. It produces devastation.

In a globally created world, it devastates the world globally. Society no longer has a vision for the future, and one can no longer demand such a thing from it. What it calls freedom – enduring liberty – means eternal devastation through the powers that sit at the controls. This is understood by most people, and dashes all hope that anything could ever change this. This despair calls for a reaction without a project, pure negation, which murders in order to be murdered. But this merely reproduces what the now meaningless society itself produces: it murders in order to move towards total suicide. Its progress is best characterized by what General Branco said after the 1964 military coup in Brazil: 'We were on the brink of the abyss and through the military coup we have taken a great step forward.' The reaction of the system to the terrorism is of a similar nature.

Martin Heidegger said: 'Only a God can still save us.' But the God that creates such a civil war saves no one. In certain cases, it promises those who would commit murder by suicide paradise, so long as they continue doing what they are already doing.

There is no such thing as the clash of civilizations. In a globalized world there are only sub-civilizations that belong to a global civilization. To speak of a clash of civilizations is only to create further excuses and confusion of language. One does not want to admit what has happened but everything serves to justify aggression. The attack on the towers does not come from outside, as if carried out by another civilization. The attack comes from within. In a certain sense it is a product of the globally dominant civilization, the centres of which it is attacking. This civilization arises out of the destruction of civilizations. Its centre is not to be found in universities and theatres. Its centre is the war ministry and the business centre of the capitalist market. Deals to increase capital ownership and war determine this civilization; everything else is simply an accessory.

The attack comes from within, not from without. The training camps of the attackers are not in Afghanistan, but in Florida and Hamburg. In Afghanistan it is not possible to plan attacks of this kind and this degree. They can perhaps be motivated and financed from there, but they are organized from elsewhere. The attack takes place in the centre of the globalized world. Today the world really is a globe, but this has not been as a result of the IMF and World Bank. Rather it is the result of the whole of human history. It has made the earth into a round globe. Nothing now happens that is outside human world

society. Everything takes place in its centre, even if certain characteristics of the source civilization co-determine the reaction. Terrorists
from the USA, for example Timothy McVeigh or the 'Unabomber',
act in this way, Arab terrorists in that. But their acts of terror are comparable. Apart from this, their nourishment has the same origin.

The origin is not the global world. A global world is the space
in which they act. The origin is rather the strategy that the IMF, the
World Bank and the G8 pursue for the accumulation of capital and
which they call globalization. The terrorists act with as much terror as
the strategy from which they emerged itself produces. Their terrorism
is merely the other side of the economic and cultural globalization
strategy. The international bodies act with incomparable fundamentalism. Even the one-time chief economist of the World Bank, Joseph
Stiglitz, describes these bodies as 'global market fundamentalists'.
They dictate to the world a *strategy for the accumulation of capital property*
which is incompatible with its global nature; indeed, it is having a
devastating effect. But this strategy allows the exploitation of people
and the earth to an extent previously unknown. In order to do this,
the international bodies systematically propagate a culture of hopelessness through their anti-utopianism and anti-humanism. The ruling
class is the global player in the casino economy. But in this casino the
game is played with the lives of human beings and the environment.

Thereby ever new global threats are provoked, which these days
frighten all of us. In the name of removing market distortions, the
barriers are dismantled so that capital is allowed to increase without
strictures. Together with the market distortions, the fundamental
human rights that guarantee right to a real life are being eliminated.
At the same time, human dignity is being lost as people are turned
into human capital. There is no longer even a sense that exclusion and
the destruction of the earth are not simply to be seen as mechanical
operational sequences, but as a violation of human rights.

The global threats are moving in a spiral of violence which the
globalization strategy cannot stop because it has created this spiral.
Rather, an automatic reflex is created, ending in the intoxication with
violence we are currently experiencing. Our empirical sciences hardly
mention this spiral of violence. They regard violence as an 'external
effect' because it is created as an indirect effect or by-product of the
direct actions on the markets.

The exclusion of large sectors of the population from the property economy creates a situation in the worst-affected regions of the world in which people can no longer survive. They emigrate. The population movements thereby created give the impression of violent expulsions. They are occurring to such an extent that they even threaten those regions previously least affected by the exclusion of populations, mostly the countries of the centre. These regions close their borders and resist the waves of migrants with violence. The consequence is an undeclared war at the borders between the countries of the centre and the excluded regions, which each year costs thousands of lives.

The more people excluded by the strategy of accumulation, the greater the pressure of the migration movement on the countries that the migrants seek to move to, and in turn the more violent the reaction of these countries becomes. The migrants that manage to get through the borders suffer discrimination and exploitation within these countries too. However, they have achieved something essential: they have managed to survive.

And in relation to the environment we find a similar pattern. The exploitation of the environment is leading to an environmental crisis, which for the last few decades has been moving towards a global crisis: the hole in the ozone layer is growing, the number of hurricanes is increasing, the deserts are expanding. Fish are disappearing from the rivers, waters are being poisoned. New technologies bring about or encourage new diseases. For the casino capitalism of property accumulation this is not a problem: each new crisis means new profits, because new investments are needed to repair the damage created by previous investments. However, the crises that arise in this way simply give more grounds for migration.

The earth is round. This seems to be something new for the United States. The bullet that we shoot kills our enemies, but comes out of their backs, circles the earth, and then hits us in the back. Because the earth is round, everyone is affected by this, including the USA. It wants to carry on shooting. But the bullets it shoots circle the earth and land in their backs too.

Casino capitalism ignores what happens to people, as well as what happens in the environment. Casino capitalism knows only the stock market index as a criterion, which it implements with fire and the sword. Whether the Gulf Wars are a success or not, is determined by the stock market. If the stock market rises then it is a good thing. The same happened with regard to the war in Yugoslavia. And if the revenge crusade for the 11 September 2001 attacks allows stock market values to increase, then it is also a good thing. Nothing else counts. No news broadcast is now complete without a report on the stock markets. The stock market shows whether the situation is developing positively or negatively. There are no other criteria.

Noticeable resistance no longer makes itself felt. The rejection of every alternative, every utopia, any humanism, has deadened the conscience of people the world over. In order to ensure peace and quiet for the global players in the casino, seeds of hopelessness were sown. This was done successfully, but much more has happened. It is not only hopelessness which is spreading: hopelessness is becoming despair. The intention was to create fatalism, but despair is not fatalistic.

Despair does not generate resistance, but aversion and socially explosive moods. How this can manifest itself can be seen with an early example: the rebellion in Caracas – the 'Caracazo' – in February 1989. There was no plan for change in that society, but the people found the situation unbearable, and an uprising took place in which the shops ended up being plundered. The societal explosion had no perspective. Such an explosion leads only to more demoralization.

The government reacted with as much blind rage as the rebels. President Perez became an executioner and gave orders to shoot. After thousands had been killed, the rebellion ended as it began – in despair. The rebellion in Caracas happened in the same year in which the student movement in Tiananmen Square in Beijing was crushed. Tiananmen Square had something of a project behind it. Caracas, several months later, did not. Despite this, Caracas became an indicator for the future, Tiananmen Square did not. But the communications media focused on Tiananmen Square, not Caracas.

Casino capitalism was unaffected, and also did not analyse the situation. The global players continued to gamble with the fate of the world. Everywhere suicide murderers appeared, originally in the USA, later across the world. No one felt concerned. The casino continued, and believed that it could continue in this way for ever because it regarded itself as the end of history. It propagated hopelessness and despondency. Despair spread.

From hopelessness to despair

But in our world, despair does not end in fatalism, as casino capitalism assumes it does. Rather, despair moves on to feverish but totally blind activity: destroy in order to be destroyed. After the execution of McVeigh, President Bush said that he had suffered the same fate as that he had pursued (through his actions). I do not think that Bush really understood what he was saying by this.

We are dealing with terrorism that has no political project behind it, with crimes that no longer have a motive. They no longer want to achieve anything, and therefore know no bounds. Were they to have a goal or pursue a utopia, they would have to set themselves limits, at least in terms of their goals. But since they have no goals, there are also no limits. The system no longer recognizes any boundaries; neither does the reaction of the terrorists.

The attack on New York was the worst consequence so far; the 1995 attack on Oklahoma was very similar. The attackers set out to destroy, and accept death as a consequence, even as the reason for their action. They accept the dominant motto of the system: there is no alternative – wanting heaven on earth results in the creation of hell, humanism is an attack on humanity. The attackers are postmodern people. But they do not lie in a hammock drinking wine, as the post-modernists preach; rather, they throw themselves into battle.

In order to recognize the parallels between Oklahoma 1995 and New York 2001 it may be helpful to recall earlier attacks. The execution of Timothy McVeigh confronts us with the problem of the new terrorism. This newly emerged form of terrorism demands our full concentration. McVeigh had no plan, did not want to achieve anything specific with his terrorist action. One could even say that his action had nothing to do with terrorism. But equally we could claim that his action was the first serious terrorist act, and all earlier acts had little to do with terrorism. McVeigh destroyed in order to be destroyed; there was no sense that through his terrorist act he might contribute to something. All earlier terrorism was derived from the idea that one destroys something in order to replace it with some-thing else. State terrorism or private initiatives announced their acts of destruction with the aim of creating something else. The new terrorist no longer has the ambition to create, but wants only self-destruction. But this self-destruction has to arise out of the destruction of other people, and so it is therefore not a simple suicide. The suicide is rather the consequence of a murder. But such a suicide neither wants to prove nor achieve anything. It also does not want to erect any sym-bols. Despite this, such a suicide is a social act. The terrorist is a subject in the community with others, even if they are a subject pitted against the others. They are also a subject with others in an opposite sense. The new terrorism has an interest only in the act of terror and nothing else. There is no longer any rationale involved.

The execution of McVeigh can be compared to a sacred act. The condemned man remained silent; he said nothing at all but claimed invincibility for himself. He asked for the poem 'Invictus' by William Ernest Henley (1849–1903) to be read to him. Those present prayed. Here, the law is being brought a sacrifice, even if execution is meant as an act directed against human sacrifices.

The story can be told briefly and clearly. In 1995 McVeigh blew up a public building in Oklahoma with two tons of explosives. In so doing, he killed 168 people, including about twenty children in a nursery in the building. McVeigh's father, when questioned, said: 'I really do not know how it could come to this. I only know that he already had this strong aversion to the government when he came home after his military service [until the end of the Gulf War in 1991 he served with the military].'[5] Indeed, McVeigh was a highly decorated soldier in this war. And when he spoke with a journalist about his act he used the language of the warring parties in the Gulf War. 'He once told me in the cruellest language: "That is 168 to one", emphasised Lou Michel, co-author of the book *American Terrorist: Timothy McVeigh and the Oklahoma City Bombing* during an interview with ABC. He saw himself as a winner, said Michel, who McVeigh has allowed to be one of the witnesses at his execution.' This, we remember, is how one spoke during the Gulf War. On 30 April 1991, *La Nación* reported: 'Without doubt Bush wanted to avoid unnecessary loss of human life. About 100 allied deaths is an excellent result against 150,000 fallen Iraqis.'

In the Gulf War the relationship was one to 1,500. McVeigh regarded one to 168 as a success. When asked whether he was not horrified that twenty children were among the dead, he answered that this was 'collateral damage'. Literally: 'I regret that people lost their lives. But that is the way of these things.' Regarding his reaction to the victims, he said: 'I feel sorry for these people in Oklahoma who have lost relatives. But that happens every day. You are not the first mother to lose a child, or the first grandfather to lose a grandchild. It happens every day somewhere in the world. I will not go into the courtroom and hide and cry just because the victims expect that of me.'

This is the language of war. During the court case he pleaded not guilty, although he admitted to having committed the crime. This is also part of the language of war. Of course, terrorism is not part of war; rather, McVeigh was bringing into daily life what happened during the Gulf War. From his perspective, that was all this was about. But that is not what it was. The Gulf War had indeed consisted of acts like those of McVeigh, but they had been accompanied by an appeal to important values. The talk was of 'war for peace', of war securing human rights. McVeigh committed his act without this justification. In this way he turned it into a naked atrocity. It is now omnipresent; it can happen at any moment and in any place – and it does indeed happen. But both types of attackers, the soldier in the Gulf and McVeigh, have a clear conscience. They regard their actions as right and plead not guilty.

If we analyse McVeigh's actions we realize that the new terrorism follows certain paradigms: destroy in order to be destroyed. 'I am looking forward to being able to leave this fucked up world at last,' McVeigh says. 'Let's call the whole thing simply a state-sponsored suicide.' Sometimes the terrorists kill themselves, sometimes they demand that the state authorities kill them, on other occasions a collective suicide takes place, in which the instigator kills themselves and everyone else as well. Clearly this started in the USA, but quickly spread to Europe and Japan. But today we find this phenomenon all over the world.

The classical analysis of terrorism does not help to understand this phenomenon. In Friedrich Nietzsche's writings we find texts that introduce us to this culture of despair:

> If a suffering, oppressed individual were to lose the faith in a right to despise the will to power, then they would step into the stage of hopeless desperation … Morality protects the worse off from nihilism, in that each individual is given an infinite value, a metaphysical value, and placed into an order that does not correspond to worldly power and ranking: it teaches submission, humility, etc. Given that the faith in this morality goes to pieces, then the worse off would no longer have their consolation – and would go to pieces. (Nietzsche 1982: vol. III, 854)

This is what is happening at the moment. The limitless value of a person, which helps to resist despair, is destroyed. People are turned into human capital. People excluded from the capitalist property society are therefore human capital of no value:

The going-to-pieces presents itself as making-oneself-go-to-pieces, as an instinctive selection of that that must destroy. Symptoms of this self-destruction of the worse off: ... above all the instinctive coercion to actions with which one makes the powerful into a deadly enemy (– equivalent to taming one's own executioner), the will to destroy as the will of a still deeper instinct, the instinct to self-destruction, the will into nothing.

Nihilism, as a symptom that the worse off no longer have any consolation: that they destroy, in order to be destroyed, that they, removed from morality, no longer have any reason to 'surrender themselves' – that they place themselves on the ground of the opposing principle, and also want power, in that they force the powerful to be their executioner. (ibid.: 855)

It seems very clear that what Nietzsche is announcing here is currently happening. The text seems to be a commentary destined to explain the case of Timothy McVeigh or the attacks on New York. There is not a single commentary in the daily press that now speaks with the clarity of this text, written more than a hundred years ago. But Nietzsche is by no means a Nostradamus. Rather he recognizes with all clarity what consequences follow a culture of despair, a culture that he himself furthered.

We are dealing with a macabre harmony. The terrorists kill themselves or are executed because they so desire it. The conflict between the executioner and the victim disappears. The executioner wants to execute and the victim wants to be executed. At long last something akin to a *coincidentia oppositorum* (a coincidence of opposites) is taking place, something that was always regarded as a sacred experience. For Nietzsche this solves the problem of nihilism. The conflict between the powerful and the underlings is overcome. The powerful punish the crimes of those below them in that they execute them, with their consent. The powerful can pursue their desire for power unhindered. Those at the bottom, 'the worse off', no longer can, nor want to, offer any resistance. 'Morality' has come to an end because it is now exclusively a matter for the powerful.

But Nietzsche's solution exemplifies a simple illusion. He destroys morality in order to destroy himself. The breakdown that Nietzsche himself experienced at the end of 1889 proves this. All those up there at the top who force those at the bottom towards self-destruction eventually destroy themselves too. The whole of society is like a merry-go-round on which everyone destroys only to eventually destroy themselves.

The new terrorism shows itself to be the reverse side of the process towards the accumulation of capital property that we call globalization. People have been reduced to human capital and every perspective beyond that is taken from them. This is where the dominant culture of despair emerges, a culture that has already permeated the souls of the people, who believe there is no alternative. But human capital remains a subject, even if now in a perverted sense: it destroys in order to be destroyed. The new terrorism represents the bloody symbol of the essence of what capitalist globalization means.

The new terrorism is paradigmatic. National Socialism itself offers a precedent. After perpetrating a frighteningly irrational violent rule over all the areas of the world that it controlled, it collapsed, and the three most important leaders – Hitler, Goebbels and Goering – killed themselves. Goebbels took his four children, his whole family, with him. Before the collapse of Germany they had threatened that were they to have to retire from the world stage they would slam the door behind them so hard that the universe would shake.

Is not our casino capitalism with its global players saying the same thing? They turn themselves into the executioners of the despairing, although they themselves have driven the people to despair. And this is how they have to act if they want casino capitalism to continue. And in doing this they themselves change: they become executioners. The dehumanization of the system and its casino forces those responsible for the system to become more dehumanized than the victims. Eventually they are simply executioners. The bullet of dehumanization that they have fired hits them in the back. The societies that regard themselves as civilized and carry the system experience an incomparable brutalization. Those who pursued war in Afghanistan were nothing but executioners.

They knew this. When the air attacks on Afghanistan began on 7 October 2001, CNN showed the large B-1, B-2 and B-52 bombers lifting off. The aircraft were painted with reflective colours. They had sharks' eyes and teeth. They looked like terrible gigantic air monsters: flying sharks, on their way to devour anything that got in their way. The flying sharks formed the backdrop against which the West proclaimed its values, and this via a president who came to power through electoral fraud. The sharks taste blood in the water and go mad. They have devoured Afghanistan and are already looking for other countries to devour. The images of the flying sharks were shown only on the first day; then they were withdrawn. But the aeroplane sharks continued flying, albeit without media publicity.

In pursuing such an analysis we are going farther than Nietzsche. The new terrorism does the same as casino capitalism, but from the opposite side. Casino capitalism is as suicidal as the terrorism that declares war on it by reproducing it. Casino capitalism is committing suicide through the irrationality of its rationalizations of capital accumulation. Terrorism, in the context of a world theatre, presents the truth about casino capitalism – it is a real Colosseum, in which people really die.

We are witnessing a *theatrum mundi*. What the mad suicide attackers produce as a cruel theatre of reality happens daily in our society. Our entire society really is carrying out what the world theatre of mad suicide attackers is presenting us with: it kills people and knows that in the end it is committing suicide. The mad suicide attackers, however, are described as the terrorists and criminals, while those who are doing the same with all of humanity sit in places of honour.

Here, then, we have further proof of our thesis that the attack on New York represents a worse catastrophe than all previous air attacks. This catastrophe reveals that the system – casino capitalism – has lost all coordinates of good and evil. Because the system itself caused the catastrophe that took place in these attacks, it cannot really condemn them without condemning itself. But because it does not condemn itself, it has to accept the attacks as a part of casino capitalism. Nietzsche, who most clearly analysed the outcome of Western society, does in fact indicate this as a solution. The executioner is only the reverse side of Nietzsche's superman (*Übermensch*). The superman, who is both the global player and the executioner, plays his game until everything blows up and ends in eternal recurrence. In this sense the system does not need coordinates of good and evil, it is already beyond them.

All people condemned the attacks by appealing to human dignity. The representatives of the system and casino capitalism also spoke in this way. But with regard to the system there is a widespread feeling that it has no authority to condemn in this way. With its strategy of globalization it has denied, condemned and trampled on human rights for decades. The people have the authority to condemn such acts because they are always defending human rights. In whose name do the representatives of the system condemn the attack? Perhaps because they have power and the attacks indicate a lack of respect for that power? The condemnation by the representatives of the system is of another kind. Many people think it has no authority.

The entire strategy of globalization has denied human dignity. This is precisely the removal of the effect of the market distortions: human dignity has been removed. For Nietzsche this removal represents the death of God. God dies when human dignity is killed. Nietzsche describes the death of God as the most significant heroic act of human history. Nietzsche is the favourite philosopher of those who represent the system. But this act is neither significant nor heroic, it is quite simply banal.

Whoever denies the essence of human dignity cannot condemn the attacks by appealing to human dignity. This is why the emperor has no clothes. This fear strikes humanity today; this is why the system is losing its orientation. It can only condemn the attacks by appealing to its own power or by appealing to the stock market values of the New York Stock Exchange, and otherwise not at all. The needle on the compass is turning in circles, and no longer shows a direction. If one is going in the wrong direction, there is at least the possibility of a correction. But when the compass needle is turning in circles, one has reached the pole, and the needle no longer offers an orientation. The system has arrived at this extreme point. The dizziness caused has us all in its grip.

Whoever condemns the attacks on New York also has to condemn the strategy of globalization that is directed towards the increase of capital property. The indirect effects of this strategy have led to the point where the reaction to the system is as extremely irrational as the system itself. In the new terrorism the system raises contradictions against itself. The opposites conflate to become one.

The mysticism of death rises up against the dignity of humanity. The dominant philosophy of the twentieth century and up to the present day centres on a mysticism of death, from Nietzsche through to Heidegger through to postmodernity. Heidegger claims that a person is a 'being towards death'. If this mysticism is the dominant theme of our civilization, can one expect any other result? Our system has turned a person into a being towards death. Is this the truth? Nietzsche said: 'We are conducting an experiment with the truth. Perhaps humanity will die out in the process! Well, well!'[6]

And Michael Novak – the official theologian at the American Enterprise Institute, the think-tank of multinational capital – claims: 'the "void" at the heart of democratic capitalism is like a battlefield, one in which the individual moves around alone in confusion and among many fallen.' Like Nietzsche he concludes that: 'Nature is not regarded as achieved, complete, finished. Creation is unfinished. There are things human beings have to do. Surprises lie in store. If there are horrors yet to face (there always have been), God is with us. The future may not have an upward slant, except as Golgotha had: So be it' (Novak, 1982: 73).

Will they carry on in this way? They know very well where they are leading us. Is this not precisely the terrorism of the system, the 'economic horror'? Everyone who supports the system is aiming for heaven on earth. This is why they hold out the prospect of their negation: extinction, Golgotha, hell.

Do they believe that the terrorists who brought down the towers believed differently? They probably even exemplify the same thinking. And with the same thinking they strengthen one another in their intoxication with violence. That one person speaks in secular language about extinction, another in Christian language of Golgotha, and yet another uses Islamic terminology: what differences are there here? A clash of civilizations? But what difference is there between those who participate in this intoxicated violence? At most their clothes are different, otherwise there is no difference. Or does it matter whether someone wears a turban or a bowler hat?

According to press reports, long before the attacks Microsoft developed and sold a computer game in which the player was an aircraft hijacker. The player had to overcome many obstacles in order to reach the goal, which consisted of making the aircraft crash into the Empire State Building. It was easy to incorporate this game into flight simulators in order to train potential hijackers. Can one still interpret the sale of such a game as a mistake, or as simple profiteering? As greed that no longer knows what it is doing? We do not believe this is the case. The loss of subjectivity transforms itself into aggression against oneself. One treats people only as 'beings towards death', aiming towards death – including one's own.

Bill Gates develops the plan, Bin Laden executes it. In a strange way – in a reverse correspondence – they act together. This obviously has nothing to do with a clash of civilizations. We are dealing rather with a global civilization that disguises itself as various sub-civilizations: turban and bowler hat, Bin Laden and Bill Gates. We are dealing with a split in which the extremes touch each other. How long will we still believe their stories? This is where the language confusion which brings down the towers of empires originates. Who is the criminal? The one who developed the plan or the one who executed it? Which powers lie behind them? Let us analyse the whole fraud. We want to see the emperor naked.

What has happened is worse than the Hollywood films that show the towers collapsing (*Air Force One, Armageddon*, etc.). But in the films, powers from outside carry out the attack. In Microsoft's computer game a player actively attacks the towers themselves. The destruction comes from within. Who failed to think, as they saw the towers in New York collapsing: 'Haven't I seen that before?' The thoughts do not come from resigned opponents of civilization. Rather, the images come out of their own inner core. In a certain sense this is a dimension of all civilizations. But our civilization brushes aside all resistance to the instinct of death. It makes the instinct of death rational and leaves it to the intoxication with violence. It is digging its own grave. Ongoing self-destruction is described as progress. Those who implement such images are executed, and with them a whole nation. But what does one do with those who develop the plan, even if they do not develop it with this intention?

Beneath the openly admitted intentions there is a level of denied desire to fulfil a dream. Goya said that the dream of reason produces monsters. This dream makes reason itself a monster. This is where the irrationality of the rationalized is to be found. Can Bill Gates or Bin Laden sit in judgment? Are there any judges who are not accomplices? We are dealing with a new kind of madness, the madness of completely reasonable people. They use their instrumental reason without difficulty. In so far as psychiatry regards the use of instrumental reason as normality, it regards these mad people as normal. It cannot even find those who are mad, because this is a madness within instrumental reason. Goya, an artist, was the first to reveal this madness.

The crisis of the West is nearing its end phase. After the crisis of the exclusion of people by the property economy, the environmental crisis and the crisis of social relationships, there is now a crisis of the human essence beginning, in which the madness of reasonable people with completely normal behaviour is spreading. This crisis will result in the war of everyone against everyone else, in which everyone will kill in a rational way, while respecting all the rules of instrumental reason and the market.

The crisis is itself getting into a crisis. If they have no anthrax, they at least have white powder that simulates anthrax, in order to spread fear and to make clear what the intention is. Back in the 1980s there was talk in the United States of terrorists lurking under the cover of the nice neighbour. The farther we progress, the more difficult it becomes to differentiate between terrorists and non-terrorists. Eventually, everyone could be a terrorist.

The system, in relation to such crises, has always tried to calculate where the boundaries of tolerance lie. It provokes chaos in order to be able to appear as a guarantor of order. In this way it has carried off one victory after another. But the boundary of tolerance cannot be calculated. This boundary is known only once it has been crossed; but after that there is no turning back. The system has now crossed this boundary. It can only carry on murdering. There is no turning back. All its victories are shown to be pyrrhic victories. Revealing the madness of reasonable people means undressing the emperor.

Is there a way out?

They promise hell on earth. But whoever wants hell will get it. They will never find heaven. This is where the difference lies in the desire for heaven. Promising heaven on earth can go wrong: it can lead to hell. But equally a good world can arise, which is closer to heaven. Promising hell – that cannot go wrong.

The issue is not to defend a civilization that is perhaps already dead and to now sing its requiem. This civilization kills on a massive scale. But this will not save it. Rather, the issue is to defend the dignity of human beings beyond the status of being an owner, so that civilization at last respects this dignity.

War has been declared. But something else should be declared – that the only way of defeating terrorism is by developing possible alternatives to the system. Further, this terrorism is only the indirect effect of the terrorism practised by the system itself. The indirect effects of the system cannot be defeated without leaving the system itself behind. Those in movements that are looking for alternatives are the only actors who, if they are successful, can stabilize our chances of life. The irrationality of terrorism can be defeated only by defeating the strategy of globalization, the irrationality of which is simply reflected in the irrationality of the terrorist. The problem is doubled, but it is ultimately a single problem. The contemporary intoxication with violence has the appearance of a supernova, which will leave a black hole behind it.

The movement that is looking for alternatives has already hinted at what must be done. The contemporary catastrophe is the proof of this. This movement has to become stronger in order to avoid worse catastrophes in the future. The system exists in its entirety as two parts: it is built on the irrationality of the globalization strategy on the one hand, and on the irrationality of the terrorist on the other, and neither of these two irrationalities can be defeated without defeating both simultaneously. This necessary defeat is the only way to stabilize our societies, by destabilizing the casino capitalism that has itself destabilized our whole lives. Without the destabilization of the casino we will not be able to stabilize our lives. We are stuck between two fundamentalist extremes. The extremes touch, and their conflict is evident. Through this conflict they affirm each other. Investors flee to 'the protection of gold'. Why do they not seek protection in a new consensus on the dignity of humanity beyond their dignity as owners? Do they think gold has a higher safety factor?

When all is said and done, the market must become more flexible, so that people and society can find their way back to stability. Casino capitalism wants to make people more flexible, so that the market can continue without any flexibility to accumulate property.

If the God of one is the Devil of the other, and the Devil of one is the God of the other, then a hopeless battle for life and death ensues. The coordinates of good and evil disappear. Everything becomes possible. We can see that Dostoevsky was wrong in saying that when there is no God everything is possible. If one accepts suicide, everything is possible. That is why in this fight for life and death anything is possible, because the opponents in this fight also accept suicide as a solution.

In the supposed battle between good and evil we can place ourselves neither on one side nor on the other. We have to avoid the battle itself. A proverb says: If there are only two alternatives, choose the third.

We have to confront this society with the fact that it is necessary to build a new consensus on the dignity of humanity in a common weal. The common weal for all people and the earth has to be the most important reference point for all parties to the conflict. In Latin America this type of common good is described using the image of a 'society in which all have space' – for non-owners as well as the environment. This theme is inspired by the Zapatistas in Mexico. Because society is global it can only be a society in which all have space. If this is not the case, then eventually nobody will have any space.

In the nineteenth century Nietzsche first articulated the motto of barbarism instead of socialism. He put it as follows: 'To fight our way out of the chaos of this form requires a need: one has to have the choice of either dying or forcing oneself through. A dominant race can only rise up from terrible and violent beginnings. Problem: where are the barbarians of the 20th century? Evidently they will only become visible after immense socialist crises reveal them and they consolidate themselves – they will be the elements capable of the greatest hardship towards themselves, and who can guarantee the strongest will' (Nietzsche 1982: vol. III, 690).

The motto of barbarism instead of socialism prevailed. First with National Socialism, and then with the barbarism of casino capitalism and its global players. Rosa Luxemburg reacted to this motto by reversing it: socialism or barbarism. That means as much as socialism instead of barbarism. But socialism too has often failed in the face of this problem.

This is why we now have to formulate the motto as follows: the common weal before barbarism, concern for the common good instead of the barbarity now prevailing. In Latin America we say a society in which all – including the environment – have space before barbarism.

Notes

1 Translator's note: the German word *Selbstmörder* means someone who commits suicide. However, literally translated it means 'self-murderer' and that is why I have tried to include a sense of that meaning in this chapter where appropriate.

2 Translation of quote from the German version.

3 Address to the nation, Internet: Office of the Press Secretary, 7 October 2001.

4 In J. P. Lucier (2000) *Sante Fe IV – Latinoamérica hoy*, Santa Fe Committee of the Council for Inter-American Security, Washington, DC. Concerning the former Santa Fe documents see Duchrow et al. 1990.

5 The following quotes by and regarding McVeigh are translations from a report in *La Nación*, Costa Rica.

6 Quoted in M. Heidegger, 'Überwindung der Metaphysik', in *Vorträge und Aufsätze*, Pfullingen, 1990, p. 79.

SIX
It is life-enhancing production which must grow, not capitalist property: Latin American approaches to a renewed dependency theory

§ For more than two decades, globalization has been sweeping over the surface of Latin America, as it has over the whole world – like a hurricane. The continent has been devastated by the privatization of state functions, free trade, the explosion in the international movements of capital, the dissolution of the welfare state, the handing over of the planning functions of the economy to the multinational companies, and the surrender of the workforce and nature to market forces.

There has been almost no effective resistance, partly because the state terrorism that accompanied globalization made this resistance impossible. Murder, torture and the 'disappearance' of people who were later buried in secret cemeteries have accompanied this process almost everywhere. At the same time, however, the apparent lack of alternatives helped to legitimize the process. Since there is clearly no more room for manoeuvre, submitting to globalization seems like realism. The dominant classes present themselves as the administrators and executors of the process, and the mass media transform themselves into its propagandists in the name of efficiency and competitiveness. The dominant economic and social theories do not analyse globalization, but glorify it. The total market seems to be the end of history and the definitive knowledge of what humanity must do. It seems to be the absolute spirit.

In the face of this situation it is no surprise that dependency theory should acquire a renewed importance in Latin America today. Dependency theory arose in the 1950s and 1960s, accompanying the politics of development as applied there from the Second World War until the 1970s. It was based on a centre-periphery model, according to which the countries of the centre (Europe, and later the USA and Japan as well) built their development for centuries on the underdevelopment of the countries of the periphery – although centres and peripheries may of course be found throughout the world. For the countries of the periphery, this implies a strategy of partial decoupling from the world market, in order to develop, before embarking on any international trade, a protected domestic economy geared to needs. From the end of the sixties this development project, which was very successful in its day, entered into a crisis that made its reformulation necessary. This was because industrialization was concentrated on the internal markets, with the result that the growing imports of capital goods could not be paid for by corresponding industrial exports. The result was a crisis in the balance of payments, which could have been resolved by reconstructing the process of industrialization. Instead, dating from the Chilean military coup of 1973, the hurricane of globalization led to the abolition and later to the renunciation of the project of industrialization and development.

The situation may be compared with that of western Europe today, where the crisis in the welfare state is turned into a pretext for abolishing it. Instead of resolving the crisis by reforming and re-creating it, the welfare state is simply denounced and declared to be the root of all evil.

The fate that befell the Latin American development project was also the fate of the theories that accompanied and interpreted it, especially dependency theory. In the 1960s, this was an important theory in Latin America, appearing in various currents of thought of which the Marxist current was only one among many. Since Latin America at this time was pursuing a policy of relative independence, the dependency/independency viewpoint was convincing because it offered an appropriate interpretation of the reality of the period. It could be found, therefore, as much in opinions of the regional UN organization (CEPAL) as in the statements of leading politicians, the declarations of social organizations of the most varied orientations, and the scientific analyses of the universities and research centres.

The hurricane of globalization was incompatible with the dependency/independency viewpoint. In Latin America, it replaced independent development by submission to the logic of the world market: development through dependency. International pressure, the pursuit of state terrorism by the dictatorships, control of the universities and the research centres – whether by police action or by a change in the policy of the foundations on whose financing many of the research activities in the continent depend – succeeded in just a short time in expelling the dependency viewpoint from the public arena. As capital relying on the logic of the world market came to prevail, theories that offered an interpretation of this domination and which are usually summed up today under the name of neo-liberalism became generally accepted. In the name of efficiency and competitiveness, they legitimize the subjection to dependency.

This repression of the dependency viewpoint within public opinion in no way demonstrated that dependency theory had been refuted or lost its importance. On the contrary: dependency had increased to such a degree that one was no longer allowed to speak of it publicly. The fact that a dependency theory appeared in the 1950s and 1960s shows rather that within the existing dependence there was still room for independent thought and action. From the 1970s onwards the dependency viewpoint was repressed, because dependency had become definitive and criticism of it was no longer accepted.

Dependency theory did not simply disappear, but it was marginalized and excluded from public opinion. As long as the logic of the world market and the present process of globalization continue to be imposed without effective resistance, it is certain that it will not return with the same importance that it had in the 1960s. For the same reason, neo-liberal theories will maintain their dominance, no matter how false they are. In fact, today they are of little use.

As Schumpeter remarked of the theory of utility, these theories are governed by a tendency towards decreasing marginal utility. The more there is of them, the less useful they are. Their theoretical utility today is limited largely to helping their authors win Nobel Prizes.

In the meantime, however, dependency theory acquires a new significance. Not only in Latin America but also in western Europe and the USA, and indeed throughout the world, we can see today a certain crisis of legitimacy in the process of globalization and its ideological justifications. The damage that this hurricane is causing both to human beings and to nature becomes more and more evident. Hence it is no longer so easy to constrain or confine public opinion.

In Latin America, this has led to new discussions on dependency theory and its development since the seventies. Included in the discussions, of course, are its weaknesses and the need to reformulate it in a changed context. In this respect, dependency theory differs remarkably from the dominant neo-classical and neo-liberal theories. These have been able to sustain themselves for more than a hundred years without any fear of contradicting reality. But this does not mean, as their representatives believe, that they are the bearers of an absolute truth. It shows rather how much these theories are based on simple tautologies. According to neo-classical theory, the market price is a rational price if it is formed in a competitive market, and a competitive market exists if prices are market prices. So far as wages are concerned, this means that a wage is a rational price if it arises in a competitive market. In this way, we arrive at a theory, abstracted from reality, that is not susceptible to any criticism. By contrast, dependency theory has had to develop constantly because it speaks of reality and not of tautologies. In this theory, a given wage is not rational simply because it is formed in a competitive market, but because it is possible to live on this wage. This puts an end to tautology and it thus becomes necessary to speak of reality.

Necessary developments of the dependency theory have taken place from the seventies to today. At present, however, there is a growing awareness that these developments must be integrated within a theoretical framework. That is indeed the purpose of the present discussions. The following problems may be included:

1) development policy as a policy of growth;
2) the new polarization of the world;
3) problems relating to a generalized policy of development.

Development policy as a policy of growth

Dependency theory in the 1960s shared the dominant opinion that the rate of economic growth can be regarded as a engine driving the whole of society which leads automatically to full employment and to the production of a social surplus that can secure the social integration of the whole workforce. Then German Chancellor Helmut Schmidt summed it up as follows: today's savings are tomorrow's investments, and the jobs of the day after tomorrow. Thus, economic policy became a policy of economic growth, whose product could, through appropriate measures of social policy, serve to integrate the whole population into the life of society.

This corresponded, in effect, to the experience of western Europe until the seventies, and in general also to Latin America's experience of the policy of development in the fifties and sixties. Latin America also found that such positive rates of growth were possible only with an appropriate policy of growth, based on a strategy of industrialization by means of import substitution.

In the second half of the 1960s, however, a phenomenon that called this experience into question was becoming apparent. In the course of that decade, industrial production grew at a high rate, but the number of people employed in industry stagnated. In Latin America, one began to speak of 'dynamic stagnation' (see Hinkelammert 1983: 138ff). It was what today is called *jobless growth*. Latin Americans spoke at that time of a crisis of industrialization by import substitution. The Marxist representatives of dependency theory saw the solution in socialist relations of production, which they thought would make it possible once more to combine high rates of economic growth with full employment and simultaneously to use the surplus product to cover the costs of the social integration of all. But the crisis of bourgeois interventionism and the welfare state linked to it was in any case visible.

The conviction that the rate of growth can be the engine of full employment has faded today, and not only in Latin America. Jobless growth has become the dominant form of growth, particularly in the developed countries of the centre. The US model of 'flexibility' seems to be an exception to this rule. Hereby new jobs are created. But these are mostly low-paid, insecure or temporary jobs. Those accepting work are forced to take several such jobs at once in order to feed their families, or they become the *working poor*. The myth of the rate of growth as a recipe for solving problems continues to be publicized by the champions of the policy of globalization, although in a completely implausible way. Similar ideas still arise in social democratic and trade union circles, which maintain that the situation can be changed by heating up global demand through public expenditure. Even though such measures might have some success, we doubt that they can solve the problems in the same way as in the 1950s or 1960s.

It is now clear that in the developed countries of the centre (the First World) economic policy is not able to determine growth rates autonomously or to increase them in the form of *extensive growth*. By extensive growth we mean growth that leads to an increase in employment, whereas *intensive growth* only improves the productivity of existing workers without creating new jobs. Intensive growth in this sense is jobless growth or growth with casualization, while extensive growth adds new and secure workers to the production process. The countries of the centre are particularly dependent on intensive growth, that is to say growth that has already reached the limits of current technology and can continue only by developing and exploiting new technical possibilities. If we ignore infrastructure investments, then new investment can realize only potential rates of growth that are determined by new technological developments. For this reason investment in productive capital can be influenced only to a limited extent by changes in interest rates (Hinkelammert 1969). If extensive growth is impossible, however, available capital cannot be employed in the sphere of production: it therefore looks for other possibilities of investment, such as speculation.

Our thesis is that it is the policy of the total market itself which makes extensive growth impossible. Eliminating 'market distortions' and, consequently, all political interventions in the market means blocking the sphere of possible productive investment. As a result, capital that is looking to invest itself must turn to non-productive spheres, notably to the service industries, the national debt and financial speculation. Hence the primary reason for this increasing orientation does not lie in the greater profits of non-productive over productive investments, but in the fact that the policy of a more total market blocks investment in the productive sphere even if this sphere offers high profits.

From this it follows that dynamic stagnation is not only a stagnation of employment in the productive sphere, but also a dynamic stagnation of productive investment.

The new polarization of the world

The dependency theory of the sixties proceeded from the thesis of a polarization between the First World (centre) and the Third World (periphery). According to this view, the First World was a world that, within capitalist relations of production, had to a great extent solved its problems of economic and social development. It appeared to have become 'capitalism with a human face'. The Third World, however, seemed to face the task of becoming what the First World already was. There was a hierarchical as well as a geographical polarization between developed and underdeveloped countries. By looking to the First World – for some, to the Second World also – the Third World would learn how to develop itself.

This highly simplified polarization can certainly no longer describe present conditions. Back in the 1960s, people began to speak of a Third World in the First World and of a First World in the Third World. The pure poles dissolved. But the more the simple polarization lost its validity, the more also the First World lost its model character. The capitalism of the First World no longer bothers to show a human

face. In fact, it doesn't have one any more. After the collapse of socialism, it no longer needs it, and it saves on the resultant costs. People
broke down walls, only to construct new ones.

So today the First World is a great archipelago found everywhere
on our planet, but surrounded by zones that cannot be integrated
either socially or economically. Although this archipelago still lies particularly in the North, the relationship can no longer be understood
as a North–South relationship. It can be designated, however, in terms
of exclusion.

There are, of course, still 'centres', although now in the form of an
archipelago, and there is still a 'periphery', although now in the form
of the sea surrounding the islands of the archipelago. Although the
globalized world market includes them all, these centres now have
the character of enclaves. A social division of labour has arisen which
presupposes this globalized world market and needs it. This globalization is based on the free movement of capital and goods and the
absence of state intervention in the movement of capital and goods;
people, however, are not similarly free to migrate. This does not in any
way imply an absence of the state. Globalization is not possible without constant and decisive action by states. But the state now works
mainly as a proponent of globalization to facilitate the flow of goods
and capital, and to promote them by means of immense subsidies
surpassing in size any subsidies ever granted by the welfare state. It is
becoming the 'nation state of competitiveness' (see Hirsch 1995), the
political representative of the total market. Competition is regarded as
the true motor of globalization, and victory in the competition is the
criterion of efficiency.

This has consequences for the productive investment of capital.
By 'productive capital' we understand capital invested, creating productive capacities, in industry, agriculture and the production of raw
materials. (We exclude investment in the infrastructure, which is governed by other rules.) What happens now is that the possibilities of
investing productive capital in an extensive growth are blocked by the
very process of globalization. The enclaves of the archipelago continue
to develop in a highly dynamic way, at the rate allowed by technological progress. The economic growth of these enclaves is fuelled
by an invested capital corresponding to these rates of growth. But
this intensive growth is mainly a growth in productivity. Extensive
growth, a growth going beyond these enclaves, appears only in lim-

ited cases. Hence the already mentioned tendency towards dynamic
stagnation of the enclaves and the whole archipelago of the centres.
Globalization, with its free movement of goods and capital, blocks
the possibility of an extensive growth of the archipelago. For this to
take place, new productive investments must be competitive from the
beginning. Since they can very rarely be competitive without protection and promotion, however, these investments are not made, The
archipelago preserves its internal dynamic, but is incapable of expanding this dynamic. Thus the tendency towards dynamic stagnation is
explained. On the one hand, the global division of labour, operated by
the multinational companies, needs the free flow of goods and capital,
but, on the other hand, the imposition of these conditions blocks the
possibility of an extensive growth of productive capital.

In this context, the *theory of comparative advantage* has become the
centrepiece of the ideology of globalization. This theory maintains
that free international trade necessarily benefits all the countries
taking part in this commerce. The worse-case scenario is where a
country obtains no advantage, but even in this case the theory excludes the possibility that a country might lose by accepting free trade.
According to this theory, buying cheap can never be the most expensive way to buy.

The transition to stagnation and later to dynamic contraction is
not foreseen in this theory. In this situation, free trade destroys incomes that are greater than the advantages derived from making a
good bargain. More is bought cheap, but this purchase leads to the
destruction of domestic production that had created larger incomes.
When this production is destroyed, and not replaced by new and
more efficient production, these incomes are also lost, without any
equivalent or greater replacement. To buy cheap becomes for many
the most expensive way to buy. The theoreticians of the theory of
comparative advantage never take these costs into account. Flying in
the face of daily experience, they speak in an indiscriminate way of
the advantages of free trade and never of the losses that it can cause.

This completely changes the character of capital investment in
general. There is much more capital than can be invested productively.
An ever-increasing proportion must be invested in non-productive
spheres. Since, however, this capital must have at least the same yield
as productive capital – assets in the capitalist system have to increase
– the hunt begins for possibilities of profitable investment in non-

productive spheres. These arise in particular as a result of the *privatiza-tion* of sectors of society that until now have been developed outside the scope of the criterion of profitability. They are to be transformed into spheres of investment for non-productive capital. This includes state activities of the most diverse kinds. Investment-seeking capital needs the privatization of the functions of the state, in order to find spheres in which to invest. This explains the worldwide pressure to denationalize all the previous functions of the state, and transform them into spheres of capital investment.

Capital now devours human beings: it becomes a cannibal. Every human activity must now become capital and bear interest, so that investment-seeking capital can live: schools, kindergartens, univer-sities, health systems, energy utilities, roads, railways, the post office, telecommunications and other means of communication, etc. The anarcho-capitalist dreams go even farther. Even the police and legisla-tion are to be transformed into capital investments. One receives a licence to live and to participate in any of the spheres of society only if one pays to capital the fees required in the form of interest. Capital becomes a 'superworld' to which sacrificial victims must be brought.

At the same time, the strategy of globalization increases the volume of capital pressing for possibilities of profitable investment. The more wage competition depresses salary levels, the greater the income con-centration that results. And high incomes have a greater inclination towards savings than low incomes. The newly formed capital, how-ever, increases the pressure towards income concentration, and thus to a further enlargement of the capital seeking to invest and the necessity to find new non-productive spheres for investment. What was looked to as a way out succeeds only in aggravating the problem, and leads finally to the reduction of the centres of the archipelago. The out-come is a dynamic contraction that is but the result of the dynamic stagnation. *We have shrunk from a one-third society to a one-fifth society, although the rates of growth are still positive, and may remain so.*

New centres also develop, however, as we have seen in the case of the Asian tigers and as we see today in some regions of China and India and in some other countries of eastern Asia. But none of these new centres arise by subjecting themselves to globalization. They arise, on the contrary, by exploiting it. These countries proceeded from a close connection between state and business bureaucracies, which aimed to promote national enterprises and enable them to penetrate by means of exports into the globalized world economy so that they might grow into multinational enterprises. Economic planning bases itself on the enterprises, integrates them in a state plan and promotes them through state policy, with the result that these enterprises can expand. The classical means of promoting development are used, particularly protective duties, import restrictions and the systematic devaluation of the currency, but also barriers to the investment of foreign capital in key sectors of production. In addition, the national enterprises are promoted directly through state subsidies and a policy of low wages, which are often supplemented, however, by a systematic national development of the education and health systems.

This policy was obviously completely successful in the countries we have mentioned. With the economic crisis of 1997, however, it has now come to an end in most of them – one of the exceptions so far is China. And now, with its entry into the World Trade Organization, the Chinese dragon may be forced to abandon the protectionist measures safeguarding its economy and could therefore end up in the same crisis as the Asian tigers.

In Latin America, however, not a single country has carried out a similar policy. Latin America is – in Andre Gunder Frank's phrase – a continent of the *lumpenbourgeoisie*. Chile, which pursued a successful and dynamic export policy, never invested its capital in relevant industrial development. Its exports are of the traditional type – agricultural and mining products – without a greater capacity for industrial exports. Mexico robbed itself of the most important instruments of such a policy by joining the North American Free Trade Agreement (NAFTA). Brazil is incapable of such a policy, despite the big industries created during the time of import substitution, because its most important branches of production are in the hands of foreign multinationals, which could never be mobilized for a policy of this type. In particular, the military dictatorship from 1965 operated a systematic policy in favour of these enterprises.

To make some comparisons:

By preventing the free movement of capital and prohibiting foreign capital investment in automobile production, as well as by the systematic state promotion of the appropriate national enterprises, Korea succeeded in creating the multinational company Hyundai. Had it allowed foreign capital to invest, Korea might have manufacturing plants for Ford or Volkswagen or Nissan; but we would know the Korean automobile industry, at best, from books or newspapers. It would have no relevance in the world market. The same holds for Japan: if it had not excluded foreign capital from its development, it would never have developed. Instead of Nissan or Toyota, it would have branches of companies like Volkswagen and Ford, which naturally would have never given it a comparable position in the world market. It would be a country like Mexico or Brazil. When the president of Nissan spoke at the opening of a factory in Mexico in the eighties, he praised the positive contribution of foreign capital to the development of Mexico. What he did not say was that if Japan had followed a policy of development similar to Mexico's, Nissan would not exist at all.

Even a successful policy of this type, however, cannot serve as a model for generalized development. It presupposes globalization in order to use it. It can do this because so many countries, indeed whole continents, are simply subjected to globalization. These Asian countries were therefore quite in favour of globalization, only they excluded themselves in order to be able to use it. It is as in the cinema: if one person stands up, then he or she sees better than the others. If some more people rise, they also see better. But if everyone stands up, everybody sees worse.

We are dealing, then, with a development policy based on the premise that the great majority of countries will not or cannot pursue the same policy. Countries that adopt this policy must be opposed to others also adopting it. It is like the drug dealers, who are against legalizing the trade in drugs because their high profits depend on the illegality of drugs.

So long as these Asian countries made use of globalization, but followed a protectionist policy and did not globalize themselves, they won. With their own increasing inclusion in globalization, they ran into trouble.

Problems relating to a generalized development policy

The dependency theory of the 1960s had a further limitation. The solutions proposed by this theory completely ignored the problem of the environment and the limits to growth that arise from the threatened destruction of the environment. Particularly from the analyses that Ivan Illich made in Cuernavaca (Mexico) during that period, this viewpoint also penetrated into dependency theory, but only later was it elaborated in more systematic form.

The dependency theory considered the problem of dynamic stagnation, which began in Latin America in the 1960s and which today
we call jobless growth. Since as yet the environmental viewpoint was
scarcely present, however, dependency theory saw the solution in a
generalization of economic growth beyond the limits imposed by
this dynamic stagnation. Growth still seemed to be the way to secure
the economic and social integration of the population, although
the theory recognized the need to overcome the capitalist limits to
growth that were becoming visible. Dependency theory shared this
central position of the politics of growth with nearly all the economic
and social theories of its time.

During the 1970s, as people became more and more aware of the
problem of the destruction of the environment, a criticism of growth
as a starting point developed within dependency theory. This criticism did not lead to the condemnation of growth as such, but it did
lead to the realization that economic growth cannot be the supreme
value of economic and social policy and that it may not be regarded
as the engine of economic and social progress. Naturally, this led to
conflict with the ideologies of globalization, which more than ever
propagated economic growth – together with formal efficiency and
competition – as the highest value of human existence. It was as if the
growing awareness that the environment was being destroyed even
increased the readiness of the representatives of globalization to continue its destruction.

Globalization in Latin America only accentuated its dynamic stagnation. Jobless growth was supplanted by economic development with
fewer workers – dynamic contraction. The workers released had to
survive somehow, however, so an increasing *informal sector* was formed,
which extends today to at least a third of the workforce, and very
often to more than half. These 'informal' workers live with the help
of precarious survival strategies and 'flexible' employment. This sector
also plays its part in the destruction of the environment.

Only a few people still believe that globalization, which is always
based on a strategy of growth, can surmount this situation of exclusion. Growth in a world economy based on the strategy of globalization can be as high as it likes, but it will do nothing to change
the exclusion of ever larger parts of the population. The more it is
accelerated, however, the more it will also destroy humanity's natural
environment. In the globalized accumulation model of capitalist

property, exclusion of the population and environmental degradation go hand in hand.

Possible solutions are therefore being discussed in Latin America today, particularly on the basis of these two problems: exclusion of the population and environmental degradation. The proposals of historical socialism no longer help much, since they were based – as completely as today's globalization strategy – on the policy of growth as the engine of progress. Today, leaving aside the issue of environmental degradation, such a policy no longer leads to the overcoming of exclusion even in the centres of the archipelago.

If the exclusion of the population turns out to be inevitable in any policy of growth, one must question the growth economy itself.

In view of the dynamic stagnation, it is impossible to maintain competitiveness as the central criterion of economic development. Competition means that one wins and the other loses. This is equivalent to a death sentence for the loser. The market decides and uses the death penalty for the loser. *Competition is a kind of war. It is not just a game that is played in the market. We are dealing with a war with the same consequences as a military war. Generalized development is possible, therefore, only through continuing interventions in the market, so that the loser in the competition is not condemned to death.*

Losers in the competition have the right to protect themselves. But not only the right: it is also economically rational to do so. If they are eliminated by the competition, they lose much more than they stand to gain from the positive effects of competition. Consequently, they do not have to accept the judgment of the market without opposition. Branches of production that are not competitive are economically rational if the advantages of competition – that is, access to cheaper goods – are counterbalanced or exceeded by the losses: the income losses from the elimination of the uncompetitive branches of production.

We see above all two spheres where the state must intervene:

- *it must protect uncompetitive simple goods production; and*
- *it must prevent the emergence of non-productive capital property.*

On the first point, this argument for the protection of uncompetitive production is completely different from the well-known protective duty argument of the Prussian economic reformer Friedrich List. He argued for tariff protection for industries during a transition period in which the developing industry is to become competitive. Our argument is for protection in the long term, and is derived directly from the thesis of dynamic stagnation.

This questioning of the growth economy and its central criterion of competitiveness is just as necessary in relation to the informal sector within an economy. These sectors must develop an economic form that liberates them from precarious strategies of survival. They can no longer aim at integration into the sector of capital accumulation, but must to a certain degree decouple themselves.[1]

Local and regional systems of dividing up the work must follow, able to protect themselves from subjection to the dictates of the worldwide division of labour. Their appropriate internal organization could perhaps best be described as being geared towards *simple goods production*. This probably represents the only realistic possibility today of giving back a stable livelihood to those excluded from society.

But this presupposes a *new protectionism*, different from the classical kind. It must take place within society, not simply at its political borders. It must permit local and regional systems of division of labour that are separated from the competition of the capitalist enterprises oriented towards capital accumulation. This can have the most diverse forms: from the protection of traditional forms of production, such as the simple goods production that still survives today in the regions of Latin America inhabited by indigenous people, to the reconstruction of forms of simple goods production in the urban sectors where all economic relations have broken down and where people survive simply by casual labour. Solutions of this sort are absolutely necessary if we want to maintain a generalized development policy. But they are by no means sufficient.

On the second point, the growth economy oriented towards the accumulation of capitalist property must itself be restructured. This means above all *reducing the mass of capital looking for investment*. It has become a 'superworld' that strangles and destroys the real world. In the budgets of Latin American countries taken as a whole, interest payments are the most important item of expenditure, representing at least a third of public expenditure. Capital must be limited to its function of productive investment, which must at the same time be made compatible with the conditions of existence of the sectors of simple goods production. The tax suggested by Nobel economics laureate James Tobin, which aims to limit the scope of speculative capital, can only be a beginning. It is also necessary to obstruct the emergence of this capital. This demands two measures that are urgent today:

- *Redistributing income and property* to those on lower incomes is the only way to limit the emergence of capital that finds no possibilities of productive investment and must therefore look for non-productive, often purely speculative, possibilities. This holds true because lower incomes have less of a tendency to form capital than higher incomes. This is particularly important in Latin America, which has the most extreme income and property concentration in the world. Therefore: property for people, not for profit.
- There is, however, yet another source of money capital that is used more than anything for speculative purposes: the formation of *large speculative money funds*, particularly those which come into being through the private insurance systems, and especially the life insurance systems. In 1992, more than half the share capital of all multinational enterprises in the United States was already in the hands of such funds (Drucker 1993: 88). One can only influence such a development, however, by strengthening the public systems of *old age pension insurance*. These are based on the principle of direct payment, so that in each period the insurance premiums must equal the insurance payments due. The contributions paid create no speculative capital funds, therefore, but are turned directly into pension payments in the same period. With private insurance systems it is different. There the contributions are accumulated as capital, while liabilities are paid from capital returns. It is precisely out of these life insurances that tremendous 'roving' capital funds have developed, which take the whole world as their playground and turn all production – even that of the multinational enterprises – into a sphere for investment and exploitation by speculative capital. This means, however, that the currently fashionable *ideology of privatization* must be questioned radically. It serves only to heat up the process of the formation of speculative capital and accelerates the speed of the avalanche that threatens to bury us all. In this respect, many pension reforms in industrial countries are going in precisely the wrong direction. They are tending to change part of the public pension provision into a system based on return on private capital. In addition – as in the case of Germany under the first 'red–green' government – they break with the basic, hard-won principle that the

employers – thus the capital owners – must pay an equal half of the old age pension insurance contributions.

These are by no means all the problems queueing up for solution, but they are the problems that are particularly discussed today in those circles in Latin America that are close to dependency theory. From these discussions a double strategy is emerging: the development and protection of sustainable local and regional forms of economy, combined with macroeconomic public interventions to block and regulate a globalization directed purely towards the accumulation of capital. In the following chapter we will try to take the discussion farther by elaborating elements of a new property order and in this way put the double strategy on a firm, extended basis.

Note

1 This problem is increasingly discussed in Europe. See Douthwaite 1996; Lang and Hines 1993.

SEVEN

Another world is possible: rebuilding the system of ownership from below from the perspective of life and the common good

§   Neo-liberal, global capitalism aims at the boundless accumulation of capital and is thus indirectly programmed to destroy life and thereby its own support systems. This logic of death must be broken, for the sake of the life of all people and the earth. This requires a fundamental change of perspective, applied in practice in alternative economic and political institutions and approaches. This is where the reorganization of ownership comes in, to overcome the ideology of privatization.

What is meant by life and the common good?

As shown in Chapter 1, the very first form of the Greek-Hellenistic and Roman property economy, driven by money and accumulating monetary value, had a destructive effect on social cohesion and the life of people and societies. Peasant farmers lost their land and their freedom through debt bondage, while the large landowners were able to live in growing luxury in the cities. Solidarity among the farmers was also eroded.

This was most strongly opposed in ancient Israel, in the Jesus movement and early Christian communities. That is why it has remained essential to recall this resistance and the alternatives it represented. Yet it is clear from the start that the economic and political questions were never just about pragmatic details. They were rooted in basic decisions on what 'functions as God', as the final authority in a society (see Veerkamp 1993: 113f; Richard et al. 1983). In Israel it was Yahweh who heard the cries of the slaves, oppressed and poor, and liberated them from the slave-owner, the oppressor and the rich. This Yahweh is a god of life, unmasking and challenging the gods legitimizing power and wealth and revealing them to be idols calling for human sacrifice. This is the fundamental perspective to which all biblical traditions related after the liberation of the Hebrews from Egypt (Exod: 3ff).

The first point of reference in this critical perspective is the social pyramid of the monarchy. It was still possible in Israel itself to establish a monarchy from *c.* 1030 to 586 BCE, albeit one that was critiqued and modified. Around this time, from the second half of the eighth century BCE onwards, it was infiltrated by elements of a new socio-economic order – a property-based economy. The prophets had already started criticizing injustice in the kingly, aristocratic system, and they immediately expressed opposition in solidarity with the farmers. The core of their criticism was: all must be able to live. This is why the biblical perspective starts from the cry of the poor and those whose livelihood is threatened.[1]

Methodologically speaking, we here encounter, for the first time in the history of civilization, an approach to knowledge, ethics and practice that has been a real alternative to this day. The starting point in every historical situation, characterized at the time by royal structures and by an incipient form of property-money mechanisms, is the experience that there are winners and losers in a given system. The winners in the ruling system present it as necessary, good for everyone and there by divine right. The Bible fundamentally sides with the loser, whose life is threatened and who must be enabled to live. The analysis of an existing system begins with a critical analysis of its negative points. At the same time the perspective of the common good fundamentally starts with the weakest, most threatened members of the community. If they can live, all can live. And finally there is liberation from oppression; all are involved and all are given a living. Justice and life are the basic perspectives and the golden thread of biblical traditions. There is no neutral place for knowledge, ethics and action, along the lines of 'neutral' scholarship. In every situation people are faced with the decision either to adopt the stance of the status quo or a critical, constructive position of liberation. This would mean checking out what is compatible with life for all and the good of all (biblically speaking, the will of God – Rom. 12: 1f).

It is precisely this approach which proponents of liberation theology try to bring out in interdisciplinary exchange with economics, social sciences and philosophy. They do this both theoretically and practically against the backdrop of capitalist history and with an eye to the future of life on this planet.[2] The starting point is criticism of the modern ideologies that justify, promote and defend the power of the market, culminating in present-day neo-liberalism. Yet first of all it is a matter of *epistemology*. As indicated in the previous chapter, the assumption of neutrality is leading the empirical sciences to draw absurd conclusions; we are witnessing the irrationality of the rational (see Assmann and Hinkelammert 1992: 90ff; Hinkelammert 1996: 12ff).

With respect to the property-based market economy this means that all rational action is reduced to a *means–ends rationality*. If the goal were profitability, i.e. maximum profit on capital assets used for personal interest, then it would be only rational to use the most efficient means to achieve this end. For example, one would need to employ as few workers as possible at the lowest possible wages and under the worst, i.e. cheapest, possible conditions to make the product or provide the service. The cost of environmental friendliness would need to be avoided and taxes kept down, or, if possible, not paid at all. Through competition action would become increasingly efficient in this means–ends rationality of the marketplace.

As indicated in Chapter 2, Adam Smith contended that actions efficiently performed (intentionally) in calculated self-interest, and in this means–end rationality, were coordinated by the 'invisible hand of the market' (non-intentionally, indirectly) so as to produce the 'wealth of nations'. Karl Marx picked up this theory and critically analysed statements by Adam Smith. In his Paris manuscripts he showed that the indirect effect of market rationality under capitalist production conditions led to misery and death among the working people and by no means to the welfare of all. The capitalist market does not coordinate the division of labour so that the basic needs of all are met (see in particular Hinkelammert and Mora 2001). As a result of his analysis in *Das Kapital* he then writes a sentence that can only be termed prophetic in the light of global capitalism: 'Capitalist production, therefore, only develops technology, and the combining together of various processes into a social whole, by sapping the original sources of all wealth – the soil and the labourer' (Marx 1887: 442f; Hinkelammert 1999b: 55f). An image of this irrationality of the rational is the man who uses all his rationality to sharpen his saw and then saws off the branch on which he is sitting (see Hinkelammert 1996: 17ff). He falls to the ground and dies, all his ends and means dying with him, along with all rationality. It then follows that the condition for all instrumental, ends–means rationality has to be a rationality of the reproduction of life, a rationality of life.

The reality of the global property market economy unmistakably reveals the instrumental logic of destruction and self-destruction. The

liberal ideology claiming that the indirect effects of intentional, egoistic, profit-maximizing competition are coordinated by the market
for the common good is disproved by the facts.[3] Naturally we now
have cynical, nihilistic capitalism (see Hinkelammert 2001: 321ff). But
this only confirms the murderous, suicidal logic of real, deregulated,
imperialistic global capitalism.

*Any reason worthy of the name must therefore come to the conclusion that
all economic structures, institutions and actions must be reconstructed according
to the logic of the survival of all.*

An ethical standpoint leads to the same conclusion. Following
Mandeville, Adam Smith had developed his economic theory from
ethics (see Gutiérrez 1998: 31ff). Believing in the 'invisible hand' that
coordinates the non-intentional actions for the common good, he
reduced ethics to the functional ethics of market action. Subsequently
Max Weber, on the basis of this inconsistency, caused a confusion
of terms that has prevailed ideologically and de facto to this day. He
claimed, on the one hand, that the capitalist market was 'non-ethical';
it couldn't have anything to do with ethics because it simply followed
the competition laws of the market that led to 'lordless slavery' (see
Duchrow 1995: 112). By contrast, ethics was either 'conviction ethics'
by which he meant the biblical 'brotherhood ethics', in its highest
form the Sermon on the Mount, which in his view applied only to the
private sphere, or 'responsibility ethics', which he defined ambiguously.
On the one hand, it simply follows the laws of the market, and is
therefore identical with the functional ethics of liberalism and neo-
liberalism (e.g. Hayek; see Hinkelammert 1994: 62ff; Gutiérrez 1998:
129ff). Hence Weber's designation of market action as 'anethical',
that is, without any ethics, is misleading. Anyone following market
laws acts according to responsibility ethics, in his view. This gives
those who do so a good conscience. They represent 'realism', while all
those taking a critical line on the market can be labelled 'idealists' and
'utopians'. Popper takes this distinction to extremes with his famous
statement that all those striving for heaven on earth bring forth hell.
This theoretical disqualification and discrimination of the 'idealists'
has dangerous consequences. In the 'national security' systems they are
equated with 'communists' and recently with 'terrorists' and eliminated,
as shown in the secret papers of the US military in 1987 (see Hinkelammert 1994: 172ff; Duchrow et al. 1990).

On the other hand, Weber defines 'responsibility ethics' in terms

of decisions involving value judgements that are not rationally accessible. These ethics have their place above all in political action. They
cannot be used with respect to the 'objective' sphere of the sciences
or of economics, where judgements must be objective. Applied to
the destructive and self-destructive logic of the market, shored up by
global imperialism, Weber's responsibility ethics accordingly mean the
legitimization of institutionalized irresponsibility – in a double sense.
The indirect effects of a market geared purely to the accumulation of
capital are not covered by the responsibility of functional ethics, and
the organizing of the political and legal conditions of the market follows from value decisions not accessible to reason. They are thereby at
the mercy of pure power. In the imperialist, capitalist global system of
today we are witnessing just this: destruction and self-destruction.

As with the critical analysis of rationality, it follows that formally
restricting ethics to the functioning of the system, and declaring all
farther-reaching ethical challenges to be either private or arbitrary
political value judgements, leads to irresponsibility and death for
people and the earth.

*This leads to the ethical necessity, the objective judgement on the basis of
facts, that action has to prioritize the creation of conditions enabling the life of
all people and the earth. Only on this basis can individual means to reach individual ends be judged and put into practice. In old-fashioned terms, this ethic
of life is called the ethic of the common good* (Hinkelammert 2001: 375ff).

Enrique Dussel (1998), the Mexican philosophy professor, outlined such an ethic of life and the common good. His work begins
with a critique of the modern Western ethical systems that confine
themselves to formal ethics, and – starting from the viewpoint of
the victims of the system (people and the earth) – calls for ethics to
be rooted in the material question of life. Only then can the question raised by discourse ethics about the communicative structures
of ethics come into its own, and again only if all those excluded from
the respective social systems can take part in the communication process. This ethic so vital to life reveals its liberating character in both its
substantive definition of the ethic of life and its comprehensive, participatory character – critically countering the existing system and its
legitimizations. It refers to the goal of a 'society in which all have their
place in harmony with nature', which was formulated by analogy
with the workings of the indigenous Mexican Zapatistas (Hinkelammert 1999b: 170ff).

Yet it is not enough for the ethic of life and the common good, defined through participation, to be recognized as necessary and elaborated critically in terms of the status quo and its legitimizations – it also has to be concerned with the *feasibility* of its alternatives.[4] Between the realization of the status quo and the utopia of unlimited possibilities lies the field of really possible alternatives. 'There is a theory of knowledge in which knowledge relates correlatively to what can be manufactured technologically, i.e. what can be made [*factibilidad*] ... If one needed to give criteria for the choice between many possibilities within the economically "makable" then the criterion that has to apply as a condition for the possibility of all others would be indispensable. Such a criterion is the fact that the human subject is a living subject with needs ... Basic human needs are absolute criteria' (Dussel in Hinkelammert 1994: 319). Only with de facto possible alternatives can the ethic of liberation effectively counter the capitalist project which cannot sustain the life of all people and the earth. This becomes all the clearer in terms of the actual economic, legal and political implementation of the ethic of liberation, which is the subject of Dussel's latest book.[5]

This is precisely where the question of means–end relations needs to be picked up again, but only with the question: What serves the life and participation of all? The response cannot be to directly derive rights, institutions, political orders and strategies, in order to declare them absolute or permitting of no alternative, as is the case in liberal and neo-liberal capitalism. Nor can one confine oneself to good intentions and choose to ignore the non-intentional, indirect effects.

Every practical proposal regarding alternative institutions and actions is to be checked and judged by whether it is de facto useful to real life and whether anyone was excluded from the process of devising it or would not benefit from its consequences.

This also applies to the basic *institution of property*. Here there can be no a priori prescribed, absolute priority for a specific form of property. There can be no natural law governing (capitalist) private property, nor can state ownership of the means of production be the only alternative. It is precisely this false, absolutized alternative which has brought the world to the almost hopeless situation in which it finds itself at present, and which is driving it farther into the abyss. Any alternative proposed below is therefore to be checked strictly against the necessary criteria of life and the participation of all, and also in terms of its feasibility. All historical, cultural, technical, political, legal and economic factors need to be considered. The results must remain open to revision. We are not replacing market fundamentalism with another form of fundamentalism. Our goal is the fullness and variety of real life.

How can the ownership system be rebuilt from below?

Historical examples What kind of new ownership system is this? To get closer to this contemporary question it would help to recall a few historical examples. As shown above, in biblical traditions no absolute model is propagated. Rather it is from the basic perspective of the God who hears the cries of creation and thus sustains the life of all that new practical forms are developed. In the ban on interest of the Book of the Covenant (after 722 BCE) the point is to prevent a threat to life through the property mechanism of debt. Deuteronomy (622) adds the periodic cancellation of debt and debt bondage, if they have come about at all through the ownership mechanism. In the holiness law of the priestly writings (sixth century BCE) property is finally stripped of absoluteness because the earth and people 'belong' to God and therefore people only have usage rights to the earth – with the consequence that every generation has to regain access to its own means of production. In the light of the political and ideological absolutization of the property-based economy brought about through the Hellenistic and Roman empires, faithful Jews and Christians can only opt to resist. They choose between God and Mammon and set up alternatives in small, attractive groups that freely share their property so that there are no poor in their midst.

Another example is offered by the Greek philosopher Aristotle. On the basis of the experience with the Hellenistic property-money economy of the fourth century BCE, he brilliantly anticipates later developments and analyses the consequences of this system, proposing practical alternative options. When it is no longer the usefulness of produced and consumed goods which drives economic activity, but their exchange value and limitless accumulation through money mechanisms, the property-owning individual falls prey to the illusion of boundless life – and the community is destroyed. With respect to property he therefore draws interesting, differentiated conclusions from the principle: property is for practical use (Aristotle 1961: 1,254a, 1–5).

The context for Aristotle is the household, the basic economic unit for the Greeks with land as its means of production. Useful property therefore relates at the same time to personal property and also to the production property that ensures the satisfaction of basic needs such as food and clothing. In this context he also allows money-mediated exchange as long as it relates to the availability of a greater range of useful goods. He also knows about the common good and the use of private property for the *polis* and caring for the poor. 'These are the objects which may be regarded as constituting true wealth; and the amount of household property which suffices for a good life is not unlimited ... and wealth may be defined as a number of instruments used in a household or state' (ibid.: 1,256b, 25–40). Künzli sums up Aristotle's view of permitted acquired property as follows: 'Acquisition may be rated naturally and positively as long as – and only as long as – it produces the utensils and provisions needed for individual and community life, and orients itself here to the elementary needs of people in the service of sustenance and a dignified, virtuous life' (Künzli 1986: 103).

So Aristotle clearly patterns the economy and, specifically, ownership on the life of persons and individuals in community. By contrast he strongly rejects the acquisition of goods and money for its own sake (*khrematistiké*): 'But there is a second form of the general art of getting property, which is particularly called, and which it is just to call, the art of acquisition. It is the characteristics of this second form which lead to the opinion that there is no limit to wealth and property ... this second form is not natural' (Aristotle 1961: 1,256b, 40, 1,257a, 5). Trading and charging interest aimed at gaining a monopoly are, according to Aristotle, the two illegitimate ways in which property is infinitely accumulated for its own sake (see Duchrow 1995: 21). They are not just to be rejected in theory but also to be politically suppressed for the sake of the life of the community, since through corruption this excessive form of wealth is the downfall of every political order. Of course, a purely legal or political solution is not enough if the citizens are not also convinced by ethical eduation that a moderate life in community enhances their self-preservation. To that extent the ethical writings of Aristotle are a necessary part of his remarks about economics and politics. An isolation of the economy from ethics and politics as in the modern age is inconceivable for Aristotle. Disregarding the indirect effects of economic mechanisms

and ways of acting on the whole of society is also unthinkable for
him.

The Bible and Greek philosophy (not just for Aristotle, but also for
Plato with his plea for common property in the cases of guards and
warriors) all underlie the complex teaching of the Church fathers on
private property. They place the accents differently – the two poles are
Chrysostomos (see Tsompanidis 1999: 189ff), a radical, and Clement
of Alexandria, who was relatively friendly towards the rich. But they
share some views:

1. The accumulation of property is greed, a major sin: 'Why, pray
   tell me, do you torment yourself to lay up every day richer treasures than the sand, to buy land, houses and baths, to even seize
   them through robbery and greed and so to fulfil the words of
   the Prophet: "Ah, you who join house to house, who add field to
   field, until there is room for no one but you" (Isa. 5: 8)' ... 'There
   is something terrible about greed, anyone guilty of it shall be ex-
   pelled from the church' (Chrysostomos, cited in Künzli 1986: 141).
2. Enjoying goods alone means losing them, harming both the social
   whole and oneself. The crucial idea here is that of benefit. Since
   everything belongs to God we are only beneficiaries of existing
   goods, and there can be no private property in the strict legal sense
   of exclusive rights, this right being limited, if not repealed, by the
   normative obligation to be useful: 'Everything belongs to God ...
   Do you not know that we will be called to account if we make
   poor use of it? Because it does not belong to us, but to the Lord,
   we are obliged to share it with our fellow servants' (ibid.: 147f).
3. In other words, if private property is to exist at all in this sinful
   world – in the Garden of Eden and under original natural law everything was shared – then at least the usage must be in common.

This means then that the Church fathers in principle held to the
biblical approach: what is not common property anyway should be
private property by relative right, so that it can be to the benefit of all.
On no account must it be misused for private wealth accumulation.

Thomas Aquinas, although often misused to legitimize capitalist
private property, knew only of a natural right to usage:

> Aquinas is not drawing conclusions about any specific form of prop-
> erty but simply offering a method for doing so: a particular kind of

property is judged to be valid if it can really guarantee to all their right
to the use of the goods of the earth. This is a matter of method rather
than a result. As conditions vary during different periods of history,
one specific form of property will turn out to be valid, and others
will cease to be valid. In essence Aquinas' method makes the property
system subordinate to the right of use and supports it only as a medi-
ation of that basic right. According to Aquinas no property system is
valid (that is, legitimate); rather its validity comes from the right of
use … Therefore Aquinas conceives of a natural right of use but not
to private property. He therefore treats the specification of property
under *ius gentium* rather than under natural law. (Hinkelammert 1986:
161).

Martin Luther, on the threshold of early capitalism, argued fiercely
for the useful character of property against the large trading and capital companies like the Fuggers (see Duchrow 1987: 59ff and 1995:
217ff). He above all fought the mechanism of compound interest and
castigated wealth accumulation as thievery and idolatry. He called
upon the powers that be to intervene in the interest of the common
good in the boundless business activities of capital owners.

By contrast with later Calvinists, who inspired Max Weber to see
capitalism as arising from the spirit of the 'Protestant ethic', Calvin
was fully in the tradition of the common good which – as in Luther's
philosophy – is ultimately defined by the need of one's neighbour.
In his study on property in the Protestant ethic – meaning Calvin's
– Dommen (1999/2000: 18) sums it up as follows:

> Firstly, property rights should be assigned to whomever is best placed
> to manage the property in the public interest. Secondly, it should not
> be assumed that it is necessary to assign all the rights over a given item,
> i.e. managerial responsibilities for it, to a single owner: they can be
> divided up and allocated in whichever way best meets the first objec-
> tive. Thirdly, efficiency is not the only goal: overriding priority is due
> to the needs of the poor. Finally, and in any event, the allocation of
> property rights is essentially a matter of public policy.

The Hebrew and Christian Bible, Aristotle, scholasticism and the
Reformation all focus decisively on the usage of property and its
usefulness for the community. However, the biblically inspired
approaches stress that the victims of the system are the criterion by

which the common good has to be defined. After all, if the conditions
for their life are fulfilled this amounts to the life of the community.
The thinker most maligned by capitalism, Karl Marx, refers to all of
these. It is no accident that Marx was converted to socialism by Moses
Hess, a Jew, and derived many ideas from the latter's essay 'On Money'
for his analysis of goods, money and capital fetishism (see Segbers
2001; Künzli 1986: 402ff).

We cannot here outline the whole development of Marx's ideas on
property and ownership (see Künzli 1986: 425ff). For our topic a few
basic observations will suffice. No one has analysed and critiqued the
implications and consequences of capitalist private ownership of the
means of production more convincingly than Marx. He demonstrated
what we can see to be a fact today, that the gearing of the economy to
the accumulation of capital not only exploits the workers, it increasingly excludes them from the reproduction of life, and likewise causes
environmental degradation. At the same time society as a whole is
directed, through the fetishization of goods, money and capital, by
laws driving the actors forward. They destroy both the proactive character of human beings and – through the competition – solidarity
among them.

As far as his proposed solutions go, he tended towards an abstract
cancellation of private property in the end, which led to the dead end
of centralist socialism (See Hinkelammert 1994: 136ff). The attempt to
replace the mistake of the abstract, reductionist market system by an
equally abstract, centralist project must be seen to have failed historically. However, two approaches rediscovered by Marx have remained
of crucial importance: that the alternative must start with the usefulness of the products and that producers must be protagonists and not
objects in the production and social processes. So it is about forming
institutions, politics and forms of action starting from the real life of
people and remaining in harmony with nature.

This is precisely the sense of the formula inspired by the Zapatistas in Mexico, that of the 'society in which all have their place in
harmony with nature', that is, a society in which no one is excluded,
which is the case by definition in a capitalist economy.

> Universalist social principles – whether they concern the market
> and private property, or a central plan and public property – will
> be checked for validity against the demand for a society in which

everyone has their place. But that implies contesting their claim to be universal. The criterion of their validity can therefore not be a fundamental one. Rather they define a valid framework. Universalist social principles are valid or may claim validity as long as they are compatible with a society in which there is room for everyone. They lose their validity when implementing them means that some members of society are excluded. The exclusion of parts of society is automatic, however, when universalist social principles are regarded as absolute. Consequently they can only be of relative validity. (Hinkelammert 1999b: 172)

The criterion 'in harmony with nature' was formulated memorably by the Declaration of the Indigenous Communities on the WTO agreement on trade-related intellectual property rights (TRIPs) in 1999, in connection with the WTO conference in Seattle:

No to patenting of Life!

We, indigenous peoples from around the world, believe that nobody can own what exists in nature except nature herself. A human being cannot own its own mother. Humankind is part of Mother Nature, we have created nothing and so we can in no way claim to be owners of what does not belong to us. But time and again, western legal property regimes have been imposed on us, contradicting our own cosmologies and values.

We view with regret and anxiety how Article 27.3b of the Trade-Related Aspects of Intellectual Property Rights (TRIPs) of the World Trade Organization (WTO) Agreements will further denigrate and undermine our rights to our cultural and intellectual heritage, our plant, animal, and even human genetic resources and discriminate against our indigenous ways of thinking and behaving. This Article makes an artificial distinction between plants, animals, and micro-organisms and between 'essentially biological' and 'microbiological processes' for making plants and animals. As far as we are concerned all these are life forms and life creating processes which are sacred and which should not become the subject of proprietary ownership.[6]

How can these alternative approaches from tradition and the present be put into practice on the basis of resistance to capitalist globalization? If the decisive point is that real life and the participation of all in harmony with nature are to be the criteria for all economic activity then it follows of necessity that the local and regional levels are crucial. All other levels – national and global – are to relate to them, and the national and global levels in turn only have a legitimate role to play if they support the level at which people take part in economic life for the sake of its usage value. To avoid any misunderstandings: these alternatives are not to be confined to the local level. All levels, from the local to the global, are to be reorganized. The question is only: from what angle and in whose interest? We say from the perspective of the local people and their interest. This is in direct contrast to the prevailing (dis)order in which large-scale owners destructively and randomly use their globalized capital to accumulate more from all over the world market (see Daly and Cobb 1989; Duchrow 1995; Korten 1995; Douthwaite 1996; Diefenbacher et al. 1997). In ancient times the household, the productive extended family, was the basis for local business and today the most diverse forms of organization are to be found at this level in the different continents and cultures. Besides the traditional extended families there are village communities, tribal communities, cooperatives and also regions. One of the principal strengths of this approach from the local level is the possibility of bringing out the cultural features of the communities. This applies not just to personal property but also to the forms of ownership of all economic factors, such as land, water, air, energy, work, industry, knowledge and money, as we shall now show.

Personal property The concept of personal property seems very clear and simple. But it contains a basic problem that is not easy: what do we understand by 'person'? In the modern, Western world we immediately think of persons in the sense of individuals. Then personal property would need to be defined in the context of the market economy and set apart from other forms of bourgeois ownership. However, it appears that there is something like personal property in all cultures. Rittstieg (1975: 319f) writes, regarding literature on African, Asian and indigenous peoples in the Americas:

> Personal property is, moreover, not a product of the market society that is oriented to private acquisition. Legal history and legal anthropology teach that even at primitive levels of social development there is recognition of ownership of objects for personal use. The property right of feudalism does not differ from bourgeois property with

respect to utility objects but through the special allocation of land, the most important means of production in an agricultural society. On the other hand, states calling themselves socialist have restricted or abolished *private* ownership of means of production while endowing personal property with constitutional guarantees. The historical and cultural ubiquity of personal property indicates that its allocation corresponds to people's basic needs. Yet it is less a matter of the dependence of human subsistence on clothes and utensils. Objects without any immediately useful function are also covered by personal property in all cultures; and with utility objects it is precisely qualities going beyond their usefulness that make them essentially one's own.

And he points to studies showing that prisoners and infants deprived of their personal objects were observed to suffer strong psychological disorders. Human beings are not just flesh and blood. They are part of a close field of relations that is like an extended part of their own body, soul and spirit, and therefore has an aesthetic dimension going beyond its own practical importance.

But precisely these fundamental observations make it so hard to say exactly what is to be understood by personal property, indeed whether the mentioned phenomena should be included in the category of property at all. This difficulty grows when one adds the fact that 'persons' are not just to be understood in the context of the things around them but also with reference to the community in which they live. In a market economy, with the struggle of all individuals against all others, personal property will have a different significance to its meaning in a society in which 'person' is understood as constituting 'person in community', in a relationship of reciprocity (see Daly and Cobb 1989: 159ff).

Without elaborating, we can just note that personal property is part of a human life led in dignity and self-reliance. It is by definition determined by personal usefulness, though usage value certainly does not mean 'utilitarian calculation' (Rittstieg 1975: 315ff). It must therefore not be seen from the angle of exchange or asset value. This is to be stressed because with the aid of Hegel's idealistic philosophy the enabling of freedom linked with personal property for self-reliant activity is also commonly seen to legitimize the property of the company owner.

A further difficulty consists in individuals needing very different degrees of personal property for their life in dignity. Anyone who has seen the famous photo of the personal effects left by Gandhi – a pair of sandals, a dhoti, spectacles and a fountain pen – will hesitate to classify the personal luxury of a sophisticated yuppy in the same legal category. And yet the band within which personal property is worth protecting should not be too narrow. The problem of luxury is less one of use than of social mechanisms enabling the accumulation of the wealth that permits the luxury. But this affects other dimensions of the ownership issue. The key point here is the personal use.

This issue should also include people's homes. This too has become embedded in the broader social context, in that the majority of the population depend on their employment or government support to pay their rent. However, a key distinction between owner-occupation and commercial use should be made when it comes to legal protection for one's home. The question of the land on which the building stands is another issue, as will be shown below.

At this point it is interesting to note that in the deliberations on the German constitution Carlo Schmid – unsuccessfully – wanted only this personal property protected by the constitution, not bourgeois property including the ownership of the means of production; that is essentially a matter of accumulation of wealth for a few at the expense of the majority, and it began with the privatization of land at the beginning of the modern age.

Land Although given present power relations it will be even more difficult to implement than after the Second World War, we should renew the insight formulated for the first time in ancient Israel in the sixth century BCE. Land is a good that should not be owned in the sense of *dominium*, of absolute private ownership; there should be only the right of usage. The long-term goal here can only be that of reversing capitalist development. This statement is founded not just on basic tenets of biblical tradition and present indigenous communities. It stems from capitalist development itself. As in Greece in the eighth century BCE the introduction of private land ownership at the beginning of the modern age was based on the attempt to justify the freedom and dignity of persons as against the dependence on feudal rule. Through capitalization of land ownership for the purpose of wealth accumulation this approach was, however, reversed. This led to an ever stronger concentration of land ownership and profit-making from it at the expense of the majority of citizens and their freedom. The most blatant example is land speculation. Capitalist development has turned into a new feudalism of the rule of the few over the many. In countries of the South classical feudalism has simply turned into capitalist feudalism.[7]

So it is no wonder that indigenous peoples and social movements like that of the landless in Brazil (Movimento Sem Terra) struggle for fundamental land reforms. 'First World' economists like Hans Christoph Binswanger from St Gallen, Switzerland, call for a fundamental revision of the constitution regarding the ownership of land (Binswanger 1978: 27ff, summarized on 58ff). With a research group he has presented proposals for a total revision of the Swiss federal constitution to bring about a phased, more or less radical abolition – or at least restriction – of dominion over land. They proposed different options:

1. Turning real estate into public property, be it that of the municipality or the state.
2. Distinguishing between property for use or for disposal, and turning the latter over to the local authority or the state; property for use would be subject to public regulations.
3. Property would be divided up in this way in urban settlements and property for disposal would be turned over to newly formed public owners' associations, consisting either of all inhabitants or of the owners but allowing the inhabitants a say.
4. Excluding the right to build on property.
5. Retaining a comprehensive concept of property but having the state or local authorities restrict the freedom of use.
6. Maintaining the guarantee of ownership but restricting the freedom of disposal by the local authorities or the state.
7. Introducing state taxes on the basic income from the landed property, which also gives direction to the market.[8]
8. Adopting state regulations on ownership, e.g. so that legal entities can only be owners in the public interest and that only restricted ownership of housing and building land is allowed – related to a proprietor's own use.

These variants clearly show that transitional arrangements are possible depending on political feasibility, but in no case is there to be a guarantee of unlimited ownership of land for unlimited wealth accumulation. The optimum solution from the angle of real life and the involvement of all local stakeholders is communal property. In this way people can decide, as a function of their cultural traditions, whether and to what extent they want to leave land to their families for their personal use, for example for agricultural use or in hereditary tenure as their own home, which has a long tradition in Germany. They can decide whether and how much is to be handled by cooperatives, indeed whether and on what terms they want to let big industry settle in their area (something that is practised in German cities). Here clashes of interest with the state are possible, even probable. It is better to work through these conflicts than to let the power of money decide over the heads of the people concerned.

On no account should the centralist solution of general state ownership be preferred as an alternative to the all-out market – to avoid conflicts with the local population. All alternatives today must be developed from below. This does not preclude the possibility of there being state ownership of land. For example, it is a good idea for large forest areas extending over the area of municipalities to be administered as state property. Likewise there will be other public facilities on state land. The essential point is that land should not be at the disposal of private wealth accumulation.

Can this be applied in practice? There is hope, if groups spring up in civil society, delegitimize the present system, fight to amend the legal situation and start to live out alternatives from below. Here the movements of indigenous peoples and the landless in Latin America have raised awareness worldwide. The initiative taken by Binswanger even led to several revisions in the course of Swiss constitutional reform.

Water and other environmental goods The following example of the struggle against the privatization of water in Cochabamba, Bolivia, shows not just the dramatic nature of the problem but also the strength of people in a local context when they act in solidarity (see Juhasz 2001 and Barlow 2001a). In 1999, at the behest of the IMF and the World Bank, the Bolivian government passed a law privatizing the water system of Cochabamba. The US Bechtel group became the owners through the local proxy Aguas del Tunari and doubled or tripled prices, before making any investments. In a country in which the minimum wage is under $60 per month the people had to pay over $20 per month for water. Those who could not pay had their water turned off. Those who had dug family wells were supposed to pay fees for them. The company had negotiated a profit margin of 16 per cent with the government, while many inhabitants no longer had access to water.

The inhabitants formed a coalition of unions, environmental and human rights groups, and local activists, called La Coordinadora de Defensa del Agua y de la Vida (Coalition to Defend Water and Life). They began with peaceful demonstrations. When the government did not react they organized a petition with 50,000 signatures. When the government ignored this they organized non-violent strikes, road blocks and protests. Whereupon the government declared a state of emergency, arrested the protest leaders, closed local radio stations and sent 1,000 armed soldiers into the city. They shot a seven-year-old and wounded many residents. On 19 April the government gave up and cancelled the contract with the company. The latter charged the government with violating the agreement. During this time no one was supplying the city with water, whereupon the workers organized the local water service, SEMAPA, by themselves. They held a series of meetings with residents to determine their needs. They reduced prices, installing new containers and pipes so that many suburbs were able to enjoy a water supply for the first time ever. The victory is by no means certain. The company left debts and sued the government, and the political and business elite reacted by boycotting SEMAPA and refusing to pay. International support for this struggle remains necessary. Together with the workers of SEMAPA and international solidarity groups La Coordinadora staged a meeting to publicize the Cochabamba Declaration (see Appendix 2).

This example again shows the lethal consequence of the globalized possessive market economy: the poor are no longer given drinking water so that a group can make a 16 per cent profit on its capital investments. But it also shows that the dealings of the IMF, the World Bank and the governments of rich countries responsible for their actions must be deemed a threat to life. What is more, this type of privatization of public services is destined to become law for all countries belonging to the WTO through the GATS (General Agreement on Trade in Services) talks, held for five years in Geneva from 2000 under the auspices of the WTO. Only worldwide resistance, which led to the demise of MAI (multilateral agreement on investment), can ward off this open assault on the life of people. In June 2001 about

500 NGOs and unions signed the declaration 'stop the GATS Attack' (*Corporate Europe Observer*, September 2001). But it is not just the IMF, the World Bank and the WTO which are in the process of pushing forward the privatization of public water supplies: so too are regional trade agreements and common markets. The North American Free Trade Agreement (NAFTA) and the planned Free Trade Area of the Americas (FTAA; Barlow 2001b) expressly plan to do this. Sun Belt Water Inc. has since 1998 been suing the government of Canada for $220 million because the province of British Columbia has generally cancelled contracts for water export. The company wants to use the new privatization efforts to secure access to the country's water (International Forum on Globalization, *IFG Bulletin*, Summer 2001).

The Cochabamba example also shows that local communities can take their water supply into their own hands against the resistance of all local, national and international forces. The source of their strength is solidarity; indeed, the globalization of these forces means it has to be the solidarity of international civil society. Since October 2001 the Ghana National Coalition against Privatization of Water, consisting of the Christian Council of Churches, the unions and different social movements and groups, has been calling for this. Here too the IMF and the World Bank have been putting the government under pressure to privatize water. A similar struggle has flared up in the Cape Town suburb of Mitchells Plain. When, on 26 September 2001, the Tafelsig area was to be cut off from its water supply, the population built barricades and the police cracked down in their hundreds. These actions are linked with an intensive campaign run by the South African confederation of trade unions, COSATU, against privatization in general. In August 2001 a countrywide strike was organized against the government's privatization policy.[9] The broad-based resistance worldwide suggests that the struggle for public, i.e. communal or state, ownership of water can be won. In Cochabamba the struggle was inspired by one of Gandhi's sayings:

> First they ignore you.
> Then they laugh at you.
> Then they fight you.
> Then you win.

Water is not the only environmental good on which people depend for survival. Binswanger (1978: 88ff) counts all goods that relate to non-economic needs. He divides them into three different categories: the biological or pre-economic needs such as breathing, eating and drinking; meta-economic needs such as harmony, beauty, conviviality, freedom from noise, etc.; and the post-economic need to save resources for posterity. The goods to satisfy these needs can simply be nature-given. But they can also relate to human activity such as buildings or the absence of noise and pollution.

Experience shows that neither private capitalist nor centralistic state ownership guarantee the availability and protection of these goods. The core of the problem is that property as asset for the accumulation of wealth and consumption is defined as *dominium* at the owner's free disposal. Binswanger sums this up as follows:

> The present environmental issue results from wealth being more and more only related to financial or capital property that gains interest through investments in securities or means of production and natural resources, and thereby increases. In this way, however, the non-monetary goods take on a merely provisional value, only 'realised' through commercialisation, i.e. by income acquisition by means of the sale of goods or through their consumption. Non-monetary things are desired less and less, things whose value lies in themselves or their immediate usefulness, and more and more focus is placed on their character as providing income and consumption. In other words, while money and financial assets increase the real wealth that we take from our environment is reduced. Yet environmental goods, as true assets, should only be used and not consumed – at least not wastefully. An environmentally sound property order must therefore have the goal of countering the 'monetarisation' of wealth and the transformation of all non-monetary goods into consumer goods. (ibid.: 97)

The attempt to solve the environmental issue while keeping a system of absolute ownership, i.e. to solve it via price hikes, has had only a very limited effect. Binswanger therefore proposes another very interesting avenue based on the idea that *the environment is a common good and the ownership system needs to be appropriately adapted.* Here he links up with the notion in Roman law of *patrimonium,* i.e. that form of ownership which, unlike *dominium,* is not based on arbitrary disposal, but on the idea of passing on a hereditary good to one's children (ibid.: 97, 102ff; Binswanger 1998: 131ff). In terms of the environment the comprehensive right of ownership would then be patrimony, eco-

nomic usage rights being derived from it and from the start environ-
mentally sound. Binswanger speaks in this context of patrimonial
owners being a 'community of heirs', i.e. All residents concerned are
joint beneficiaries of the estate.

Such approaches also exist in European tradition. Binswanger
names traditional state (royal) rights, such as exclusive rights to a
mountain, or to salt, hunting or fishing. Here the state is the trustee
for the population concerned; it gives concessional rights for the use
of resources only on condition that they are used in the public interest. Another example is forestry rights. Here, too, the crucial requirement made by the state as trustee is the requirement to use the forest
sustainably. Finally there are the traditional Allmend corporations, in
which farmers use a mountain together, for example. It is wrong to
derive from these commons the belief that it is all right for individual
members to over-graze to their heart's desire. On the contrary, the
system is structured in such a way that ownership rights of partners in
a mountain are adapted to the respective grazing capacity, and sustainability is guaranteed.

According to Binswanger, this is the decisive model for handling
common environmental goods. He compares this cooperative appropriation of the environment, which is thereby liberated from dependence on the arbitrary *dominium* of private owners, with the abolition
of slavery. In fact a new right of ownership should be created for
common environmental goods, but one that is linked to the remnants
of the old forms of property:[10]

- '*Expanding exclusive rights*: The non-renewable resources and the
  scarce renewable ones whose renewability is threatened (exploitation of mineral resources, water use, fishing, hunting etc.) are to be
  managed by the state as a trust for the environmental owners.' The
  state grants conditional concessions for economic usage.
- '*The principle of sustainability*: The basic obligation behind forestry
  law – sustainable management – is to be extended to all soil and
  land management, i.e. Above all to agriculture.' This prevents overuse by monoculture, desertification, etc., and makes it clear that '*all*
  soils in their totality belong in a non-economic sense to the citizens of a country'. Economically speaking, this approach supports
  small-scale agriculture rather than capital-intensive agro-industry.
- '*Creation of regional environmental authorities*: The patrimony will

be organised by associations of owners with a cooperative character, with a regional connection not identical with the state. We
are thinking of regional environmental bodies as relatively autonomous self-managed entities. Their members would be the residents of the region.' These environmental cooperatives can then, in
turn, grant concessions for economic use, e.g. including limited
pollution rights. But this can only be decided jointly (i.e. democratically, with one vote per resident).

*Unlike the tradition of dominium and common law, this new conception of
law does not assume that private property is absolute and thus that restrictions
should possibly be imposed. Instead the preservation of the natural environment is fully integrated into the very concept of ownership, and priority in
decision-making is given to the cooperatives of local and regional residents
affected by decisions.*

Means of production, corporations and labour In the classical liberal view there are three interlocking factors in a company: labour,
capital and the entrepreneur, who exploits the first two, in the face of
market risks, to achieve maximum profit.[11] If we relate this approach
to the different articles of the German Basic Law (constitution),
capital ownership in the sense of fixed assets and money is the basic
constitutional institution. It is by no means the case that the important role of managers has eclipsed property as the ultimate authority.
Managers enjoy exclusively the right to the 'free development of their
personality' (Art. 2 [1], Basic Law), while owners enjoy the guarantee
of free disposal of their property. The entrepreneur (owner-manager)
finds a legal place in freedom of industry. The workers are only protected by law through the free choice of vocation and place of work
in which to offer their labour on the market. The law allows them to
freely enter into employment contracts to this effect.

Owing to the owner's freedom of disposal the workers have a say
only in the company if it is structured in such a way that performance-related remuneration is at least part of their pay. In a situation
such as that pertaining today, in which most work for a fixed salary,
owning property is fundamentally connected to commanding working people. Legally speaking, the protagonist (subject) of the company
is the property, while the workers are the object. As shown above,
as bourgeois society developed, the owning class soon succeeded in

limiting the equality of citizens exclusively to political rights – and even these had to be fought for.

A particular but central problem now arises from the fact that from the nineteenth century capital companies arose to replace personally owned companies, and they went on to become the now widespread public limited (or joint stock) companies (Binswanger 1978: 122ff; Rittstieg 1975: 346ff). The guarantee of property ownership, previously legitimized with free personal development, was therefore continually expanded until finally it became an institution under the protection of the constitution. In this way its original sense was turned upside down. Since the liberal market concentrates property in fewer and fewer hands a large part of the population is excluded from this development of personal freedom. Conversely, boundless accumulation was placed under the protection of the constitution. In addition, the concentration of property continually reduced political options through its economic power. How can this unfortunate development be countered?

Let us first again present the argument for depriving the present system of its legitimization (see Binswanger 1978: 134ff; Rittstieg 1975: 374ff). There are basically two claims: 1) that the common good arises through market coordination of the companies aiming for profit maximization, and 2) that private property serves to safeguard freedom. Real life itself refutes these claims. The reality is that there are huge differences in market power. The working people bear a much greater risk than the company owner in an exclusively property-based market economy – not just in terms of wages but particularly in terms of the exclusion from gainful employment. The self-fulfilment of the few free owners creates a lack of freedom for the majority. The concentration of ownership is destructive of democracy.

Existing proposals for reform with respect to the property issue start from two central tenets: the involvement of workers in the wealth and profit development of a company and co-decision independent of ownership. For the former, *asset formation in the hands of the employees,* constitutional preconditions need to be created for involving the workers in profit-making. The second solution, *property-less co-decision,* would involve a problem of compensation if the legislator were to intervene in the substance of the right to ownership. The problem can only be solved if the compensation guarantee is expressly limited to a suitable amount, not related to market value.

Given the connection with different articles of the constitution relevant to economic law, Binswanger proposes the formulation of clear goals to which individual matters can be uniformly related. He here proposes 'relating the production of goods to the *common good* as the goal and pivot of all economic law' (Binswanger 1978: 146ff). Three consequences follow from this:

- 'The supreme goal besides the production of goods is *personal development* and the *economic safeguarding of all* those working in the company ...
- A further goal is the *granting of participatory (codecision) rights* in the undertaking.' The latter is central, not just with respect to personal development but also for the sake of democratization and balancing power. Binswanger even goes so far as to demand the constitutional goal that '*all those affected by company decisions are to be guaranteed appropriate rights of codecision*'. This would mean that people living next door to a company would need to be brought into the decision-making process if an issue affected them.
- Finally he calls for 'the broadening of entrepreneurial ownership and the formation of company ownership in the hands of the workers to be made an issue and a constitutional right'.

In the words of Greffrath (2001: 4), it is about 'deciding on the democratisation of all conditions in which power and property decide on the opportunities and participation of people in the life of society'. As long as all life-determining securities and rights depend on normal employment there must be equal access to paid work and the expansion of rights of co-decision and ownership by the workers.

For some time now, however, there has been a new model for the realization of the welfare state which, going beyond previous approaches, could constitute an important milestone on the way to a post-capitalist society: *a tax-financed basic income for all citizens* (see ibid.: 5f; Kessler 1996: 113ff). From the perspective of life and the common good, this is of prime significance. It would expressly benefit not just needy members of society but everyone. Additional paid work could be freely sought, either full time or part time, linked with personal work, civil society commitment, public work or leisure. That is, people would have the freedom of flexible employment and personal activity without any pressure on their livelihoods. The many individual social benefits (except for those such as housing support) would be unnecessary. Conversely, the appropriate amount would be subtracted from the income tax on paid work.

A precondition for the implementation of such a model would be a 'tax system starting from productivity and wealth' (Greffrath 2001: 6). The present fiscal system, as shown above, is shifting the burden of tax increasingly to work and away from capital. This by no means corresponds to productivity development, which is increasingly being determined by capital investment. Hence taxation on the basis of value added would be the appropriate form in the productive sphere. Progressive taxation of wealth would not only reduce unbridled enrichment on the basis of a neo-liberal economy, it would slow down unproductive and dangerous use of this wealth in finance speculation. In other words it would feed this social wealth back into the productive sphere. An additional instrument along the same lines would be a progressively higher inheritance tax on all wealth going beyond an appropriate level of personal needs. The Swedish model shows that all these instruments are possible in practice. *Now under fire!*

There are two objections here. The first is that the tax sovereignty of states is being increasingly undermined and sometimes abolished by globalization. The solution can only be the restoration of tax sovereignty worldwide. Second, this model is hardly applicable in poor countries, owing to the lack of social wealth and also the traditional power positions of the ruling classes.[12] Here priority must be given to setting up a productive sphere not deformed by the world market. We are reminded of the proposal made in the previous chapter for making a new start with the production of simple goods by the majority of the excluded world population, goods that would be protected from the global market driven by competition and solely serving capital accumulation. This would not only comply with Binswanger's basic criterion of gearing the production of goods to the common good, it would also create broadly spread income and property, and thereby purchasing power.[13]

If through tax incentives simple goods were produced according to ecological criteria this could ease the burden on the environment. But it would, above all, stop the constant deterioration of the quality of life in most of the world. Thus it would be a form of development policy, and – being rooted in economics – would provide a way out of the 'development of under-development' (Rodney 1972) dependent on the global market.

The only loser from this basic turn-around would be casino capitalism, with its huge, unproductive amounts of capital. In this model, profits cannot be won at the gambling table. On the contrary, devouring capital would find no prey if its speculative bubble were already burst by self-generated crises. Productive capital could have a long-term interest in this model, however. Macroeconomic planning would not rest in the hands of big groups, as is the case now. In this model private interests would clearly be subject to democratic planning according to the criterion of life and the common good. In this framework, however, a limited form of private ownership of the means of production is conceivable if subject to political co-decision, particularly in a regionally adapted setting. It would, for example, be subject to the social obligation entailed in owning property entrenched in the German constitution, and not just formally to the stabilization of a capitalist economy. It would be able to operate only in a work-related, productive sphere, however, and no longer in the sphere of unproductive, speculative wealth accumulation (see Fischbeck 1996).

In connection with the above local and regional forms of economic activity, and with democratic, macroeconomic planning from the perspective of life and the common good, this model would lead beyond the capitalist market approach which regulates itself on the basis of private property and contracts.

Implementation would need to be democratically monitored at all levels – local, national and global. It is not enough for alternatives to be developed only at local level. The dual strategy proposed here is about regaining political control of the economy. Setting up a new order from below must be provided with macroeconomic safeguards, precisely so that local and regional economies can blossom and not be destroyed by the world market.

Regarding global control, this concerns the area of finance policy, to be considered further below, and, above all, the WTO. The trend here towards liberalization, deregulation and privatization must be reversed if humanity is to survive. It must be replaced by planning and regulation guided by a concern for life and the common good. Probably this can only be achieved by subjecting the WTO to a more democratic UN. This would mean a reversal of the neo-liberal approach. The democratic UN and its economic organizations (UNCTAD, UNDP, ECOSOC) have been increasingly upstaged by global economic institutions such as the WTO, which are increasingly dominated by the industrial countries. The UNDP's Human Development Reports of 1992 and 1994 illustrated what a new allocation of responsibility could look like (see also Duchrow 1995: 288ff).

Fundamental services The same move towards life and the common good is necessary in the ownership of basic social services. It has already become clear how disastrous the consequences are for the majority of people, particularly in poor countries, when water supplies are privatized, i.e. transferred to the ownership of the capitalist market of profit maximization. But this applies to other basic social services, not just to water: public transport, basic communication systems, education, healthcare and energy supply.

In all these areas it is not a matter of permitting *additional* private facilities. The central point is that appropriate public institutions must be available to guarantee that *all* members of society have affordable access to basic provision in these areas. It is a question of practicability as to whether local or central government is the owner. Local public transport has proved itself to be in good hands if run by local authorities.

An especially interesting field is the issue of energy supply. Here a highly monopolized energy industry has arisen, partly with state assistance, but structured so that profits are privatized. You can study the results in California, where the privatized – and therefore more expensive – power supply periodically collapses and has to be rationed. The *Wall Street Journal*, not known for its anti-capitalist tendencies, reported tersely after the collapse of Enron on 30 November 2001 (p. 1):

> It was one of the great fantasies of American business: a deregulated power market that would send cheaper and more reliable supplies of electricity coursing into homes and offices across the nation.
> But look what's happened instead. Enron Corp., the vast energy trader at the center of the new freewheeling U.S. power markets, now faces collapse amid a blizzard of questionable financial deals. And California, the first big state to deregulate its electricity market, has watched its experiment turn into a debacle, with intermittent blackouts and retail power rates as much as 40% higher than they were a year ago.

At the same time the energy industry has had dangerous ecological and social consequences. The nuclear industry, as has become clear since Chernobyl, poses infinite dangers for populations and the earth.

The construction of large dams has evicted whole populations and plunged them into misery. The depredation of non-renewable resources such as oil is proceeding apace. CO_2 emissions consequent on the burning of this oil are causing global warming and the disaster of climate change. The Western imperial powers and Russia are waging war for the control of these oil sources in Iraq and the Caucasus, in Chechnya and in Afghanistan, at the cost of hundreds and thousands of lives.

There is now an alternative in the form of energy generation from solar panels, windmills, hydroelectric plants and biomass (see Douthwaite 1996: 179ff). However, we should carefully distinguish between whether this is done on a small or a large scale. It would be raising false hopes to assume we could cover, or meet our excessive energy consumption in a capitalist industrial society simply through solar energy. Although solar energy has a positive energy balance,[14] besides generating new, renewable energy in the North we must also save energy, i.e. change our consumerist lifestyle.

On a small scale alternative energies have great potential at the local level and with simple technologies. They are decentralized forms of energy and are available as commons, albeit in differing intensities in the different regions. This will enable municipalities or small regions to provide themselves with energy in some cases independently of the world market. Places such as Schönau in the Black Forest and others along the Danish coasts are some of the most well-known examples of the use of good wind conditions. At the same time this has been an incentive for manufacturing industry to develop simple, durable technology, allowing individuals and communities access to these decentralized energies, starting with the simplest and cheapest solar cookers, so that the poorest of the poor can be spared having to fetch firewood from far away or chopping down forests. At the other extreme are wind energy towers. In any case, local and central government must be responsible for the energy supply so that all people can have a share in it and sustainability is guaranteed.

These examples show what madness it is that the USA and the EU especially are pressing in the WTO for local and central services to be privatized – in the interests of big money. So, as has been said repeatedly, it is most urgent for all responsible people, social movements, unions, Churches, etc. to publicly combat these GATS plans of the WTO.[15] As happened with the MAI, it must be possible to stop this attack on the welfare of the global population by private capital ownership and its state promoters. The WTO succeeded, by moving its meeting in November 2001 to a dictatorship, in preventing people's resistance going public, as happened in Seattle in December 1999. It launched a new round of liberalization, without meeting the demands made by the social movements and many governments from developing countries that the (indirect) effects of the previous round be examined and publicly debated. Yet these dictatorial and sometimes blackmailing approaches will only cement and strengthen the resistance of the people affected and those in solidarity with them.[16]

Intellectual property and culture The WTO also plays the key role in the question of intellectual property. As shown above, a decision of the US Supreme Court broke the barriers that had prevented the patenting of life forms, thus turning them into private property for profit maximization. The TRIPs agreement means that all countries wanting to become members of the organization have to bow to this privatization diktat in the interests of big business.

Here too fundamental resistance is called for. The alternatives are clear. With Macpherson, Jeremy Rifkin has underlined the reasons why the elements of life, the commons, must not go into private ownership. The central reason is that private property excludes, and allows access only to well-off buyers, while public ownership guarantees (at least in principle) access to the good in question, in this case to knowledge. Rifkin writes, quoting Macpherson: 'He argues that in a complex, highly interdependent world, the most important form of property is "as an individual right not to be excluded from the use or benefit of the accumulated productive resources of the whole society". Macpherson favours bringing back the older definition of property that existed before the days of industrial capitalism. Property needs to be broadened … to include the "right not to be excluded from access"' (Rifkin 2000: 238; Macpherson 1973: 133).

In practical terms this means that privatization through *patenting life forms must be reversed*. It is not enough, for example, for it to have been decided at the WTO conference in November 2001 that governments grappling with pandemics like AIDS or malaria should be given discounts on costly medication by pharmaceutical companies in order to make them more affordable to their citizens. Conversely, governments must have stewardship over the healing forces of nature and award private industry concessions for their economic use in the general interest, or take in hand the development of medicines in public universities and research institutes. All research in the private sphere builds on foundations laid by public tax funding, and it is not at all acceptable for the subsequent profits to be privatized.

Another example is seed. When TNCs steal the grain or rice varieties developed by farmers in countries of the South with traditional methods, modify them genetically and then establish a monopoly, the devastating social and ecological consequences described above follow. States must therefore take back stewardship of seed to enable all farmers to cultivate their own.

The issue is even more pressing in terms of the human genome. It is horrible to think of what could follow from privatization through patents in this field. Public, democratic control must at all costs prevent the commercialization and manipulation of the building blocks of human life.

In all these fields the range of problems goes beyond the local and national levels. This is why these dangers emanating from WTO-promoted privatization and liberalization must be combated at the global level.

The same applies on the level of culture. Here the global commercialization of local and regional cultures is destroying its very sources. Cultural creativity grows out of the direct relations of people in particular landscapes, communities and traditions. Freedom from purpose is the essence of culture, which is now being marketed in homogenized form by a handful of gigantic corporations according to the criterion of profitable usefulness.

This is why the cultural and ecological resistance movements have to form links, which is already happening. Here Rifkin (2000: 257f) writes convincingly:

Preserving biodiversity and cultural diversity are the two great social movements of the twenty-first century. The two forces are closely linked. All cultures share common roots in nature because all cultures arise out of an intimate connection to the earth … Cultures are born out of an abiding respect for and devotion to the wellsprings of life that make up the natural world. Our many contemporary cultural expressions all trace their lineages back to our first cultural connections to the earth itself. Cultural practices and institutions are, for the

most part, life-affirming. They speak to our indebted relationship to
nature and wed us to the larger life forces of which we are a part. The
reaffirmation of life is at the heart of what intrinsic value is all about.
Culture, then, exists in sharp contrast to the commercial sphere, in
which all phenomena are reduced to utility, and expropriation and
expediency become the accepted behavior norms …

Weaken or eliminate cultural diversity, and capitalist markets will
eventually tumble because, as described, social trust and social capital
will dry up and no longer be available as a foundation for building and
maintaining commerce and trade.

This text clearly shows that these issues centre on the future of life.
At the same time they make it clear that the capitalist economy is
destroying itself by destroying the bases of creative life in nature and
culture for the sake of wealth accumulation. Rifkin proceeds to point
out that the destruction of these areas by the fetishist fundamentalism
of the property-based market economy is encouraging blind, violent
counter-fundamentalism. But how is the core of capitalism, money
and capital fetishism to be controlled and overcome?

Money and finance Money, in its connection with property, has been
the centrepiece of the most varied market economies since the eighth
century BCE, as we have seen. Property serves as a basis for a new
credit system centred on interest. The system increasingly operates by
means of interest-bearing money. Aristotle sees in the mechanism of
property accumulation by money the tempting instrument for the
boundless striving for wealth of individuals at the cost of the community. Jesus identifies it with Mammon and thereby uncovers its
pseudo-religious function. The capitalist society arising in the modern
period is precisely defined by the fact that increasingly all that exists
has been seen as capital, i.e. 'property generating profit'.[17] Hobbes calls
money the blood pulsing through the veins of the market economy.
Locke justifies and legitimizes the unequal distribution of property
with the 'tacit agreement' on the introduction of money. With inimit-
able lucidity Marx analyses the way in which the fetish character of
money, by its very nature programmed to multiply itself, drives the
whole of the life of society behind the backs of the actors – with the
indirect effect of direct and indirect destruction. This can be seen
today by anyone prepared to look.

From the perspective of life and the common good, this orientation of society to the value of money is first and foremost to be fundamentally challenged, before we turn to examining the alternatives to individual aspects of money and finance. Economically speaking, measuring economic success exclusively from the angle of monetary growth (Gross Domestic Product: GDP) is based on a wrong perception. After all, destructive elements are included in this measurement as something positive. A traffic accident (due to additional services and goods), pollution of a river by a chemicals factory (due to necessary cleaning) or a rise in share prices (due to job redundancies) raise the monetary value of GDP. So there have long been attempts to introduce social and ecological indicators into the measurement of economic progress. The most well known in this respect are the annual Human Development Reports of the UNDP, which have established a human development index (HDI). The most far-reaching model of an alternative measurement was suggested by Diefenbacher and his reseach group (1997; see also Anderson 1991), the 'magic disks of sustainability'. These measure results in the economic, social and environmental fields with six indicators each with a view to their practical (not purely monetary) use for real people and environmental situations. So it is about a change of awareness in society. Economic activity should not be seen purely from the angle of wealth accumulation but in terms of its effects on the life of people and the environment.

There is a second fundamental question regarding the role of money in the property market economy: *added value*. Back in the nineties the Dutch economists Goudzwaard and de Lange (1995: 137ff) pointed to the structural injustice implicit in the fact that countries with hard currencies – in particular the USA with the dollar – can trade and go into debt in their own currency. Yet the currencies of most of the southern countries are not accepted in international trade and debt management. These countries must therefore earn hard currency through exports or take out loans – with the consequences of unpayable debts. The two authors therefore propose a similar reform of the global monetary system to that sought in 1944 by Keynes at Bretton Woods. Keynes had suggested establishing a currency for the world central bank, called Bancor, and using it as the world reserve currency instead of the dollar. However, the USA succeeded in imposing its own currency to which the other hard currencies were tied until 1973 with fixed exchange rates (see Duchrow 1995: 95ff).

The International Monetary Fund, founded at Bretton Woods, did introduce special drawing rights (SDRs) but their distribution again favoured the richer countries. Goudzwaard and de Lange therefore propose that the 'distribution rules must be revised in favour of the poor countries' (Goudzwaard and de Lange 1995).

The problem has another, sensational dimension, though, as shown with horrifying clarity by Rowbotham.[18] Who actually owns the money that is put into circulation? The majority of the population certainly think it is the state. We superficially note that the issuing of coins and notes is a state privilege. In reality the state now contributes only about 3 per cent of the money supply in circulation. The rest is obtained in different ways from private financial institutions, primarily banks.

The core process is adding value on the basis of encumbered property. For example, the banks issue money as a loan in exchange for a mortgage on a home. The same applies to land, industry, public institutions and services, and, above all, to the state budget itself. That means that the banks make money on the basis of the debts of citizens and the public sector. The 1998 figures for the money in Britain, for example, are very clear: £411 billion sterling was made from home ownership, £300 billion from industry, agriculture and services, £80 billion from public assets and public debts (Rowbotham 1998: 35). This 'debt-money' (Rowbotham) owned and controlled by the banking system entails two decisive disadvantages for citizens and the public community as a whole. First, their property moves increasingly into the hands of capital owners and their agents, the banks. Second, the money used to repay debts always involves interest payments to the capital owners. If the banks grant loans and thereby make money (on the basis of only a small share of their own capital), repayment means the debt is cancelled but not the amount created by making money on the loan.[19] This means that we, the political community, allow the capital owners, represented by the banks, to create further property for themselves by making money on debts without doing a stroke of work. Through the permanent self-multiplication of money, with the assistance of the debts of the population and the public sector, property is going automatically to the capital owners represented by the banks – quite apart from the additional economic processes that reinforce the process of redistribution towards the capital owners further.

Thomas Jefferson (third US President, 1801–9) understood this problem of the self-expropriation of a people by leaving the power of making money to the banks:

> If the American people ever allow the banks to control the issuance of their currency, first by inflation and then by deflation, the banks and the corporations that will grow up around them will deprive the people of all property *until their children will wake up homeless on the continent their fathers occupied.* The issuing power of money should be taken from the banks and restored to Congress and the people to whom it belongs. I sincerely believe the banking institutions having the issuing power of money are more dangerous to liberty than standing armies. (ibid.: 34f)

Nothing could be clearer. And it is interesting that this wording reminds us of what Isaiah observed in the seventh century BCE (Isa. 5: 8).

Rowbotham then analyses, step by step, the destructive effect of this privatized monetary system with respect to the drive towards unbridled growth, consumption, arms proliferation, industrialization of agriculture, debts incurred by industry and the states, free trade, etc. He traces the historical origins of this development in Britain and the USA, then comes up with proposals for a reform of the monetary system. There are different approaches:

At the heart of the alternatives lies the fact that the share of 'debt-money' must be reduced and the share of debt-free money in circulation increased.

Rowbotham links his practical proposals to Abraham Lincoln (the sixteenth US President) and C. H. Douglas, the founder of the social credit movement in Britain in the 1920s. Abraham Lincoln drew up a statement on monetary policy in 1865. It says:

> Money is the creature of law, and the creation of the original issue of money should be maintained as the exclusive monopoly of national government. Money possesses no value to the state other than that given to it by circulation. Capital has its proper place and is entitled to every protection. The wages of men should be recognised in the structure of and in the social order as more important than the wages of money ... Government should stand behind its currency and credit and the bank deposits of the nation. No individual should suffer a loss of money through depreciation or inflated currency or Bank bankruptcy ... Money will cease to be the master and become the servant of humanity. Democracy will rise superior to the money power.[20]

A few weeks later he was assassinated. The motive for the murder has never been established but there are grounds for suspecting that bank circles were behind it (ibid.: 216ff). His goal was to take money and loans completely out of the hands of banks and to establish a national system. Douglas, by contrast, started with the idea of creating purchasing power by circulating debt-free money among the population.

Rowbotham links both approaches in one proposal that aims to show the way forward but not necessarily to be introduced everywhere in the same way. He is concerned not to make the proposal so revolutionary that it will be rejected from the beginning, but to show possibilities for evolution. The key question here is how much debt-free money the state should create (ibid.: 264ff).

In 1998 3 per cent of the money supply in Britain was debt-free and government-issued. But since the overall debts of £780 billion are £100 billion higher than the £680 billion in circulation, the debt-free money supply is therefore minus £100 billion. At the other extreme, too great a debt-free money supply would fuel inflation. Between 1950 and 1963 the debt-free share of the money supply was 21 per cent, inflation was low, employment high, the economy was continually growing, and international trade less aggressive (ibid.: 309). However, since many complex factors are in play it would be wrong to give a statistical percentage. But how is the balance to be calculated? Without going into detail here Rowbotham's approach can be described as follows: the supply of debt-free state money should every year correspond to the rise in the money supply created by loans (called M4). That is, this additional money supply would not be created by 'debt money' but through debt-free, state-acquired funds (ibid.: 366f). We would therefore have a state-controlled, 'compensatory' money supply, in addition to the traditional private money obtained from bank loans, etc.

Where is this money to go? It would be used, first, to reduce government debts and, second, to provide a basic income for the population (see above). One can envisage four phases after the introduction of such an arrangement until the new system has taken over (ibid.: 269ff). The advantages for the majority of the population and the state are clear. The state can assume its responsibility for education, health, transportation and culture free of debt. The population can, on the basis of such a basic income, organize its work flexibly, so that working-time reduction and part-time work, linked with free social activities, ease the pressure for constant growth. Lasting, qualitative and thereby sustainable production would also increase through the reduced pressure to produce to pay interest. Countries introducing such a system would also have the advantage that their products would have less interest to deal with. However, the more countries introduce it, the better it will be for all, precisely because this monetary system is not based on shake-out competition. The debts of the 'two-thirds world' could then be repaid – as long as they were legitimate – by the rich countries making available debt-free means of payment via special drawing rights.

Once again: however the problem is to be solved in detail, it is a scandal that banks are entitled simply, with the stroke of a pen, to increase the property of capital owners, thereby increasingly expropriating the citizens, getting the state deeper into debt and doing more economic and ecological damage. It must be put on the political agenda immediately.

On the basis of this fundamental change of perspective further individual possibilities are to be sought by which monetary mechanisms connected to property can be changed. They should no longer benefit the minority of owners of financial assets, as at present, but should benefit all, not least the natural life support systems.

The age-old question of money has first and foremost centred on the linking of property and *interest*. The owner who lends money wants more back. Since, in the 'static' economy of the ancient world debtors could not produce any added value to pay the interest, this meant an infringement on their livelihood. They had to work off debt as a slave and/or lose (landed) property, i.e. their means of production, to the creditor, if they could not extract the money for repayment from their own families. Because of the fatal consequence of interest the Bible, Aristotle and others called for it to be banned.

What would a ban on interest mean under today's economic conditions? If it is a matter of not attacking the substance of the debtor the demand today, if ecologically sustainable at all in our growth economy, would be that real interest should not exceed the added value produced, i.e. the real growth attained after deduction of costs and adjusted for inflation. This would mean that the high-interest policy set in motion by neo-liberalism is *structural usury*. Since 1980 the real interest rate (adjusted for inflation) on the capital markets on average far exceeds the rate of growth of the real economy – with the consequent destructive effects on countries, indeed for 90 per cent of people and the economy itself, of unrepayable debts.[21] The mere proposal of an additional debt-free money supply would certainly push interest rates up. What is also needed is a reintroduction of state interest regulation on the transnational as well as the national markets.

So if the use of property for mere wealth accumulation is not stopped in respect of real interest – allowing interest rates to exceed real growth rates without commitment to society and life – the re-linking of captial to the productive sphere of usage value will not be successful.[22] *The first practical demand following from this is the political re-regulation of interest rates on loans in transnational capital markets, i.e. the abolition of a monetarist policy.*

There are farther-reaching demands. They include the old demand for 'self-decreasing' money, raised by supporters of a 'natural economic order' as propounded by Silvio Gesell (1862–1930) in Switzerland. This holds that retained money increasingly loses value, so that it should circulate as a pure means of exchange. Kessler (1992: 14ff) has put together the arguments against this well-meant proposal. It would effectively lead to even more consumption. Above all, however, interest is only a reinforcing factor in the mechanism of property, interest, money, competition and profit maximization. It is coordinated by the market that is understood to be self-regulating – this complex mechanism that promotes so much inequality within society.

In the short term the call should simply be to demand compensation for the investors' run on international money markets since 1980. Priority here goes to *the cancellation or – as described above – the repayment of debts of all developing countries through interest-free special drawing rights.* Developing countries have already repaid much more than they originally borrowed, owing to the mechanism of compound interest and the simultaneous high-interest policy, and yet they face higher interest every year and demand more sacrifices from their people. This measure must, of course, be linked to the return of the money belonging to the elites of these countries, who themselves participate in plundering their countries through the flight of capital to Western banks. In individual cases like South Africa there must be another demand, besides debt cancellation. Banks that financed the oppressive policy of the white minority (their loans constituting 'odious debts') must provide compensation instead of requiring that debts incurred to support apartheid be repaid by its victims.[23]

All these necessary steps towards a new monetary policy call for the cooperation of governments at the global level. But before global arrangements start to work there are many options for people *at the local level* itself (see Douthwaite 1996). They can, for example, organize bartering groups to exchange goods and services without money and interest, which is already successfully practised internationally in Local Exchange and Trading Systems (LETS). The crucial thing, however, is the development of alternative bank systems and credit cooperatives. In Europe over thirty alternative banks are members of INAISE.[24] They vary in their conditions. Those going beyond ecological concerns to specifically raise the interest question, such as the GSL Gemeinschaftsbank in Germany, have gained very interesting experience of the readiness of investors to adapt interest levels to the above-mentioned criteria in the interests of promoting a social economy. This potential has by no means been fully tapped by persons and institutions that by their very nature should call for a just interest system, such as trade unions and Churches, naturally including their members. If they did so, this would have a powerful influence on public awareness.

Besides interest, and in combination with it, there is another central issue – *speculation*. The end of currency regulation in 1973 led to an incredible degree of speculation in foreign exchange. As we know, daily foreign exchange transactions, worth about US$1.5 trillion, are over 95 per cent speculative in nature. The most accepted counter-measure under discussion today is a turnover tax on all currency transactions, known as the Tobin tax (see Kairos Europa/WEED 2000: 50f). Nobel laureate James Tobin, back in 1978, suggested imposing a tax of 0.5 per cent on all currency transactions in order to reinstate a balance in the finance markets and cool inflation. With a tax rate of between 0.25 and 0.5 per cent, a further side effect would be collection of an annual tax revenue of between US$150 and 300 billion. This could be devoted to both the reduction of public debts and the productive sphere, particularly in developing countries. The UNDP's 1994 Human Development Report proposes paying the amount collected into a world social fund to benefit poorer regions, as happens with the European structural funds. The tax would be easy to collect because all foreign exchange transactions are dealt with via the SWIFT clearing system of central banks. The governments of Canada and Finland, and other government leaders in Europe, have expressed support for the Tobin tax, and movements like Kairos Europa, Attac

and Jubilee South are campaigning in many countries for its introduction.

The Tobin tax is no panacea for speculative accumulation of capital, but it would be a beginning – in compliance with the market and
yet a strong symbol. In financial crises such as the Asian one, where
profits from speculation were around 40–60 per cent, this small fee
would be insignificant. Further instruments such as *capital movement
and currency controls* should be used (ibid.: 51f). China was able to avoid
being sucked into the Asian crisis in 1997 only because it had not yet
abolished them. It remains to be seen how China can save itself in the
next crisis now that it has joined the WTO, which like the IMF and
the World Bank forces its members to deregulate markets.

Further, stricter measures need to be taken against increasing
speculation at the *stock exchanges* as a means of work-free property
accumulation (ibid.: 51). The issuing of shares and loans for real investments is being increasingly misused for speculative secondary trading.
Germany and other countries should introduce a stock exchange
turnover tax (of about 1 per cent) as is usual in the stock exchanges
of London and Singapore. In Germany the public budgets would
thereby gain about €12.5 billion. In addition speculative gains would
be subject to tax without limitation for a year, just as losses can be
deducted without limit from taxes. It is quite irresponsible, moreover,
that among the tax reforms of the German governing coalition has
been the abolition of the tax on the sale of company shares. This en-
courages mergers of companies producing no real economic growth.
It promotes only the concentration of capital property and, to add
insult to injury, is costing thousands of jobs, which in turn burden the
state budget. The public loses out doubly and triply – through taxes,
jobs and the heightened public debt, which in turn calls for more
interest payments. This amounts to a multiple upward redistribution
of property. This taxation should be reintroduced at a higher rate.

Finally, in the field of the speculative abuse of capital property and
the question of getting it under control, a completely different point
still needs to be mentioned: the *pension system* (ibid.: 39ff). So far old-
age pensions have been based on solidarity between the generations.
The young, working population paid part of their salary and employers had to make an equal contribution – with an express reference to
the social obligations of property. This income enabled the payment
of pensions. Through the inversion of the age pyramid the burden on

income from work has increased. The red–green coalition in Germany responded in 2001 with a reform of pensions: it introduced a 'third leg', partial coverage of pensions by private capital contributions from workers, and it waived the social commitment of employers. The consequence is that they no longer have to pay on a parity basis. This is a scandal and a violation of the Basic Law, which a conservative, neoliberal government could never have imposed because it would have run up against the resistance of unions and a social democratic opposition. It is well known that Anglo-American pension funds are already active on the capital markets, and for the sake of beating the competition have joined the global players of casino capitalism. A further inflation of the finance markets will not just reinforce the destruction caused, it will raise their insecurity. What will happen to pensions if there is another big crash?

Even if after the turn-about of German Social Democratic and Green policy there is no realistic chance of an alternative to this 'reform' visible in the near future, in the long run it must be clear that there is an alternative that it is feasible, and that it must be fought for from the perspective of the common good. After all, it is highly symbolic in character. Realpolitik is the art of making the seemingly impossible possible – especially if the alternative is destruction and self-destruction. The alternative is to reintroduce a modified version of the parity system of solidarity that has been partly diminished by the system of capital income accumulation. The counter-argument that, owing to the age pyramid, the cost of labour would increase even more does not hold water. Studies have shown that it is possible to finance pension funds such that the employer contribution is calculated not via wages but via added value. So it is not just labour but also technology, as a proportion of the respective productivity gain, which contributes to social insurance. This puts paid to the argument of non-financeability (see Kessler 1996: 102ff and 2002: 114ff).

There are other feasible models for social security (pensions, health, unemployment), as the examples of different countries show. The key criterion is: all citizens have to finance the system and to benefit from it. Scandinavia has tax-based systems. In Switzerland all income groups are members of the pension fund. This includes income from capital and assets and thus leads to the lowering of labour costs.

Naturally there will be a greater burden on capital in these models. But this makes sense in order to divert it from speculation and, via the redistribution of income in favour of the workers, to lead it back to the real economy. The same applies to the question of the tax burden on capital.

Besides interest, currency, stock exchange and pension funds, we must raise the topic of *tax flight and tax avoidance*. The important thing here is that the population should grasp that the neo-liberal governments are simply not telling the truth when they claim that big capital owners could be prevailed upon to create jobs by cuts in top tax rates and similar give-aways. This was claimed from the 1980s up to the tax reform of the German governing coalition around 2000, and it has been belied by the facts. At least since the 1996 UNDP Human Development Report, dealing with jobless growth, it should have become generally known that companies invest their capital gains, if not in speculative finance transactions, in rationalization, and thereby eliminate jobs. Capital gains and income from assets must be taxed on a progressively higher scale. That would slow down speculation and productive industry would be freed from the pressure of financial dividends and would therefore become more attractive. In addition, necessary public services can be financed without debts, which will also create jobs. So before we come to illegal tax flight, we must emphasize that legal tax avoidance must be brought under control. Only thus can the social obligations of property called for in the German constitution be restored (see Roth 1999; Hengsbach and Möhring-Hesse 1999: 195ff). This applies equally to all other countries, however, as stated by Christian de Brie with respect to France:

> The personal, progressive income tax is the republican tax par excellence, the only one corresponding to our constitutional consensus that 'No citizen is relieved of the duty to make a contribution to the burden of public spending according to his/her ability'. Yet half of the citizens are not subject to this obligation and with the other half the burden is unjustly distributed. The tax burden of the 10% of tax-payers with the highest incomes – who criticise the top tax of 54 percent as daylight robbery – has constantly diminished and fell between 1988 and 1996 from 19 to 15 percent. The share of income tax in inland revenue is only 10 percent; the remaining 90 percent in no way corresponds to the principle of ability to pay and places an above-average burden on the poorest groups of tax-payers.[25]

This is particularly true of the states' reluctance to combat the *tax flight* of capital property. As described in Chapter 4, states do not employ enough tax inspectors. Apart from the self-financing of their salaries, they could bring into public budgets and thus to the general public many billions of additional taxes each year (estimates vary between €15 and 50 billion in Germany). Hence the prime call to the state is to equip the Inland Revenue with sufficient staff.

National action is inadequate here, admittedly. The key problem is an international one, that of *tax oases and offshore finance centres* (see Kairos Europa/WEED 2000: 52f; Bracewell-Milnes 1979 and 1980). Their only purpose is to withdraw the commitment to society and the common good from capital property. They must be abolished, not just from the alternative perspective of human and natural life, but also for the self-preservation of the state and even of the real economy. According to an Oxfam study, the developing countries alone lose an annual US$50 billion to tax oases. Contrary to the claim that their abolition is not possible, it can be stated that even the publication of 'black lists' by the OECD has led to visible efforts being made by such centres to be regarded as 'clean'. The campaign should start with the banks, companies and individuals that use the offshore financial centres. This can be achieved by different means:

- the announcement of tougher controls, which would lead to more caution;
- sanctions for banks and other financial institutions if they work with tax oases;
- the abolition of anonymous trusts, no-name, numbered accounts, etc.;
- taxing of TNCs on a universally uniform basis;
- setting up a global tax inspection authority.

National governments can and must cooperate on this. In particular the USA, Japan, Germany, Britain, France, Austria, Luxembourg, Ireland, Switzerland, and other European countries to a lesser degree, bear the main responsibility for tolerating these facilities which are patently harmful to the common good. In the case of Germany it would be helpful to examine the possibility of a constitutional appeal against the federal government for not acting sufficiently vigorously to counter the violation of Art. 14 (2) of the constitution, which stipulates that 'property entails obligations. Its use shall also serve the public good.'

The international financial institutions (IFIs) How is one to deal with the forces of 'finance-driven imperialism' (see Bond 2000: 196ff; Negri and Hardt 2000), the IMF and World Bank, from the perspective of life and the common good? There are several strategic options here on which civil society groups cannot yet agree:

* critical dialogue;
* replacing the undemocratic present IFIs by new democratic institutions, under the oversight of a reformed UN, regulating the global economy;
* return to national, or development of regional, regulation.

Critical dialogue has been taken up by Churches and some NGOs, and also by the Jubilee North campaign. Since the attendance of James Wolfensohn, president of the World Bank, at the Lambeth Conference in 1997, the Anglican Churches have launched a broad-based initiative called World Faiths Dialogue on Development.[26] In addition, different dialogues are being held at the national level. The synod of the Evangelical Church in Germany (EKD) issued a statement on globalization in November 2001, stating: 'The churches must make it clear that they consider transnational companies, the International Monetary Fund and the World Bank as partners, not as opponents, albeit requiring critical dialogue.'[27] The Jubilee North campaign is far more critical, but argues that to gain a broad base in the northern hemisphere it is necessary to start from specific issues like 'debt relief for the poorest countries' on the heavily indebted poor country (HIPC) list. From there they aim to work towards structural transformations such as an international insolvency law.

A working group of the World Council of Churches (WCC) has produced a document warning the Churches not to swallow the rhetoric of the IMF and the World Bank when they respond to growing criticism by claiming that their policies now focus on combating poverty (WCC 2001). This is a real danger as the World Bank offers churches in Asia, Africa and Latin America co-financing for their social work. The framework is the new Poverty Reduction and Strategy Paper (PRSP), which governments and World Bank staff are working on. That this is a purely tactical measure is clear from the following. The last stage of the structural adjustment programmes (SAPs) of the IMF is called Enhanced Structural Adjustment Facility (ESAF). After strong criticism of these programmes the IMF, after the

Cologne G8 summit in 1999, changed the name to Poverty Reduction and Growth Facility (PRGF). This means that the IMF and the World Bank are simply continuing their neo-liberal structural adjustment policies which increasingly produce structural poverty. In order to hide this they spend some money to mitigate the consequences of this policy and thereby silence their critics.

It is not a matter of deluded naivety that the EKD synod should clearly have set itself apart from the critical NGOs and the WCC by calling the TNCs, the IMF and the World Bank its partners (not 'opponents'), thereby defending them despite their undemocratic character and destructive policies. This phrase is a deliberate statement of loyalty towards (absolute) power, and shows that the economic and political interests in the synod are stronger than the facts and the biblical message. That the bitterly poor Churches in impoverished societies of the South are tempted to accept money from the World Bank is understandable in human terms, but should still be avoided. Critical dialogue is only possible as a balancing act if we go beyond the HIPC cancellation initiative, for example, and call for fundamental transformations such as a new international insolvency law, the abolition of the impoverishing SAPs and the democratization of world economic institutions.

The second strategic option is the demand for *democratization of the IMF and the World Bank.* There have been many descriptions of the profoundly undemocratic organization of the IFIs (ibid.; Duchrow 1995: 95ff and 288ff). They are comparable to joint stock companies – one dollar, one vote – and in addition the USA has reserved the right of veto for itself through the volume of its shares. It is most improbable that these institutions could be transformed from within. On the other hand, it is indisputable that in many respects institutions at the global level are absolutely necessary in order to regulate the existing global markets, now programmed to pursue pure profit maximization, from the perspective of life and the common good. This applies equally to interest, currencies, stock exchange, pension funds and tax systems. Here the only long-term prospect seems to be expanding the economic competences of the UN, which at least has a democratic constitution. The 1992 UNDP Human Development Report presented a comprehensive plan regarding the global economic and financial order (Duchrow 1995: 288ff). It is still unsurpassed, although it has been forgotten following the victory of neo-liberal powers over the last decade. Along the lines of Keynes's proposals at Bretton Woods, it provides in the long term for a global central bank, a global system of progressive taxes, a socially oriented international trade organization, and an international security council for economic questions – all this under the aegis of the UN. In this way the IFIs and the WTO would – after a transitional phase – become superfluous. In terms of power politics these proposals clearly do not have a chance. In the medium and long term, however, they will prove useful. In view of the existing global interdependency of business and finances it is essential for there to be global planning and regulation.

What are the chances of the option of *national and large-scale regional control?* This does not exclude long-term global democratic regulation. On the contrary, control of the economy, starting from the priority of the life of local people in their natural and cultural environments, must take place from the local to the global levels. In the short term, however, there will be more chance of success at the national and regional levels. Bond (2000: 251) puts it pithily: 'The global scale may one day appear as a likely site of struggle (for example, through the United Nations system which at least conceptually could be democratised, unlike the Bretton Woods Institutions). But realistic "alternatives" are probably going to have to be fought for and won at national and regional scales.'

This is not founded simply on the realistic assessment that in view of the global rule and accumulation strategy of capital property no transformation is to be expected from above. This 'bottom-up' approach is itself a substantive part of the alternative. Only if people take economic, political and cultural action at the local and small-scale regional levels can the property system and the industry based on it ultimately be reorganized in the interests of all people and of life as a whole. In practical terms, at the global level the movements can, under present conditions, only offer resistance in the interests of life and the common good, delegitimize the present system and at most formulate long-term goals regarding global socio-ecological control. At the national and possibly large-scale regional levels (e.g. in southern Africa, East Africa, the Andes, the EU, etc.) they can, besides resisting neoliberal policies, perhaps push through individual socio-ecological and democratic re-regulations of the property and economic order. One form of resistance in the rich countries could be, for example, winning over parliament to defund the Bretton Woods organizations.

In his latest book Bond (2001: 282) sums up his demands for a new political economy from below in the context of a democratization of economic policy as follows:

> In general, not merely in South Africa, a feasible menu of developmentalist-state interventions along these lines would include imposition of watertight exchange controls; careful reflation of the economy through strategic state spending; imposition of prescribed assets on financial institutions so as to redirect finance to social uses; increasing nationalisation of strategic sites of the economy; creative juggling of import/export requirements so as to avoid foreign debt and wastage of resources on luxury consumption; default on illegitimate foreign debt; and a more general commitment to 'get the prices wrong' in financial markets through interest rate subsidies and directed credit to socially-useful producers, if need be, to assure the maximum developmental return on democratic investment.

Economists such as Amin (1990) propose regional delinkages from the world market, in order to be able to push through autonomous social and ecological regulations against the predominance of imperial financial forces more easily than at the national level. Here the European Union has unique opportunities which unfortunately it has not taken so far, despite the great efforts of social movements. Quite the contrary – with Economic and Monetary Union (EMU) it has allied itself with a monetary 'stability pact' instead of with a European welfare state. Given Europe's social traditions it would in principle be possible to oppose neo-liberalism and its religious myth of immutable globalization, American-style (see Bourdieu 1997). Forcing Oscar Lafontaine out of the Social Democratic–Green coalition of neo-liberal Chancellor Schröder after 1999 and the alliance with the equally neo-liberal Tony Blair have ruined the chances for the foreseeable future of turning Europe into a welfare state model that stands up to the self-destructive course of social Darwinist capitalism in at least a neo-Keynesian, if not post-capitalist, mode.

No one can say how things will develop. The system of casino capitalism may collapse at any time. The crises in Asia, Russia and the different countries of Latin America are only symptoms of the global crisis of the predominant system itself. It was only after the world economic crisis of 1929 that Keynes was able to gain a hearing in the West, although his critique of the liberal system and its proposals were known before. So post-capitalist alternatives could be in demand quite quickly. But if people are not prepared for such alternatives there is again the danger of seductive populist fascism, of which there are already worrying signs in Europe. In practical terms this means that even if the EU is currently allowing itself to be a channel for the global, neo-liberal property-based market economy, the social movements must persistently keep at it, endeavouring to forge it into a welfare state instrument – as it were, turning swords into ploughshares.

Whether the downfall of the system or life-enhancing political interventions come sooner or later, people at the local level can start now – and use all available opportunities to organize and harness property, industry and money. Whether they do this in cooperatives or through their municipalities they will at least be committed to life in all its fullness.

Notes

1 On life as the ultimate theological reference point in the economic question, see Duchrow 1987.

2 In this context the following are particularly recommended: Hinkelammert 1986; Assmann and Hinkelammert 1992; Hinkelammert 1994; Hinkelammert 1996; Hinkelammert (ed.) 1999a; Hinkelammert 1999b; Hinkelammert 2001; Hinkelammert and Mora 2001; Duchrow 1987; Duchrow 1995; Duchrow and Liedke 1989; Boff 1998; Dussel 1998; Dussel 2001; Gutiérrez 1998; Gutiérrez, 2001; Dierckxsens 1998; Dierckxsens 2000; Tamez 1998.

3 David Jenkins (former Bishop of Durham) has analysed all these ideological claims in a penetrating analysis and comes to the damning conclusion that in view of clear counter-proof one must assume that those further defending these claims are deliberately lying: Jenkins 2000.

4 Hinkelammert 1994, systematized in the epilogue by Dussel: 309ff (in Spanish in Dussel 1998: 258ff). See also Picht 1966.

5 Dussel 2001: 24ff. See also Dussel 1999: 87ff. concerning *factibilidad/* feasibility.

6 The full text is in Appendix 1.

7 It is naïve or ideologically motivated to believe that poverty in the Third World can be cured by giving property rights (in the meaning of *dominium*, i.e. Absolute property ownership) to the poor as H. de Soto (2000) does. He recommends imitating the settlers in North America in former centuries. This proposal neglects two basic arguments, one historic and the other systematic. Historically North American wealth creation was founded on stealing the land and murdering the indigenous people of the continent. This cannot be repeated by the impoverished majority of the world's population, nor should it be. Systematically absolute property ownership linked to interest, money and cut-throat competition in unprotected markets leads to a growing gap between rich and poor, exclusion and ecological destruction. This is why H. de Soto's work is being hailed and used as propaganda by the think tanks of neo-liberal capitalism, but not by the poor. Certainly the poor need access to the *use* of property for their needs, but not to the mechanisms of the *exchange value* of property. This would mean drawing them into the

greed systems of (unequal) wealth accumulation and would only co-opt them ideologically, break their resistance and weaken their struggle for sustainable alternatives to global capitalism.

8 Fred Harrison and others have taken up the legacy of Henry George, *Progress and Poverty* (1889), suggesting a 100 per cent tax on the annual rental value of all land plus natural resources and a simultaneous reduction in other forms of taxation. They present astonishing calculations showing that these measures would allow for a public budget satisfying all social needs. See Harrison 1998.

9 See the two special issues of the *South African Labour Bulletin*, vol. 25, nos 4 and 5, August and October 2001, Johannesburg.

10 See Binswanger 1978: 111ff. This approach goes farther than the UNDP Study on Global Public Goods, 1999, which envisages only a global regulation and not local forms of ownership.

11 See ibid.: 116ff; Rittstieg, 343ff; also Chapter 4 on the German Basic Law.

12 See Hinkelammert 1999b: 39ff on the weakness of Latin American governments in collecting taxes.

13 See also Dierckxsens 2001, particularly 174ff; Roth 1999 follows a similar approach.

14 Contrary to the opinion of Sarkar 1999: 102ff; cf. Bernreuter 2002.

15 See Chapter 4, note 7).

16 This was forcefully demonstrated at the WTO meeting in Cancun in 2003 where the combined resistance of the sothern countries and social movements prevented further liberalization.

17 Buchan 1997: 70: ' ... capital ... we define as property capable of generating profit'.

18 Rowbotham 1998. The concept of 'grip of death' is a literal translation of the medieval concept of mortgage. It relates to the custom of someone leaving their house to someone else mortgaged by shaking hands ... until death.

19 Ibid. 29f: 'When money is repaid into an overdrawn account, the bank cancels the debt, but the money is not cancelled or destroyed. The money is regarded as being every bit as real as a deposit; it is regarded by the bank as the repayment of money that they have lent. *And that money is held and accounted an asset of the bank* ... this money is accounted and treated as the bank's own property.'

20 Abraham Lincoln, Senate Document 23, 91, 1865, in Rowbotham 1998: 220f. On Douglas and social credit, see also Hutchinson 1998.

21 The original theory behind these comments is developed by Hinkelammert in Füssel and Hinkelammert et al. 1989: 147ff.

22 This is an additional factor to those featured by Dierckxsens 2001. See also Altvater 2001.

23 See Aktion Finanzplatz Schweiz 2000. Further questions in connection with legitimate compensation demands, e.g. regarding slavery, colonialist exploitation, etc., cannot be followed up here. See also Dierckxsens, 2001: 176ff.

24 The International Association of Investors in the Social Economy. Concerning ethical investments, see Ethical Investment Research Service (EIRIS), <www.eiris.org>

25 *Le Monde diplomatique*, October 2000.

26 See the website <http://www. wfdd.org.uk>

27 EKD 2001. English translation published separately in May 2002.

EIGHT

God or Mammon? A confessional issue for the Churches in the context of social movements

The social movements

The Multilateral Agreement on Investments (MAI) was prevented when there was a leak of secret negotiations in the OECD, sparking worldwide campaigns. Since then the global networking of social movements has become a visible factor in the struggle against neo-liberal globalization. At the WTO conference in 1999 in Seattle they helped to stop the initiation of a new round of liberalization. At the different summits of the IMF or G8 their protests have gone from strength to strength. Mies has described the different events and campaigns and has published their documents.[1]

The shooting of a demonstrator at the protests against the G8 summit in Genoa in 2001 marked a new stage of violence against those dismissed by the spokespersons of the other side as 'anti-globalization activists'. The question of counter-force and how to handle it is a difficult one. 'Peaceful' alternative events and statements are given hardly any media coverage, if any. If a few violent people mingle with the large numbers of non-violent demonstrators the media report only on the violence of the small minority but not on the message of the non-violent majority. This is a dilemma for which there is no general solution. This problem will certainly increase now that President Bush has proclaimed from his imperial heights that 'either you are for us or you are against us' – without distinguishing between populations and government policy. All those who cannot agree with this over-simple view are considered either terrorists or their sympathizers – a situation familiar from the secret strategy papers of the American military in 1987, which dubbed human rights groups like Amnesty International, liberation theologians and aid organizations 'communists', and thus to be combated (see Duchrow et al. 1990). An old rule dictates, though, that the more an empire has to rely on direct force and totalitarian methods to shore up its power the closer it is to its end. This is a sign of internal weakness and a loss of legitimacy. Such a situation calls for stubborn resistance (not with the same imperialist means).

It is just as important to work on alternatives. Here the first global

event to mention is the World Social Forum that took place in Porto
Alegre in Brazil in January 2001/2002/2003, in parallel with the
World Economic Forum associated with Davos.[2] As of 2002 it has also
been held at regional levels to achieve broad-based attendance. The
first European Social Forum was held in Florence and attracted half a
million people for its concluding demonstration. Through the spatial
separation of the counter-events from Davos (and from New York,
where the World Economic Forum was held in 2002) the infiltration
of violent minorities was excluded from the start, and it was possible
to obtain better media coverage for the message of the World Social
Forum.

A key issue regarding the success of alternatives to neo-liberal
globalization is the *behaviour of large institutions within civil society*,
such as the trade unions, the Churches and other religious communities. The success of Seattle was due not least to the surprisingly
strong participation of the North American unions. The fact that in
Europe the attempts of social movements to renew the social policy
of the EU have had little effect is, conversely, due to the fact that the
European unions have had little to do with them so far. The problem is on both sides, as was seen in the example of the 'European
marches against unemployment, precarious jobs and social exclusion'
(www.euromarches.org). The European Kairos Document, expressly
designed to appeal to alliances between social movements, unions and
Churches, was not signed by the unions (Kairos Europa: 1998). The
Erfurt Declaration for Another Policy of 1998 and the subsequent
Alliance for Another Policy in Germany are an attempt to overcome this lack of contact.[3] In France the sociologist Pierre Bourdieu
worked particularly hard for a union-led alliance at the national and
European levels (see Bourdieu 1997).

The ecumenical context

The following thoughts are about the Churches. The reason for
their importance in this matter is twofold. On the one hand, property-
based capitalism is not just an economic or political phenomenon
but a religious one, as will be seen more clearly later. On the other,
the Churches can be forceful actors in civil society once they work
together with social movements. It took the Jubilee 2000 campaign to
bring them in on a large scale at the national and international levels.
This focused on the issue of neo-liberal globalization in the form of

the hopeless over-indebtedness of poor countries. Even in the North many Church members attended the two big events centred on the G7/G8 in Birmingham (UK) in 1998 and in Cologne in 1999 – 20 million signatures were collected. And the reduced number of staff continuing to work on the campaign since 2000 are trying to get governments to keep their promises in view of the halting process of implementation.[4]

Jubilee South and Kairos Europa have from the start tried to make it clear to the Churches that the Jubilee 2000 campaign is dealing only with one symptom of the effects of neo-liberal globalization – in other words that it is only a beginning and the campaign cannot be considered over. In particular the issue of the financial markets and the whole financial system is a cause of the 'debt crisis' and many other social and ecological disasters.[5] The fundamental significance of the property issue, the topic of this study, became clear precisely in the context of these efforts.

At the same time, however, a notable dynamic arose at the international ecumenical level that needs to be described in more detail because it is continuing and offers the opportunity to implement many of the proposals developed here. In 1997 the twenty-third General Council of the World Alliance of Reformed Churches (WARC) took place in Debrecen, Hungary. Several regional preparatory conferences had preceded it, including one in Kitwe, Zambia. The latter issued the following statement:

> Today, the global market economy has been sacralised and elevated to an imperial throne. It has changed places with the human beings who created it. By redefining what it means to be human, it has become the creator of human beings. Thereby it usurps the sovereignty of God, claiming a freedom that belongs to God alone. For us as Christians, this raises the question of idolatry and of loyalty to God or mammon. … It is our painful conclusion that the African reality of poverty caused by an unjust economic world order has gone beyond an ethical problem and become a theological one. It now constitutes a *status confessionis*. The gospel to the poor is at stake in the very mechanism of the global economy today. (WARC 1995)

This means that this African consultation classed global economic injustice and destruction of nature in the same category as National Socialism in Germany and apartheid in South Africa. It called upon the WARC assembly to mobilize a movement of Churches and others in the South in solidarity with them.

The Debrecen General Council responded to this call in 1997 and decided to invite member Churches to engage in a *processus confessionis* against global economic injustice and the destruction of nature. This was to be a process of recognition, education, confession and action in the context of globalization. The eighth assembly of the World Council of Churches (WCC) in 1998 in Harare, Zimbabwe, welcomed the *processus confessionis* and called upon member Churches to join in. There were two programmatic emphases: alternatives to neo-liberal globalization and the Ecumenical Decade to Overcome Violence. Together these represent the continuation of the 'conciliar process of mutual commitment to justice, peace and the integrity of creation' that was launched at the sixth WCC assembly in Vancouver in 1983 (see Duchrow and Liedke 1989). In the meantime there has been intense cooperation between WARC and the WCC in the *processus confessionis*. Other world communities such as the Lutheran World Federation (LWF) have joined this process. The member Churches and ecumenical councils in the different regions of the world have also begun to give a committed response to the calls of Debrecen and Harare. In all continents consultations have taken place or are being planned.

- In Asia symposia were held on the consequences of economic globalization in Bangkok and Seoul in November 1999. The Bangkok symposium sent messages to the Churches, faith communities, the WTO and the IMF, calling on them to take clear action against economic injustice and environmental degradation.[6]
- The second symposium took place in June 2001 in Budapest with the main emphasis being on the consequences of economic globalization in central and eastern Europe. The message of the symposium was 'Serve God, not Mammon'.[7]
- The Pacific region held its consultation in Fiji in August 2001. The theme was: 'The Island of Hope: An Alternative to Economic Globalization'.[8]
- In western Europe a global 'Colloquium 2000' was held under the motto 'Faith Communities and Social Movements Facing Globalization' (see Duchrow 2002). It was organized by an international alliance made up of WCC, WARC and Kairos Europa, an ecumenical grassroots network on economic justice, assisted by a

large support group in Germany including the Gossner Mission, Pax Christi, the Franciscan Mission Centre, and the Institute for Theology and Politics. It became surprisingly clear here that representatives of the Buddhist, Muslim and Hindu faith communities completely agree with the criticism and the positive initiatives emanating from the Judeo-Christian tradition. In the process of getting the Churches to work for the democratic control of financial markets, Kairos Europa organized workshops and produced educational and liturgical material (Kairos Europa 1999, 2000, 2001 and 2002). The climax was the conference on 'Economy in the Service of Life. Western European Churches' response to globalization and the financial system' in the Netherlands in June 2002.[9]

- In April 2003 two important events took place in Buenos Aires: the continental consultation for Latin America and the Caribbean, and the South Membership Forum of WARC for representatives from Asia, Africa, Latin America, the Caribbean and the Pacific region. The theme of the former was 'Globalizing Life'. The final document declared '*basta*', 'enough is enough', to neo-liberal globalization. The latter formulated a most important 'Faith Stance on the Global Crisis of Life', rejecting the ideology and practice of neo-liberalism as a matter of faith and committing the Churches in the South to work for alternatives (Kairos Europa 2003).
- A further consultation is being planned for North America.

The organizational goal of this process is the assemblies of WARC in 2004 and the WCC in 2006. The key question is whether the Churches will become – spiritually, theologically and practically – 'confessing Churches' in this process. Will they prove that they belong to Jesus Christ on the basis of the biblical traditions of the God of life and justice? How can they do so in the face of the (self-)destructive, all-out market?

Becoming a confessing Church?

If this issue is really on the same level as the challenge of the Churches to National Socialism and apartheid it is really one about the 'being', and not just the actions of the Church (see Duchrow 1987). It is a question of whether the Church is a true Church. Biblically speaking the question here, as in the book of Daniel or the Revelation of St John, is whether the community of the faithful adapts to the anti-God, totalitarian empire or holds true to God even unto

martyrdom (see Richard 1995; Howard-Brook and Gwyther 1999).
Dietrich Bonhoeffer, a dissident theologian under the Nazis, studied
this most difficult of all questions for the Church in a way that is still
relevant.[10] His argument – in the face of a totalitarian state – may be
briefly summarized as follows.

There can be two basic perversions regarding the state's mandate,
in theological terms: 'too little' or 'too much' influence on the part
of the government or 'state'. In the case of the Nazi state both forms
were to be identified. There was 'too little' state influence in that it did
not protect some of its citizens, indeed persecuted them, particularly
the Jews; there was 'too much' state influence when it declared itself
absolute and thereby an idol. Normally the Church relates only indirectly to the state, but if the state is perverted in this sense the Church
has not just to tend to the victims that fall under the wheels of a
coach driven by a drunken driver – it must 'put a spoke between the
wheels'.[11] Here we have a *status confessionis*, i.e. the Church must make
a clear decision. Bonhoeffer expected the Church to take a strong
stand, with all the consequences this entailed. The confessors did so
with the Barmen Theological Declaration (1934). They then had to
constitute themselves as the Confessing Church because the institutional German Evangelical Church was a Reich church, with a Reich
bishop, in conformity with National Socialism.

This led to the 'Question of Church Community' (Bonhoeffer
1936). Bonhoeffer does not begin by asking who belongs to the true
Church. Rather, he says, the Church must wrestle with giving visible witness to Christ in real-life situations. It will be the reaction of
others which will determine whether they belong to the Confessing
Church or whether they are an errant or false Church. Accordingly,
the confession must be a strong invitation to take part in a process of
communicative decision-making in the synods. This is precisely the
meaning of the present ecumenical *processus confessionis*. Bonhoeffer
goes so far as to say that when the decisions have been made: 'those
who knowingly separate themselves from the Confessing Church
will be separated from salvation.' He distinguishes the errant and false
Church through their reactions to the Confessing Church. The errant
Church shies away from a final decision in order to prevent conflict;
here the Confessing Church must keep up an intensive dialogue with
it. The false Church is revealed in that it is actively involved in perse-
cuting the true Church through the perverted state.

What does all this mean today in the total market and under the US-led empire, which is becoming more and more total? Undoubtedly the situation today is much more difficult to understand than National Socialism and apartheid, although the struggles there were difficult enough for Christians. Why does the situation seem so much less easy to grasp? Before the Reich court, presiding judge Freisler openly asked a defendant: 'From whom do you take your orders: Jesus Christ or Adolf Hitler?' And Hitler made it plain through what he said and wrote and how he acted that he wanted to eliminate the Jews. It must have been clear to anyone with eyes to see: there was both 'too much' and 'too little' state action. Bethge (1982) later put it as follows: 'it was a matter of "only" – only one *volk*, one *reich*, one *führer*' or 'Christ alone' (*solus Christus*), as stated in the Barmen Theological Declaration. Later, in South Africa, the white Reformed and Lutheran Christians stated quite clearly that they wanted apartheid, i.e. separation. And this was not just in public or social contexts but also within the Church. And the black and Indian populations were clearly robbed of their civil rights. Therefore, the true Church had to clearly say: '*unum*', one Church and one humanity (ibid.).

By contrast, what person in the management boards of the TNCs and commercial banks, in the IMF, the World Bank and the WTO, in the US government or in other Western governments or in Japan, would say: I want through my business activities and decisions to make my contribution to the deaths of 100,000 people who die of hunger every day, my contribution to the extinction of species, to global warming and the resultant hurricanes, to flooding and the disappearance of islands and coasts under the ocean, my contribution to the spread of deserts? No one (except perhaps for some completely hard-boiled cynics). They all say: we want the best – welfare for nations, poverty reduction, environmental technologies, etc. But they also say – as was stated recently by the US representative at the preparatory committee for the UN conference on Financing for Development: this wealth is only achievable if you accept (globalized) capitalism. But this means property accumulation through the absolute mechanisms of capital in the global market. Everything else, the unintentional, indirect effects, is placed in parentheses or called 'collateral damage'.

So this is the difference between now and the ages of National Socialism and apartheid: it was intentional, visible and audible acts which caused exclusiveness and murder, separation and discrimination, while in the global market it is the indirect effects of an intentional system that promises wealth, while admitting to being absolute and without alternative, which destroy life and are causing the deaths of people and nature.

The ideological rationale for this system is unequivocal. We recall the words of Hayek in Chapter 3: 'A free society needs morality that is ultimately reduced to the maintenance of life – not the maintenance of all life, as it could be necessary to sacrifice individual life in order to save a greater number of other lives. That is why the only rules of morality are those leading to a "calculation of life": property and contract.' In other words: only those who own private property and/or are capable of contract (for example, workers) have a right to life in a pure market economy. Private property and contract are the two mainstays of the market. Very few people own private property as a means of production and more and more people are being deprived of the opportunity to contract their labour in order to make a living, given the increasing role of technology. Moreover, in a neo-liberal system the state is unable to subject property to a policy of social concern in the interests of losers. For all these reasons, the system as such means more suffering, exclusion and death for more people.

Consequently, it is not enough to attack the present disaster in purely moral terms and attribute it primarily to the intentional evil actions of the actors. Instead we must realize that making private property an absolute necessity leads to the destruction of human and natural life – especially if coupled with the capital mechanisms for money accumulation in the absolute market, leading to the systematic reduction of political oversight regulating the economy according to the criterion of the common good.

Of course, this does not mean that the actors do not bear any responsibility. But their responsibility is not purely individual. They cannot remedy the effects of the system through better individual behaviour. A company owner who employs an arbitrary number of people in a competitive market will lose out and the system will not change. It was in this sense that Max Weber spoke of the 'non-ethical' market. Responsible action will be directed to changing the system, and making life and the common good the all-defining criteria – not the 'neutral' profit maximization on private property in a self-regulating market. Practical steps should follow, along the lines described here. Refusing to change a system that, through its indirect effects, patently kills is morally wrong – and economic, political and social actors must be charged with just that, rather than with their individual actions within the system.

This is a most difficult challenge for the Churches. The roots of this system, which is only now revealing its fatal consequences, lie centuries deep in our societies, and are embedded in our own psyches. They continue to be inculcated into our young people at schools and universities. The media are, with few exceptions, completely under the sway of the language and thought structures of this property- and competition-driven system, since they are paid by the god of capital that calls for its human sacrifice. And many Churches in the North are even paying public relations companies to help them become more customer friendly and to keep well-off members on board.[12]

Confession begins with *confessing our own guilt and complicity*. Jesus Christ sheds light on what we have not done to help the victims – we are saddened and this leads to a change of heart and then the struggle. Bonhoeffer's confession of guilt on behalf of the Church, following the Ten Commandments, includes the following:

> On the First Commandment: 'The Church ... has often denied its office of guardianship and consolation. It has therefore often refused to render to the outcast and to the despised the mercy it owes them. The Church was silent when it should have cried out because the blood of the innocent was crying to high heaven.'
>
> On the Third Commandment, on the Sabbath: the Church 'has made itself guilty of the restlessness, the disquietude, and also of the exploitation of labour beyond the working week'.
>
> On the Seventh Commandment, about stealing: 'The Church confesses that it has looked on silently while the poor were exploited and robbed, and while wealth and corruptness increased among the strong.'
>
> In sum: 'The Church confesses itself guilty of all Ten Commandments. It confesses therein its apostasy from Christ.
>
> • It has not so borne witness to the truth of God that all quest for truth, all *science* did not recognize its origin in this truth;
> • It has not so proclaimed the righteousness of God that all human *law* must see there the source of its own essence;
> • It has not been able to make the loving care of God so believable that all human *economic activity* would have accepted its commission from it.' (Bonhoeffer 1940-43: 129ff)

Science, in our case the economics of autonomous laws and the self-regulation of the market, *law*, the making of exclusive property an absolute, *the economy*, geared to the exclusive accumulation of capital – all are here opposed to God's truth, justice for all and generous caring for life. Can there be a clearer statement of what the choice between Mammon and God means today? Why can't the Churches join in this confession of guilt? Isn't everything much clearer now, in terms of facts and consequences, than for Bonhoeffer after the experience of classical liberalism leading up to 1929? Of course, he knew what few in the Churches know – that evil takes on the angelic figure of light and goodness. He says: 'The huge masquerade of evil has thrown all ethical concepts into confusion. That evil should appear in the form of light, good deeds, historical necessity and social justice is completely bewildering for one coming from our traditional world of ethical concepts. For the Christian who lives by the Bible, this is the very confirmation of the abysmal wickedness of evil' (Bonhoeffer 1943–45).

Where the Churches have adapted to the current market ideology and its ethics they do not understand that the IMF and the World Bank talk of 'fighting poverty' but by imposing structural adjustment programmes continue to uphold the interests of creditors and the capital accumulation of world market actors, creating and deepening systemic poverty (see WCC 2001); they do not comprehend the fatality of an economic model that defines success as growth measured in monetary terms, and methodically excludes the real effects of this success as being (only) indirect effects on the life of human beings and the environment. Only when the Church turns both to the Bible and the actual victims will it grasp the depths of evil glimpsed by Bonhoeffer.

Here there arises a social, psychological (and also theological) issue, which Müller-Fahrenholz (1995) has brilliantly highlighted following the insights of US psychologist R. J. Lifton. When we sense the global threats to life created when the total market turns everything into capital, our panic turns to paralysis. Here – according to Müller-Fahrenholz – the only thing that helps is the experience of the Holy Spirit, *spirit power*. She (in Hebrew *ruach* is feminine) 'comforts' us (does not command abstractly like the law), can lead us 'into all truth' and the truth will 'make us free' (see John 8: 32). The pouring out of the Holy Spirit brings people of all languages and cultures into a new community – in which even property can be shared (Acts 2 and 4).

So Bonhoeffer's confession of guilt gives pride of place to the *experience and affirmation of God's truth, justice and loving care freely given*. In theological jargon this means that: the gospel, the good news for the poor, takes precedence over the law, while the necessary provisions of the law lose their abstract and deadening character and reveal their importance for real life. God's truth turns the uneasy fear of threat into the clear-sighted fear of that which really threatens life. God's righteousness justifies by empowering people to see and seize the real opportunities to act. God's generous care shows what fullness the earth has in store for our lives, as long as money and property accumulation do not bring scarcity and hardship.

Paradoxically, the Church can have this spiritual experience of God's truth, justice and care only *side by side with the victims of the system fighting for survival*, and not side by side with the TNCs, the IMF and the World Bank. This God has revealed himself since the time of the Hebrew slaves (Exod. 3) in the context of the 'crying people' with God's name, 'I am there' (Yahweh), at your side, not at the side of Pharaoh from whose hand I will free you. The life of Jesus also reveals just that. He is present among the victims of the Roman empire and its local collaborators, radiating healed, comforted, courageous new life – which is so infectious that some of the elite even catch it.

Clearly changing places to side with the victims – the Jews in National Socialism, the black people in South Africa under apartheid, those who are today excluded from the all-out market and the doomed human beings and creatures on this earth – will continue to enable the Church to experience God's truth, justice and care. From here, the confession of guilt may grow into freedom from the fetters of the past.

The classic structure of the confession of guilt does not entail just insight into the guilt of the past. It involves *a present-day rejection of the evil recognized and confessed as guilt*. This is not just the ethical evil but, as we have seen, by fatally making itself absolute, it is *an idol with a political, economic and ideological dimension*. Bonhoeffer said on this (according to his lecture notes):

1. Imperial religion. The human being is God. It is mission of the West in the East, mission of the idea of power.
2. Capitalist religion. Capitalism and certainty of salvation are siblings nurtured by the same milk. Both are a) seizures of property b) seizures

of God. Therefore, with reason, protest by Bolshevism against the capitalist Christ. (Bonhoeffer 1932–33: 159)

With amazing clarity and precision he went to the heart of the problem: the connection between Western imperialism and capitalism, and not just as politico-economic powers but also as powers in the religious context.

Concerning 'imperial religion' it was horrifying to see with what directness, after 11 September 2001, God was again identified with the United States. Everywhere there were flags, and posters saying 'God bless America'. And whoever is not with us – that is, with God – is of the Devil.

As to the 'capitalist religion', President George W. Bush, like Ronald Reagan before him, obtained the votes of the moral majority and neo-Pentecostalist movements. Then there are the preachers of 'prosperity religion'. If wealthy, they feel chosen by God, and if poor, they pray to become rich. These types of spirituality are continuing to flood Central and South America. But are we proof against them in Europe? Certainly not. Here there is less directly religious legitimization of capitalism. Yet we have long been used to restricting faith to the private sphere and considering it private property. We take possession of God just as we take possession of things (and people), says Bonhoeffer. Through this kind of religiosity individual Christians and Churches legitimize the competition-driven system of capitalism, without even having said a word in its defence.

In the processus (status) confessionis *the Churches must publicly and unequivocally reject:*

1. The global market, permeated by the empire and its institutions under the sway of the idol of power. This market makes an absolute of the mechanism of capital accumulation based on private property and contract, idolizes itself and systemically excludes those who neither have property nor can contract their labour. It is increasingly destroying the life of people and the earth – and finally it will destroy itself.

2. All religious, mostly individualistic forms of piety and faith that – directly or indirectly, consciously or unconsciously – legitimize power in the sense of absolute authority, in particular imperialist power, along with the accumulation of property, and in particular the politically deregulated mechanisms of capitalism that aim for this.

But confession is not just the verbal affirmation of God's truth,

justice and care, it is not just a confession of guilt and a rejection of
the life-destroying idols of the property-based market. All of this must
lead to a personal change of heart without which all outward action
will lack credibility. To what extent must we *as Churches* change direction ourselves when it comes to property in combination with capital
accumulation by means of the total market?

The Barmen Theological Declaration of 1934 made it clear in its
third article that the Church in general, but particularly in the event of
confession, should reflect the fact that 'it is his (Christ's) alone' (Duchrow 1987: ch. 6) – not just in its proclamation but also in its *form*, i.e.
in its orders and institutional acts. What does this mean in the context
of the global market that is structurally geared to the accumulation of
capital property and thereby to destroying life and the common good?
In Germany many Churches have an article in their statutes providing
that Church savings are to be invested 'at a profit'. So their finance of-
ficers can hardly experience a bad conscience when they do this with
the billions of euros that all Germany's Churches taken together hold
as reserves.

Having said this, the Churches in the processus confessionis *must take
practical steps:*

1. They have to change their statutes so that their reserves will not
just be invested profitably but also with social and ecological responsibility.

The old statutes were apparently premised on responsible stewardship in an age in which the money economy was socially regulated
by the state. However, the deregulation and liberalization of the
global money markets are aimed precisely at discarding all social and
ecological barriers for the sake of profit maximization. This is why
the mere reference to profitable investment is simply incompatible
with being the Church. Luther said that a Church that charges interest should stop calling itself a Church because this was taking part in
usury. This would mean today that a Church accepting more interest
than what is produced by the real economy is participating in usury
and misusing the name of Christ.

2. The Churches must immediately withdraw their money from
all commercial banks engaging in financial transactions for property
accumulation on the transnational markets, and invest their money
in their own cooperatives, local and regional banks that do not operate on the world market, or in alternative banks with interest rates

not exceeding the growth rate of the real economy and which invest responsibly in social and ecological causes.

By withdrawing their funds from commercial banks the Churches would not be saying that those who staff these banks are acting immorally, just that monetary and financial transactions in the global market no longer comply with a structural commitment to society and life. Through socially and ecologically responsible reinvestment the Churches will give an encouraging example of possible alternatives and show that there is a demand for them. In this way they can link up with their old, cooperative traditions. For example, in German Churches there are still cooperative 'congregational reserve funds' used for building projects. The congregations receive just as much 'interest', usually between 2 and 3 per cent, as they have to pay in fees when they take a loan out of the fund for a building project. Through cooperative activity they save the difference between this and the interest they would have to pay for a normal loan. Cooperative local and regional savings used to be organized in this way too, with the savings remaining in the region. Today such schemes have often succumbed to the temptation to imitate the commercial banks. Individual monitoring must show whether they satisfy Church criteria. With alternative banks this is usually clear, although some respect only ecological criteria and not the level of interest.

3. Churches must sell all their stocks in companies that make their profits by the rules of the global market, i.e. without a commitment to society and life, and invest only in projects in the ecologically responsible social economy, i.e. in those that do not offer work-free profits at the expense of the working population and the environment.

By withdrawing investments from transnational companies the Churches would not be saying that their workers are acting more immorally than those in other institutions. However, they would be saying that the global market that is increasingly immune to the social obligations of property ownership is, thanks to competition, forcing them to serve shareholder value instead of the common good through transfer price manipulations, financial deals, tax avoidance and mergers leading to redundancies. The Siemens group, for example, makes about 70 per cent of its profits through financial transactions and only 30 per cent through productive work. Conversely, cooperation with ecologically oriented companies in the social economy is an encouraging sign that there are alternatives. This area includes development projects for micro-companies that are, for example, co-financed by Oikocredit, an ecumenical development cooperative society.

4. Churches should also call upon their congregations and members to do the same regarding banks and companies.

It is clear that the *processus confessionis* cannot just concern the Churches as large institutions. The congregations and members are the Church and, ecclesiologically speaking, the institutions are only service facilities for the people in the pews. The experience of the Church struggle under National Socialism and against apartheid teaches us that a decision can only be arrived at from below. Public announcement of the above steps would probably create a sensation in society. This challenge to the system would in itself give significant support to the struggle of victims and social movements worldwide. Before even raising any specific economic or political demands, the Church would create an enormous public impact through this mere act. Luther called it 'setting a good example to the world', meaning in this context the economic and political institutions. People would see that the accumulation of capital property need not be the goal of business activity and that the latter can be life-sustaining and for the common good.

5). The issue of the *Church's landed property* could be addressed similarly. Is church real estate, both land and buildings (rents!), being used for the usual market-led accumulation of property, or for life and the common good? This topic would be particularly significant in the countries of Asia and Latin America in which wealth and power have traditionally depended on large land ownership. But at this point we would simply like to mention that here too present order and practice have to be measured by the criteria of life and the common good and, if necessary, changed.

The political demands of the Church with respect to a new property system

Besides delegitimizing the present global economic order, confessing to and ending our own complicity in it, and taking alternative economic action as a symbol, the Church has little chance of impacting directly on the economy. However, since the problem lies precisely in the fact that policy-makers do not even assume their constitutional responsibility to guide the economy in a social and ecological sense, it is a central mission for the Church to address this question. In terms of Bonhoeffer's theological categories, this is directly about there being 'too little' state action, which the Church has to respond to. The state, by hiding behind the myth of the constraints of globalization, allows people to be excluded from the dignity of paid work and therefore a living. It also allows the tax burden to weigh increasingly on employees while the owners of the means of production and assets increasingly enjoy tax relief and subsidies. Further, it allows real interest to greatly exceed the growth rate and thereby monetary property to move from the real economy into speculation. It allows tax avoidance and evasion far more than necessary. It allows, through the patenting of seeds and life forms, the common resources of the earth to move into private hands and be dangerously manipulated in the interests of capital accumulation. It permits public services such as water supplies and transport to be privatized in the same interests so that the poor in many countries can no longer afford them.

However, there is also 'too much' state, which the Church must likewise relate to, at least in terms of the rich countries. This is because all these indirect effects are created by the all-out race for capital accumulation in the global property-based market, its social and ecological deregulation being actively supported by the G8 governments through their undemocratic international institutions such as the IMF, the World Bank and the WTO. Neo-liberal globalization is basically political. It is the responsibility of the governments of the rich countries, in particular the imperial hegemonial power of the only remaining superpower. But the European governments cannot simply withdraw because of the dominance of the USA. If they resolutely acted and voted together in the European Union, a powerful economic bloc, and used their voting shares in the IMF, the World Bank and the WTO to promote social and economic commitment, there would be grassroots groups in the USA that would also constantly remind their government of its responsibilities. Moreover they would have a large number of the now frequently blackmailed developing countries on their side.

Certainly the constitutional differences between the different countries need to be considered. Nevertheless the Churches, particularly in Europe, which has traditional welfare states, can publicly challenge their governments to end and change their new-found neo-liberal policies of cutting down on the social commitment of property. They could also point out that this demand is urgent even in a capitalist system, since the indirect effects of the global market are turning the destruction into self-destruction. This gives rise to the following demands (which are intended to show a general direction):

1. The Churches should call upon their governments (and if appropriate the European Union) to end their neo-liberal policies with regard to the global market, where they are structurally abolishing the constitutional commitment of property ownership to social justice and the common good; all of life is being subjected to the sole purpose of the accumulation of capital ownership and is thus being continually destroyed. In order to push through this vital and constitutional transformation of politics in terms of economic interests they should demand, above all:

- the *promotion of municipal and cooperative ownership at the local and regional levels,* in order to give people the opportunity to organize production and services to satisfy their basic needs in the context of their respective ecological and cultural conditions;
- consequently immediately to *end the GATS negotiations in the WTO* which aim to privatize public services; the privatization of water supplies has particularly fatal consequences since in the poorer countries transforming water into a means of accumulating capital property excludes the poor from the most fundamental human right, access to fresh water;
- rescinding the *WTO TRIPs agreement on the patenting of intellectual property in terms of seed and life forms,* in particular the protection of people and their genes from patenting, in order to prevent the monopolization of life, the threatening world food crisis and the commercial manipulation of the future of humankind;
- *increasing the share of debt-free public money* in contrast to the increase in debt-based money created by the banks through credits;
- *moving environmental goods into public trusteeship* or cooperative common ownership with strict social and ecological requirements for any economic usage;
- *linking private productive property to strict criteria* of social usefulness, encouraging participation in decision-making by employees and other stakeholders, and particularly promoting investment in the production of simple, durable utility goods;
- the *reintroduction of visibly progressive taxation of incomes from entrepreneurial activity and assets* in the sense of the constitutional commit-

ment of performance-related contributions to the common good,
and the extension of this system to the global level;

- the *ending of the monetarist policy introduced in 1979 and re-regulation of the interest rate* on the transnational markets in order to adjust real interest to the level of real growth;

- the *consistent combating of speculation* on the financial, particularly currency, markets, with instruments such as the Tobin tax, capital flow controls and regulation of derivatives;

- the *prevention of tax avoidance and consistent combating of tax flight* at the national and international levels, since the loss of tax revenue harms the common good not only directly but also indirectly, through the resultant public debt;

- the immediate *abolition of the structural adjustment policy of the IMF and the World Bank*, which in order to pay interest to capital owners plunges whole societies into poverty and misery, plus the cancellation of all illegitimate ('odious') debts;

- the *phased restructuring of the international system* into democratic institutions *within the framework of the UN*, which needs to be re-formed accordingly.

2. Should governments continue not to implement the constitutional commitment of property to the common good in the direction indicated and continue via capitalist, global market mechanisms to renege on this central constitutional provision, the Churches should announce that they are taking appropriate *legal action*, for example appeal to the federal constitutional court (in Germany) in conjunction with other concerned groups (see Chapter 4).

3. Going beyond existing constitutions and legal practice, they should suggest that *land* be transferred to public, municipal and state ownership.

All these demands and proposals are meant to get the economy and, specifically, the markets to serve the self-reliant life of all people, present and future, and of the earth. They are intended to free the economy from the compulsion to transform people, their cultures and the earth with its rich resources into a means of accumulating private capital property, a process that is leading indirectly to the destruction of all life and hence to self-destruction.

These calls and proposals are not intended to lay down the law. They are meant to show the directions and goals that the different

Churches in the *processus confessionis* can use to develop the demands
that suit their respective contexts. Everything they undertake along
these lines will contribute to promoting public awareness and the
necessary processes of reflection and transformation. Above all, however, it will strengthen the struggle of the victims of the system and
the social movements.

It is clear that in the Churches a major conflict is to be expected
on these issues. Above all, at least some of the Churches in the North
will try to prevent decisions along these lines since many of their
members still believe they can continue to be on the side of the winners. In this system there are no long-term winners. In order to give
an impression of how the necessary learning and decision process
could be organized in the Churches, I would like to cite the example
of the Lutheran Churches in the USA, after the Lutheran World
Federation at its sixth assembly in Dar-es-Salaam in 1977 decided
that apartheid constituted a *status confessionis*. This example shows that
talk of 'the' Church in general is too abstract. The Church has five
'social manifestations' (see Duchrow and Liedke 1989: 179ff): the local
congregation, discipleship groups (for example, religious orders), regional Church institutions, worldwide ecumenical structures and, in a
hidden and unintentional way, people who respond to the basic needs
of their neighbours (Matt. 25: 35ff). The necessary conflicts in the
Churches about true discipleship take place in interchange between
these social manifestations.

Following the 1977 assembly a Lutheran Coalition for Southern
Africa was formed in the USA. Committed Church members set up
groups all over the country. They developed information material
and a motion for discussion and took them to as many district synods
as possible. The motion contained the following three points: 1) We
have found, on theological grounds (outlined in the text), that we
are in a 'state of confession' regarding apartheid as formerly regarding National Socialism. We affirm this decision. 2) In order to take a
stand we will withdraw all our money from banks and companies that
are not willing to break off their business relations with South Africa.
3) We will ask our national synods to adopt these decisions.[13] The
Lutheran Coalition won the votes in two-thirds of all district synods.
Although the whole Church government was against it, and the treas-
urer resigned, the national synod of the American Lutheran Church
approved the motion. This shows the need for a process of recognition

and of learning before confession and action can follow. But it cannot remain just a process if what is really at stake is the question of being the Church on a biblical basis and not just questions of economic or political detail. Eberhard Bethge wrote to the author (on 18 February 1983), after the latter had suggested the concept of the confessing process (*processus confessionis*):

> The *processus* concept is helpful but it cannot replace the *status confessionis*. Only with the latter (which can also hardly be forgotten) is it expressed that there is a necessary prehistory with unavoidable stages and then also a post-history with reception and consequences – also financial, but in the centre stands the element of a decision, which ends the non-committal debate. The introduction of the '*processus*' concept should be a certain relief – why not, in order not to over-estimate oneself! – but it should not 'talk away' the decision that will be necessary one day, that in this process there is a left or right of the fork towards the true or false church, which is no longer only an 'errant' church. (Sorry, I'm sure you have known this for a long time, better than me!) Who could imagine themselves to be beyond the threat of the respective temptation to become the false church! Perhaps the distinction between false and errant church will also help in the really difficult problem of the so different social manifestations of the church with their different reactions in different periods?

In South Africa the confessing struggle of the Lutheran and Reformed Churches led to the overcoming of apartheid (and also to the credibility of the Churches!). Now, however, the population is all the more disappointed for having to suffer under the dictatorship of capital ownership, the financial markets, the IMF and the World Bank – a dictatorship that is implemented by their own government with its neo-liberal policies.

South Africa is only one example. The whole earth is suffering. What is at stake is neither more nor less than victory over a market that has made private property an absolute and which has imposed itself with ever more totalitarian, imperialist means. This must be possible – after all, National Socialism and apartheid were defeated. Now the Churches, acting ecumenically, can help to replace the (self-) destructive 'economic horror' by a commitment of property to life and thereby a life-enhancing economy. They can do this by taking clear positions simply by virtue of their being the Church. Will they be willing to risk conflict with power and wealth, even if they have to pay the price that always awaits those who tread in Jesus's footsteps by standing up to the empire, big property and the temples that legitimize it (Mark 8: 27–38)?

Notes

1 Mies 2001. Wielenga (1999) also offers important thoughts about the need to link justice and ecology movements (Eco-Justice) and the way in which this should be done.

2 See Dierckxsens 2001 and <http://www.forumsocialmundial>

3 Erfurt Declaration, 1997, in Dahn et al. 1997.

4 In the UK the continuation of the campaign is now linked to the New Economics Foundation, London. Jubilee South in Africa can be contacted at: <www.jubileesouth.net>

5 Kairos Europa in conjunction with church aid agencies, Pax Christi, different religious orders, the WCC and WARC organized several workshops and conferences to prepare for follow-up on the topic. Kairos Europa Documentation, 1999, 2000.

6 Documented by WARC 2000. These documents can be consulted at <www.kairoseuropa.de>.

7 Documented in WCC, Dossier 7 on Globalization. See the *Ecumenical Review*, vol. 53, no. 4, Geneva, October 2001.

8 Ibid.

9 Kairos Europa 2003, and at <www.kairoseuropa.de>.

10 See Bonhoeffer 1933: 349ff. Bonhoeffer's works are being translated and published by Fortress Press, Philadelphia. This edition indicates the volumes and pages of the original German edition, which we are using here. Thanks to Dr Ilse Tödt, we have drawn on the English manuscript.

11 Bonhoeffer said this in an image attributed to Luther, also quoted by Bishop Berggrav in Norway at the time of resistance to Nazi occupation.

12 See working group Church in a Competitive Society 1999, 'Against the commodification of the Church … '

13 In summary, district and national synods were recommended to give: 'Formal recognition by Lutheran Churches in the US that a situation of *status confessionis* exists in southern Africa, and the disinvestment from corporations and withdrawal from banks involved in South Africa as concrete signs of taking such a stand of faith' (Occasional Paper 1: *Status Confessionis*).

APPENDIX 1
No to patenting of Life!

Indigenous Peoples' statement on the Trade-Related Aspects of Intellectual Property Rights (TRIPs) of the WTO Agreement
Adopted in Geneva on 25 July 1999 by 87 representatives of organizations of indigenous people, NGOs and networks from Asia, Africa and Latin America

No to patenting of Life!

We, indigenous peoples from around the world, believe that nobody can own what exists in nature except nature herself. A human being cannot own its own mother. Humankind is part of Mother Nature, we have created nothing and so we can in no way claim to be owners of what does not belong to us. But time and again, Western legal property regimes have been imposed on us, contradicting our own cosmologies and values.

We view with regret and anxiety how Article 27.3 (b) of the Trade-Related Aspects of Intellectual Property Rights (TRIPs) of the World Trade Organization (WTO) Agreements will further denigrate and undermine our rights to our cultural and intellectual heritage, our plant, animal, and even human genetic resources and discriminate against our indigenous ways of thinking and behaving. This Article makes an artificial distinction between plants, animals, and micro-organisms and between 'essentially biological' and 'micro-biological processes' for making plants and animals. As far as we are concerned all these are life forms and life creating processes which are sacred and which should not become the subject of proprietary ownership.

We know that intellectual property rights as defined in the TRIPs Agreement are monopoly rights given to individual or legal persons (e.g. transnational corporations) who can prove that the inventions or innovations they made are novel, involve an innovative step and are capable of industrial application. The application of this form of property rights over living things as if they are mechanical or industrial inventions is inappropriate. Indigenous knowledge and cultural heritage are collectively and accretionally evolved through generations.

Thus, no single person can claim invention or discovery of medicinal plants, seeds or other living things.

The inherent conflict between these two knowledge systems and the manner in which they are protected and used will cause further disintegration of our commercial values and practices. It can also lead to infighting between indigenous communities over who has ownership over a particular knowledge or innovation. Furthermore, it goes against the very essence of indigenous spirituality which regards all creation as sacred.

We are aware of the various implications of the TRIPs Agreement on our lives as indigenous peoples. It will lead to the appropriation of our traditional medicinal plants and seeds and our indigenous knowledge on health, agriculture and biodiversity conservation. It will undermine food security, since the diversity and agricultural production on which our communities depend would be eroded and would be controlled by individual, private and foreign interests. In addition, the TRIPs Agreement will substantially weaken our access to and control over genetic and biological resources; plunder our resources and territories; and contribute to the deterioration of our quality of life.

In the review of the Article 27.3 (b) of the TRIPs Agreement, therefore, our proposals are as follows:

This Article should be amended to categorically disallow the patenting of life forms.

The provision for the protection of plant varieties by either a patent, a *sui generis* system, or a combination of both should be amended and elaborated further. It should

- ensure that the *sui generis* system which may be created will protect the knowledge and innovations and practices in farming, agriculture, health and medical care, and conservation of biodiversity of indigenous peoples and farmers;
- build upon the indigenous methods and customary laws protecting knowledge and heritage and biological resources;
- allow for the right of indigenous peoples and farmers to continue their traditional practices of saving, sharing, and exchanging seeds; and harvesting, cultivating, and using medicinal plants;
- prevent the appropriation, theft and piracy of indigenous seeds, medicinal plants, and the knowledge around the use of these by researchers, academic institutions, and corporations, etc;

- prevent the destruction and conversion of indigenous peoples' lands which are rich in biodiversity through projects like mines, monocrop commercial plantations, dams, etc. and recognize the rights of indigenous peoples to these lands and territories;

...The implementation of the TRIPs Agreement in its present form will have devastating social and environmental consequences which will be irreversible. It is an imperative, therefore, that this Agreement be amended to prohibit the patenting of life forms and the piracy of indigenous peoples' knowledge and resources.

APPENDIX 2
The Cochabamba Declaration[1]

We, citizens of Bolivia, Canada, United States, India, Brazil: farmers, workers, indigenous people, students, professionals, environmentalists, educators, nongovernmental organizations, retired people, gather together today in solidarity to combine forces in the defense of the vital right to water. Here, in this city which has been an inspiration to the world for its retaking of that right through civil action, courage and sacrifice standing as heroes and heroines against corporate, institutional and governmental abuse, and trade agreements which destroy that right, in use of our freedom and dignity, we declare the following:

For the right to life, for the respect of nature and the uses and traditions of our ancestors and our peoples, for all time the following shall be declared as inviolable rights with regard to the uses of water given us by the earth:

1) Water belongs to the earth and all species and is sacred to life, therefore, the world's water must be conserved, reclaimed and protected for all future generations and its natural patterns respected.

2) Water is a fundamental human right and a public trust to be guarded by all levels of government; therefore it should not be commodified, privatized or traded for commercial purposes. These rights must be enshrined at all levels of government. In particular, an international treaty must ensure these principles are noncontrovertible.

3) Water is best protected by local communities and citizens who must be respected as equal partners with governments in the protection and regulation of water. Peoples of the earth are the only vehicle to promote democracy and save water.

Note

1 International Forum on Globalisation, *IFG Bulletin*, Special Water Issue, Summer 2001, San Francisco.

Bibliography

Aktion Finanzplatz Schweiz (ed.) (2000) *Odious Debts*, Zurich: Hinterlassenschaft der Diktatoren.

Albertz, R. (1992) *Religionsgeschichte Israels in alttestamentlicher Zeit*, Göttingen: Vandenhoeck & Ruprecht.

Altvater, E. (2001) 'Die neue Finanzarchitektur. Zur Regulation und Reform der internationalen Finanzmärkte', *Widerspruch*, 40(1), Zurich: 13–24.

Altvater, E. and B. Mahnkopf (1996) *Grenzen der Globalisierung. Ökonomie, Ökologie und Politik in der Weltgesellschaft*, Münster: Westfälisches Dampfboot.

Amin, S. (1990) *Delinking*, London: Zed Books.

Anderson, V. (1991) *Alternative Economic Indicators*, London and New York: Routledge.

Aristotle (1961) 'Politics', in E. Barker (trans.), *The Politics of Aristotle*, Oxford: Clarendon Press.

Arrighi, G. (1994) *The Long Twentieth Century: Money, Power and the Origins of Our Times*, London and New York: Verso.

Assmann, H. and F. J. Hinkelammert (1992) *Götze Markt*, Düsseldorf.

Barlow, M. (2001a) 'Water Privatization and the Threat to the World's Most Precious Resource: Is Water a Commodity or a Human Right?', in International Forum on Globalization, *IFG Bulletin*, Special Water Issue, summer, San Francisco, CA.

—(2001b) *The Free Trade Area of the Americas: The Threat to Social Programs, Environmental Sustainability and Social Justice*, San Francisco, CA: IFG.

Barnet, R. and J. Cavanagh (1994) *Global Dreams. Imperial Corporations and the New World Order*, New York and London: Simon & Schuster.

Bauhaus Dessau (ed.) (1996) *Wirtschaft von unten. People's Economy – Beiträge für eine soziale Ökonomie in Europa*, Dessau.

Bernreuter, J. (2002) 'Mehrfache Ernte', *Photon*, December.

Bethge, E. (1982) 'Status confessionis – was ist das?', *Evangelischer Pressedienst (epd)*, Dokumentation Nr. 46(82).

Binswanger, H. C. (1978) *Eigentum und Eigentumspolitik. Ein Beitrag zur Totalrevision der Schweizerischen Bundesverfassung*, Zürich: Buchverlag Neue Zürcher Zeitung.

—(1995) 'Die Marktwirtschaft in der Antike. Zu den ökonomischen Lehren der griechischen Philosophen', in K. Füssel and F. Segbers, '… *so lernen die Völker des Erdkreises Gerechtigkeit'. Ein Arbeitsbuch zu Bibel und Ökonomie*, Lucerne and Salzburg: Exodus/Pustet.

—(1998a) 'Dominium und Patrimonium – Eigentumsrechte und Pflichten unter dem Aspekt der Nachhaltigkeit', in M. Held and H. G. Nutzinger (eds), *Eigentumsrechte verpflichten. Individuum, Gesellschaft und die Institution Eigentum*, Frankfurt: Campus.

—(1998b) *Die Glaubensgemeinschaft der Ökonomen*, Munich: Gerling Akademie Verlag.

Boff, L. (1998) *Die Stunde des Adlers. Wie der Mensch das Fliegen lernt*, Düsseldorf: Patmos.

Bolz, N. and D. Bosshart (1995) *Kult-Marketing. Die neuen Götter des Marktes*, Düsseldorf: Econ.

Bond, P. (2000) *Elite Transition: From Apartheid to Neoliberalism in South Africa*, London and Pietermaritzburg: Pluto Press/University of Natal Press.

—(2001) *Against Global Apartheid: South Africa Meets the World Bank, IMF and International Finance*, Cape Town: University of Cape Town Press.

Bonhoeffer, D. (1932–33) 'Vorlesung' (Mitschrift), in D. Bonhoeffer, *Werke* (DBW) 12, Munich: Chr. Kaiser, 1997, pp. 153ff.

—(1933) 'Die Kirche vor der Judenfrage', in DBW 12, 1997, pp. 349ff.

—(1936), 'Zur Frage nach der Kirchengemeinschaft', in DBW 14, Munich: Chr. Kaiser, 1996, pp. 655ff.

—(1940–43) 'Ethik', in DBW 6, Munich: Chr. Kaiser, 1992.

—(1943–45) 'Widerstand und Ergebung', in DBW 8, Munich: Chr. Kaiser, 1998.

Bourdieu, P. (1997) 'Die fortschrittlichen Kräfte', in P. Bourdieu et al., *Perspektiven des Protests. Initiativen für einen europäischen Wohlfahrtsstaat*, Hamburg: VSA.

Bracewell-Milnes, J. B. (1979) *Tax Avoidance and Evasion: The Individual and Society*, London.

—(1980) *Economics of International Tax Avoidance*, London.

Breuer, S. (1987) *Imperien der Alten Welt*, Stuttgart: Kohlhammer.

Buchan, J. (1997) (1998), *Frozen Desire: An Inquiry into the Meaning of Money*, London: Picador.

Cockett, R. (1994) *Thinking the Unthinkable: Think-Tanks and the Economic Counter-Revolution 1931–1983*, London: HarperCollins.

Cranston, M. (1957) *John Locke, a Biography*, Harlow: Longmans.

Crüsemann, F. (1983) *Bewahrung der Freiheit. Das Thema des Dekalogs*, 'Sozialgeschichtlicher Perspektive', Munich: Chr. Kaiser.

—(1992) *Die Tora. Theologie und Sozialgeschichte des alttestamentlichen Gesetzes*, Munich: Chr. Kaiser.

—(2000) 'Gottes Fürsorge und menschliche Arbeit. Ökonomie und soziale Gerechtigkeit in biblischer Sicht', in R. Kessler and E. Loos (eds), *Eigentum: Freiheit und Fluch. Ökonomische und biblische Einwürfe*, Gütersloh, pp. 43–63.

Dahn, D. et al. (1997) *Eigentum verpflichtet. Die Erfurter Erklärung*, Heilbronn: Distel Verlag.

Daly, H. E. and J. B. Cobb (1989) *For the Common Good: Redirecting the Economy toward Community, the Environment, and a Sustainable Future*, Boston, MA: Beacon Press.

Davis, M. (2001) 'Furcht vor der Fünften Kolonne. Zur Zukunft der Angst: Mit dem neuen amerikanischen Patriotismus droht der Weg in die Kontrollgesellschaft', *Die Zeit*, 39, Hamburg, 20 November.

De Soto, H. (2000) *The Mystery of Capital: Why Capitalism Triumphs in the West and Fails Everywhere Else*, New York: Basic Books.

Diefenbacher, H. et al. (1997) *Nachhaltige Wirtschaftsentwicklung im regionalen Bereich*, Heidelberg: FEST.

Dierckxsens, W. (1998) *Los límites de un capitalismo sin ciudadanía*, San José, Costa Rica: DEI.

—(2000) *Del neoliberalismo al postcapitalismo*, San José, Costa Rica: DEI.

—(2001) 'Porto Alegre: camino al postcapitalismo', DEI, *Pasos*, 93, San José, Costa Rica.

Dillon, J. (1997) *Turning the Tide: Confronting the Money Traders*, Toronto: Ecumenical Coalition for Economic Justice.

Dommen, E. (1999/2000) 'Property and the Protestant Ethic', *Metanoia*, 9(4), Prague.

Douthwaite, R. (1996) *Short Circuit. Strengthening Local Economies for Security in an Unstable World*, Dublin: Lilliput Press.

Drucker, P. F. (1993) *Post-Capitalist Society*, Oxford (USA).

Duchrow, U. (1987) *Global Economy – A Confessional Issue for the Churches?*, Geneva: WCC.

—(1995) (1998), *Alternatives to Global Capitalism – Drawn from Biblical History, Designed for Political Action*, Utrecht: International Books.

—(2000a) '"Eigentum verpflichtet" – zur Verschuldung anderer. Kritische Anmerkungen zur Eigentumstheorie von Gunnar Heinsohn und Otto Steiger aus biblisch-theologischer

Perspektive', in R. Kessler and E. Loos (eds), *Eigentum: Freiheit und Fluch. Ökonomische und biblische Einwürfe*, Gütersloh, pp. 14–42.

—(2000b) 'Zivilgesellschaftliche Gegenstrategien zur Globalisierung in Westeuropa und die Rolle der Kirchen in ihren verschiedenen Sozialgestalten', in R. Fornet-Betancourt (ed.), *Kapitalistische Globalisierung und Befreiung. Religiöse Erfahrungen und Option für das Leben*, Frankfurt, pp. 273–88.

—(2000c) 'Die unvollendete Befreiung vom imperialen Geist – Kirchen und Theologie am Ende des 2. Jahrtausends', in R. Fornet-Betancourt (ed.), *Kapitalistische Globalisierung und Befreiung. Religiöse Erfahrungen und Option für das Leben*, Frankfurt, pp. 389–405.

—(ed.) (2002) 'Colloquium 2000: Faith communities and social movements facing globalization', *Studies from the World Alliance of Reformed Churches*, 45, Geneva.

Duchrow, U. and G. Liedke (1989) *Shalom – Biblical Perspectives on Creation, Justice and Peace*, Geneva: WCC.

Duchrow, U., G. Eisenbürger and J. Hippler (eds) 1990, *Total War against the Poor: Confidential Documents of the 17th Conference of American Armies, Mar del Plata, Argentina, 1987*, New York: CIRCUS Publications, Inc.

Dussel, E. (1998) (2000), *Ética de la liberación en la edad de la globalizción y de la exclusión*, Madrid: Editorial Trotta.

—(1999) 'Six Theses toward a Critique of Political Reason: The Citizen as Political Agent', *Radical Philosophy Review*, 2(2).

—(2001) *Hacia una filosofía política crítica*, Bilbao: Desclée de Brouwer.

EKD (2001) *Shaping the Global Economy with Responsibility*, background information and declaration of the 9th Synod of the Evangelical Church in Germany (EKD), Amberg, 4–9 November.

Fischbeck, H. J. (1996) 'Heiligtum Eigentum', *Junge Kirche*, 12(96): 666–75.

Fornet-Betancourt, R. (ed.) (2000) *Kapitalistische Globalisierung und Befreiung. Religiöse Erfahrungen und Option für das Leben*, Frankfurt: IKO.

Forrester, V. (1999) *The Economic Horror*, Oxford: Blackwell.

Füssel, K., F. J. Hinkelammert et al. (1989) '…in euren Häusern liegt das geraubte Gut der Armen', Lucerne: Exodus.

Georgi, D. (1992) *Der Armen zu gedenken. Die Geschichte der Kollekte des Paulus für Jerusalem*, Neukirchen-Vluyn: Neukirchener Verlag.

Gorringe, T. (1999) *Fair Shares: Ethics and the Global Economy*, London: Thames & Hudson.

Gorz, A. (2001) 'Vom totalitären Vorhaben des Kapitals. Notizen zu Jeremy Rifkins "The Age of Access"', *Widerspruch*, 40(1), Zurich: 30–9.

Goudzwaard, B. and H. de Lange (1995) *Weder Armut noch Überfluß. Plädoyer für eine neue Ökonomie*, Munich: Chr. Kaiser.

Greffrath, M. (2001) 'Und wo bleibt die Gerechtigkeit? Über soziale Gerechtigkeit, gesellschaftliche Ungleichheit und die Zukunft sozialdemokratischer Grundwerte', *Frankfurter Rundschau*, 53, 3 March.

Grey, M. (2003) *Sacred Longings: Ecofeminist Theology and Globalization*, London: SCM Press.

Gundlach, G. (1958/1959) 'Die Lehre Pius XII. vom modernen Krieg', *Stimmen der Zeit*, 59(1).

Gutiérrez, G. (1998) *Etica y economía en Adam Smith y Friederich Hayek*, San José, Costa Rica: DEI.

—(2001) *Globalización, caos y sujeto en America Latina : el impacto del neoliberalismo y las alternativas*, San José, Costa Rica: DEI.

Harrison, F. (ed.) (1998) *The Losses of Nations: Deadweight Politics versus Public Rent Dividends*, London: Othila.

Hayek, F. (1952) *Individualismus und wirtschaftliche Ordnung*, Zurich: Erlenbach.

—(1981) interview in *Mercurio*, Santiago, 19 April.

Heinsohn, G. (1984) *Privateigentum, Patri-archat, Geldwirtschaft. Eine sozialtheo-retische Rekonstruktion zur Antike*, Frankfurt: Suhrkamp Taschenbuch Wissenschaft.

Heinsohn, G. and O. Steiger (1996) *Eigentum, Zins, Geld – Ungelöste Rätsel der Wirtschaftswissenschaft*, Hamburg: Rowohlt.

Hengsbach, F. and M. Möhring-Hesse (1999) *Aus der Schieflage heraus. Demo-kratische Verteilung von Reichtum und Arbeit*, Bonn: Dietz.

Hinkelammert, F. (1969) *Plusvalía e interés dinámico. Un modelo para la teoría dinámica del capital*, Santiago: Editorial Ensayos Latinoamericanos.

—(1983) 'Dialéctica del desarrollo desi-gual', in F. J. Hinkelammert, *Dialéctica del desarrollo desigual*, San José, Costa Rica: EDUCA, pp. 138ff.

—(1984) 'Die Politik des "totalen Marktes". Ihre Theologisierung und unsere Antwort', *epd-Entwicklungspoli-tik*, 12(84): a–f.

—(1985) 'The Politics of the Total Market, Its Theology and Our Response', *North & South Dialogue*, 1(1), EPICA, Washington, DC.

—(1986) *The Ideological Weapons of Death*, Maryknoll, NY: Orbis.

—(1994) *Kritik der utopischen Vernunft. Eine Auseinandersetzung mit den Hauptströmungen der modernen Gesell-schaftstheorie*, Lucerne and Mainz: Exodus/Grünewald.

—(1996) *El mapa del emperador*, San José, Costa Rica: DEI.

—(ed.) (1999a) *El huracan de la globaliza-ción*, San José, Costa Rica: DEI.

—(1999b) *Kultur der Hoffnung: Für eine Gesellschaft ohne Ausgrenzung und Naturzerstörung*, Lucerne and Mainz: Exodus/Grünewald.

—(2001) *Der Schrei des Subjekts. Vom Welttheater des Johannesevangeliums zu den Hundejahren der Globalisierung*, Lucerne: Exodus.

Hinkelammert, F. J. and H. M. Mora (2001) *Coordinación social de trabajo, mercado y reproducción de la vida humana. Preludio a una teoría crítica de la racionali-dad reproductiva*, San José, Costa Rica: DEI.

Hirsch, J. (1995) (1996), *Der nationale Wettbewerbsstaat. Staat, Demokratie und Politik im globalen Kapitalismus*, Berlin and Amsterdam: Edition ID-Archiv.

Hitchens, C. (2001) *The Trial of Henry Kissinger*, London:Verso.

Hobbes, T. (1651) (1986) *Leviathan*, Har-mondsworth: Penguin Classics.

Hoogstraaten, H. van (2001) *Deep Economy. Caring for Ecology, Humanity and Religion*, Cambridge: James Clarke & Co.

Horne, T. A. (1982) *El pensamiento social de Bernard Mandeville*, Mexico.

Howard-Brook, W. and A. Gwyther (1999) *Unveiling Empire: Reading Revelation Then and Now*, Maryknoll, NY: Orbis.

Hübner, U. (1997) 'Bemerkungen zum Pfandrecht: Das Ostrakon von Mesad Hasaoyahu, alttestamentliches und griechisches Pfandrecht sowie ein Graffitto aus Marissa', *Ugarit-Forschun-gen*, 29.

Hungar, K. (2000) 'Antike Wirtschaft-skrisen und die Ökonomik des mod-ernen Patriarchats der Brüder', in R. Kessler and E. Loos (eds), *Eigentum: Freiheit und Fluch. Ökonomische und bib-lische Einwürfe*, Gütersloh, pp. 145–61.

Hutchinson, F. (1998) *What Everybody Really Wants to Know about Money*, Charlbury: John Carpenter.

Initiativkreis 'Kirche in der Wettbewerbs-gesellschaft' (1999) (2000), *Evangelium hören: Wider die Ökonomisierung der Kirche und die Praxisferne der Kirch-enorganisation. Ein theologischer Ruf zur Erneuerung*, Nuremberg.

Jenkins, D. (2000) *Market Whys and Human Wherefores: Thinking Again about Markets, Politics and People*, London: Cassell.

Juhasz, A. (2001) 'Bolivian Water War Presents Alternative to Globalization of Water', International Forum on Globalization, *IFG Bulletin*, Special Water Issue, summer.

Jupp, Sir K. (1997) *Stealing Our Land*, London:Vindex.

Kairos Europa (1998) *European Kairos document for a socially just, life-sustaining and democratic Europe. A call to: faith communities, trade unions, people's movements and individuals working for social, political and economic change*, Brighton: Sarum College Press/Delta Press.

—(1999) *Alternatives to the Global Financial and Economic Mechanisms of Debt and Impoverishment. What are the Next Steps for Churches and Social Movements in Europe?*, documentation of strategy workshop, Copenhagen, Heidelberg: Kairos Europa.

—(2000) *Towards a Just International Financial System. European Churches in the Process for a Democratic Control of Financial Markets*, documentation of conference, Frankfurt, Heidelberg: Kairos Europa.

—(2001) *Short and to the Point, a series of popular materials for congregations and groups on finance and economy as a matter of faith*, Heidelberg: Kairos Europa.

—(2003) *Economy in the Service of Life*, Heidelberg: Kairos Europa.

Kairos Europa and WEED (2000) *Kapital braucht Kontrolle. Die internationalen Finanzmärkte: Funktionsweise – Hintergründe – Alternativen*, Heidelberg and Bonn: Kairos Europa/WEED.

Kessler, R. (1992) *Staat und Gesellschaft im vorexilischen Juda – vom 8. Jahrhundert bis zum Exil*, Leiden, New York and Cologne: E. J. Brill.

—(2000) 'Arbeit, Eigentum und Freiheit. Die Frage des Grundeigentums in der Endgestalt der Prophetenbücher', in R. Kessler and E. Loos (eds), *Eigentum: Freiheit und Fluch. Ökonomische und biblische Einwürfe*, Gütersloh, pp. 64–88.

Kessler, R. and E. Loos (eds) (2000) *Eigentum: Freiheit und Fluch. Ökonomische und biblische Einwürfe*, Gütersloh: Gütersloher Verlag.

Kessler, W. (1992) 'Freies Geld für freie Bürger?', *Publik-Forum*, 22, Oberursel, November: 14–16.

—(1996) *Wirtschaften im dritten Jahrtausend. Leitfaden für ein zukunftsfähiges Deutschland*, Oberursel: Publik-Forum.

—(ed.) (2000) *Geld und Gewissen. Kompaß für ethisch motivierte Sparer*, Oberursel: Publik-Forum.

Khor, M. (2001) *Rethinking Globalization: Critical Issues and Policy Choices*, London: Zed Books.

Kinsler, R. and G. (1999) *The Biblical Jubilee and the Struggle for Life*, Maryknoll, NY: Orbis.

Kippenberg, H. G. (1977) 'Die Typik der antiken Entwicklung', in H. G. Kippenberg (ed.), *Seminar: Die Entstehung der antiken Klassengesellschaft*, Frankfurt: suhrkamp taschenbuch wissenschaft.

—(1978) *Religion und Klassenbildung im antiken Judäa*, Göttingen: Vandenhoeck & Ruprecht.

Klingebiel, R. and S. Randeria (eds) (1998), *Globalisierung aus Frauensicht*, Bonn.

Kofler, L. (1974) *Contribución a la historia de la sociedad burguesa*, Buenos Aires.

Korten, D. C. (1995) *When Corporations Rule the World*, West Hartford and San Francisco.

Koshy, N. (ed.) (2002) *Globalization: The Imperial Thrust of Modernity*, Karnataka.

Krölls, A. (1988) *Das Grundgesetz als Verfassung des staatlich organisierten Kapitalismus*, Wiesbaden: DUV.

Künzli, A. (1986) *Mein und dein: zur Ideengeschichte der Eigentumsfeindschaft*, Cologne: Bund.

Kurz, R. (1999) *Schwarzbuch Kapitalismus. Ein Abgesang auf die Marktwirtschaft*, Frankfurt: Eichborn.

Lafontaine, O. (1999) *Das Herz schlägt links*, Munich: Econ.

Lafontaine, O. and C. Müller (1998), *Keine Angst vor der Globalisierung*, Bonn: Dietz.

Lang, T. and C. Hines (1993) *The New Protectionism: Protecting the Future against Free Trade*, London: Earthscan.

Lappé, M. and B. Bailey (1998) *Against the Grain: Biotechnology and the Corporate Takeover of Your Food*, Monroe, USA: Common Courage Press.

Le Goff, J. (1986) *Wucherzins und Höl-lenqualen. Ökonomie und Religion im Mittelalter*, Stuttgart: Klett-Cotta.

Leutzsch, M. (2000) 'Das biblische Zins-verbot', in R. Kessler and E. Loos (eds), *Eigentum: Freiheit und Fluch. Ökonomische und biblische Einwürfe*, Gütersloh, pp. 107–43.

Lindsey, H (1970) *The Late Great Planet Earth*, Grand Rapids: Zondervan.

Lisbon, The Group of (1993) *Limits to Competition*, Lisbon: Gulbenkian Foundation.

Locke, J. (1690a) (1988) *The Second Treatise of Government*, ed. P. Laslett, Cam-bridge: Cambridge University Press.

—(1690b) (1959) *An Essay Concerning Human Understanding*, 2 vols, New York: Dover.

Luhmann, H. J. (2001) 'Sicheres Wissen – der Gott, dem wir heute Menschen opfern', NDR 3/WDR 3, *Gedanken zur Zeit*, 5 May.

Luhmann, N. (1974) *Rechtssystem und Rechtsdogmatik*, Stuttgart: Kohlhammer.

Lyotard, J.-F. (1979) (1984), *The Postmod-ern Condition – A Report on Knowledge*, Minneapolis, MN: University of Minnesota.

Macpherson, C. B. (1962) *The Politi-cal Theory of Possessive Individualism: Hobbes to Locke*, Oxford: Oxford University Press.

—(1973) *Democratic Theory: Essays in Retrieval*, Oxford: Clarendon Press.

Maissen, T. (1998) 'Eigentümer oder Bürger? Haushalt, Wirtschaft und Politik im antiken Athen und bei Aris-toteles', in M. Held and H. G. Nut-zinger (eds), *Eigentumsrechte verpflichten. Individuum, Gesellschaft und die Institu-tion Eigentum*, Frankfurt: Campus.

Mandeville, B. (1729) 'The Fable of the Bees: or, private vices publick benefits', in *Collected Works*, Hildesheim and New York: Georg Olms Verlag.

Marx, K. (1887) (1990) 'A Critical Analysis of Capitalist Production', in K. Marx and F. Engels, *Gesamtausgabe*, Berlin: Dietz Verlag.

Mayer, L. (1992) *Ein System siegt sich zu Tode. Der Kapitalismus frißt seine Kinder*, Oberursel: Publik-Forum.

—(1999) *Ausstieg aus dem Crash. Der radikale Wegweiser in die Wirtschaft der Zukunft*, Oberursel: Publik-Forum.

Menedez, A. (2000), *In Redistributive Taxa-tion We Trust*, Florence: EUI.

Mies, M. (2001) *Globalisierung von unten. Der Kampf gegen die Herrschaft der Konzerne*, Hamburg: Rotbuch.

Mofid, K. (2002) *Globalisation – for the Common Good*, London: Shephard-Walwyn.

Müller-Fahrenholz, G. (1995) *God's Spirit. Transforming a World in Crisis*, New York and Geneva: Continuum/WCC.

Myers, C. (1988) (1994), *Binding the Strong Man: A Political Reading of Mark's Story of Jesus*, Maryknoll, NY: Orbis.

Negri, T. (2001) 'Empire – das höchste Stadium des Kapitalismus', *Le Monde diplomatique*, 1 January: 23.

Negri, T. and M. Hardt (2000) *Empire*, Cambridge, MA: Harvard University Press.

Nietzsche, F. (1982) 'Aus dem Nachlass', in K. Schlechta (ed.), *Werke in drei Bänden*, Munich.

Novak, M. (1982) *The Spirit of Democratic Capitalism, an American Enterprise Insti-tute*, New York: Simon & Schuster.

Picht, G. (1966) 'Prognose, Utopie, Pla-nung', in G. Picht, *Zukunft und Utopie (Vorlesungen und Schriften)*, Stuttgart: Klett-Cotta.

Pirker, T. (ed.) (1963) *Die Moskauer Schau-prozesse 1936–1938*, Munich.

Polanyi, K. (1945) *Origins of Our Time: The Great Transformation*, London: Gollancz.

Poliakov, L. (1983) *Geschichte des Antisemitismus. V. Die Aufklärung und ihre judenfeindlichen Tendenzen*, Worms.

Renoux-Zagamé, M.-F. (1987) 'Origines théologiques du concept moderne de propriété', *Pratiques sociales et théories*, 5, Geneva.

Richard, P. (1995) *Apocalypse: A People's Commentary on the Book of Revelation*, Maryknoll, NY: Orbis.

Richard, P. et al. (1983) *The Idols of Death and the God of Life*, Maryknoll, NY: Orbis.

Rifkin, J. (1998) *The Biotech Century*, New York: Putnam.

—(2000) *The Age of Access: The New Culture of Hypercapitalism, Where All of Life is a Paid-for Experience*, New York: Tarcher/Putnam.

Rittstieg, H. (1975) *Eigentum als Verfassungsproblem. Zu Geschichte und Gegenwart des bürgerlichen Verfassungsstaats*, Darmstadt: Wissenschaftliche Buchgesellschaft.

Rodney, W. (1972) *How Europe Underdeveloped Africa*, London: Bogle-L'Ouverture.

Roth, R. (1999) *Das Kartenhaus: Ökonomie und Staatsfinanzen in Deutschland*, Frankfurt: DVS.

Rowbotham, M. (1998) *The Grip of Death: A study of modern money, debt slavery and destructive economics*, Charlbury: Jon Carpenter.

Santa Ana, Julio de (ed.) (1998) *Sustainability and Globalization*, Geneva: WCC.

Sarkar, S. (1999) *Eco-Socialism or Eco-Capitalism?*, London: Zed Books.

Schneeweiss, A. (1998) *Mein Geld soll Leben fördern. Hintergrund und Praxis ethischer Geldanlagen*, Mainz and Neukirchen: Grünewald/Neukirchener Verlag.

Segbers, F. (1999) *Die Hausordnung der Tora. Biblische Impulse für eine theologische Wirtschaftsethik*, Lucerne: Exodus.

—(2001) 'Karl Marx im Lehrhaus des Moses', in U. Eigenmann et al. (eds), *Suchet zuerst das Reich Gottes und seine Gerechtigkeit. Kuno Füssel zu Ehren*, Lucerne: Exodus, pp. 95–107.

Smith, A. (1795) *An Inquiry into the Nature and Causes of the Wealth of Nations*, ed. R. H. Campbell et al., Oxford: Oxford University Press, vols I and II.

Stegemann, W. (2000) 'Christliche Solidarität im Kontext antiker Wirtschaft', in R. Kessler and E. Loos (eds), *Eigentum: Freiheit und Fluch. Ökonomische und biblische Einwürfe*, Gütersloh, pp. 89–106.

Tamez, E. (1998) *Gegen die Verurteilung zum Tod. Paulus oder die Rechtfertigung durch den Glauben aus der Perspektive der Unterdrückten und Ausgeschlossenen*, Lucerne: Exodus.

Todorov, T. (1985) *Die Eroberung Amerikas. Das Problem des Anderen*, Frankfurt: Edition Suhrkamp.

Tsompanidis, S. (1999) *Orthodoxie und Ökumene – Gemeinsam auf dem Weg zu Gerechtigkeit, Frieden und Bewahrung der Schöpfung*, Münster, Hamburg and London: Lit Verlag.

UNDP (1999) (I. Kaul et al., eds) *Global Public Goods: International Cooperation in the 21st Century*, New York and Oxford: Oxford University Press.

Veerkamp, T. (1993) *Autonomie und Egalität. Ökonomie, Politik, Ideologie in der Schrift*, Berlin: alektor.

—(2001) 'Gott/Götze', in *Histor.-krit. Wörterbuch des Marxismus*, vol. V, pp. 918–31.

WARC (World Alliance of Reformed Churches) (1995) *Reformed Faith and Economic Justice*, documentation of consultation in Kitwe, Zambia, Geneva.

WCC (World Council of Churches) (2001) *Lead Us Not into Temptation. Churches' Response to the Policies of International Financial Institutions*, background document, Geneva: WCC.

Weber, Max (1956) 'Vom inneren Beruf zur Wissenschaft', in E. Baumgarten (ed.), *Max Weber, Soziologie, Weltgeschichtliche Analysen, Politik*, Stuttgart: Kröner.

Wielenga, B. (1999) *Towards an Eco-Just Society*, Bangalore: Centre for Social Action.

Williams, G. H. (1983) *La reforma radical*, Mexico: FCE.

Wörner, B. (2000) 'Von Gen-Piraten und Patenten', in Brot für die Welt (ed.), *Welt Themen 1*, Frankfurt: Brandes & Apsel.

Zinn, K. G. (1989) *Kanonen und Pest. Über die Ursprünge der Neuzeit im 14. und 15. Jahrhundert*, Opladen: Westdeutscher Verlag.

Index